RYE SPIRITS

Thomas Hamon, Mayor of Rye, 1605-7

RYE SPIRITS

Faith, faction and fairies in a seventeenth century English town

Annabel Gregory

The Hedge Press
London

Published by The Hedge Press
246 Alexandra Park Road
Wood Green
London N22 7BG

www.thehedgepress.co.uk

Copyright © Annabel Gregory 2013
The moral right of the author has been asserted

Print and Production managed by Jellyfish Solutions, Swanmore

All rights reserved. No part of this publication may be reproduced or transmitted, in any form or by any means, electronic or mechanical, including photocopying, recording or any information storage or retrieval system, without prior written permission from the publishers.

British Library Cataloguing- in-Publication Data
A catalogue record for this book is available from the British Library

ISBN 978-0-9571080-0-4

In memory of my father

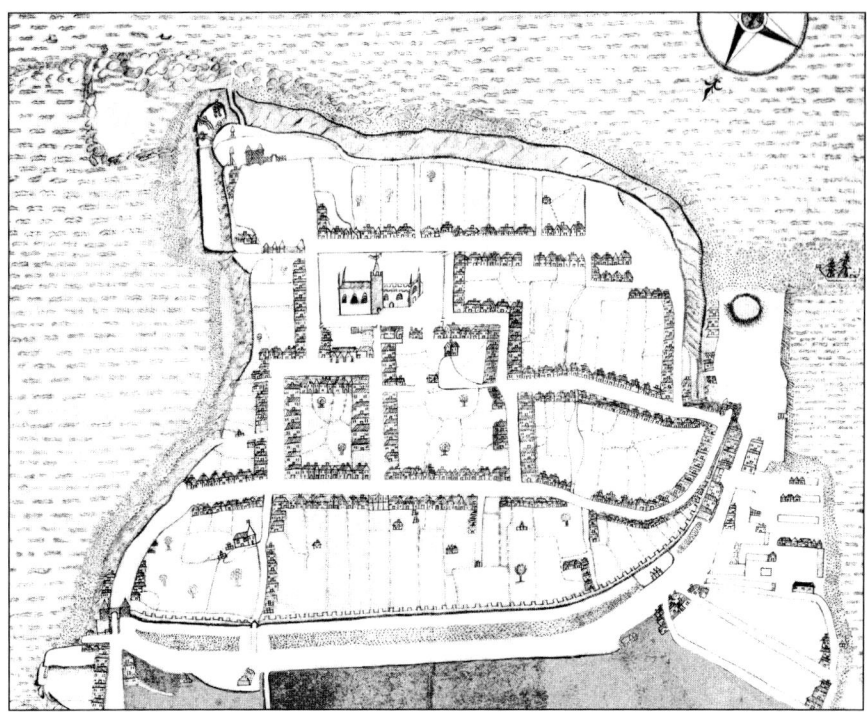

Samuel Jeake's map of Rye, dated 1667, copied 1728.

South and the Camber are at the top, with the river Rother flowing into it from the left, and the Tillingham from the right. The Ypres (Baddings) Tower and gungarden are at top left, and below these Watchbell Street runs east-west. Below the Church is the Court Hall in the market place and butchery. The Strand (quay) is on the right of the town, with the fishmarket just below. The Landgate is bottom left, whence the road runs along the causeway, up Playden Hill, and into the Weald.

Contents

List of illustrations ix
Preface xi
Acknowledgements xiv
Note on quotations xv

Part 1: The Story

    Prologue   1
1. Approaching Rye   6
2. Susan's Story   21
3. The Interrogators   46
4. Anne Taylor   70
5. Faith and Faction   78
6. Attempts at Reconciliation   99
7. Healers   108
8. Entertaining Fairies   121
9. Many Eyes Fixed upon this Case   137
10. Economic Decline   156
11. Thomas Hamon and the Crisis of the 1590s   163
12. The Accusers   181
    Epilogue   202
13. The Wider Context   208

Part 2: Of mirth and godliness

    Introduction   224
    Ritualised Speech   227
    Plaindealing and Bodily Control   235

Back to Rye	242
Afterword: the social sandwich and 20th century fundamentalisms	245
Conclusion (to the essay)	248
Appendix 1: Time Line	249
Appendix 2: Tax Lists	252
Notes	254
Bibliography	279
Names Index	293
General Index	301

Charts and Tables
(all relate to Rye)

Banishments and proclamations for suspected felonies	66
Dramatis Personae in riot of 1577	90
Boats owned by inhabitants of Rye, 1560-1660	156
Shipments of goods in and out of Rye, 1560-1660	157
Price of bread and labourers' daily wage rates in Rye, 1554-1602	171
Wealth of Fagge supporters relative to other freemen in disputed election of 1577	177
Number of visits of the players of noblemen and of local towns/villages, 1485-1620	191

Illustrations

Plates follow page xvi

The copyright illustrations on the pages listed below are reproduced with the kind permission of the specified institutions or individuals:

Plot of the Town of Rye, 1591, Sussex. (The National Archives, MPF 1/3). Details on the cover and pages 2, 18, 46 (2nd) and 164.

Thomas Hamon, Mayor of Rye, 1605-7; from a brass in Rye Church. (Rye Museum Association and East Sussex Record Office; plate III opposite p.16 in *The Records of Rye Corporation: a catalogue*, ed. R.F. Dell, Lewes, 1962). Frontispiece.

Samuel Jeake's map of Rye, dated 1667, copied 1728. (East Sussex Record Office, Rye 132/15). Page vi, with details on pages 19 and 91.

Plate Section:

1. The coast at Rye. *The Ypres Tower at Rye, seen from the South*, Anthony Van Dyck. (The Fitzwilliam Museum, Cambridge; PD.282-1963).
2. The parish church from the sea. *A View of St. Mary's, Rye*, Anthony Van Dyck. (Gabinetto disegni e stampe degli Uffizi, Florence; 762P; photo: Bardazzi Fotografia).
3. Rye from Playden hill. *View of Rye from the Northeast*, Anthony Van Dyck. (The Pierpoint Morgan Library, New York; III, 178; photo: The Pierpoint Morgan Library).
4 and 5. The Market Hall, from Titchfield, Hampshire, 1620s; Shops from Butchers Row, Horsham, Sussex, 15th century (buildings exhibited at The Weald and Downland Open Air Museum, Chichester, West Sussex; photos: Alex King).
6 and 7. A Rye Window; Site of the 'riot' in 1577: St. Anthony's, Church Square, Rye. (photos: the author and Alex King).
8. Baddings Tower: the prison and courthouse. Detail from *The Ypres Tower at Rye*, Anthony Van Dyck (Museum Boijmans Van Beuningen, Rotterdam; V18 (PK); photo: Studio Buitenhof, Den Haag).
9 and 10. Prison window on the ground floor, Baddings Tower; a corner-turret room in Baddings Tower (photos: Alex King).

11. Members of the Privy Council signing the peace treaty with Spain in 1604. Detail from *The Somerset House Conference, 1604*, by an unknown artist. (National Portrait Gallery; NPG 665).

*John Speed, *A Prospect of the most famous parts of the world … together with all the … shires, contained in … Great Brittaines empire …*, 1631. (The British Library Board; Maps.C.7.c.6, 2 vols., map of Kent vol.2 opposite page 7). Detail on page 8.

Map of the country and marshland around Rye and Winchelsea, ?1595, Sussex, drawn by John Prouez. (The National Archives, MPF 1/212). Details on pages 17, 46 (1st), 158 and 163 (for full map, see the cover of Mayhew 1987).

Anonymous, *The Great Frost: cold doings in London, except it be at the lotterie*, 1608. (Houghton Library, Harvard University; STC 11403, title page). Whole woodcut on page 21, and details on pages 85, 122 and 189.

*Thomas Hill, *The Gardener's Labyrinth*, 1577. (The Bodleian Libraries, The University of Oxford; Douce M 399, woodcut on p.22). Page 31.

*John Gerard, *Herbal*, 1633. (the Syndics of Cambridge University Library; Whipple Library Store 119: 11, engraving on p. 591). Page 127.

M.A. Lower, Pillory and Cucking-stool in Rye Church, *Sussex Archaeological Collections* **9** (1857), pp. 361-3. (Sussex Archaeological Society; woodcut on p.361). Page 160.

*Anonymous, *A Mad Crue;* broadside ballad. (Pepys Library, Magdalene College, University of Cambridge; woodcut on p.1). Page 190.

Rye Corporation MSS. Extracts from Rye 13/1 x2, 7, 3, 5, 6, 17, 21, 25 x2 (on pp. 22 and cover, 40, 52, 77 (2), 105, 110, 119 and 153 respectively); Rye 47/75, 1/8/73v and 99 (on pp.64, 68 and 142), and Rye 47/74/9 or 12 (on p.152). Also extract from Rye Parish Register PAR 467/1/1/2 (on p. 172). (East Sussex Record Office).

Many thanks to Ellen King for the drawings on pages 23 (after a woodcut in J. Fox, Acts and Monuments (1610) Vol.3 p.1789), 25, 29, 73 and 93.

* These four images are published with the additional permission of ProQuest, who produced them as part of *Early English Books Online* (STC (2nd ed.) 23040, 13485, 11751 and 6038.5); address for enquiries: 789 E. Eisenhower Parkway, Box 1346, Ann Arbour, MI 48106-1346 USA.

Preface

man cannot inherit the past; he has to re-create it
Arthur Koestler, *The Act of Creation*, p. 266

Many small ports around the long coastline of Britain have suffered over the centuries from changes in the shape of that coastline—their harbours have silted up and become useless, or alternatively their houses have been swept away by the encroaching sea. The town of Rye in Sussex was one such port, but its experience in the 16th century was particularly remarkable because for a couple of decades before the harbour started silting up, it experienced a sudden prosperity (partly because its neighbour, Winchelsea, had already suffered the same fate). The population of Rye at least doubled in size and it became one of the most important ports on the south coast, before subsiding back into its earlier role of small port and market town, with little more than 1500 people.

Such dramatic economic changes were not likely to be seen as the result of an impersonal fate, in the heated religious climate of the 16th century—with Reformation being over-taken by Counter-Reformation, predictions multiplying about the coming of Antichrist heralding the end of the world, and paranoia about witches building up across Europe. In a godly town like Rye, in particular, disasters were seen as punishments from God (too large just to be sent to try us), or alternatively as the work of the devil, who had been drawn into the fray by the machinations of some local witch.

It was witchcraft that some amongst Rye's social and business elite pinpointed as at least one of the evils afflicting their fortunes. These people were the merchants and capitalist tradesmen who had been able to survive better than most the declining fortunes of the town, until around the turn of the 17th century they too were swept under by a tide of disasters. Their scapegoat was a local healer named Anne Taylor who had close ties with their political opponents in the town—a faction in which small independent artisans and retailers were dominant, known at this period as the urban *middling sort*. These tried to distance themselves from the pervasive influence of the big merchants in local affairs—refusing to *lean to the bent of their bow* and *hang on their sleeves*, in the words of one inhabitant—by emphasising their own honesty and godliness, and evincing an outspoken, defiant rejection of traditional forms of deference, conformity and controlling rituals (both religious and social).

The middling sort were much more vulnerable to economic decline than the merchants, and sunk into political oblivion as soon as Rye's fortunes started to plummet. But some of the elite feared the resurgence of this faction following their own catastrophes. They had experience of this—back in the time of prosperity, the members of the middling faction had become so confident and numerous that they had dominated local politics for a short time, and remained a present threat to the elite's grip on power in the town. So who more likely to be causing trouble to the elite than a sharp-tongued cunningwoman from the middling sort—the daughter of an indebted butcher—who had made an extraordinarily good marriage to a local gentleman, by which that faction's political fortunes might have been restored?

We might not have known anything about the prosecution of Anne Taylor for witchcraft, were it not for another extraordinary feature of Rye's past. As a member of the semi-autonomous enclave of the Cinque Ports (along the coast of East Sussex and Kent), which had special privileges as a recompense for its ancient role of defending the kingdom from invasion and providing ships in time of war, the mayor and aldermen (known as *jurats*) had the authority to try all crimes except treason. They thus had the power, in this very small town, to inflict the death penalty on their neighbours. Some of the Rye elite were therefore both principal accusers and judges in this witchcraft trial, and they collected a *massive* amount of evidence—compared with most such cases—with which to bolster their case. Part of the reason for this was the need to fight off attempts by the central government and others to challenge their right to try it.

This large cache of documents tells us little, however, about the political and economic context which I have outlined—that only emerges when the participants and their statements are linked with other records. It tells us, instead, about the arrival of spirits in the town, as well as a myriad of little details about life and social relations. Much of this detail is in the words of a poor sawyer's wife—Susan Swaffer—the second scapegoat in this case, who seems to have got caught up in it almost by mistake. She was too recent an arrival in Rye to have much awareness of the ancient conflicts that periodically divided the townspeople. It is rare indeed to have such a record of the words and beliefs of a poor woman before the advent of newspapers or of much antiquarian interest in folk beliefs and customs (the middle and end of the 17th century respectively).

Most of this book just tells the story—although I pay considerable attention to teasing out its different strands, as well as revealing the confusions between spirits and real people, and the uncertainties and surprises that this extraordinary material presents us with. Chapter 13 relates the case—which is unlike any other in the annals of English witchcraft—to the history of European witchcraft, and suggests that it is not so peculiar when set in a European context. There is a Time Line of the events in the story (or relevant to it) in appendix 1, and some biographical details of the people involved are included in the Names Index.

With a background in social anthropology, in which people are directly observed and questioned about their lives, I do at times find the local records very frustrating, because it is so difficult to find out the assumptions that people made about their world. In particular to understand the *godliness* that was such a major feature of life in Rye, and which has a large role to play in this case (although not in a way that you might expect!). It was utterly different from the nonconformity of the 19th century, that so automatically comes to a modern mind—as often noted by historians—when we think of puritanism (hence the epigraph at the start of this preface). So in the essay at the end of the book I venture out of the local context, using a wide variety of printed sources to explore a particular aspect of godliness—its rejection of laughter—and use the findings to interpret the behaviour of people in Rye. The essay is something of a scamper through a wide range of ideas—a narrative that is intended to make suggestions rather than to prove a theory. But an important aspect of proving anything is to get the hypothesis right in the first place, and that is what I have tried to do here. A more complete treatment of these ideas may be the subject of another book.

London *Annabel Gregory*
March 2013

Acknowledgements

It is many years since I started doing research on Rye, and at that time I was overwhelmed by the size and richness of the town's archive. Since then, publications on various aspects of its early-modern history have appeared, and I am grateful to be able to refer, in particular, to the works of Graham Mayhew and Stephen Hipkin—which make it much easier to both focus on a case study, and relate it to the broader history of the town.

I am grateful to the staffs, past and present, of West Sussex Record Office, Kent History and Library Centre, the National Archives, the British Library, and in particular East Sussex Record Office, who have gone out of their way to be helpful. Many years ago Michael Burchall kindly lent me his transcripts of the early Rye parish registers, Christopher Whittick helped me understand the Rye court records, and Judy Brent allowed me to use an archivist's desk to type up the evidence for this witchcraft case on my manual typewriter. My early research benefited from the generous advice of Malcolm Kitch, Ann Whitehead and Michael Hunter, and the encouragement of the late David Pocock, who was an enthusiast for interdisciplinary anthropology, as also for rigorous analysis. On the publishing side, I and Alex are enormously grateful to John and Indijana Harper for their help in getting The Hedge Press started, and to Peter Holloway of Jellyfish Solutions for his patience with complete novices.

Jean Whitehead read early, incomprehensible drafts of chapters as they were written and made encouraging noises, George Yerby's comments were very helpful, and Jessica Mayer has been a great support. Many thanks also to Veronica Browning, Janice Williams, and the Women Writers and Artists Network (sadly no more). Tony Ryle with typical generosity read the whole book more than once and gave invaluable advice on improving its readability. My conversations with Miranda Chaytor have been a source of inspiration for many years.

My greatest thanks must go to my partner Alex King, who has diverted endless time and effort from his own projects to reading and commenting on the whole book, putting heroic efforts into restructuring parts of it, and giving encouragement. He has also done wonders with the pictures. It would have been a leaden and unwieldy object without his help. Finally, thanks to my daughter Ellen for her drawings, and for putting up with my absorption in this project, on and off, for much of her life. She must have never expected it to see the light of day.

Note on quotations

Spelling, punctuation and capitalisation have been modernised. Contractions have also been expanded, including *Mr.* and *Mrs*, which had very different connotations from their meanings today. They were the titles of gentryfolk and of the mayor, aldermen and town clerk. *Mistress* was used of single as well as married women, and the word *Master* would also be used of somebody who was in charge of others. That these meanings merged into each other is illustrated by the comment of a Rye inhabitant who was accused of taking bribes, that he called *Master Beveridge* 'Master' *as he doth diverse other men in the town*, and that this did not imply that he served him nor received any wages.

The townclerk had to translate what witnesses said into reported speech, which makes the language seem remote, and adds extraneous verbiage to the text. I have therefore edited quotations to try and restore a sense of somebody speaking. For example, *this examinate* becomes *[she]*, and reported speech is italicised. When on occasion the town clerk forgets and writes speech in the first person, this is put in quotation marks *as well as* italics. He often crossed words out, and when on occasion these are interesting, they have been retained. Dashes indicate that the handwriting is illegible, or the paper has been torn.

The main characters in the story are referred to—anachronistically—by their first names, but I think it seems unnatural to us, and laborious, to repeatedly refer to e.g. *Mistress Taylor*.

All Old style dates have been rendered as New Style, with the year starting on 1 January.

A note on some occupational terms:

feter: a local term for wholesale fishmonger
yeoman: in Rye, this usually referred to status (just below a gentleman), not occupation, since no-one in the town was involved in agricultural work

Part 1

The Story

Plate 1. The coast at Rye
[*The Ypres Tower at Rye seen from the South*, 1630s, by Anthony Van Dyck; Fitzwilliam Museum, Cambridge]

Plate 2. The parish church from the sea
[*A view of St Mary's, Rye*, 1634, Anthony Van Dyck; Uffizi Gallery, Florence]

Plate 3. Rye from Playden hill
[*View of Rye from the north east*, 1633, by Anthony Van Dyck; Pierpont Morgan Library, New York]

Plate 4. Market hall from Titchfield, Hampshire, 1620s (Weald and Downland Open Air Museum, West Sussex).

Plate 5. Shops from Butchers Row, Horsham, Sussex, 15th century (Weald and Downland Open Air Museum, West Sussex).

Plate 6.   Site of the 'riot' in 1577: St Anthony's, Church Square, Rye

Plate 7.   A Rye window

Plate 8. Baddings Tower: the prison and courthouse (now called Ypres Tower)
[Detail from *The Ypres Tower at Rye*, 1630s, by Anthony Van Dyck; Museum Boijmans Van Beuningen, Rotterdam]

Plate 9.

Prison window on the ground floor, Baddings Tower

Plate 10.

A corner-turret room in Baddings Tower

Plate 11. Members of the Privy Council signing the peace treaty with Spain in 1604, including Henry Howard, Earl of Northampton, Lord Warden of the Cinque Ports (second from front), and Thomas Sackville, Earl of Dorset, who was patron of Rye vicarage (nearest the window).

[Detail from *The Somerset House conference, 1604*, by an unknown artist; National Portrait Gallery, London]

Prologue

The best time to visit Rye is on a misty winter evening, when the tokens of the modern world—tacked on to old buildings—are obscured. Your restricted vision makes you more aware of the lumpiness of the cobbles under your feet, and, over your head, the protruding jetties on some of the half-timbered houses. On one such gloomy damp November evening I walked up the hill from the station through the dimly lit streets. Through a lighted window, a 16th century wall painting of a ship was visible. Near the top of the hill, I turned a corner towards the churchyard, and was brought up short by a sudden brilliance—the church lit up by floodlights. On down Watchbell Street, I merged again with the grey wetness. It was raining in earnest by the time I reached the door of my weekend bed-and-breakfast.

The looming physical presence of the old buildings seemed to evoke the town's past—yet this was misleading. Something essential was not there. The streets are indeed still laid out as in the 17th century town plan, and many of the houses survive, even if some are fronted with 18th century brick facades. Other changes are more superficial—the half-timbered houses which would traditionally have been whitewashed are now marked out in black-and-white; there are no dunghills outside the houses being picked over by dogs and pigs, nor precarious wooden chimneys. But the ancient source of the town's life is missing—the sea, which has disappeared beyond the horizon.

In the 16th century the sea surrounded the town at high tide, and you could have smelt the salt water, and the rotting fish on the Strand, from Watchbell Street (see town plan on page vi). Walking back to the churchyard and down a few yards to the Gungarden, you would have had a commanding view of the huge estuary—the *Chamber*, or *Camber*—which extended a couple of miles south to the main sea, fed by the rivers Rother and Tillingham sweeping down on either side of the town. In the early 16th century, this estuary had been the main harbour of refuge in foul weather for Channel shipping.

On the cover of this book is shown a delicately drawn 16th century plan of the town and harbour at low tide, when mudflats, rocks and sandbanks were exposed by the retreating sea. If you look closely, two men can be seen playing bowls on the gungarden below the 14th century

The Story

castle, Baddings Tower, and two cannons are trained over the Rother where it opens out into the estuary. The Strand is denoted *the Key*.

Rye was virtually an island, connected to the mainland over the saltmarshes to the north only by a causeway. As the sea gradually receded during the 17th and 18th centuries, taking with it the livelihood of most of the population, the town was left stranded, like a piece of jetsam abandoned on the mudflats.

* * *

Not that the sea has always been receding. Over the centuries it has engaged in a complex dance, redrawing the coastline according to its whim, unimpeded by any natural obstructions on the vast expanse of Romney Marsh stretching out to the east. The one constant point in this part of the marsh is the hill on which Rye stands, a lump of sandstone rising up from the soggy clay below. Even while I was there, the river—swollen by a freak high tide—threatened to flood the children's playground, below the town's cliffs, on what had been the old saltmarshes (dried out enough by the 18th century for the gallows to be sited here).

Back in the 14th century Rye had had too much water swirling around its feet. The tidal reaches of the River Rother so undermined the side of the hill that—over a couple of centuries—the streets near the cliff gradually subsided into the waters. The Rother was, however, a relatively new factor at that time in Rye's fortunes. It had changed its course following some violent storms a century earlier, abruptly abandoning the erstwhile port of Old Romney, and taking a more direct route to the sea past Rye.

The antics of the sea often benefited one port at the expense of a rival. In the early 16th century it left neighbouring Winchelsea bereft, high and dry above the waters (this was the second Winchelsea to fall victim—'Old Winchelsea' is now sunk deep *under* the waters). Winchelsea's trade transferred to Rye, which by the middle of the century was experiencing a level of prosperity unparalleled in its history.

Prologue

For fifty years at most, the sea lavished its favours on Rye, and it became one of the busiest ports on the south coast. Grain was shipped from west Sussex, coal from Newcastle, wine from Gascony, woodfuel, timber and iron shipped to London and woodfuel to the Netherlands, and woollen cloth to Antwerp and later France. Numerous other products were imported and re-exported, ranging from pepper, raisins, dyestuffs, salt, glass, silk, ivory combs, spectacles and quails to elephant tusks. Its fishermen ran the main passenger service between London and the continent (via Dieppe), and often carried the royal posts. They also supplied the Royal household with most of its fish. By the end of the 16th century, however, Rye was being abandoned in its turn. It was towards the end of this period of prosperity that the events occurred which form the subject of this book.

* * *

My arrival in Rye on that damp November evening was by no means my first visit. It was in fact about 25 years since I had first encountered Rye—not in its physical manifestation, but through its archives. These are extensive, providing materials for many a historical research project. But there is one curious cache of 17th century documents of which nobody has attempted to make sense, even if many people have looked at it. Twenty thousand words of evidence, or thereabouts, collected for a single witchcraft case—a phenomenal amount for the period. The problem is that the documents do not tell a clear story, but appear to be an aimless collection of anecdotes about spirits, buried treasure, unneighbourly opinions, and eventually (two years after the first evidence had been recorded), accusations of black witchcraft—of harming and killing people in the town by the utterance of angry words or some other unspecified supernatural method.

I was meant to be working on a different topic at the time, and the witchcraft case remained at the back of my mind while I explored other avenues. But these covered the same period as the case—the turn of the 17th century—and on looking at it again, these other materials gave me new ideas about the case. Gradually pieces of information began to fit together, comments made by the witnesses gained meaning, and a story began to emerge.

So most of this book just tells a story—an extraordinary story that I try to 'make sense' of in terms of the culture and economy of early modern England. I was tempted to call the penultimate chapter *Whodunit*,

The Story

if it had not sounded so flippant, because it is not till then that the identities of the accusers become evident. If this sounds contrived, it is to a great extent a consequence of the problems of reconstruction. Very little can be gleaned about the accusers from the case itself—other than that some, at least, of the magistrates seem to have been rather more involved than was compatible with their roles as justices. It is not until you delve into the relationships between those involved, going back decades, piecing together information from a wide variety of sources, that the main instigators of the court proceedings are revealed, and the reasons for their involvement. As I explored the prehistory of the case, it became clear that this was just one episode in a series of social dramas, as the anthropologist Victor Turner dubbed such events, which periodically, over a couple of centuries, rent the town into competing factions.

* * *

Before turning to the story itself, I would like to consider for a moment what the town looked like in the early 17th century. We are able to do this because of the improbable survival of holiday snaps taken by one contemporary traveller. Anthony Van Dyck travelled through Rye on more than one occasion during the 1630s, en route between Antwerp and London. He was escaping from the towering shadow of Rubens to the court of Charles I, where—over the next decade—artist and king would each reign in splendid isolation in their separate spheres.

During his brief sojourns in Rye, Van Dyck sketched the town from different viewpoints, and in plate 1 you can see the town's cliffs surmounted by Baddings Tower (now known as *Ypres* tower), and in plate 2 the Church, as he would have seen them from a passenger boat sailing up the Camber before veering west towards the Strand.

The cliffs in plate 2 are rather lower than they would have been in reality, but in general Van Dyck is likely to have sketched what he saw — there was little or no market for landscape drawings at this period, so he would not have needed to compose his drawings to please potential clients. He used them instead as source material for the backgrounds to his portraits. Indeed his most evocative sketch of Rye (plate 3)—much copied by other artists—is captioned *Rie del naturale, li 27 Aug 1633* ('Rye from nature'). It is a view of the town as the traveller would have seen it as he started his journey by road to London (perhaps after staying overnight in one of the town's inns). Riding north through the town walls at the Landgate, along the causeway, and up Playden Hill, he might have stopped for a moment to look back and admire the view spread out below. The negligent spray of bramble in the foreground emphasises how high we are above the town, and below can just be seen the causeway, with groynes in the sea to its left, curving back towards the Landgate.

As he got back on his horse (travelling by carriage was an unlikely choice on this road, rutted as it was by the combined effects of winter rains, clay soil, and the ironmasters' heavy carts), and set off into the Weald, he might have passed one of the daily cavalcades of horses carrying fish in panniers to the London fishmongers and the Royal Household. The fish must have been seriously jaded by the time it reached the capital, its reputation sealed in a quip by one of the Privy Councillors that some so-called 'news' was *as stale as Rye fish*.

1   Approaching Rye

The youngish woman who was at the centre of the rumours circulating in Rye in 1607 was not in other ways a central figure in the town. In fact she was a newcomer, as well as poor. She may, therefore, have been unknown to many of the inhabitants, until her blabbing tongue set off a train of events in September of that year. Susan Swapper was a catalyst, reopening old conflicts in the town to which she and her husband Roger were strangers. At least, this is what the evidence suggests—the Swappers were not mentioned in the town's records before that autumn, when she was examined by the magistrates, and as recently as 1604 there had been someone else living in the house which they rented in the Butchery.

    Where did they come from? If they were really called *Swapper*, they must have materialised out of thin air, because *Swapper* is not a name. Or at least not a name used by anyone else. It is not in any of the name dictionaries, nor in the International Genealogical Index (which indexes a large proportion of the English baptism and marriage registers), apart from three people who are probably the children of this couple, and, much later, half a dozen who suddenly materialise in 19th century Ontario. One local historian clearly had problems with the name because he rendered it *Snapper*, although there is no doubt about the spelling. A variation which makes more sense is *Swaffer*, which they were called by Roger's employer, a gentleman named George Taylor. He was likely to know, because—as I shall suggest below—he may have been acquainted with Roger before they came to Rye, and because George himself came from the precise point in Kent where the name *Swaffer* is said to have originated—Willesborough, near Ashford.

    Historians of Kentish names assure us that the name *Swaffer* or *Swafford* derives from *Swatford* or *Swatfield Bridge*, which was where the old Roman road crossed the River Stour in Willesborough, on its way from Canterbury to the Weald. There are certainly Swaffers on 18th century gravestones in Willesborough churchyard, and a large group in one corner of the tiny churchyard of nearby Sevington (whence the M20 can now be heard roaring over the hedgerows). Three *Susan Swaffer*s were later baptised in neighbouring Kingsnorth in the 1730s. Indeed all the 16th and 17th century Swaffers in the IGI come from Kent, apart from a handful from London, and another handful from a village in Cheshire. A more fanciful suggestion makes *Swatford* the ancient river crossing of the

Kentish tribe of *Swaefa*, who were led by the King of Kent, *Swaefheard*! We seem to have moved all the way from granting this rather marginal couple no forbears at all, to raising the possibility of a grand and ancient ancestry.

Leaving such fancies aside, what is more certain is that the town clerk of Rye, who wrote down their name as *Swapper* (even when quoting George Taylor), would not have been well acquainted with Kentish names, since he came from Berkshire. He may have been the first person to write down their name in Rye. It is also possible that *Swapper* and *Swaffer* sounded similar—both *swape* and *swafe* were apparently used to refer to a pumphandle.

Even if *swapper* was not a common *name*, it was a common *word*, and there are several senses in which it might have been used as a nickname. It meant a thumping great lie—what we call a *whopper* today. Was Susan being mocked for telling whoppers—*swappers*—around the streets of Rye? Some witnesses certainly suspected her of twisting the truth. Roger could also be described as a *swapper* in another sense. *Swap* basically meant to *strike*—thus, you cut corn with a *swaphook* (and, incidentally, a swathe of corn was a *swaff*—but that was cut with a scythe!). So perhaps it was an appropriate nickname for a sawyer who travelled round chopping wood for other people. A *swapper* was also a large man—perhaps somebody whose *swaps* you should avoid! Was this descriptive of Roger—or was the joke, rather, that he was so *small*? Whether or not any of these meanings attached themselves to the couple, the name *Swapper* stuck—we find a *Jane Swapper*, presumably the daughter of Susan and Roger, marrying in Rye in 1633.

If we hypothesise that their name was really *Swaffer*, I can suggest where they came from: the village of Headcorn, in the Kentish Weald, which was 16 miles due north of Rye as the crow flies, and a few miles west of Willesborough. Here lived another Roger Swaffer (also known as *Swafford*), who could well have been our Roger's father, judging by the dates at which his children's baptisms were entered in the parish register. True, these did not include a *Roger*, but there are many gaps in parish registers, and it was very common for an eldest son to be named after his father. If *Swaffer* was an unusual name, *Roger* was not a common first name either (but curiously, George Taylor had two siblings called *Roger* and *Susan*). Roger's birth might, also, have been registered in his mother's natal parish, since mothers sometimes went to their parental home to give birth to their first child. In which case we could surmise that he was born about 1566, since six siblings (of whom two died) were baptised at

The Story

roughly two-year intervals between 1568 and 1578. So an origin has been reconstructed for Roger, but Susan's forbears remain a mystery, since no record of their marriage has survived (they probably married in her village).

Below is an early 17th century map showing *Hedcorne, Willesborow* (top left and right respectively) and *Rye* (bottom):

Detail from John Speed's map of Kent

The map is fairly accurate, but disconcerting because the villages appear to be set in the middle of nowhere—they are not connected by a network of roads, as in modern maps. The arteries of this map are, instead, *rivers*—a much more practical method of getting from one place to another at this period. The trees indicate wooded areas (mostly the High Weald, described below).

* * *

Approaching Rye

To the north of Rye, the land rose into a country of wooded hills and streams. This was the *Wild* (or *Weald*, as we know it today), which was dotted with small, scattered farms, each surrounded by small, irregular fields. These in turn were bounded by narrow strips of trees and brushwood known as *shaws* where pigs rootled in the undergrowth. Here the villages were not compact like those on the Downs to the West, each presided over by church and manor. There were no common fields, divided into strips rented or owned by villagers, nor common sheepflocks like those roaming the sheepwalks on the tops of the Downs. Few manorial customs regulated the rights and obligations of the inhabitants of the Wild.

In the past, according to the contemporary William Lambarde, the Wild had been

> nothing else but a desert, and waste wilderness, not planted with towns, or peopled with men...but stored and stuffed with herds of deer, and droves of hogs only.

A 'desert' was a wilderness. The land was indeed shunned by many of the larger gentry, because the heavy clay soils were too labour-intensive and cold to make the growing of wheat a profitable enterprise. By the 17th century, however, the Wild was becoming well-populated with smallholders and artisans—or even over-populated, judging by the complaints about cottages being erected on the waste. For if it was not good farming country, it had those essentials of early modern industry—wood and water. Wood was required for fuel (coal being a recent innovation) as well as for such products as barrels, spoons, dishes, baskets, buckets, furniture, house frames, roof shingles, arrows...the list goes on.

Industrious people might devise many different employments with which to make a living in the Wild. In the summer, cattle farming engaged those who had some land (the grassland was rather too rank and damp for sheep), and woodworking and manufacturing were common activities in the quieter winter months. Some by-employments were also provided by the two major industries which flourished in the Wild—iron production (for which charcoal was required in large quantities) and clothmaking. Ingenuity brought rewards—though few can have been as versatile as the *Archimedes of Wadhurst* (as he was denoted in the parish register), who

> was by trade a glover, a joiner, a carpenter, an instrument maker, a curious workman for jacks, clocks, pieces, stoves and vices for glaziers

Those who were not so ingenious might, however, find it hard, because they had to make enough from these employments to be able to buy wheat or other cereals for bread, when their own cereal production was inadequate. Bread was the mainstay of their diet—at least half a labourer's wages was spent on it.

Contemporaries were often suspicious of the inhabitants of such woodlands—not only of the criminals harboured in the areas of dense forest, but also of the smallholders and artisans in the cleared areas. *The people be given much to rudeness and wilfulness,* according to a report to the Privy Council in 1587; the authors therefore recommended the provision of more justices in the area.

> people bred amongst woods are naturally more stubborn and uncivil than in the champion countries [*i.e. fielden areas*]

commented another writer. Any mention by contemporaries of the characteristics of the inhabitants of woodland regions conjured up unfavourable comparisons with those of the contrasting, fielden, regions.

John Aubrey related such differences of character to what the inhabitants ate (a common viewpoint), and thence to the soil from which the food originated. He noted sourly of a similarly *dirty, clayey country* in Gloucestershire, and of parts of Wiltshire, that the

> Indigenae, or Aborigines, speak drawling; they are phlegmatic, skins pale and livid, slow and dull, heavy of spirit: hereabout is but little tillage or hard labour, they only milk the cows and make cheese; they feed chiefly on milk meats, which cools their brains too much, and hurts their inventions. These circumstances make them melancholy, contemplative and malicious…
> and…they are generally more apt to be fanatics: their persons are generally plump and feggy: gallipot eyes, and some black: but they are generally handsome enough. It is a woodsere country, abounding much with sowre and austere plants, as sorrel, etc which make their humours sour, and fixes their spirits.

What these people needed, according to Aubrey, was more hard labour, like those engaged in arable farming:

> On the downs… where 'tis all upon tillage, and where the shepherds labour hard, their flesh is hard, their bodies strong: being weary after hard labour,

they have not leisure to read and contemplate of religion, but go to bed to their rest, to rise betime the next morning to their labour.

The *dirty, clayey country* described by Aubrey specialised more in dairying than the Weald, but otherwise it shared with it the usual features of a wood-pasture economy: cattle farming and whatever industries were supported by local resources (both had clothmaking districts).

* * *

Aubrey was writing at the end of the century, so when he referred to *fanatics* he may have been thinking of the proliferation of religious radicals during the Civil War. Pastoral areas are known, however, to have fostered independent-mindedness in religion, and evidence of radicalism in the Weald goes back a couple of centuries, increasing from the end of the 15th century. Such *lollards* (as they were dubbed) wanted more direct communication with God than was made possible by the Church—to be able to read the scriptures in English, to pray without relying on the mediation of priests, and without using the intercession of saints. It was more an attitude than a set of doctrines, though one belief was commonly held—that the consecrated bread did not literally become the body of Christ, but was only a symbol—a *remembrance of his passion*. It typified their opposition to mechanistic rituals. They held meetings to discuss the scriptures, and were encouraged and guided by travelling evangelists, who provided a link between lollard communities in different parts of the country.

The Wealden lollards, like those elsewhere, sometimes expressed themselves in earthy and abusive language—one said he would no more wish to hear the mass of a bad priest than that of a barking dog. They also evinced a variety of more or less eccentric and extreme views—such as that Christ was a man as others are and not divine, or that the soul is only breath. A few of those who refused to recant suffered the ultimate punishment—death by burning.

The protestant Reformation introduced few novel beliefs to these radicals, and they already had contacts with protestants on the continent before Henry VIII initiated his early reforms. In particular, some of the inhabitants of the clothing township of Cranbrook were corresponding with one of their number who was in Antwerp, assisting William Tyndale to translate the Bible into English. The clothiers had long-established trading links with Antwerp.

The Story

There were again religious martyrs from the Weald during Queen Mary's reign, although the martyrologist John Foxe had to gloss over the occasional extreme belief that did not quite fit within the confines of mainstream Protestantism—such as rejection of the Trinity. One extremist from Headcorn (where the Swaffers came from), John Fishcock, did not hold with the rejection of the Trinity, but went so far as to want to separate himself from those whom he considered ungodly.

By the late 16th century, some of the more godly inhabitants of the Weald had introduced their own distinctive indicator of popular piety. Ben Jonson may have located his preposterous character *Zeal-of-the-Land Busy* in the town of Banbury, but it was actually in the Weald where such names appear to have originated and were most numerous. So we have *Repentance Coperthwaite* of Cranbrook, and *Smallhope Bigge* of Tenterden. In Rye also, a few parents gave their children such names—for example *Renewed Wood*, and *Hopewell Gill*.

Not all the inhabitants of the Weald were godly. In fact, these may well have been spurred to greater fervour by the ungodliness of their neighbours. Take the Swaffers. Roger was no John Fishcock. In fact he was called a *wicked liver* by one of the godly in Rye, and Susan was called *lewd* by another (meaning *unlettered, ignorant, rude*, and consequently, perhaps, *ribald* and *lascivious*—but the latter was not the core meaning, as we think of it today). And Susan was certainly not averse to the old rituals, judging by her use of *measuring*. This involved taking the length of someone in ribbon or other material, and using it in a ritual—usually to cure them of some illness. For example, there was a widespread custom in the Middle Ages of taking the length of a sick person in a taper, coiling it in front of the statue of a saint, and lighting it. This offering made a connection between the saint and the sick person (particularly useful if you could not write their name), thus invoking the saint's power to bless and cure the invalid. Susan used measuring in a similar way, but the power that was being invoked was more ambivalent than that of a saint.

Such beliefs were much more widespread in the downlands to the west, an area that was as notorious in the later 16th century for the *old religion*—Catholicism—as was the Weald for godliness. I would just like to briefly introduce this region, which was so interdependent economically with the Weald, and yet was such a contrast in many ways. We will return very shortly to the nitty gritty of *why* and *how* the Swaffers came to Rye.

* * *

Near the western border of Sussex, north of Chichester, were the large estates and seigneurial households of some of the richer gentry and nobles. They held to a type of Catholicism that was

> less concerned with doctrinal affirmation or dramas of conscience than with a set of ingrained observances which defined and gave meaning to the cycle of the week and the seasons of the year; to birth, marriage and death…[Here] the liturgical cycle merged indistinguishably with the cycle of hospitality. At Easter or Christmas there would be a large company and sung Masses…. Here was a religion of communal observance and mutual obligation, binding the living to one another and to the dead.

This was a type of Catholicism that was well suited to the downland economy. The complex farming methods required close co-operation to manage efficiently the shared fields and communal sheepflock. Mutual dependence, and the importance of reducing strife, was particularly apparent at harvest-time, when so many hands were required for the harvest that labourers were drawn in from elsewhere, including the Weald. Disloyalty at this time—in the form of withdrawal of labour—could jeopardize the following year's profits. The rituals of Catholicism, that emphasised (among other things) reciprocity between God and man, and peacefulness and reciprocity between neighbours, reinforced the more earthy rituals of drinking and festivity that were thought to encourage *good neighbourhood*.

Some of these Sussex catholics defied the protestant status quo by refusing to go to the parish church, and the occasional landowner even went so far as to harbour a popish priest in the inner recesses of their mansion. But the most influential catholic magnate in the region, Viscount Montagu, managed to persuade Queen Elizabeth of his loyalty even after the Pope had released all English catholics from allegiance to her. In 1588, when Philip II of Spain was about to unleash his crusade against England, she permitted Lord Montagu to turn up at Tilbury with his catholic troop of tenants and neighbours, to help defend the country against the catholic threat from abroad.

Good neighbourhood, hospitality, loyalty—all words associated in contemporary ballads with the golden age of *Merry England*. But the later sixteenth century was a hard time for the small arable farmer. If he did not grow enough surplus wheat to tide him over years of bad harvests—of which there were several in the 1590s—he had to buy wheat when prices were high, and this would have been exacerbated by the relentless rise in wheat prices during the 16th century (5-fold on average, driven by increased demand and expanding population). Unlike the Weald, these small farmers had nothing to fall back on if their profits from sheep-corn husbandry were inadequate—there were no opportunities for other types of employment. Consequently, the compact little villages in this part of Sussex were not as well-populated as they had been, and a few were empty—sometimes with only the manorhouse occupied, or inhabited by farm servants.

The larger landowners, on the other hand, found the same price rises profitable, and an incentive to consolidate their holdings. They helped fill the voracious maw of London, which devoured ever larger quantities of wheat, as its population expanded at least 3-fold during the 16th century. Wheat was shipped coastwise from Chichester and Arundel to London, and also to other ports on the south coast. Rye was another large consumer of wheat, because, being surrounded by water, none of its population were engaged in agriculture (unlike most towns). In bad years, wheat was also disembarked at Rye to feed its Wealden hinterland.

* * *

Roger Swaffer the elder brought up his family in a low-lying part of the Weald known as the *Vale of Kent*. Here the clays were soggier, although also more fertile, than in the High Weald to the south, where, amongst the numerous streams, were concentrated most of the ironworks and clothmaking (and religious radicalism). The focus in the Low Weald was more on cattle farming and woodworking, and these were the activities engaged in by Roger and his sons.

He must have been reasonably well off in 1595, since he is described as a *yeoman*; his son William was simply described as a *sawyer*, like our Roger, his supposed brother. *Yeoman* was as much a description of status as of occupation, so their occupations may in practice have been similar. The only other information we have about William is that other people were twice indicted for assaulting him with apparently no blame being attached to him. One explanation might be that he held some position of responsibility in the village—perhaps a constable, or sidesman. Being beaten up was a perennial hazard of holding minor offices.

Perhaps the epithet *yeoman* no longer truly described the old man's circumstances, however, because only 8 years later he had fallen on hard times. It was ordered by a county magistrate that he be

> charged with the maintenance of his daughter's child, as grandfather of the child. ...He is unable to do this because of his age and want of ability, as the parishioners of Headcorn have certified to the justices, [and it is therefore] ordered that the said Roger shall contribute 2d weekly toward the sustenance of the child, during his life or until the child is self-supporting.

The daughter's husband had presumably died (if the child had been a bastard, the father would have been asked to pay). An obvious cause of hardship to Roger senior would have been the terrible harvests of 1596-7, when Wealden smallholders would have had to buy wheat, and other cereals for their bread, brought from outside the region at sky-high prices.

It was only a few years after this that Roger and Susan Swaffer arrived in Rye. So it was probably hardship that drove them to try their luck in this bustling port. Other inhabitants of the Weald may also have been migrating out of the area during the 16th century, because the number of people baptised exceeded the number of those who were buried there. By contrast, Rye attracted migrants like moths to a candle, because it promised much—wages were quite high, and it was still busy enough to offer much employment in the service industries, providing for merchants, and travellers taking the Channel crossing.

There may also have been more personal reasons for coming to Rye—Susan's sister lived there, and Roger's future employer, George Taylor, was a dealer in wood (Roger being a sawyer). George seems to have specialised in exporting *billets*, which were short lengths of wood used for firewood (wood was the town's main export).

George was a son of John Taylor, gentleman, of Willesborough, whose coat of arms consisted simply of two boars' heads (most appropriate for a Wealden gentleman, though the lack of any other emblems suggests a lack of distinguished predecessors). His stepmother was the daughter of a Rye jurat (i.e. alderman), so he may have been well-acquainted with the town when he moved into the house in the Butchery owned by the mother of his new wife, Anne, in 1603. He was always referred to respectfully as *Master Taylor*—indicating his gentle status—and he later demonstrated his ability to pull strings in high places when necessary. Few other inhabitants were given the title of *Master*, apart from the mayor, jurats and town clerk, who were given it by virtue of their offices. Curiously, the Taylor household paid no more in tax after George

and Anne's marriage than before—suggesting that no expensive items of furniture, objects of silver or gold, or jewels were added to the contents.

* * *

The big downside to living in Rye—as the Swaffers were soon to experience—was the unhealthiness of the surrounding saltmarshes, where malaria (*ague* or *marsh fever*) was endemic. Everyone in Rye would have experienced the ague (the word derives from *fièvre ague*, acute fever, but was used almost exclusively to refer to malaria). Even a seasoned inhabitant like the wealthy merchant Samuel Jeake, living in the town at the end of the century, suffered frequent agues. One bout that lasted fully 8 months he recorded in meticulous detail, in order to study its astrological causes; it released its hold when *Spring coming on apace, and nature [i.e. his body] growing stronger, it finally expired on May 2 [1671]*.

Many more people died in Rye than were born there. Romney Marsh was *one of the most deadly places in the country*, according to a modern expert, and even at the start of the 20th century it was found that the *anopheles* mosquitoes which carry the disease were present *in as great numbers as I have ever seen in tropical countries, and are more numerous than in any other locality I have examined in England* (this type of mosquito particularly favoured brackish water).

In earlier centuries contemporaries did not need experts to tell them about the deadly effects of marsh fever, even if they had different ideas about its causes. An 18th century commentator explained that

> the large quantity of stagnating water… engenders such noxious and pestilential vapours, as spread sickness and frequent death on the inhabitants… the sickly countenances of them plainly discovering the unwholesome air they breathe in

16th century theories of causation were similar:

> All the infections that the sun sucks up
> From bogs, fens, flats on Prosper fall, and make him
> By inch-meal a disease!

William Lambarde in the 17th century thought the area *evil in winter, grievous in summer, and never good*.

In Rye, conditions on a crowded hilltop that had no natural springs contributed to the unhealthy environment. All the water had to be piped from the surrounding hills, and there were seemingly endless payments made by the corporation for canvas and wax to mend the pipes.

When a vagrant tried to account for his presence in Rye by saying that he came *to see the fashions of the day*, he presumably meant travellers passing through, not the inhabitants, because very few gentry lived in this unhealthy place (apart from the maverick George Taylor), even though it may have been the largest town in East Sussex in the 1560s and '70s. Most local gentry had their town houses in the county town of Lewes, which was located among salubrious hills on the border between the rolling chalklands to the west and the Wild to the east. They could hunt in the woods, attend the Quarter Sessions (presided over by those gentlemen who were Justices of the Peace), and send their merchandize for export down the river Ouse to the new port of Newhaven. At Lewes market, smallholders from the Wild came to sell their wood, and farmers from the downlands came to sell their wheat—each had essentials that the other lacked.

* * *

The Swaffers had little choice of where to settle—Roger had a young family to support and needed work. We never learn how many children they had, let alone their names—only that they had more than one. The *Jane Swapper* who got married in Rye in 1633 was presumably their daughter.

When they travelled from Headcorn to Rye, the first few miles would have been over muddy tracks, but from the quay at Small Hythe, near Tenterden, they may well have sailed down the Rother in one of the narrowboats known as *lighters* that plied the navigable rivers in the region, because Susan's sister Elizabeth was married to a lighterman named Nicholas King. Normally lighters carried not people but Wealden goods downriver to Rye (wood, cloth, iron), either to provision the town, or to be exported further afield. On the return journey upriver, they carried such necessities as wheat, and also wool and dyestuffs (madder, brasell, woad) for the clothiers.

As the Swaffers sailed south through the Rother Levels—the river sweeping round the Isle of Oxney in a wide curve—and then straight

down to Rye, the countryside on their lefthand side changed from wooded hills to the flat, wet lands of Romney Marsh, stretching out to the horizon. Not many people lived in this unhealthy region, apart from the *marsh lookers*, who were employed to watch the grazing animals. There were few even of these in the winter, but in the spring, herds of cattle and sheep started to appear, driven from different parts of the south-east to fatten on the new, succulent grass. This land was enriched by occasional doses of silt brought in by the sea, which made it the most valuable in Sussex and Kent—*wealthy but not healthy*, as a contemporary put it. The closeness of London enhanced its value, with much of the fattened stock (some of which had been bred as far afield as Wales and the North) being sold to London butchers, sometimes through agents (butchers) living in Rye or other local places. The butchers were an influential group in Rye.

Rather than sailing round the hill on which Rye perches to the Strand, which was where the larger ships disembarked, the lighter may have pulled in just north of the town, where the ferry from East Guldeford—a village on the edge of the marshes—crossed the Rother. Then it was a short walk down the causeway and into the walled town at the Landgate, passing under the portcullis that had been installed in the mid-16th century (replacing an older one).

The Swaffers' destination—if this had been decided in advance—was a part of Rye known as the Butchery. Here a market was held on Wednesday and Saturday mornings for all produce other than fish (which had its own market on the Strand). Bread, butter, cheese, eggs, meat, fruit in season, tallow, hides, cattle and horses were sold in the market, as well as, on occasion, such products as sickles, edgetools, seeds, coverlets, shoes, laces and glasses. Some of the market stalls were set up under the Court Hall, which had an open ground floor, as was typical of Sussex town halls (see plate 4). Above it was the room where the mayor and aldermen—who were known as *jurats* in Rye— together with the freemen, held their fortnightly assemblies. At these assemblies prices were set, officers elected, summary punishments

Approaching Rye

ordered, relations with the outside world discussed, decrees passed, and many other functions dealt with relating to the corporation of Rye.

The freemen (also known as the *commonalty*) were a privileged body of men who, as well as taking part in the government of the town, had trading privileges—in particular, paying half as much in the way of customs duties on goods passing through the port as non-freemen. They constituted about a third of tax-paying householders—there had been at least 149 freemen when the town was prosperous. A man did not have to pay for his freedom if his father had been free when he was born, but others—if they were accepted by the corporation—paid for the privilege (40s for strangers, about the same as a year's wages for a servant, or 20s for residents). The mayor (with the consent of the jurats) could also bestow one free admission to the commonalty per year. Each year the freemen chose one of the jurats to be mayor, and the mayor chose new jurats from amongst the commonalty if there were any vacancies (maximum twelve)—only occasionally did jurats *not* continue to serve until they died or retired.

About a third of households were too poor to pay any tax—these included the Swaffers. And then there were those who too poor even to be described as *householders* in the burial register—how many there were of these can only be guessed.

The Swaffers moved into a house just down the road from the marketplace and Court Hall (house *c* in the drawing below), next door but one to the Taylors (house *a*). It was owned by Anne Taylor's mother, Widow Bennett, whose late husband had been a butcher. She also owned the house in between, which was let to a sailor and his wife (house *b*). Two of the houses were fronted by shops—presumably butchers' shops (see plate 5 for similar shops, with counters in front of the open windows). You can see the arches of the Court Hall in this extract from Jeake's map (south is at the top; the full map—almost—is shown on p. vi).

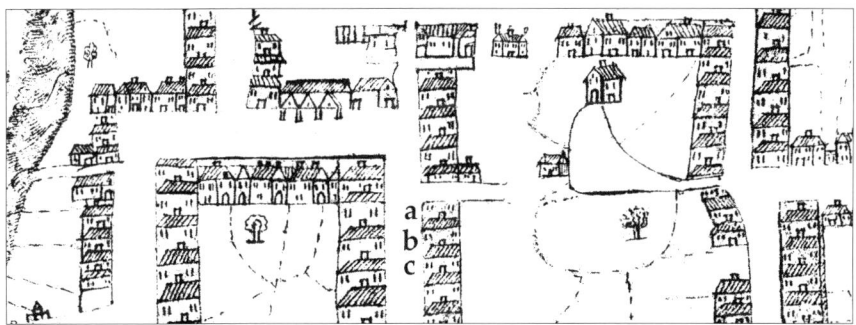

The Story

The Swaffer's house was medieval in layout, with a *hall* which was the main living area, and next to it a *parlour*. Banish all thought of Victorian parlours—the 16th century parlour was an unheated room that was just smaller and more private than the hall, and therefore a suitable room in which to talk—from the word *parler*. It was probably also used for sleeping and storage, and Susan would keep her spinning wheel in it.

There is no mention of a kitchen, which does not necessarily mean it did not exist—but they may have done all their cooking on the hearth in the hall. The smoke would have escaped through a smoke-bay or chimney; if they had a chimney, it would have been a hazardous wooden one, bricks being little used because they were so expensive (and stone was out of the question).

The hall would originally have been open to the roof, but above it and the parlour had been built two or more chambers, as was commonly done in the 16th century, and there was a garret above these, where hemp was stored. Also in the garret were *weasels*, according to Roger—perhaps hunting mice in the packs of hemp (or possibly in the thatch—but thatched roofs had been forbidden in a 16th century byelaw, because of the danger of fire). One chamber was not let to the Swaffers—Susan said that Anne Taylor kept them unlet so that the *spirits could walk there*.

*　*　*

The Swaffers probably enjoyed a couple of years in Rye of comparative well-being—Roger had work, chopping firewood for George Taylor (amongst other jobs). But then in the cold winter of 1606-7 they both became ill, and this precipitated an extraordinary series of events, beginning with the arrival of spirits. The mayor and jurats (aldermen) of the town became alarmed, and interrogated Susan and others about the spirits the following autumn. I will tell the story as Susan told it, with some input from other witnesses (or to be more precise, it is the town clerk's version of what was said, because he wrote most of it down).

2 Susan's Story

The Swaffers succumbed to the *pestilential vapours* of the marshes during Lent in 1607. It was *a great shake of sickness which Swaffer's wife and her husband and her child had*, according to George Taylor—an evocative description which leaves little doubt as to what they were suffering from. The *shaking ague* was a common term for it. Uncontrollable shivering and extreme cold are the initial symptoms of malaria, after which the victim's temperature shoots up and the body is wracked by fever. Heavy sweating brings the temperature down to normal, and there is then a respite until the next fit, a couple of days later. The Swaffers were likely to have been worse affected than most people, for

> fresh-incomers...run a great risk, who having been brought up and accustomed to a clear healthy air, remove to fenny, wet, sickly soil; for people born in, and inured to bad air, bear it much better

as was noted in the 18th century.

A fair held on the frozen Thames in the winter of 1607-8.

The Story

The tail end of winter was the worst time for the poor—fatalities from fever were at their highest, and even the rich took medicines to prevent them getting ill. And winters were colder then—the winter of 1607-8 was particularly cold, when the Thames froze in London, and a fair was held on the ice. These were the lean months when the cows were giving little milk and the hens had stopped laying. Cheese and eggs were the staples of the poor (apart from bread and beer)—the prohibition on eating meat during Lent would have been of little significance to those who could not afford to buy it. If the Swaffers came to Rye because of a downturn in their fortunes, they must now have felt that they had hit rock bottom.

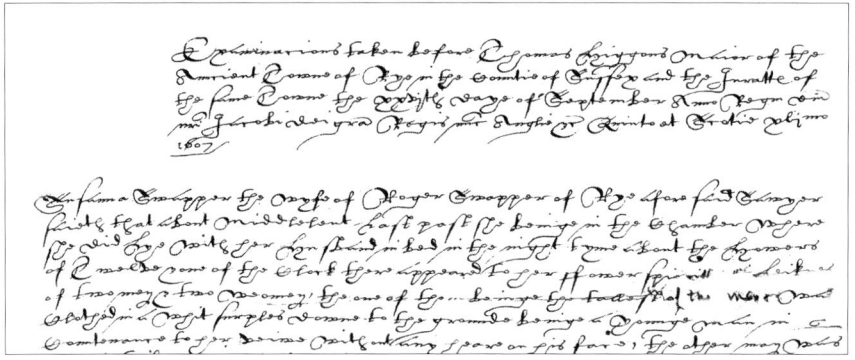

Susan Swapper's first examination [Rye 13/1]

It was one night when the Swaffers were lying *sick a bed togethers* (as Roger put it), in the chamber where they usually lay, that Susan had her vision. The time was between midnight and one a'clock—the most likely time (apart from noon) for spirits to appear. Perhaps it was during a spell of high fever, delirious, that she became aware of the presence in the room of two men and two women. She described their appearance in detail. The tallest man wore *a white surplice down to the ground, being a young man in countenance (to her view), without any hair on his face*—so possibly a minister of the church, or student. *The other man was a short thick man clothed all in white, with a satin doublet and breeches pinked* [studded with holes] *and a long grey beard*—a very rich and fashionable older man. One of the women was clothed with a green petticoat and a white waistcoat [jacket, not sleeveless], with a rail [kerchief] about her neck, and a white kerchief upon her head—a young woman, to her judgment. This woman was lower in status than the men. The other was a young woman likewise, clothed all in white. This was a grand company to grace a poor woman's chamber!

The next day Susan told her landlady, Anne Taylor, about them. She must have felt reassured that this woman lived next door, because she and her mother, old Widow Bennett, were reputed to have healing skills. When Anne heard the tale, she wanted to know if Susan had been dreaming, and asked her

> *Whether she were a wake or a sleep when they did appear unto her?* and she said
> *She was awake*, and then Mistress Taylor willed her to
> *Call upon god, for that they were illusions which she had seen.*

Good protestant advice—they were illusions created by the devil.

The spirits appeared again to Susan over the next three nights. If she did *call upon god*, it had no effect. Their repeated appearances must have seemed increasingly ominous—did they have a message, or a warning for her? Were they ghosts who needed to unburden themselves of some hidden knowledge before they could rest—a murder or theft, or a legacy that had been withheld, or buried treasure? Whatever type of secret it was, people feared the need of the dead to make contact with the living—their refusal to let go of this world. The Catholic church had tried to limit the wanderings of ghosts by consigning them to purgatory—but neither then, nor since purgatory had been officially abolished by the protestants, could popular fears be corralled into the neat categories of clerics.

A woman wearing kerchiefs

After the third night, Anne advised Susan to speak to the spirits with these words:

> *In the name of the father, son and the holy ghost, wherefore come you to trouble me, or what will you have?*

If they were evil spirits, calling on God would hopefully scare them away, while if they were ghosts or other types of spirit with a message, it would invite them to divulge why they had appeared (Anne did not specifically tell Susan to ask *who or what* the spirits were, which was the more usual approach, to ascertain whether they were good or evil). But it required courage and a strong faith in God to challenge apparitions. Even Parliamentary Commissioners during the Civil War were described as *bold* when they addressed an extremely noisy and violent spirit in this way.

On the fourth night the spirit-woman in the green petticoat did eventually speak to her. Her words were threatening:

> '*Sue, come and go with me, or else I will carry thee!*'
> Whereupon [she] being affeared with that vision, and the calling of her by her name, called to her husband, and waked him, and *willed him to hold her*.
> And he awaking turned unto her, and answered her
> '*Wherefore should I hold thee?*' and she replied unto him again and said
> '*Here is a thing that will carry me away!*'

As she was thus calling out in fear to her husband, another of the spirits

> … took hold of her by the arm and gripped her. And …her arm was lame by reason thereof two days, that she could not help herself.

This was 'spirit Richard', who was the tall young man who wore a surplice. Susan could provide the names of the others as well, which were Robert, Margery and Catherine. Perhaps spirit Richard was punishing her for seeking her husband's help. Roger, however, was totally oblivious:

> And he said again unto her,
> '*I see nothing*', and so turned about from her.
> And then the … vision, which she so did see, departed from her. And afterwards the same night, a little before day, the … two men and two women app[eared] unto her in form as they were before.

This time Susan plucked up the courage to speak.

> '*In the name of the father, the son and the holy ghost, what will you have me do?*'

Not quite the same question as Anne had suggested, but it seems to have been the right one to ask, because the spirits had a curious task for her. The woman in the green petticoat said to her:

> '*I would have you go unto young Anne Bennett, and call her, and go into her garden with her, and dig and set sage; and then you should be well.*'

It seems that the spirit was promising to cure Susan of her illness by getting her to plant sage cuttings! *Young Anne Bennett* was none other than Anne Taylor, *Bennett* being her maiden name, and 'young' because her mother, Widow Bennett, was also called Anne, and lived in the same house.

How can a man die who has sage in his garden? The ancient saying overstates the point, but sage was indeed considered to be a cure-all. More pertinently, sage was thought to be a febrifuge, and Susan was probably taking it for her ague—a Sussex remedy requires you to eat sage leaves nine mornings in succession while fasting. Perhaps Susan felt that anything to do with sage might help her illness—even just planting sage cuttings.

* * *

The account thus far of the events of the previous four nights has been Susan's. Roger's recollection was rather different. He had been unaware of his wife's visions at first, until woken by his wife calling him and saying that a spirit was threatening to carry her away. He could not see the spirits, but he had done his best to help, and had even suffered for it:

> he did take hold of his wife and lay his arm over her, but did [not] see nor hear anything; [but] that hand which he did lay over his wife was so benumbed and lame, that he could not help himself there with.
>
> And [...] Mistress Taylor by the space of two days togethers did cut [Roger's] bread, for that she was daily at his house.

So while the couple were suffering the effects of the spirits' spite, Anne came daily to attend on them, and was clearly very interested in the spirits. On one occasion she came round to the Swaffers' house with her mother, and Roger overheard Susan telling them about more specific threats from the spirits:

> Two spirits in the likeness of two women did appear unto her that night, and...they said
> *They would carry her away and lay her under an appletree in Mistress Taylor's garden...*

—as if she were going to be *buried!* The spirits' meaning was not as threatening as it seemed, however, for they then revealed news of a most interesting kind:

The Story

> The spirits did certify her that *there was money hid under the appletree near unto the summer house, and that they did mean to bring Mistress Taylor unto her in the said garden.*

So the spirits, Roger said, had come to tell Susan where treasure was buried. Anne now reassured her that

> *She should fear nothing, for [the spirits] would not hurt her. And that if they required her again to go with them, she should go.*

She had abandoned the idea that these were devilish illusions, and now took a more positive view of them.

Anne was clearly considered to be an expert in dealing with spirits. Such *wisewomen* or *cunningfolk* (from *con*, know) were consulted not only on medical matters, but also on divining the whereabouts of buried treasure and lost or stolen goods, identifying a thief, and providing love potions. What linked these apparently disparate functions was the ability to conjure spirits, talk with the fairies, or have some other means of accessing the spirit world. Many cunningfolk claimed to get their knowledge from the fairies. Dr. Faustus was not the only person to believe that knowledge—*cunning*—was something you got as much from spirits as from books.

*   *   *

Anne Taylor does not seem to have taken exception to the spirits' suggestion that Susan should dig in her garden, or to the curiously insulting way in which this was expressed—referring to her as *young Anne Bennett*. As the wife of a gentleman, she deserved the title of *Mistress*, and was also married with two children.

The next day (in Susan's words):

> In the afternoon after dinner, Mistress Taylor did pull open two pales [from the fence between their two gardens], and sent for [Susan]. And so they went both together into the garden, and [she] did dig in the garden with Mistress Taylor.
>
> And Mistress Taylor did thrust a spit into the ground where they did dig, and they heard a sound. And [Susan] being very sick, could stay but a very little space, but departed away without setting any sage.

Susan is still referring to *setting sage*, but they were clearly doing something quite else. At the back of her mind may have been the thought that what they *ought* to have been doing in the garden at this time of year was planting sage cuttings (so said the author of the first English gardening manual). This was an essential task for cunningfolk, who grew a great deal of sage, not just the odd plant.

> But Mistress Taylor said (at the thrusting in of the spit the first time)
> *It was there when they heard the sound*. And she thrusting in the spit the second time so far as she could, said
> *It was in vain to dig, for now it is farther off.*
> And also the same time Mistress Taylor went into the Summer house, and did take up a stone, and thrust in the spit. And so departed without digging any farther, but put in the earth in the place again where she digged.

Could *setting sage* be a euphemism for digging for buried treasure?

* * *

The existence of treasure was not news to everyone, for Roger reported that:

> Mistress Taylor [said]…that she
> *Did know that there was money hid in her garden, and also did know where the same did lie*

There had in fact been at least two attempts to dig for treasure in the garden already, though Susan and Roger only heard of these later. The first was made by a former tenant of the house which the Swaffers now occupied, a Robert Pywall. A tailor called Philip Williams who had done some gardening for the Taylors also claimed that Anne had asked him to dig for treasure there, but he had refused.

Robert Pywall had been hired by George Taylor to make them a garden and orchard—this must have been not long after their marriage in 1603, when George had moved into the house. Pywall, being *greatly troubled in the night with treasure that should be hid in [the Taylors'] garden near unto the summer house* (George's words, when questioned on the subject, which were echoed by Anne), had asked *for the satisfying of his mind, that he might dig in his garden to search for the [treasure]*. George agreed (insisting in his examination that he had *not* hired him to dig for treasure).

The Story

Anne said that one of the symptoms of Susan's illness was (like Pywall's problem) being *troubled with treasure,* for which the cure—so Susan told her—was to *go and dig in [Anne's] garden, and then she should be well.* Perhaps we can imagine Susan, whilst wracked by the shaking ague, also tormented by the thought that there might be money in the next-door garden, there for the taking. It was Susan alone who did the digging, in Anne's account, but she was not successful—she *could find nothing but stones, neither did she hear any sound of any thing but as a stroke upon a stone.* Anne told her that she would only *make herself a fool* as Robert Pywall had done—thus further distancing herself from the hunt for treasure.

After Susan became too sick to continue digging, they both went into Susan's house and Anne told her about Robert Pywall having also been *troubled with treasure.*

When Pywall had tried his hand at digging, George said he provided him a with short spit, at his request, with which to sound the ground, and they (he and Pywall—Anne is not mentioned in George's account) heard a *sound as if the spit had hit uppon some brass pot.* But when he dug again, they found nothing. Pywall then again sounded the ground with the spit and

> found the [sound] to be two foot lower. And then he digged the third time, and he found the sound to be very near in his judgment. And then he digged further, but as he digged further so to his judgment…the sound was further off…. Pywall saying *he did labour in vain,* gave over his work and filled up the hole again.

The treasure kept *going away,* just as Anne and Susan had found.

* * *

Why this obsession with buried treasure? First and foremost, people *did* bury money and valuables in the ground. What else was there to do with them? There were no banks, and locked chests could be broken open or carried away. Before the Reformation, people used to leave money for safe keeping in abbeys, monasteries and convents. Since the monks and nuns were not supposed to have personal possessions, it was harder for them either to spend the money or pass it on to others—and of course they were expected to be less venal than ordinary people. But all such sacred institutions had been dissolved. Money could be—and often was—loaned out by rich people to others in small sums, but then there was the problem of getting it back.

Take the predicament of the Vicar of Halifax, who in 1537 owned the huge sum of £800 in coins. Keeping the money from thieves was a particular problem because catholic rebellion had broken out in the northern counties (the Pilgrimage of Grace). Yet he simply hid the coins in the ground, in a brass pot with short feet (metal pots with three feet were common, since all cooking was done over open fires).

His neighbour Thomas Lacey, emboldened perhaps by the general lawlessness, and hearing that the vicar *was wont to hide money in the ground*

> Took a piked staff and struck into the ground and at the first stroke hit the pot. Took the money home in his sleeve.

Large sleeves were fashionable at that period, and Lacey was no pauper.

Thomas Lacey used the same method, then, as the Rye treasure-hunters, but unlike them, he actually found the money. There is a further twist to the story, however. Anxiety about spiritual retribution appears to have got the better of him, because he confessed the theft to a priest during Lent, and returned most of the money. He defended his actions by saying it was treasure trove, and did not belong to the vicar.

This curious twist in the tale does not just illustrate the peculiar psyche of Thomas Lacey. Spiritual retribution—not necessarily of a godly kind—was of much wider concern, as was the associated belief that treasure usually had a rightful owner.

*   *   *

That stony, sunken spot under the appletree in Anne's garden had special qualities. There was not only treasure hidden there, but it was also haunted by spirits, as Anne told Philip Williams when he was gardening for them.

Appletrees were associated with fairies in medieval stories and songs—Tam Lin, in the ballad of the same name, was carried away by fairies when sleeping under an apple tree, as was Sir Lancelot, and Queen Meroudys in the medieval poem of *King Orfeo*. Apples were perhaps the pre-eminent English symbol of fruitfulness—so the English translators of the Bible chose to translate the non-specific *fruit of the tree of good and evil* as an apple.

The Story

Both humans and spirits were interested in the apples on the Taylors' tree. Susan's neighbour on the other side from the Taylors, Phyllis Swan (the wife of a sailor), asked her to get some of them for her. She was pregnant, and had a craving for green apples. Then again a

> spirit in the likeness of a woman great with child did appear unto [Susan] in her house in the day time, and did wish that she had some apples, whereupon [she] went to Mistress Taylor and teld her of it …

There was something else under the ground next to the appletree. Susan said in a later examination that one of the spirits told her that those

> things that [Susan] was troubled withall was true… it was money that was hidden amongst the thyme in Mistress Taylor's garden. And that Mistress Taylor did know thereof, and did tell [her] that the ground where the thyme grew is hollow, and that the same had been vawted.

Vaulted stone cellars were not unusual under the houses of Rye—often used by merchants to store their Gascon wine—and they were often much older than the buildings above. The houses were built with frameworks of wood, so they burned down easily, leaving the cellars behind. One cellar was mentioned earlier in the century which only had a garden above, so the foundations of an old medieval building may have lain under the Taylors' garden.

There had, indeed, been a medieval mansion beyond the end of their garden which must have dominated the town at one time. It was owned around 1500 by the King's Bailiff and courtier John Shurley, whose main seat was at Isted in Sussex—he probably only descended on Rye with his retinue for occasional visits. He was also briefly one of the town's jurats—in those days the advantages of having an important man as jurat outweighed the lack of independence which it entailed for the corporation. This mansion would have had extensive wine cellars, and was later broken up into smaller units, so it is possible that since that time some of its land with an abandoned cellar beneath had been bought by former owners of the Taylors' garden.

Anne and Susan may, of course, have had quite other ideas as to what was buried under the thyme. Spirits were often thought to haunt ruins—had there been a burial in unconsecrated ground? When one of the spirits later brought back a sheet that Susan had given him, there was clay on it, as if it had been taken underground. Anne could have planted the thyme there to increase its potency in medicines, because herbs grown in burial grounds were thought to be more powerful. Thyme was also said to be associated with fairies.

The *summerhouse* next to the appletree, in which Anne had tried digging for treasure (according to Susan), is a curious ingredient in this scene. Summerhouses (*summerhalls, arbours*) were very popular in the 16th century, whether in private gardens, or as a centrepoint for village games, where the summer lords reigned, and cakes and ale were served. This one must have been more substantial than the usual flimsy structures made from boughs and creepers, because it appears to have been mentioned in the will of Anne's grandfather back in 1564 (an unusual item in a Rye will). It is there called a *herber*, which was a common medieval word for a sheltered pleasure garden, planted with flowers and possibly herbs, and usually surrounded by high fences or walls. It could also be spelt *arbour/harbour*—meaning a shelter, whether for people or ships. During the 16th century the meaning of the word narrowed—now referring to a sheltered part of the garden, rather than the whole of it. This one might therefore have been the remains of the old building whose vaulted cellar had been left below ground, together with, perhaps, the nearby herb beds and apple tree. Remnants of an old house frame would have provided an ideal support for creepers.

A Herber.

The Story

Buried treasure seems to have spawned spiritual guardians as readily as bad meat bred maggots. The connection is spelt out by a cunning woman who told a wealthy widow that her late husband had buried money around their house, *for which cause there are sprites now that haunt your house.* Sussex folklorists record many tales of treasure guarded by spirits which took various forms, such as a black hen, snakes, or simply the devil. The origins of most of these stories are lost in the mists of time, but we could take as an example one which was reported in a 19th century newspaper. A couple of Sussex hills were reputed to have Aaron's golden calf buried there, and a writer in the West Sussex Gazette reported that *my Dad* said that his grandfather had got up early one Easter Sunday to dig for it in one of these hills (did he think that digging on such a holy day would provide some spiritual protection?). He did catch sight of a lump of gold, but was *almost deafed by a clap o' thunder, an' when he looked again, the gold was gone.* Another 19th century countryman said that several people had attempted to find the treasure, but *he* (presumably the guardian spirit) always moves it away. Other people thought that the calf was the guardian spirit of a Viking hoard, and could be heard lowing on certain nights.

In the 16th century, shape-changing spirits of dubious morality were not the only kind of spirit who might provide protection for treasure. One reason why people left their savings at abbeys, monasteries and convents before they were dissolved was that these places were sacred—and those who violated them would be cursed. The wayside crosses which dotted the pre-Reformation countryside were also thought to be a good place to hide money—they were not only sacred, but had the advantage that you did not have to rely on the honesty of monks and nuns.

The dissolution of the monasteries perhaps dealt a blow to people's faith in this form of protection, because there was a spate of treasure-hunting at this time—in particular, digging up wayside crosses. Crosses were easier to dig up than ex-monasteries, and less obviously belonged to anyone. The authorities were not sure what to do with such troublemakers. When some glovers and labourers were examined in 1538 about the digging up of a cross at Willington in Sussex, the examining magistrate wrote to Thomas Cromwell (Secretary of State) to ask whether they should be sent up to London. One of the men was quoted as saying in a scoffing manner, as they left an alehouse

> *There be many crosses digged up hereabouts, and men say there is much money under Willington Cross, which, if thou wilt be ruled by me, we will have.*

Another said that he had often dreamed there was money under the cross. They attempted it with a shovel and three mattocks, but found no money. Some other Sussex artisans were examined about digging up a cross near Chichester in 1547 in search of treasure; they were pardoned. If Henry VIII could plunder religious buildings without spiritual retribution, why not ordinary people? Such activities generated the phrase *cross-digger*, meaning a man on the make—comparable to *hill-digger*, which referred to those who dug for treasure in ancient burial mounds or hills frequented by fairies.

The authorities reacted with considerable alarm to this treasure-hunting, as is evident from the extraordinary act passed in 1542 which made the conjuring of spirits to find buried treasure a capital offence on the first conviction.

Note that treasure-hunting *without* conjuring was not targeted by any particular order or regulation—they were either assumed to go together, or it was thought that successful prospectors for buried treasure were most likely to have used conjuring to achieve their ends. The best negotiators with guardian spirits were other spirits, and early modern treasure hunting groups often included somebody experienced in conjuring spirits, or who at least had a book on the subject—he was usually a priest or schoolmaster who could read latin.

The Act of 1542 was also the first time that murder by witchcraft entered the statute book—but it was *treasure-hunting* that was the first item in the Act (followed by detection of lost and stolen goods). Making such crimes statutory offences was not in itself peculiar—the secular courts were taking over some types of criminal and civil cases in the early 16th century that had formerly only been actionable at church or local courts—but infliction of the death penalty was an extreme response. Concern about it soon relaxed, however, and the Act was repealed only five years later. Six years after this (in 1563) another Act was passed making it again a statutory offence to conjure spirits in order to find buried treasure (amongst other crimes), but the death sentence could only be imposed for a second offence, and cross-digging was not mentioned.

The legal owner of all such *treasure trove* was the Crown (if the original owner was unknown), and the Tudor monarchs were not slow to take advantage of this. A succession of people were licensed by them to search for treasure in different parts of the country. The metal was to be used by the Crown for coining, and the finders were permitted to keep a certain proportion for themselves. Conjuring was acceptable for those who were thus licensed (since they were unlikely to be successful without it).

What the Rye treasure-hunters were doing was therefore technically illegal—but there were many activities that were illegal that were nevertheless rarely prosecuted. Thief-detection with the help of spirits or rituals was similarly illegal, but this did not stop some cunningfolk being bold enough to inform the authorities who to charge with theft, after they had used their divining skills to reveal the culprit. Anne and Susan were not, it is true, actually *conjuring* spirits—or at least not as revealed by the evidence considered thus far…

* * *

If they had succeeded in finding the treasure, Anne would not, anyway, have defined it as *treasure trove* (if she knew what this meant), since she considered herself *heir* to it (according to Susan). It was, in some unspecified sense, hers by right. This was not a simple question that could be sorted out by the law of inheritance, however, because in a flash of antagonism towards her husband, Anne said *it was god's will that he should not enjoy it,* and the *he* appears to refer to George! She said this (according to Susan) when Robert Pywall was trying to dig for treasure:

> … Master Taylor coming to the place where he digged, [Anne] said
> *The further they digged, the further the money was off. But,* she said, *she was heir to the money, and therefore it was god's will that he should not enjoy it.* …

This curious juxtaposition of statements seems to imply that the treasure had *gone away* when George arrived, because he had no right to it. It is possible that she meant that *Pywall* should not enjoy it—but if that were the case, why did she then ask him to carry on digging? Pywall did not perhaps really count, because he was just hired labour. Roger also heard Anne say that they could not hear the *sound* after George arrived on the scene *nor knew not what became thereof.* The implication seems to be that Anne thought she had a *moral* right to the money, even if, by law, George acquired all her possessions at marriage.

George appears to have been unaware of the effect of his presence on the treasure (or does not admit to it)—in fact, they get closer to finding it in his account than in any other, because Pywall actually hits something that might be a brass pot.

There is a Somerset tale that illustrates the meaning of a *moral* right to treasure—a folklorist recorded it as recently as the 1920s. As in Rye, the treasure was buried under an appletree. A man who had been deprived of his inheritance rented an orchard that was rightfully his. One Christmas he had wassailed the trees with his last mug of mulled cider, and the oldest apple tree (known as *appletree man*) told him:

> *'You take and look under this gurt diddicky root of ours'*. And there was a chest full of finest gold.
> *''Tis yours, and non one else'*, say the Apple-Tree Man. *'Put'n away zafe and bide quiet about'n'*. So he done that.

The coming and going of treasure, therefore, has to do with the moral right of the person digging. The role of the guardian spirit (in the above example, *appletree man*) appears to be tied up with this in a manner that may not be altogether straightforward. Those who are chancing their luck might expect spiritual retribution, unless they can command a more powerful spirit to defend their interests.

* * *

Robert Pywall was gripped by fear when he was digging for the treasure, so Anne told Susan. This is not surprising given that spirits were guarding it, and only those who had a moral right to it were likely to be successful. But she told him:

> fear not, for she was with child, and I hope in god nothing will hurt us

Being pregnant was clearly thought to provide some protection.

George too said that because he was frightened, Pywall had wanted him to stand there while he dug. As far as George was concerned, that was the end of the story. But his wife read more into it, for she told Susan that:

> Pywall was fearful, and his colour vaded away, and she thought in her conscience that he died of it.

Indeed, Pywall died soon after, in May 1605. Fear was a recognised cause of death at this period—about one such death a year was listed in the London Bills of Mortality (drawn up by local women, not physicians).

The Story

Perhaps it was because Susan's house was haunted, along with the garden, that Pywall had had a similar symptom to Susan's when he had lived in it. For him, instead of curing his symptoms and making him rich, digging for treasure had had fatal consequences.

All this talk of fear, and cravings for treasure, did not wash with the prosaic Roger. Identifying, perhaps, with another lowpaid worker, he said that Pywall had been arguing with Anne about how to divide the proceeds, and had downed tools because she would not make a definite offer. Pywall wanted half, and refused to continue until George came.

Anne made a more attractive offer to Susan than she had to Pywall:

> [she] willed her that *If the spirits should appear unto her again, in regard they had digged already and could find nothing, that she should ask them the sum of it, and in what place and wherein it was. And whether there were any more in any other place…If she did find the money she would give unto [Susan] one hundred pounds, and that she and her children should never want whilst she lived.*

What reassuring words! Susan does not say whether or not she ever put Anne's question to the spirits.

Susan had had a better experience than Robert Pywall, since in spite of having to stop digging early in the day because she felt ill, she *did sleep in quiet* that night, and *was not any ways troubled.* And again the next night she *did sleep in quiet and heard nothing.* It seems the spirits were as good as their word—she had no symptoms of any sort, and the spirits themselves no longer haunted her. Indeed, shortly *after that time she was not troubled in a long space, but she grew to be well.* Her spirits did not in fact depart, but they stopped being threatening.

* * *

The spot in Anne's garden under the appletree was not the only place where treasure might be found. One of the questions which Anne had wanted Susan to ask the spirits (so Susan said) was whether or not there was *any more [money] buried in any other place.* Susan does not say if she passed on the query, but an answer came nonetheless in a typically gnomic pronouncement. A spirit man first asked her:

> *What [Anne] had in the Summer house.* And [Susan] answered,
> *She could not tell.*

A curious question—were not the *spirits* the ones most likely to know what was in the summerhouse?

> And then he said unto her again, that
> *Those things that [Susan] was troubled withall was true. And that the field at Weeks G[reen] was ploughed and the crock was broken, and some part thereof was found and the rest was left behind.* And so [the spirits] departed.

Weeks Green was a hamlet situated about a mile north of Rye, where the London road entered the Weald (there is a Houghton Green there now—perhaps it was just renamed after a different inhabitant).

> And then in the morning Mistress Taylor came unto her again, and asked
> *'What news?'* And [Susan] did tell her as before is said. And then she said
> *'Is it even so? Well I have a groat of the same money'*, which she said she gave sixpence for.

Must be a joke—since a groat was only worth fourpence! So a farmer had found some treasure buried in a pot in the field at Weeks Green when he was ploughing, but there was still some left that had not been dug up. Nothing further came of this disclosure, however, until later in the year.

* * *

When spring was turning into summer, Susan did pursue the matter—again prompted by the spirits:

> And after Whitsontide last, the two men and women appeared unto her again. And the two women came into her chamber, and the two men went up into another chamber …. And one of the women said unto her,
> *'How now, now thou art well!'* and she answered
> *'Yea, I thank god'*. And then she said,
> *'Thou must go with me'* and I answered
> *'In the name of god, whether must I go with you?'* And [her] girl coming up [to?] the chamber, the woman vanished away.
> And then she went unto Mistress Taylor and told her of it. And Mistress Taylor said
> *'Well, you shall hear more soon'*, and willed her that
> *If they should require her to go any whither with them, that she should have a strong faith in god, and so go with them.*
> And the next night following, two of them came unto her, and one of them asked her
> *Whether she would go with them*, and she said

The Story

> *No, she would not go with them that night, but the next day she would go with them, by gods help.*
> And the next morning she went to Mistress Taylor and told her what had passed that night. And Mistress Taylor then asked her
> *Why she did not go with them?* And she answered that
> *She was too much afraid to go by night, unless she had some to go with her.* And then [Anne] said
> *I promise thee, I should be afeared to go, too.*
> And the next day between twelve and one of the clock, [she] being a lone in her house, did hear a great stamp in the loft over the hall. And then she went up, and the tall man asked her
> *Whether she would go with him?* and she answered
> *'Aye, by the grace of god, if you....[will] tell me whither'.* And then he said
> *She should go to Weeks [Green], and asked whether she would go with him or a lone?*
> And she answered
> *She had rather go alone, if she knew the way.* And then she went to Mistress Taylor and teld her of it, and Mistress Taylor told her
> *'The way is easy to be found'*, and so she directed her the way, and told her *by what token she should know the house.*

Even though Anne appears to be so interested in the spirits, there does not seem to be any question of *her* going to Weeks Green—yet she knows the way, and Susan does not.

The house. This was a farmhouse that used to belong to Anne's father Robert—another connection with the Bennett family. Robert Bennett had been burdened by debt when he died—a victim of the plague epidemic of 1596—and the *house, barn and orchard beneath Weeks Green* and other lands in the same parish had had to be sold to pay the debts off. He had left these properties directly to Anne (his only surviving child), not first to her mother for her life, as with his properties in Rye. He had hoped that the profits from the farm would cover his debts.

Widow Bennett had tried to keep the farm in the family—she and her daughter had been betrothed to marry one of their creditors and his son—Thomas and John Lashenden. The Lashendens were tanners, to whom Robert Bennett (butcher) had presumably sold his hides—and perhaps also received loans from the richer man. I do not know when these dual betrothals had been broken off—perhaps when Anne landed her gentleman suitor. But in spite of this extraordinary achievement, perhaps Anne still felt that the disasters that befell them in the 1590s were unjust. That crock full of money in the field at Weeks Green was rightfully *hers*.

* * *

The scene that unfolded when Susan got to Weeks Green was, however, all her own.

> And thereuppon [she] went to Weeks Green by the house. And there she did see the tall man stand in the street by the orchard, and he willed her to
> *Follow him,* thorough a rye field into the greenfield next to it, which she did. And in the middle of the field there was a valley of th'one side, and a bank of th'other. And there he did tell her
> *In that valley there was a pot, and in that pot there was gold, and upon the top of the pot a chain. And beside the pit under a little stub, there was a crock, metal with three legs, and [in] which there was money.*

This sounds like a mythical landscape—*in the middle of the field there was a valley of th'one side, and a bank of th'other*—but it is actually a realistic description of the lie of the land around there, where several fields rise up in the middle, and then slope down on the other side, like a very large bank.

Susan has made her (or the spirit's) purpose very clear, but what actually happens is something else (rather like a dream):

> And then he bade her
> *Set down upon a bank,* and she did set down. And then she saw a man all in black on the on[e] side of the hedge, and a woman in green on the same side, one going to meet another (as she thought). And as she set, she thought the ground did move under her, and then she cried
> *'Lord have mercy upon me, what shalbe come of me!'* And then the tall man came to her again, and bade her
> *Be not afraid, for she should have no harm.* And then she looked about her again, and did see the two persons which she did see by the hedge side, and she asked the tall man what they were. And he said *the woman in green is the [Queen] of the Fayries, and that if [Susan] would kneel to her, she would give her a living.* But she did not kneel unto her. And then she looked about, and they were gone. And the tall man came to her again, and willed her to
> *'Rise, and go home',* but she could not rise. And then he willed her
> *In the name of god, to rise,* and then she rose and went home, and the men [sic] vanished away.

Was Susan too proud, or too scared, to ask the Queen of the Fairies to be her patron?

> And so [she] went home sick to bed, and sent for Mistress Taylor, and told her all the discourse. And she asked her

The Story

> *Whether she did see nothing else,* and she said
> *No.* Then Mistress Taylor said
> *She had been troubled with that before, and wished she had a hundred pounds to buy her farm again.*

So Anne hoped that the treasure could be used to buy the farm back—she clearly thought it was her due. She got too demanding, however, and earned a reproof from the spirits (through Susan). She had asked Susan to

> *Demand of them when she could have some money of them, for if she had a thousand pounds she could tell where to have a purchase for the same.* And [Susan] accordingly, the next time her familiars appeared unto her, did ask them
> *When the said Mistress Taylor should have money of them.* And the tall man, who named himself to be Richard, said that
> *If she be so hasty, she shall tarry until she had a child of her body, should live to be six years old.*

They might indeed consider her greedy to demand a *thousand pounds*! (the largest houses in Rye cost £80-90). Her punishment was a long wait—over 4 years, since her son George was only 19 months old. She also had a 5-year-old step-daughter, Elizabeth (her husband's daughter by a previous marriage), so perhaps this is why the spirit specified a *child of her body*.

After this incident, Susan made no more attempts to find treasure—or at least none that she told the magistrates about.

[Rye 13/7]

Above is Susan's mark, at the bottom of her examination. She has carefully written an S—not the careless cross that people often made—pressing so hard on the paper that she has spattered ink drops (her S is in a common style, although different from that of the town clerk, who has written her name next to it). Each witness and examinate had to sign or make their mark at the bottom of their deposition or examination.

The copy of Susan's mark shown above is actually from her *second* examination, since the original of the first has not survived—what we have is a copy, written in the very neat handwriting of one of the jurats, with none of the usual crossings-out. Perhaps the original document was sent to the town's counsel, Serjeant Shurley, when the magistrates later wrote to him to check the legality of the trial.

*   *   *

Susan's relations with the spirits had improved. Spirit Richard was now acting as her guide, and giving her useful advice. There were no more episodes of lameness.

About the time that spirit Richard acquired a name, he was also given, on occasion, a new identity—as her *familiar* (he could hardly be familiar if he were nameless). Is this an ominous development? Was it Susan who had used that word, or had the town clerk substituted it for a different word? Most people have heard about familiars—they are those little imps in the shape of toads, cats or other small creatures, with names like Piggin and Pyewacket, who carry out foul deeds for witches in return for suckling hidden teats on their bodies. Or are they? If you rely on the tabloid press of the period—the pamphlet accounts of witchcraft trials—this is the type of story that you get. But there are few such animal familiars in the surviving legal evidence (except those relating to the witch-hunt which occurred during the Civil War). Instead, the witches themselves sometimes appear to their victims in the shape of an animal (or indeed in their own shape)—a rather more frightening witch-image, perhaps, than the old woman who is somewhat at the mercy of her little imps. These records are admittedly not very representative, because the only examinations and evidence for the Assize courts that *do* survive are for the northern counties of England.

This at least suggests that we do not have to struggle to fit spirit Richard into the mould of an animal familiar when he is referred to as a *familiar*. The word means *one of the family* (in the loose sense used at that period), and he certainly seems to have acquired a special relationship with Susan. He was her special guide, and only she could see him—as indeed all the spirits (Robert Pywall had no such privilege).

That spell of fever in the early months of the year had melted the boundaries between the ordinary, material world and more nebulous realities, and enabled the spirits to make their presence felt. After that, Susan was sensitised to their existence. She could see them not only in her own house, but also in the street, in a crowd of people, on the gungarden, going into the church. And no-one else could—though there is a question mark over Anne Taylor. Susan often implies that Anne will not have dealings with them because she is *frightened*, but it seems to me that the overall implication of Susan's account—and everyone else's—is that Anne is not able to see them. So even though Anne feels that the treasure is *hers*, it is in *her* garden, and in *her* field at Weeks Green, and she knew about the spirits and the treasure before Susan arrived, she cannot deal with the spirits because they have chosen Susan to be their medium (if you can use the same word as in spirit possession). Yet Anne appears to know much more about how to deal with them than Susan—or that is what the latter implies, emphasising her own ignorance and innocence.

Susan's experience might be compared with that of practitioners termed *shamans* by anthropologists (borrowing the Siberian word), who, on recovery from a spirit-induced illness, manage to tame that spirit and then employ it (or them) to help cure others suffering from similar illnesses. Would she rise to this vocation? And might those cunningfolk who obtained their knowledge from the fairies also have been fairy-taken or fairy-gripped at one time?

Even if other people in Rye could not *see* the spirits, they could *hear* them, so they did not have to rely entirely on Susan's words. There were those noises in the upper chambers of their house that Roger thought were made by weasels—*great stamping, knocking, lumbering* (must have been heavy-footed weasels—though some people thought that weasels *were* fairies). Anne Taylor and Susan's sister Elizabeth also heard the noises. We have a term for such spirits today—*poltergeists*—but what did the people who heard them think they were? What did Susan think these spirits were, that she nearly always referred to as just that—*spirits*?

* * *

The word that was occasionally used of Susan's spirits was *fairy*—both by Susan and others. George Taylor added an extra *s* to the word—*faireses*—in a letter to the magistrates. Adding an extra *s* to plurals was a Sussex custom (like *waspses* and *ghostses*), and it has been said that in the 19th century, fairies were implicated with the Biblical *pharisees*! The town clerk, however, was not a local man, and did not use this spelling when he recorded the examinations and evidence.

Banish any thought of diminutive beings with gossamer wings. Fairies were generally about human-size, although they could vary. And the commonly used euphemisms *fair folk* and *good neighbours* were not descriptions, but terms of *flattery*. These terms were intended to deflect any malice that these beings might harbour against us, and encourage them instead to act in ways appropriate to the titles that we use—to be our helpers.

There were various tokens which would suggest that these spirits were fairies—apart from the give-away of meeting the Queen of the Fairies. The spirits were dressed in green and white, which were often considered to be fairy colours (and it was *green apples* that were desired—unripe apples, because it was still summer, the time *when apples were green*); they inflicted lameness by gripping the victim—perhaps a more severe form of the *pinching* that was often said to be typical behaviour; they haunt a spot under an appletree, where thyme grows—both associated with fairies; and finally, they threatened to *carry her away*, which is a typical fairy action, even if it was not to a fairy hill (and she was not the typical victim, a baby or nursing mother).

But we should not be too dogmatic about what type of spirit these were. After all, Scottish fairies were often people who had died—so ghosts and fairies were not clearly distinguished there. The well-known Scottish cunning woman Bessie Dunlop had a familiar named Thom Reid, who had died at the battle of Pinkie, fighting the English (1547). She told the widow of the Laird of Auchinskeyth, who had died a few years before Bessie was interrogated (1576), that her late husband was with the fairies.

These Scottish catholics presumably *also* thought that the dead might be in purgatory, waiting for the prayers of the living to wing them heavenwards (or perhaps purgatory was the state of remaining *here* in this world). But reality is muddy—or at least not as clearcut as the various churches would have liked it to be. *Theologians like their spirits* out *of this world, and either good or evil* according to one historian, whereas for ordinary people spirits were more often ambivalent and local—the souls of people who had been known when they were alive.

Spirit Richard has some similarities with Scottish familiar spirits. Bessie describes her familiar's clothes in as much detail as Susan does; like her, she sees him sometimes amongst all the people in the marketplace, as well as when there is no-one there; she meets the *Queen of Elfame, his mistress,* who had told Thom to *wait upon [Bessie]* and *do her good*. Bessie claims to get all her skills in healing from Thom—she herself knows nothing, like Susan. And like Susan, she had been in a vulnerable state when her familiar first appeared to her—newly risen from childbed.

Thom's relations with God are contradictory—he reprehends Bessie for displeasing god on the one hand, and then demands that *she deny her christendom* and go with him. One may suspect the influence of the interrogators here, since they found her guilty, amongst other things, of

The Story

invoking and being familiar with *sprites of the devil* (the terse marginal note *convict, and brynt* [burnt] is the only record of her fate). The idea of the *pact with the devil* would soon be a spur to the witch-hunt in Scotland, as also in the other worst-affected areas of Europe (more on this later).

It may seem perverse not to be discussing other *English* fairies—but there is just nothing comparable in English court records. Why this should be so we will return to in the next chapter. Court records are *the* major source for popular beliefs in an era before newspapers, and before the growth of antiquarian interest in folklore (starting the middle and end of the 17th century, respectively). There are, it is true, some legal cases that I have not mentioned—of fraud, brought against cunningfolk who had claimed to be able to make their clients rich by applying to the Queen of the Fairies. On these cases, I refer you to Ben Jonson, who has the phenomenon drawn to a *T* in his play *The Alchemist*.

* * *

Thinking of those Scottish fairies—who were often, like Thom, dead heroes—suggests an origin for spirit Richard's name, and his curious dress (a *fairy* in a *surplice*?!). Susan no doubt wanted to present him as nearer to God than the Devil, but the idea of the surplice may have had a deeper resonance. The name *Richard* would have been associated by local people—at least those who hankered after the old religion—with holiness, in the person of Saint Richard of Chichester, who had been a popular local saint in Sussex and Kent before the Reformation. In Rye, money had been collected quarterly for Saint Richard's shrine, which was located in Chichester cathedral, together with relics of the saint. His hat would have been an appropriate relic for ague-stricken Rye, since a man was miraculously cured of the ague by having the saint's hat put on his head at the *exact* moment the next fit was due, and he never suffered from it again.

We can not know what Susan knew about this humble but determined man, but one thing that she might have been familiar with—perhaps in a picture or image that had survived the iconoclasm of the Reformation—was the token by which he could be identified, the chalice at his feet. This represented the miraculous occasion when he dropped the chalice while administering holy communion, and not a *drop* of the consecrated wine was spilt. To someone interested in searching for buried treasure, however—not just a pot of money but also silver cups and spoons (according to George Taylor)—this chalice might have suggested something quite else. Susan may not have consciously identified her spirit with the saint, rather ideas about the saint, or his image, might have been in the back of her mind, and informed her depiction of the spirit.

Then there is the saint's *whiteness*—when he died, his body apparently shone brilliantly white. Susan mentions twice that she saw her familiar spirit in white—once when she first saw him, and then again later when she saw the spirit going into the Church for the funeral of Anne's son. In medieval thought, whiteness had been a sign that a spirit had reached heaven. If a ghost had asked for masses to be said to help him (rarely her) get to heaven, and then subsequently appeared in shining white, it would indicate that the efforts of the living had been effective.

The whiteness was particularly important at the funeral, because he appeared to Anne—as reported by Susan—to be in *black*, in a flat cap (sitting in the gallery of the church, during the sermon). The flat cap had been fashionable in the middle of the 16th century, but by this date was only worn by tradesmen, so Susan is depicting him as a merchant, in a typical merchant's black gown. Or does the blackness indicate that Anne is seeing the devil (a man in early 16th century Switzerland recognised a figure in a church to be a demon because it changed from white to black)? This occasion was, incidentally, the only time that Anne saw him, as reported by Susan.

A *saint* may seem a long way from a *fairy*, but medieval saints could on occasion be as capricious as non-saintly spirits, inflicting the illnesses that they professed to cure.

* * *

I have suggested that Bessie's account may have been influenced by the interrogators—but what about Susan's? Did her interrogators ask her questions, prompt her for answers? And what did they make of her story —did it reek of irreligion, as Bessie's story did to her Presbyterian interrogators (who were probably members of the local Kirk)? Who *were* Susan's interrogators…

3 The Interrogators

Each September, a fleet of twenty or so fishing boats—and a few larger vessels—set sail for the deep-sea herring fishery in the North Sea, carrying in their bottoms nearly half the men of Rye. It was the equivalent of the harvest in arable areas, drawing in people who did not usually engage in fishing (sometimes these landlubbers became too seasick to work, and were put ashore to make their own way back to Rye). This year there were the *John* and the *William*, the *Hawk* and the *Diamond*, the *Mayflower* and the *Rose* …only 15 boats in total, because by this date the harbour was becoming seriously decayed. The small boats *Ninnyhammer*, *Small Brains*, and *Friday Afternoon* were perhaps *too* small to go on such a voyage.

The boats negotiated the treacherous sandbanks which had been thrown up by storms and currents from the silt collecting in the Camber, past Henry VIII's castle (from which a shot had never been fired in earnest), and sailed out into the main sea. They would not be back for a couple of months—the fish that were caught being sold at the Herring Fair at Yarmouth.

So the town would have been rather empty of men on 26th September 1607, when the mayor and jurats gathered to interrogate Susan Swaffer—possibly in the Court Hall, only a few yards from her house. Well, not quite all the jurats—for two of them were fishermen, and John Styner had left for Yarmouth in his boat the *John*. Robert Swayne, however, was still in town—an elderly, outspoken man, and rather a thorn in the side of some of the others on the bench. His place had been taken on the Yarmouth voyage by his sons Henry and John. Robert concentrated now

(now called Camber castle)

on trade rather than fishing, his merchandize—including salt, coal, boards, pitch and tar—carried in other people's boats.

There was a more crucial absence from the magisterial bench that was still very keenly felt—at least by some of those who sat round the table. A couple of months earlier, the man who had been at the top of the aldermanic hierarchy—the mayor and MP for the town, Thomas Hamon—had died suddenly (probably from a stroke). A brewer by trade like his father before him, he was the richest man in Rye, owning valuable marshland in different parts of Romney Marsh, as well as some farmland in the town's hinterland. He had been an impressive representative for Rye in Parliament, and nobody else on the bench could now approach him in wealth or prestige. His passing was symbolic of the recent decline of the town, which had been more successful than most members of the Cinque Ports in resisting the demands of the Lord Warden to choose their representatives in Parliament. At least one of the two MPs had always been a Rye jurat during the second half of the sixteenth century, but after Hamon's death, an influential Kentish gentleman managed to foist one of his relations on the town to replace him as MP. At least this saved the now impoverished town from having to pay their MPs' expenses—a not inconsiderable sum—and *some* of the gentlemen who were to represent it during the 17th century made efforts to promote the town's interests, employing their undoubtedly serviceable connections in high places.

Hamon's importance is expressed in the brass set up by his young widow Martha in his memory, behind the altar in Rye church (see frontispiece)—no other such memorials survive from this period. He was buried little more than a month after the two had got married—he in his late fifties, and she in her late twenties.

The bench managed to retain, however, at least some of Hamon's wealth and what you might call political capital within their ranks, when the new mayor, Thomas Higgons, married Martha Hamon—a mere fortnight after her husband's death. Higgons had been the government's customs officer in Rye, and owned the town's principal inn—the Mermaid (inherited from a deceased jurat, whose daughter had been Higgons' first wife). He dealt in a wide variety of merchandize—including wine, vinegar, wheat, sack, wool, salt, hops and prunes. Not being one of the more senior jurats—he had been on the bench for only 3 years—marriage to Martha may have helped convince the rest of the bench and freemen of his suitability for the role of mayor (Martha was also the daughter of another jurat, William Tharpe or Thorpe).

The Story

Thomas Hamon and the fishermen-jurats were extremes in the social hierarchy of the magistrates, although they all engaged in trade, and could therefore be described as in some sense *merchants*. On that autumn day there were in total: a goldsmith, 4 non-specific merchants, two brewers, a draper, a feter (which was a local name for a wholesale fishmonger) and a fisherman. Not quite the *butchers, bakers, and silver candlestick makers* that some wag (a goldsmith, which perhaps explains the 'silver'!) later accused them of being in some abusive verse, but lower in status than the usual Justices of the Peace who examined those suspected of criminal activity—these latter were chosen from the more *substantial* landed gentry. And rather than the usual one or two JPs questioning the suspect, the whole bench was present (apart from Styner) to hear Susan's story. Even if these magistrates were not county gentry, they must have seemed very grand to the poor woman standing on the opposite side of the table (in what follows, *Rye magistrates* and the *mayor and jurats* are used indiscriminately to refer to the same people).

* * *

Am I being disingenuous to keep referring to *Susan's Story*? This was not, after all, a gossipping session at the town's conduit—the woman was being interrogated! You would expect her account to be influenced by what they asked her. But there are various reasons why I see Susan's account as all of a piece—carried along by a momentum that was hers, rather than structured by the interrogators' questions.

It appears that Susan had already told at least part of the story in a more informal setting to George Taylor and the Vicar, John Bracegirdle—so the story had been rehearsed, and perhaps acquired a shape. It is Anne Taylor who mentioned this, after claiming that Susan had told her *nothing* about the trip to Weeks Green,

> but as she heard [Susan] tell unto Master Bracegirdle and unto [my] husband in [our] house

Susan is unlikely to have felt very threatened, telling her story in the Taylors' house—after all, the Taylors were themselves implicated in treasure-hunting.

Bracegirdle was on good terms with the Taylors (more on this later), and it may even have been one of them who spoke to him about the spirits, as is suggested by Anne's comment when Susan first told her about the spirits

> [she] *was altogethers ignorant what such apparitions should mean, and that she ... would, if ... [Susan] did think it convenient, make Master Bracegirdle acquainted therewith.* But [Susan] answered ~~me~~ ... again
> "*Do not so, for it is as much as all our lives are worth, if you should make him ~~or your husband~~ acquainted therewith.*"

Susan, however, denied that Anne had said any such thing, instead making her *swear that she should not disclose the same to any body*. Anne and Susan often accused each other of wanting to keep the spirits secret, with the implication that if they did so, the spirits would punish and forsake them (an oft-repeated belief about fairies). Perhaps the town clerk crossed out *or your husband* to give the impression that it was human prosecutors who were feared, rather than spirits.

On another occasion, it is speaking about the spirits in front of *Susan's* husband which is the problem. The conversation takes place when Susan starts to get well and the spirits stop haunting her. She says that she told Anne *Now I hope I am rid of them*. But Anne is (reportedly) alarmed that the spirits might have forsaken them, and accuses her of speaking to somebody about them. Susan replied that

> *She had said nothing unto anybody, but that Mistress Taylor and [she] had said before [Susan's] husband.* Then Mistress Taylor said that
> *She doubted [i.e. feared] that the speech which we have made before your husband hath hurt us.*

* * *

Cases involving spirits and popular magic would in most places have been heard at the church courts, but the town of Rye had made a special arrangement with the ecclesiastical authorities for church court cases to be heard in Rye before the magistrates and vicar jointly. Accordingly, Bracegirdle attended the interrogations in October, but does not appear to have attended any more.

If the case *had* gone to the church courts and Susan had been found guilty of something, the punishment would only have been to stand in church on a Sunday, holding a white wand, and making an apology.

The Story

What was this compared with the fame that she was acquiring from the local gossip about her *communication with spirits*?

* * *

So Susan had told her story before others at least once, and when she repeated her story before the magistrates, they appear to have mostly just *listened*. The story kept the shape that it had acquired when told before the vicar. There were only *two* questions which the magistrates definitely asked her. First, *what the four spirits' names were* — to which she answered, *the eldest named himself Robert, the tallest of them Richard, and the two women Catherine and Margery*. Presumably they wanted to ascertain if these were familiar spirits. The second was why she had not told anyone about the spirits, to which she answered that *Mistress Taylor had caused her to swear to reveal the same to no person.*

This lack of questions contrasts with the examinations of other people recorded later in the autumn, in which the interrogators' questions are clearly set out — in fact, the phrase *examined upon certain Articles or Interrogatories* is included in these documents, and the answers are often numbered to correspond with the questions. Many of the interrogatories survive.

But did Susan's story include responses to more informal questions from the magistrates, which are less apparent to the reader? I think this unlikely, because of the way the magistrates treated the narrative when they came to interrogate Anne Taylor, three weeks later. They asked Anne fully *31 questions*, and all but two repeated Susan's story — often verbatim — in the order in which she had told it. Anne was simply asked for her knowledge about each incident, except for an *Any comments?* question at the end, in which she was asked what else she knew about Susan's *communication or dealing with spirits*. But the question about the *names of the spirits* was extracted from the narrative and put in a different place in the interrogatory — it had moved from the end of her story to near the beginning, suggesting that not only did they consider this a particularly important question, but also that it was not really integrated into the rest of the narrative. Anne did, incidentally, know the names of the spirits, and told them to the interrogators — one of the few questions that she agreed to answer. The other question put to Susan by the magistrates — about her failure to tell anyone about the spirits — remained in the same place in the interrogatory as in the original narrative.

Susan's examination before the magistrates was much more formal than that before the vicar, but it is not clear what anyone thought the issue was—certainly nothing straightforward like a theft, or murder, or death or maiming by witchcraft. True, using spirits to find buried treasure was defined by statute as a crime, but in practice very few people were indicted for it. Probably fewer than a hundred cases of using magic (as opposed to black witchcraft) were heard at the national Assize courts between 1563 and 1736. Even the magistrates may not have been sure what to make of Susan's account, because three weeks elapsed before they examined anyone else.

Did Susan know why she was being examined? Feeling intimidated, she might well have made an effort to give the interrogators what she thought they wanted to hear—and what this was may be indicated by the embellishments to her tale. *Every* little incident that she related was followed by a report of what Mistress Taylor had to say about it. Then after telling her story, she recounted numerous anecdotes—unrelated to the main story—which all focused on Anne. In part, she no doubt wished to make clear that responsibility for all interaction with the spirits lay with her richer and more knowledgeable neighbour. But such extensive efforts to implicate Anne Taylor may indicate where Susan thought the magistrates' concerns lay.

I was intrigued to discover recently another, contrasting, version of Susan's first examination (revealed while checking references—I had assumed it was just a copy). In this version, nearly all mention of Anne has been *omitted*—the whole narrative revolves around Susan. Otherwise, much of it repeats the original almost verbatim. Where this document originated is not clear—it has found its way into a manuscript collection in the British Library. But it is clearly a later re-working by Susan herself of the story, because she incorporates bits from later evidence into earlier sections (and even from other people's evidence), a couple of extra bits of information are added to one incident, and the spirits have names right from the start. This is a reworking that is too detailed and complex for it to have been done by somebody else. When Anne is mentioned, she is simply referred to by Susan as *Anne*, not *Mistress Taylor*—a somewhat insulting way to refer to her. Perhaps this examination was recorded when George Taylor later tried to get the case removed to an appeal court, since it provides no basis for suspecting Anne of anything.

* * *

The Story

If the interrogators were interested in Anne, they were certainly not very interested in Susan, as is evident from how they examined Susan's husband. You would think he would be a prime source of information both about his wife's involvement with the spirits and, perhaps, the spirits themselves, since he was the person most directly affected by them after Susan—after all, they gripped his arm so hard that he could not use it. Yet he was asked only five questions in all, four of which concerned Anne quite as much as his wife.

In his replies, Roger mentioned Anne frequently, saying that *she was daily at his house*, and that he blamed his wife for talking to Anne so often, for *when [he] was at Mistress Taylor's and when he was from home, then commonly Mistress Taylor would be at [his] house with his wife. But he heard not their conference*. So even when he was chopping wood for George, Anne would be at his house.

He distanced himself from the spirits, saying that, yes, he had heard *lumbering and a noise in his chamber and lofts*, but that he thought they were weasels, which he had often seen in the house. Yes, Anne had paid him a penny a night to sleep out of the house for a week, but he did not know why. There is no doubt that Anne *had* done so, and *she* declared that it was because the spirits had said that he was a *Lewd and wicked Liver* (and because they were both ill), and she thought the spirits might go away if he was not there: *Susan* ~~would then be well~~ *should be no more troubled with them*. Susan, however, thought that Anne's motive was the reverse of this: she did it *to the intent that the spirits might have more familiar conference with [Susan]*. She said he was away for a fortnight.

Roger scribbled his mark carelessly at the bottom of his examination, unlike Susan's careful effort:

[Rye 13/3]

No great efforts were actually required by the interrogators to link Anne with the spirits. Several witnesses said that Anne spent much time at the Swaffers' house, and much of her and Susan's activity involved attending to the spirits. Susan's sister Elizabeth said she was often present *at her sister Swapper's house in the company of Mistress Taylor and her sister* (although nobody else mentioned Elizabeth). Elizabeth's deposition is torn, but the sense can be reconstructed:

> knocking in the chamber over their heads as though one ... And upon that knocking Mistress [Taylor said to] sister Swapper *that she must go* ... and whispered to her in her [ear] ...Her [sister went] down to Master Taylor's summer[house], and in the mean time Mistress Taylor [did her] sister's work till she return[ed]. And ... after they had whispered togethers ...that she was so heavy asleep

The sense is not altogether clear—*who* was asleep—was this when Susan was still very ill? What was Elizabeth doing while Anne was doing Susan's work—or was she not there at that point? But it confirms Susan's presentation of herself as just doing what Anne and the spirits wanted her to do.

Anne was so often in Susan's house, according to Susan, that the spirits got annoyed:

> Mistress Taylor diverse times came unto [Susan's] house, and sent away [Susan's] children to her house. And then cause [Susan's] doors to be bolted that none should come in. And after ... t[he] g[rou]nd did move, when the said ~~Anne~~ -------- did go or sett [i.e. walk or sit] And then she willed [Susan] to go up to the spirits to
> *See what news they brought, and what they would have.* And thus the said Mistress Taylor most days did use.
> And sometimes likewise at Mistress Taylor's own house, when [Susan] and she did sett togethers, the ground did move where Mistress Taylor did sett. And likewise she would then send [her] up to
> *Know what they would have.* And sometimes when [she] was sent up, the spirits would say nothing. And sometimes at [her] house, when Mistress Taylor sent [her] up, the spirits would will her to
> *Bid Mistress Taylor go home.* But wherefore she knoweth not, but then Mistress Taylor would presently run home.

Susan seems to have been completely at Mistress Taylor's command—no wonder the spirits, as relayed by Susan, sometimes told her landlady to *go home*!

* * *

There was one occasion when the usually impassive Roger got angry. He had been locked out of his own house, with Anne Taylor apparently inside with his wife! Roger was the first to mention this incident, and it suggests more serious wrongdoing by Anne than we have encountered

The Story

thus far. It was midsummer (about the time when Susan went to Weeks Green) when

> he coming from his work from Winchelsea unto his house about candlelight, did find his door locked up, and did knock at the same a pretty space, and none would come to the door. At last his little girl did come to the door, and he willed her to open the door. And she said she could not open the door, for Mistress Taylor had the key. And then [he] did knock hard again at the door. And then Mistress Taylor came to the door and said [he] should
> *"Stay awhile, you shall not come in yet,"* whereupon [he] said that
> *He would come in,* and so ram with his foot against the door, but could not open it. Then at the last with much ado, she opened the door and went away. And [he] did ask her
> *Where his wife was?* and she said
> *She was gone out of the town.*

Roger was not only angry, but very alarmed by the apparent inability of anyone in the house to open the door, according to their neighbour Anne Moore (a labourer's wife). He said to her, *they came to the door and from the door, and he thought the divell was within with them, that they had no power to open the door.* A more serious matter than weasels, this! But he did not himself reveal his concerns to the interrogators.

Once he had managed to get into the house, Roger tried to find his wife:

> Then [he] went in and looked up and down his house in his own chambers, but could not find her. So [he] went out of doors, and as he went down the street, John Moore's wife and one Mittimor's wife did tell him that
> *They were assured that she was within the house, and that Mistress Taylor had been with her all the day.* Thereupon [he] went into his house again, and did go up into Mistress Taylor's chamber, and there he found [Susan] standing against the garret door. And then he demanded of her
> *How chance she did not come and open the door?* and she answered she was very busy for Mistress Taylor above in the garret and did not hear him knock. But what her business was there she did not tell him.

Roger seems to be blaming Susan as well as Anne, but when Susan was later asked about this incident by the interrogators, she explained that she could not come to the door because she was *paralysed*. Her account of this very frightening incident begins peacefully enough, with her and Anne spinning and carding in Susan's parlour (perhaps they were spinning some of the hemp that was stored in the garret—it was commonly used to make such household items as cloths and aprons, the thread for which would have been spun at home):

> … true it is, that the same time her husband knocked at the door, Mistress Taylor was in the house with [her]. And there Mistress Taylor stayed the most part of the afternoon, and part of the time did spend in spinning. And sometimes Mistress Taylor was above in the chamber alone where the spirits did resort, and did wash the glass windows.
>
> And towards the evening, she and Mistress Taylor going togethers in the parlour a spinning and a carding, of a sudden they did hear a great stamping in the loft [i.e. floor above]. And then Mistress Taylor said to [her]
> "Hark! Now they be come, you see what they lack". But [Susan] answered her,
> "You have been a great while above alone there your self, and there fore you may go up to them again". Then she prayed
> [Susan] to go up to them, and in the mean time she would have [her] children to bed.
>
> Whereupon at [her] request, [Susan] went up into the chamber where the spirits did use, and there she saw a light like a candle in the midst of the chamber, which did suddenly depart. And then [she] seeing nothing there, did think to go up into the garret. And when she was got up to the garret door, she was taken in such sort, as she could not wag hand nor foot, but leaned to the wall beyond the garret door. And her speech was taken from her. And in such sort she remained, as she thinketh, the space of one hour, until such time as her husband did come and find her, and took her by the arm. And then she felt her limbs, but could not speak till she came down. And then her husband asked
> *How chance she did not open the door when he knocked?* And she answered him,
> "I did not hear you, neither could I move from that place till you took me by the arm".

Susan and Roger both agree on what he said to her when he found her, if not on much else. When Anne was asked about this occasion, she was evasive: *she saieth she cannot remember that she was at Swappers house when he knocked at the door.*

The two women whom Roger had met in the street confirmed (when interrogated) his problems of getting into his house, and that when he did get in, Mistress Taylor came out. Anne Moore said *there was common speech made thereabouts that Swapper's wife had communication with spirits,* and Elizabeth Michenor made a similar point, which suggests that they had both been asked this by the interrogators. The latter also confirmed that

> [she] hath very well observed that Mistress Taylor did often use and frequent the company of Swapper's wife, and was commonly at Swapper's house with her.

Elizabeth was not, however, a disinterested neighbour—she was none other than the widow of the previous tenant in the Swaffer's house, Robert Pywall, who had been *troubled with treasure*, and apparently died from fear after trying to dig for it. Elizabeth had since married the laborer Nicholas Michenor.

Neither of these neighbours saw as much of what was going on inside the house as Goodwife Beale, who, according to Anne Moore, went into the house with Roger, and told her afterwards that Susan was upstairs. Yet the only other thing Goody Beale told her was that they had a *great coal fire*. Why did she pick on this item of information? If they cooked in the hall, it would have been normal to have had a fire there; if they had a kitchen, on the other hand, they would certainly not have needed a big coal fire (hotter than the traditional wood) in the hall in midsummer. But there was a more dubious reason why they might have had a fire—they could have been conjuring fairies, for which a hospitable fire was a necessary ingredient.

* * *

Before starting the conjuration, according to a ritual described in one 17th century manuscript, you must create an ointment with which to anoint your eyes to enable you to see the spirits. To do this, sweep the hearth very clean *in the house where [the fairies] use* and leave on the hearth a *bucket of fair water* the night before the new or full moon. In the morning, there will be a fat or jelly upon the water, which you should remove with a silver spoon and put in a silver or tin vessel. Then when you are ready to *work* (i.e. conjure the spirits), the night before a new or full moon,

> set a new bowl full of new ale upon the board [i.e. table], and three new white loaves, with three new knives with white hafts. This done make a fair fire of sweet cloven wood, then sit in a chair with your face towards the fire. Then take the [ointment] and anoint your eyes therewith, and sit silent, and see all the house be quiet and at rest. And when you have sitten so awhile, you shall see three women come in. But say nothing, but nod your head at them, as you shall see them do to you. And they will go to the table, and eat and drink. When they have done, let the first pass, and the second, but the third you may take and ask what you will of her.

This may not describe exactly what Goody Beale thought they were doing—but it tallies with other accounts of attempts to conjure fairies, in emphasising *hospitality* (attempts to conjure other types of spirits required more erudite, and less homely, methods). A similar technique in the same manuscript has an additional suggestion: if you fear that you might conjure up an evil spirit, you should write a circle on the floor, and move the part of the table where you sit inside it, to protect yourself from the spirit.

Goodwife Beale herself was never questioned about this incident—perhaps she had only been visiting the town, because Anne Moore was not even sure if she had her name right.

The experience certainly had a much more serious physical effect on Susan than previous encounters with the spirits, so perhaps she and Anne Taylor had unleashed more dangerous powers than they had intended. We will return to conjuring matters in a later chapter.

* * *

By the middle of October 1607, the magistrates had decided—if they had been unsure before—to pursue this case, and pursue it they certainly did. They had already collected nearly 4 thousand words of evidence in Susan's first examination, and between October and the Sessions of the Peace held in December, they collected another 8 thousand words. If this case had gone to the Assize courts—where most serious crimes were tried—the judges would not have thanked any county magistrate for presenting them with such a mountain of paper. The King's Justices sallied forth twice a year from the Inns of Court in London to do the rounds of the county towns, and they had about a fortnight to cover the Home Counties. So there was not much more than a couple of days to try all the prisoners in each county gaol, as well as anyone who had been bailed. The length of each trial would then have been no more than *thirty minutes*. In this time the witnesses repeated orally, to the trial jury, the evidence that had previously been recorded by a magistrate, following which the accused and accuser argued it out at the bar. The judge therefore required just so much evidence as would convict the accused, if found by the trial jury to be factually correct—usually a couple of pages at most.

The Story

Most boroughs in England came under the jurisdiction of the Assize courts—the aldermanic bench in a few of them *also* had the authority to try crimes, but ultimate authority rested with the King's justices at the Assizes. In the Cinque Ports (which included Rye and several other ports and towns in East Sussex and Kent), by contrast, the mayor and jurats had the authority to try *all* crimes except treason, as one of the privileges consequent on their ancient role of helping to defend the country against invasion, providing ships in time of war, and transporting troops to the continent. The Rye magistrates could therefore inflict the death penalty on their neighbours—an extraordinary responsibility in a small community. Miscarriages of justice in the courts of the Cinque Ports were dealt with in the court of St. James in Dover, under the overall authority of the Lord Warden of the Cinque Ports.

* * *

Some of the evidence collected that autumn has already been mentioned, including Susan's second examination, when she was questioned about points arising from her first examination, as also on points made by other people. At the start of December, however, the interrogators' questions became more directed. The first question had no relation to anything previously said by her or anyone else who had been examined:

> 1 The said Susanna being again examined whether she knew any thing by the spirits or otherwise concerning the sickness and death of Master Thomas Hamon, late mayor of Rye, or of the death or sickness of the children of Master Taylor, confesseth and sayeth as followeth

The interrogators are here almost consulting her as an intermediary—the spirits could be expected to know the reasons why Thomas Hamon and the Taylors' children got ill and died. In answer, Susan started with an obscure ramble about *planet water*, apparently implying that Anne or the spirits had sent a bottle of it to Hamon, a day or two after he fell sick. There then follows a grim litany of accusations against Anne—mostly by innuendo—which were quite different in tone from her comments in previous examinations. Except for one item in her second examination (on 20th November), concerning a turkey that Anne said she would kill and eat the next day if Thomas Hamon died that night. He had been so ill that the bells were ringing out for him, and he did not last the night. Turkeys were rather special—they had been introduced by seafarers returning from the New World relatively recently, and were rather troublesome to keep, so only members of the gentry generally did so.

Most of Susan's anecdotes concerned Hamon:

Mistress Taylor did then tell her that
She heard that Master Mayor was taken sick, and that he should die of the said sickness. For she knew it well, and that she did know and could tell all what was done in Master Mayor's house, and in every house in Rye, if that she ... would trouble herself about it.

And she further said to [Susan] that
Every body should see that after Master Mayor was dead, what an ugly corpse he should be to look on. And that one side of him should die before the other, and that there was one of the spirits with him at times. And that one of the spirits before his death should give him a gripe upon his members [i.e. would grip his limbs tightly], and that they should look very black after his death.

So this was a much more serious *gripping of the members* than the spirits had inflicted on Susan and Roger, resulting in a seizure down one side of Hamon's body—presumably a major stroke. Anne had foretold not only his death, but the manner of his death—could this suggest that she had some responsibility for it?

The origin of the word *stroke*, incidentally, is *fairy-stroke*, according to the Dictionary of Celtic Mythology. The OED has instead *the stroke of God's hand*, but this appears to be translated from the German—either way, the word would seem to be derived from a spiritual strike.

Susan had yet more to say on Anne's evil speeches:

... And after Master Mayor's death ... Mistress Taylor did further say to [her] that
It were no matter if the divell did fetch away his body for, or to be, an example for others, for she doubted that the divell had his soul already, for that he was an evil liver.

Why this inventory of evil? The obvious explanation was provided by George Taylor:

[Neither] upon her first examinations before Master Braceg[irdle]---------[nor] ... before Master M[ayor]--------, spake [she] any one word of accusing my wife or any of my------ [until] such time, as she had been a pretty while in prison.

The Story

Susan had spent at least a fortnight in the town's gaol, and this experience transformed her attitude to Anne Taylor—and no doubt to everything else that was going on. The accounts that she now gave to the interrogators of Anne's behaviour were radically different in tone from her previous accounts. If Susan did not know why she was being interrogated at her first examination, she was left in no doubt now.

* * *

Rye prison was in an old 14th century fortification known then as *Baddings Tower*, which surveyed the Camber from the outer corner of the gungarden. Taller than today, with an extra floor and a thatched roof, it had very thick walls and little turrets in its four corners leading from one central room (see plates 8 and 10).

One corner of the prison was referred to by Susan as the *place of little ease*, a term referred to by a nineteenth century historian as a euphemism for torture. The town's chosen form of torture was said to have been a tight boot of leather, which was wetted before being put on the victim, and then heated up so that it shrank and constrained the calf muscles, causing intolerable pain. Perhaps this was used during the endless medieval wars with France, to get information from the French prisoners. Whatever the truth of this, it must have been a grim place to be incarcerated.

It was in these circumstances that Susan started making much more serious accusations against Anne—of cursing and witchcraft. These were made in her own voice, and not attributed to the spirits. For example:

> Also she sayeth that after Master Mayor's death, Mistress Taylor did in [the Swaffer's] hearth,
> *Pray unto god that his widow might die within one month next after her husband, that the right heirs might have the land.*
> And [she] further sayeth that she was present when Mistress Taylor did speak these words following, in the presence of Jeremy Talherst, before Master Thomas Hamon (being then mayor) fell sick, viz
> *Master Mayor and his ---------repent it a------vaines in their hearts, that he would not -------husband to pass away his billets.*
> And as concerning Master Taylor's children that died, whereas Mistress Taylor did say that
> *She doubted that [Susan] had bewitched her children*, [Susan] sayeth that if any of them died by any evil means, they died by the evil dealing of her ~~self~~.

Susan is accusing Anne of cursing Hamon's widow, cursing Thomas Hamon and his brethren the jurats, and—in a rather indirect manner, taking her cue from the question put by the magistrates—of bewitching to death her stepchild and her own child. The issue of the *right heirs* was an explosive one that concerned others in the town (if you recall, Thomas and his wife Martha had only been married a month), and we will return to it later.

The conflict over the billets, however, was just between George Taylor and the aldermanic bench. Billets were firewood, which according to local regulations had to be chopped to a standard size (specified as *Calais* billets, so-named because Rye used to supply such vast quantities to Calais, when it was the last English possession in France), and sold at a set price. George exported substantial quantities of billets (probably chopped by Roger Swaffer)—one of his consignments of 21 thousand to a Dover merchant in exchange for a gelding may have been about a tenth of the annual exports of billets for the whole town (and wood was the main export). We only know about this deal, however, because the merchant did not receive all his billets—only 8 thousand had been delivered—and he was suing George in the Dover common court for damages.

It is possible that Rye corporation might have intervened to prevent George fulfilling his bargain—for example if he had been underselling. There was a corporation decree on this matter that same summer (1607)— that *if wood is delivered under the rate, it will be seized by the clerks of the market and converted to the use of the poor.* Another reason for them intervening might have been if he had tried to avoid paying the local customs (*maltods*) by shipping them from another port—which some people were reportedly doing. He would have had good reason for so doing because, as a non-freeman, he had to pay *double* the dues of those who were free of the town.

Restrictions on the export of wood were considered to be necessary by the corporation because the large quantity of wood used by the Wealden ironworks limited the amount available for firewood and shipbuilding. The previous year (1606) it had been decided to *draw up a bill for Parliament for renewing and revising the statute for the preservation of woods within 5 miles of Rye.*

So there were many possible sources of conflict between George and the corporation over their economic regulations—although it could not *actually* have arisen in relation to his bargain with the Dover merchant, because that was not to take place for another couple of months.

The Story

But there were two other actions for debt initiated against George in 1607, the details of which are unspecified—perhaps a similar issue had arisen in relation to one of these. This level of litigation, incidentally, was by no means unusual in this very litigious town—although the fact that he was the defendant in all these cases suggests that he may have been having problems.

* * *

Susan's accusations against Anne could in principle have been enough to substantiate a charge of killing by witchcraft, given that Hamon had died not long after the utterance. But nobody else gave evidence of *maleficia* (harm or death caused by witchcraft). If the magistrates asked Jeremy Talherst (who heard Anne curse Hamon over the issue of the billets) to give evidence, he must have refused to do so. So the only accusations were made by a poor prisoner, and the alleged incidents had only happened in the last couple of months. Most witchcraft cases at the assizes involved accusations going back *decades*, not months—which gave time for suspicions to either evaporate, or harden into certainty.

Perhaps these were the reasons why the indictments that were preferred against Anne and Susan at the December Sessions of the Peace did not actually refer to killing by witchcraft. Instead, Susan was indicted for *counselling with, entertaining and feeding evil and wicked spirits with the intention of acquiring treasure*, and Anne for *aiding and abetting her*. These indictments closely followed the wording of the recent witchcraft act passed in 1604, which made it a felony (i.e. punishable by death) to *consult, covenant with, entertain, employ, feed or reward any evil and wicked spirit, to or for any intent or purpose*, whether or not they resulted in harm to a victim. This could have paved the way to prosecutions for devil worship, on the lines of the trials that were multiplying in Scotland and on the continent—conjuring spirits was now a crime *whatever* its purpose.

The new Act was in line with the views of James I, crowned King of England only the year before, although it is not known whether he had any influence over its content. In Scotland, he had become very caught up in fears of witchcraft (in particular when he thought it was directed at himself), and was personally involved in a few of the interrogations. His book *Daemonologie*, written in part to refute the work of the Kentish sceptic Reginald Scot, was well known in England (*Macbeth* was undoubtedly also written to appeal to him, for its use both of Scottish history and the scenes with witches). The King's paranoia appears to have subsided, however, around the time that he left the volatile political and religious climate of Scotland. So much so that rather than detecting witches, he took to detecting imposters among possessed children—the alleged victims of witchcraft.

Whatever the King's attitude to witchcraft, the Assize judges were little swayed by the introduction of the new Act. The cases that were tried continued to be mostly concerned with death or maiming by witchcraft. The Rye magistrates were not to know about this conservatism, of course—it was early days, and for all they knew there might have been a rash of cases at the Assize courts based on the new Act. Even allowing for this, however, the case against Anne Taylor—for *aiding and abetting* Susan—was extremely flimsy.

* * *

In Van Dyck's drawing of Baddings Tower in plate 8, the only proper windows peer out from an upper floor. It was in this smallish room that the trial of Anne and Susan would have been held, presided over by the magistrates and town clerk—so different from the pomp of the Assizes, where the cream of the county gentry sat in attendance! The mayor's sergeant, appointed by the mayor, was responsible for making sure that witnesses, juries and accused women were also all present (as well as arresting people when necessary). Susan would not have been a problem, since she was imprisoned in the basement.

What did the two juries think about the case—the *grand* and *trial* juries? The Grand Jury—who were impannelled from the more substantial inhabitants—had the authority to throw out the accusation, if they did not think there was a case to answer. Their judgment is written as a full sentence—not the usual scrawled formula *true bill, ignoramus*, or whatever—on the strip of parchment which would become the indictment if they found it to be a true bill. *We find this bill a bill of error*. The writing would have been that of the foreman of the jury, the fish wholesaler Henry Godsmark—59 years old and born in the town.

Grand Juries at the Assize courts in East Sussex threw out at least a quarter of all such bills, but this judgment is problematic. The grand jury were supposed to be assessing whether there was sufficient evidence for the trial jury to reach a verdict, but instead they appear to be rejecting the bill on legal grounds, which did not come within their remit.

The Story

You can see why the jurymen might have had a problem with the bill. To most people, the crime of witchcraft was about harming people or animals, not about dealing with spirits (as a Sussex physician complained, in a manuscript deploring the attitude of ordinary country people who saw only *black* witches as evil, not *white*). The town clerk must have told them about the new statute, and it was presumably him who crossed out their judgment, and wrote on the back *billa vera*—i.e. true bill.

Or is this interpretation totally misconceived? *Bill of error* sounds exactly like *billa vera*. Perhaps Henry Godsmark had just got the spelling wrong—he knew what the legal formula sounded like, but not how to write it down! On other occasions, also, a grand jury had had problems with the latin—they made a valiant effort on one strip of parchment with *A bell a vera*. The town clerk could just as well have allowed them to write it in English, *true bill*.

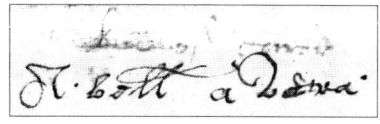

At least one of the jurymen may have had reasons to be ill-disposed towards Anne Taylor—the tanner John Lashenden had been betrothed to her nearly 10 years earlier (see p.38 above). Certainly his brother Robert was later included in a list of witnesses for the prosecution.

* * *

Assessing formal accusations of witchcraft would not have been part of the experience of this Grand Jury, even if most of them had served before (there was only a small pool of reasonably well-off inhabitants from which the mayor's sergeant could choose). In late 16th century Rye, just over 3 formal accusations of felony were made on average each year, but only 3% of these concerned any crime other than theft, murder by non-supernatural means, and infanticide.

Only one indictment for witchcraft had ever been preferred in Rye— in the same year as the Witchcraft Act of 1563 was passed. The accused woman had been acquitted by a local jury. In the 40 years since then— nothing. Which is not to say that witchcraft was never a problem—but the magistrates had a remedy that was not available to the county magistrates or Assize courts. They simply *banished* troublemakers from the town.

In principle, any such ex-inhabitants of Rye found wandering the country could simply be sent back to the town by a county magistrate, in line with the recent Poor Law legislation (which specified that vagrants should be returned to their place of birth). But this did not deter the Rye bench. People were banished for a wide variety of minor offences and immorality: for fornication, adultery and bigamy; for being an *evil doer* and for *ill demeanour*; maidservants who had been mistreated by their master; for keeping an unlicensed alehouse; for raping and attacking a woman; for stealing strips of leather from the shoemakers' hides that they had brought to be curried (the currier's whole family was banished); for witchcraft; suspected felons whom the victims refused to prosecute, or who were acquitted by a local jury; and finally, for being vagabonds—the only reason valid in law for banishing people (if they were returned to their place of birth).

There is one notable case in the early 1560s of an old woman—one *Mother Margery*—being whipped and banished for practising witchcraft. Notable because somebody has clearly challenged the mayor and jurats' right to banish her—possibly with the intention of returning her to the town. In the 1560s town clerks had not bothered to record very much in the town's assembly books, so we only know about the case from a document written fully 10 years' later, in which the mayor and jurats defend their predecessors' actions. After a preamble about *truth* and *making the ambiguous clear*, they describe her *notorious offences*, which included burying raw beef in the ground near the town's almshouses where she dwelt to the intent (as by examination appeared) that as that beef decayed, so the bodies of divers persons whom most wickedly she bore malice unto, should also decay in their bodies. Which thing was so in deed, for one among the rest being by the witchcraft most cruelly tormented in his body, at last hanged himself …. But sithence her banishment we have not been troubled with the like … If she continue in her former folly she is not worthy to remain among the people in the common weal; for a more wickeder woman than she was (in that abominable faculty) while she dwelt with us, in our country hath not sithence been heard of.

They suggest in the document that the woman would have been indicted if this remedy had been available then. But one reason why they used banishment so much may have been because they often found it difficult to get victims to make formal accusations against their neighbours. The magistrates could not try anyone for felony (other than murder) unless the victim would make a formal accusation against them—leading to an indictment—and in the middle years of the 16th century (when such records began) there were numerous instances of the mayor and jurats issuing proclamations for accusers to come forward, to no effect. After the third proclamation had been issued, the case had to be dropped. Such proclamations almost cease in the later 16th century.

This may indicate a change in record-keeping, but if the magistrates were continuing to have problems getting people to make formal accusations, there is no doubt that this would have been mentioned in a period when records were in general *so* much fuller than earlier in the century. They may of course have become more willing to bind the victims of crimes over to prosecute the law against suspected felons. Whatever the reason, the number of indictments had almost tripled between the 1550s and the 1590s, during a period when the population may have halved:

| | Banished || Proclamations which do not result in formal accusation | Formal accusation |
	vagrant	not vagrant		
1550s	dk	dk	19	13
1570s	5	15	3	20
1590s	17	9	0	37

Banishment was such a regular method of purging social ills that there was a standard punishment for those who returned (and some did)—standing on the pillory with an ear nailed to it. If they returned *again*, they were threatened with having one or both ears cut off. You can see the attraction of this method of punishment—in particular in the case of the currier whose behaviour (see above) incited others to a fight in which somebody was killed. The killer was sentenced to be hanged, but it was the currier's behaviour that seems to have been considered the *real* problem.

Sometimes witchcraft may even have been considered just an unavoidable evil, and not dealt with at all. Take the case of Mother Rogers, in the early 1590s. A woman had visited a cunning man named Zacharias in Hastings about her sick child, who she thought was bewitched. He confirmed her suspicions, naming Mother Rogers as the culprit, and advised the woman to thrust a *knife* into the unfortunate suspect's buttock. The woman took the kinder course of pricking her in the hand (a common remedy), and *thereupon presently [immediately] her child took rest*. Nothing appears to have been done about Mother Rogers, however—it was the cruel counsel of the cunning man which was the focus of the questioning (presumably the magistrates were carrying out the interrogation for the magistrates of Hastings).

Witchcraft was not, therefore, necessarily considered to be an appropriate subject for indictment. Banishment would have been a possible way of dealing with Susan Swaffer, who had only arrived a couple of years earlier, but Anne Taylor was a quite different matter—she was not only married to a gentleman, but had freemen on both sides of the family—her father and his father on the one side, and her mother's brother and father on the other. Yet her husband had not been offered the freedom of the town—the magistrates clearly did not want him in the commonalty (he was unlikely to have refused such an offer, if only for the economic benefits).

* * *

The Trial Jury was a mixed bunch, of varying wealth. The foreman, Matthew Young, was a rich yeoman, and then there was a fish wholesaler, two shipwrights, miller, baker, shoemaker, sawyer, 3 unknowns and an attorney in the town court (who would later become town clerk). Matthew Young was unusually rich to be on a trial jury—but then Anne Taylor (or rather, her husband) was also well off, and the ideal was that

The Story

juries should be of similar status to those they were trying. Anne might well have been shocked to see him there, however—standing only a few yards away—because he had earlier that year been in controversy with her husband in Rye common court over a debt of £40. Shocked and surprised—because only the previous April, in the records of that same action for debt, he had been described as *of East Guldeford*, which was a village on the marsh just across the Rother. So he was a *very* recent incomer, and possibly interested in winning favour with the magisterial bench.

A couple of years later—after he had been made a freeeman—he was complaining that *he looked to be a jurat long before this time, and to have been two jurats*. The reason for this outburst (which included abusive language against the bench, enough to get him disfranchised for a time) was that he had again been chosen for the onerous role of land chamberlain—an office that often left the incumbent in debt (in his case, £14), but which usually had to be served before the man was chosen to join the privileged few. The land chamberlain dealt with most of the income and expenditure of the corporation, and it could be difficult calling in all the debts that they were owed—including rents, fines and duties (income and expenditure pertaining to the *sea* were the responsibility of the *sea* chamberlain). His expectation of being made a jurat was probably also bolstered by his marrige to the widow of a former jurat earlier the same year.

Well, Anne might have been shocked and surprised if she had actually been there. In fact she had forfeited her bail, and fled—to her husband's relations in Kent, beyond the reach of the mayor and jurats of Rye. They could only proceed with the case if she was returned to them by other authorities.

Susan, however, had no such favour. The verdict of the trial jury is not difficult to interpret—they declared on their oaths that *Susanna Swapper est culp' de felonia*. Her sentence was to be *suspend' per collu' quousq' mortua esse*—hanged by the neck until she is dead.

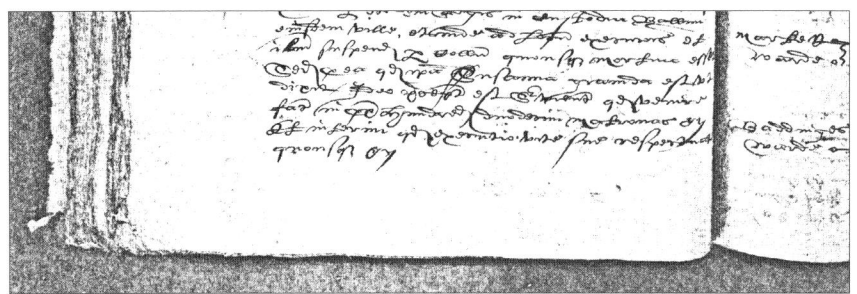

It was, however, remitted for the moment because she claimed to be pregnant. The magistrates ordered the Sergeant to fetch a panel of 12 matrons to examine her. Convicted women often claimed to be pregnant, because it could earn a temporary reprieve which often became permanent (*benefit of the belly*). But in her case, it happened to be true—for baby Agnes was baptised the following May. Meanwhile, Susan was returned to prison.

* * *

After Christmas, outside influences began to make themselves felt—and the case moved out of the local arena. Before following it, let us look closer at the woman who is now emerging as the main focus of the magistrates' concern—a shadowy figure, who has now left the stage altogether.

4   Anne Taylor

I will admit at the outset that I have a problem with Anne Taylor. The more I learn about her, the less real insight do I gain into her character. The feelings and motivations of her poorer neighbour, Susan Swaffer, seem transparent in comparison. It is partly that Anne seems so unsympathetic (though you can of course dislike someone, and understand their motivations only too well). Uncaring and harshly critical of her family and neighbours, Anne was apparently willing to sacrifice them to serve her avarice and social ambition.

This is, of course, grossly unfair. No evidence was taken down in her defence (as in most criminal cases at this period), and she refused to answer most of the questions put to her—unlike the voluble Susan, who no doubt had less inkling of how her answers would be used against her. And this is a *witchcraft* case. We may be hearing only the fears and projections of others, and nothing about the woman at all. Perhaps their characterisation of her was just a paranoid fantasy (in so far as it was not a cynical fabrication—more on this later).

But we *do* know quite a few facts about her—much more than about Susan. That she appears to me shadowy is, I think, not entirely due to lack of evidence, but also to a cultural prejudice that clouds my vision—a prejudice that I am sure many readers will find that they share, relating to her puritanism (to be introduced in a moment). I cannot disperse these clouds by focusing entirely on one woman, but will try to get a firmer take on the concerns and preoccupations of her and her allies (for she did have some) by looking at them in a broader historical context. And in the process, I hope to expose more of the accusers' motivations as well—but this will take us beyond the witchcraft case to other issues, raised in chapter 13 and the second part of the book.

What we have learned about Anne thus far comes mostly from Susan, whose views often reflected her own concerns, or what she thought the interrogators wanted to hear. We need to move beyond *what Susan said*. Taking another vantage point, let us go back to an autumn day shortly before the interrogations began.

* * *

Anne Taylor

September 15th 1607 was a sorrowful day for the Taylors. On that day their only surviving child, George, was buried in Rye churchyard—not quite 2 years old—only two months after his half-sister, 5-year old Elizabeth. He was possibly Anne's second child (the first had died in infancy), and George's fifth. *I have now no child, nor I shall have no more*, she told the town clerk's wife, Margery Convers. Whatever her reason for saying this (which may have had something to do with her husband's health), it would prove to be only too true.

She was talking to Margery about it because Margery had also suffered a loss—her maidservant Philip Binwen was buried on the same day, and she was deeply affected by the maid's death. *I think in regard of her great pains and pangs in her sickness, and the manner of her sickness, will be a cause that I shall never forget her whilst I live*. Such maidservants were not necessarily lower in class, just other people's teenage daughters. Parents were too ready to spoil their own children, so it was thought, and other adults could discipline them more effectively. *Apprenticed to huswifery* was how apprenticeship indentures put it (although these were generally only drawn up for the poor and orphans, to make sure that *somebody* took responsibility for them).

Anne was more stoical than Margery, and said even of her own children that *as freely [as god] gave them her, as soon she gave them to god again*. It was all part of God's providence—she knew this not only from her own strong convictions, but also because there had been *signs*. Only that day the Taylors had seen them in the glass windows of the house opposite, and it was because of *the report of Master Taylor himself of strange and miraculous sights which he ... had seen in the windows*, that Mistress Convers and other neighbours had come to see for themselves (a similar window is shown in plate 6). None of them could see anything, however, and Margery would have departed with the rest, had not Mistress Taylor asked her to sit down next to her, and *stay with her a little while*. They then talked about sickness, death and other matters (which we will return to in a later chapter). Anne must have little suspected that this conversation would be written down by Margery's husband Robert—in his wife's words—for use in evidence against her. Perhaps because the witness was his wife, Robert Convers forgot to put the conversation into reported speech.

Anne had seen the strange sights on several occasions since midsummer. The first time she saw them was two days before little Elizabeth died. She saw *the picture of death* and *shapes of men and women at diverse and sundry times after*.

The Story

The *picture of death* was perhaps the deaths head, or skull, that George mentioned. It was he who gave the most detailed description—not once, but *twice*. He first described them when he was examined in October, and then again in an undated letter which he wrote to the magistrates. I think this letter was mainly intended for the trial jury, however, because at one point he addresses them directly:

> My masters, you that be of the jury, I beseech you mark how many devices this ... Swaffer's wife had. Which, if it please Master Mayor, he is likewise able to certify you, and Master Bracegirdle, what report she made upon her confession before them ...

i.e. at her first formal examination before the magistrates and vicar. Presumably George wrote this letter as a substitute for giving verbal evidence directly to the jury, when he and his wife had left Rye to avoid the trial. There was a very remote possibility that she might be tried *in absentia*, and he probably also felt the need to supply more evidence in her defence, in case his attempts to get the case removed to the appeal court in Dover fell through.

The apparitions, as George describes them, are like a motionless tableau, and his two accounts are almost identical, even though there was a 4-6 week gap between them. The following is taken from the examination:

> About midsummer last past, and divers and sundry times sithence, [I] ... did see in the ... window ... a grave man in show, setting in majesterial sort in a chair, having a book before him. And at his right hand, to [my] seeming, one sitting. And at the left hand, one man and one woman. The woman ... was apparelled in black, with a hat upon her head, and a ruff about her neck. The other in a shayish colour.
>
> At the back of the man and woman, a deaths head appearing like a skull newly taken out of the ground, with diverse persons standing round about the skull, as if they were desirous to hear something. Behind these in an other pane of glass, there appeared unto [me] very glorious shows. A person apparelled in very rich attire, bedecked to [my] seeming with sundry jewels. Underneath [the] deaths head, in a casement, there appeared one in show to [my] thinking holding before him or her a very goodly child.

This account can be filled out. The *very ancient grave man, sitting very majestically in a chair with a book before him* (the terms used in George's letter) was probably Thomas Hamon, and the man on his right—said to be either reading or casting of accounts in the letter—may have been the mayor's sergeant, Angel Shaw, judging by Susan's report that Anne had seen these two men in the windows. The following November, Angel would arrest and imprison Susan. He had previously had another role — as the town's drummer, who for many years played in the evenings with the fife-player to summon the town's watch to their posts (inhabitants were chosen on a rota basis to watch for invaders or pirates).

The only person whose clothes are described is the woman in black — who is she? The man next to her appears to have been clothed in deep red, so they must have presented a very striking couple. At least, the only gloss I can suggest for *shayish* (*shayiches coloured apparel* in the letter) was a deep red Indian dye from the *chay* or *shaya* root, which was unusual and probably, therefore, expensive. The couple appear to be part of the group centering on Thomas Hamon, but are also linked to the deaths head — for the latter is behind *them*, not behind the whole group. I would therefore suggest that the couple may be the Taylors themselves — for it is they who are warning people about the pronouncements of the deaths head. And a woman dressed in black, with a hat on her head and a white ruff, suits Anne Taylor's gravity and godliness. George's red apparel — if it really is him — does seem rather incongruous, though it would advertise his wealth and status.

The black attire contrasts with the *shadows of people in as rich and gorgeous apparel as could be devised* above the deaths head (as described in the letter). These were no doubt those who should have been listening to the deaths head. Such a one was the jurat and tailor Stephen Harrison, who had drowned recently (such accidents were common in the dangerous floes of the Camber). *Master Harrison went out in his bravery* [swaggering, ostentatious clothes], *but his body shall never be found and … his head did lay under a certain stone*. Not only his clothes, but his body was gone — God's judgment suited the sin. The words were Anne's (as reported by a grocer from Dover). Godly people were much given to such pronouncements, but it must have hit hard when those being judged were their neighbours.

The *goodly child* is not difficult to identify — Anne said that she had seen *the picture of her own son a senight* [week] *before he died*. In the letter, George refers to *the shadow of a woman holding a child standing up against her knees*, which suggests too small a person to have been his 5-year old daughter Elizabeth.

Many of these apparitions seemed to portend the deaths of the people portrayed. There was the image of Thomas Hamon — Anne said she also saw *a shape of a man very like unto Master Hamon* in the window of another man's house shortly before Hamon's death, and the vision of the child. Did the threat extend to others depicted, such as Angel Shaw, who would not in fact be on this earth much longer, and the Taylors themselves?

The deaths head was like those apparitions in the sky, warning of God's anger, and portending some doom, that were frequently publicised in the pamphlets and almanacs of the period. These prognostications were usually rather general—such as heavenly battles foretelling the outbreak of war. Although particularly associated with the godly, they were an old idea.

* * *

Anne only gave a short statement about the apparitions, in response to a couple of questions from the interrogators. But this included a strikingly audacious pronouncement:

> Some [apparitions] are yet to be seen, but not so plainly as heretofore they have been seen.

She appears to be claiming the power to forecast future sightings—the words spoken directly to the interrogators, not referred to some other spirit or human being. Nor was it attributed to her by other people, unlike most of the statements of her thoughts and feelings with which we have to deal.

* * *

What did Susan have to do with these apparitions? This was one of the things the interrogators wanted to know. The answer is—very little. On the day that little Elizabeth was buried, when Susan was in the Taylors' house and Anne was upstairs, she heard Anne call down to George, to come and look at the sights in the windows of the house opposite (it was the parlour window of Alexander Fowkes, the Royal Purveyor of Fish, who bought fish for the royal household every day in Rye market).

The next person to be called upstairs to look was Widow Bennett—who, when she came down, told Susan that she could not see as much as the Taylors. Only then was Susan asked to go up and see the sights. She could only see the shape of a man's head at that time, but later saw more shapes (*two gentlewomen* and *a man drinking with a napkin before him*). Anne was not interested in Susan's views on the matter, and the only time she mentioned Susan in relation to the apparitions was to avoid answering (it would seem) the interrogators' question as to why she thought the apparitions had appeared. She said that Susan told her it was because of the Taylors' lack of belief in what Susan had told them about her spirits (George also mentioned this).

So the Taylors were the only people who could see very much in the windows. When Master Fowkes first came to look, he could see nothing, and laughed—but later when Anne and her mother were there, he could see *diverse sights*. They told him *you must believe or you can see nothing*. The importance of their presence perhaps connects with the idea that if somebody with second sight puts their foot on somebody else's, then the other person can also see the spirits that are visible to the first person.

Fowkes must have been on good terms with the Taylors, because he and George were currently partners in a trading venture—at least, they were later taken to court for a debt of £100 by a yeoman of Winchelsea. Fowkes had not lived in the town long, but was important enough for the magistracy to wish to absorb him into the select few. He had been made a jurat just the previous month, and it was only two years since he had been granted his freedom *gratis* by the mayor, Thomas Hamon. How different from George's experience, who was not even a freeman!

* * *

Not all the visions were still and silent. In the chamber frequented by Susan's spirits more illustrious beings appeared, in the form of two angels, bearing tidings of the impending cataclysm. Susan told Anne that:

> [The] two angels had each of them a prophet, and … those angels would reveal unto the [two] prophets, to [no] other person, the cause of their coming. And … their coming was to cut off the wicked from the yearth. And … [Anne] and her husband should see the angels hereafter.

When Anne made this declaration, she no doubt had the Book of Revelation in mind—where Saint John set down the things which must shortly come to pass. Angels and prophets had crucial parts to play in the working out of the last days, as revealed to John.

There was a general sense among the godly in the early 17th century that the end of the world was imminent, but for some there was more sense of urgency, and the Book of Revelation was earnestly scanned by them for indications of what form the cataclysm would take, and when it would happen. A common view was that the Antichrist described by John was currently reigning, would be overthrown before the end of the century, and then bound for a thousand years while the elect lived and reigned with Christ. Antichrist was the Pope—as was explained in the annotated Bibles provided in parish churches in the late 16th century—though this was self-evident to the godly.

Anne says that it was *Susan* who saw the angels, but Susan herself never mentioned angels or prophets in her examinations, and I do not imagine that the Book of Revelation would have appealed to her. Giving Susan responsibility for the vision enables Anne to make the apocalyptic message seem impersonal, independent of her own views. Through the mouth of a poor sawyer's wife, she implies, it is decreed that Anne and her husband will be saved, and will hereafter meet the angels who have destroyed the wicked.

Anne thus expresses in her own way a widespread belief of the period, while George is much more precise about when the great event was predicted to occur:

> until eleven months were expired I should never have any more revealed unto me. But at eleven months end, I should have that revealed unto me that never Abraham nor Salloman had, nor any man living upon the earth. And that at eleven months end, there should no man living be left to tread upon this earth.

The end of the world will happen within the year! This is much sooner than most predictions. But this is not *exactly* his opinion. It is yet another instance—according to him—of *what Susan said*. And she has also revealed that in the Last Days he will receive revelations that nobody else has received—not even Abraham or Solomon. Does he see himself becoming a spiritual leader? Perhaps one of the prophets that Anne said Susan had seen—in which case will she be the other one? These kinds of extreme beliefs are more typical of the Civil War period than the early years of the 17th century. But the extraordinary changes in economic fortune which the town of Rye experienced during the previous century—which will be described in due course—could have prompted apocalyptic alarm, not just in the Taylors, but in others as well. Hence the Taylors' eagerness for the neighbours to see the apparitions for themselves.

Mistress Anne Taylor has thus emerged as a radical puritan. It seems hard to believe that she was the very same woman who had been trying to get hold of buried treasure with the help of spirits whose morality was at best uncertain. But if the Taylors were claiming to have such powerful spiritual allies, it does help explain why their opponents on the aldermanic bench should have become so alarmed.

[signatures: Annea. Taylor   George Taylor]

I have suggested that apocalyptic concerns arose out of current ecoonomic circumstances, but these radical beliefs also had a pre-history. Strident religious radicalism had characterised some of the inhabitants of Rye for many decades past—including some of the Taylors' forbears. During this earlier period these beliefs and behaviour were inextricably entwined with political struggle. Looking at these earlier conflicts gives a historical background to the current dispute between the Taylors and the magistrates—indeed, similar issues kept recurring over the decades. The tale takes us back to the time of the Taylors' grandfathers, and the upheaval in the English Church created by Henry VIII's reforms, out of which the Taylors' brand of godliness had eventually developed.

5 Faith and Faction

The 1530s were a confusing time. Beliefs that had been considered heretical for centuries past were being recategorised. But such changes had not yet come into effect when one Thomas White of Rye was tried for heresy at the church court in 1533. Some unnamed heretical (protestant) books had been found in his inn, which—so he claimed—had been left by a merchant of Norwich some 18 months before. He did not know the merchant's name, he had not read the books, and he did not know that they were heretical (note that he did not try to claim that he *could not* read them). The accusation was made by a friar from the Augustinian friary in Rye (soon to be dissolved by Henry VIII's commissioners)—though the books had actually been found by the rector of West Blatchington (presumably when staying at the inn). West Blatchington is 60 miles to the west of Rye, in the most traditional part of the county.

No witnesses could be found, however, to make accusations against White, and he was therefore allowed to purge himself with four honest neighbours in Rye church during service time—in other words, they had to swear that they thought he was telling the truth. Presumably he found enough neighbours to support him, since nothing more was done. If he had wanted to obtain heretical books, he certainly did not need to rely on merchants from Norwich to bring them. Just to the north of Rye, some of the Wealden radicals were heavily implicated in smuggling protestant books into England.

The hollowness of White's denials is evident from another case four years later. This time it is not him and fellow protestants who are being investigated, but instead their opponent, the curate of Rye, William Inold. The protestants complained to Thomas Cromwell, Secretary of State, that Inold insisted on observing the old saints' days that had recently been abrogated by Henry VIII—*and some of them kept as though it had been the highest day in the year, with solemn ringing, singing, procession, and decking of the church*. He preached that people should *remain and do as of old time they had done* and *boasted that their old fashions should yet flourish*. The attitude of the government to the accusations is clear from the endorsement—*The misbehaviours and evil preaching of William Inold, Curate of Rye, defending Popery*.

Inold's supporters included the mayor and jurats of Rye, as well as the *best and most substantial commons* (i.e.freemen), or so they claimed.

They fought back by accusing their opponents of heresy. These people, so they said, were of *very simple and … small substance, rude both in their communication and behaviour*—perhaps like the lollards in the 15th century, most of whom were artisans. These 'heretics' included the butcher Robert Bennett, Anne Taylor's grandfather, and Richard Ruck, George Taylor's step-grandfather (if you can call him that). George's father (John Taylor, gentleman of Willesborough, Kent) would later marry Ruck's daughter Bridget after his first wife died.

A list of the beliefs of those whom Inold's supporters called 'heretics' was included with the complaint. These were not only protestant but—now—broadly acceptable to Henry VIII's government. Although referred to as *protestant*, the similarities between these beliefs and those of the fifteenth century lollards are more evident than the differences. The 'heretics' were opposed to the type of worship that they considered meaningless rituals, such as going on pilgrimages, and giving oblations to the images of the Virgin Mary and Saints. When they took communion, they considered the Eucharist to be *not the very body of god*, but just a symbol. Praying for the souls of the dead to get them out of purgatory and into heaven—or paying for priests to do so—served no purpose since purgatory did not exist. These men proclaimed their own powers to communicate with God, they did not need intermediaries such as priests, saints or the Virgin Mary—every man was a priest, and there was no need to make confession to one.

Occasionally there was a more unusual belief—such as one man declaring that his body *needeth not burial in church or churchyard*. The only really challenging aspect of their statements, however, was the earthy and abusive language in which they were allegedly couched. The language was perhaps rather more abusive than lollards were usually reported as using, since it was their opponents who accused them of speaking the words (they denied saying them):

> there is no purgatory, for purgatory is pissed out
> the mass was of a juggler's making
> the image of our blessed lady and other saints in the Church be as idols, and
>   have mouths, and can not speak, hear nor see
> the divine service sung in the Church of God is of no more effect than the
>   blething of a cow to her calf, and the calf again to the cow
> he had rather have a dog sing for him than a priest
> our lady being the mother of god was a sinner in this world as we be

One statement was so extreme, however, that somebody has written in the margin *no man would say so, therefore a forgery to make them odious*—a neat excuse for accepting these protestants' denials of having spoken the words. The objected statement was that *If our lady were here in earth, I would no more fear to meddle with her than with a common whore*. Even this document is treated favourably—it is endorsed: [list of names] *for speaking against Popish superstitions.* It was Inold who ended up in prison.

* * *

These pioneering protestants cannot have been of *very* small substance, because they managed occasionally to oust the catholics from control of the magistracy—although the interference of the Privy Council was also an important factor in determining the choice of mayor at this period. Richard Ruck (George Taylor's step-grandfather) was made a jurat in 1548, when the protestant Edward VI was on the throne.

By the time Queen Mary came to the throne in 1553, the town's elite had become decisively protestant, and were often in conflict with her attempts to reimpose Catholicism. The freemen refused to accept the Privy Council's nominee as mayor (on the second occasion) in 1557—the Queen's 'servant' (i.e. client), George Raynolds—and chose the protestant Alexander Welles instead. Robert Bennett (Anne Taylor's grandfather) was one of those whom Welles chose to fill the three vacancies on the magisterial bench.

The new mayor was not, however, left to enjoy his success in peace. Four times in the next few months he had to travel to London to answer questions put to him by the Privy Council, and was even thrown into the notorious Fleet prison for a few days, for refusing to allow the collection of a forced loan in Rye to finance the war with France (the Cinque Ports were supposed to be exempt from taxation, other than their customary duty of providing ships in time of war). This was a dangerous time for protestants to defy the government—one of the inhabitants of Rye, Thomas Ravensdale, was martyred for being a protestant and refusing to recant, according to the martyrologist John Foxe. The local records do not mention this—although the parish register does have a man of this name getting married and having two children baptised during this decade.

Bennett was also chosen to be church warden, and one can imagine the fury with which he had to oversee, together with his fellow protestant Robert Fowler, the continuing re-installation of catholic furnishings and ritual objects in Rye church. There was the lamp to be re-hung in the choir; many candles and tapers to be bought and placed in front of the new images of saints, and on the new altar in front of the new cross; frankincense for Easter, the annual mending of the Easter sepulchre, and payments to those who maintained the lights round the sepulchre for two nights. Some parishioners now wanted the best cross at funerals to stand on the hearse, as well as Saint Crispinian's cloth to be placed over it — perhaps this was the cloth of yellow silk which had been bought back in 1525 for this purpose, with a picture of the saint painted on it. Crispin and Crispinian were a pair of local saints, who, so legend had it, had been Roman gentlemen. They escaped from persecution by the heathens, first to France, and then to Faversham in Kent, where they got their livings by being shoemakers. The artisans of the Cinque Ports could thus claim some truly illustrious forbears.

It was not long, however, before there was a protestant monarch again on the throne. The altars, images, crosses and rood loft were taken down again, a plain communion table and desk for the preacher set up, the picture of the Day of Judgment whitewashed over, and passages from scripture written on the whitewashed walls. All very much plainer than the interiors of parish churches today, and a truly dramatic transformation from the splendid accoutrements of the pre-Reformation church. The last remnants of the church plate and vestments were sold off, and new servicebooks in English and books of sermons were purchased.

Only a year after Robert Bennett was made a jurat, he was chosen with three other jurats to represent Rye at a celebratory occasion that must have confirmed for him his new stature — the coronation of Queen Elizabeth. Wearing something similar to the long scarlet gowns lined with crimson satin, hose, crimson silk stockings, crimson velvet shoes, and black velvet caps ordered for James I's coronation, they and representatives from the other Cinque Ports held the traditional silk canopy supported by silver staves over the young Queen, as the procession made its way to Westminster Hall, where these *Barons of the Cinque Ports* (as they were known) later dined with the rest. Just as the canopy protected the Queen from the elements, so the Cinque Ports protected her country from foreign invaders — perhaps somesuch symbolism was implied. Whatever it was, it was ceasing to reflect a fast changing reality. *Master Bennett* was granted expenses of two shillings a day for a fortnight by the corporation while he was in London for the celebrations.

The Story

Robert Bennett left a personal statement of his faith in 1564 in the preamble to his will (written three years before he died), which resonates with the confidence that he is one of God's elect (a true Calvinist):

> trusting assuredly to be saved by the merits of christ's passion, and to be raised up again at the day of judgment with the righteous people: and this I protest before all the whole world, to be my faith.

* * *

When Bennett died in 1567 he left his wife, three sons and a daughter very comfortably off, with a farm at Weeks Green, and other lands in Playden (known as *Parisgarden*) and Iden, as well as various properties in Rye, most bought recently. The eldest son—Anne Taylor's father—was another Robert, and a butcher like his father, so the slaughterhouse near the dwelling house which he inherited would have still been used for its original purpose, and the watercourse (drain) that came with it would have been very necessary to wash away the detritus of slaughter. The property also had a barn, as well as the herber which was later said to be haunted by spirits. Robert married the same year as his father died, to Anne Radford, the daughter of a Rye shoemaker.

The 1560s and 70s were a prosperous time not only for the Bennetts, but for many inhabitants of Rye. Trade flourished—partly because Rye benefited from the decline of neighbouring Winchelsea, whose port was silting up—and immigrants flocked to the town. Rye became for a brief period one of the main ports on the south coast. The population rose dramatically from just over a thousand at the start of the century, to over three thousand. The file of records for the town's court for private actions bulges with litigation initiated by merchants and others.

The corporation were so satisfied in 1576 with the income generated by a local tax—and the readiness of the inhabitants to pay it—that they even decided to waive the fines for minor misdemeanours listed in the annual presentment by the Grand Jury (apart from fines for wearing *hats* at the wrong season—hats in winters, caps in summer, according to a recent regulation, intended to benefit cappers). A townsman reading the minutes of this meeting thirty years later would have been astounded at how rich the corporation felt itself to be at this time.

Increasing concern about the state of Rye harbour is nevertheless evident from the corporation records. Severe storms in August 1572 destroyed jetties and threw sand up onto the quay, exacerbating the effects of the gradual build-up of silt. The corporation were alarmed at *this unseasonable weather*, which was a *token of god's great displeasure, threatening no small miseries and calamities to fall upon us.* Practical remedies were not enough—God's forgiveness had to be sought. All the inhabitants were ordered to take part in communal prayers and fasting:

> it is ordered ... that for our loose life and neglecting to do our duties, as we ought, to serve god, on Mondays next and so forth every Monday, till it please god to stay this unseasonable weather, the people ... of this town of all ages and sorts diligently repair unto the church, both to call upon god by prayer, and also for the hearing of his word, both forenoon and afternoon at such time as the bell shall be tolled. And there with all christian reverence, to continue, until the end of prayer, and the sermon ...
>
> Item for the better continuance of the people in godly fervency of prayer, it is ordered ... that a general holy and solemn fast be kept ... that day to the Lord, of all sorts [of people] from 16 years to 60 (sick folks and labourers in harvest only excepted), [who] are wished only to content themselves that day with bread and drink, if the health of their bodies will bear the same, that they may be the more apt to prayer.

And each householder was to show the fruits of their christian faith by giving alms to the poor. Afterwards, people could return *in the fear of god* to their work, but should not spend any part of it in *plays, pastimes or idleness, and much less in lewd, wicked or wanton behaviour*. Fines were to be administered to those who did not comply.

Rye was now a fervently godly town, employing a preacher to make up for the deficiencies of the mostly absentee vicar. Religious differences between different groups are less evident than they had been, and the large numbers of protestants fleeing catholic persecution in France were on the whole welcomed (particularly those with skills and money— the magistrates did object to the numbers of *poor* people that the fishermen were bringing over from Dieppe).

* * *

Curiously, relations between the two factions were particularly fraught at this time, even though they do not seem to have been deeply divided over religious matters. I will not go into detail about who belonged to which faction, which would involve lists of names and relationships with only the barest clues about the personalities involved. Suffice it to say that this has been teased out in detail by Graham Mayhew, taking into consideration such matters as voting patterns, appointment to office, conflicts, bequests in wills, kinship, marriage, apprenticeship, godparenthood and guardianship.

Faction was a dirty word in this period—*rivalry that over-rode all other considerations*, as one historian has put it. It was *the dark side of the system of personal loyalties and dependence that the society prized so much*. Ties of patronage and neighbourliness (*good lordship* and *good neighbourhood*, as they called them) linked people together by many different types of personal ties. But some groups were more densely intertwined than others, and occasionally faultlines opened up between them as they competed for power and resources. The faultlines might be entirely local, or the tentacles of faction might reach right up to the court itself. Townspeople tried to use these ties of *good lordship* to influence events which concerned them (such as in Parliament), just as noblemen did the same to manipulate town politics. It was the town aldermen, usually, who had formal ties with particular noblemen (in the Cinque Ports as elsewhere, although it was contrary to their regulations). The patrons would sometimes intervene on behalf of their clients—referred to as their *servants*—when, for example, the latter did not want to serve in an office that the corporation had asked them to take on.

These faultlines between the factions in Rye were persistent—Graham Mayhew has demonstrated that continuities in the membership of the two factions can be traced throughout the 16th century, even though they ceased by the 1570s to be characterised as *catholic* versus *protestant*. This persistence was partly because allegiance was not *simply* determined by personal ties—since the Reformation, religion was an overarching (indeed an international) issue. No longer were the French simply the enemy, as they had been for centuries—the French protestants were considered deserving of help by the inhabitants of Rye. And it was the more radical faction which continued to evince the most godliness—as Mayhew has again demonstrated, from analysis of the preambles to wills.

* * *

The factions in Rye perhaps deserved the contemporary opprobium attached to the word *faction*, and the Bennett brothers were in the thick of the conflicts. References to Robert and John start springing up like mushrooms in the records of the corporation assemblies in the '70s—references to trouble, affrays, abuse. These two were the angry young men of the town—no others seem to have been quite such a problem (brother William died in 1573, at the age of 21 years). Such substantial inhabitants could not, of course, be so easily banished as the poorer sort. John, who was a tailor, was probably not as well off as his elder brother Robert, but he could nevertheless boast a gold signet ring, and some rich clothes—a *doublet of changeable taffeta, gaskins* (baggy breeches) *laid with velvet and blue lace,* and *black paned hose guarded with velvet* (slashed trunk hose decorated with bands of velvet).

Trunk hose on the left

First in the chapter of incidents was a *night of illrule,* as the town clerk puts it, in September 1575. Robert and John had been out drinking with Edward Harris (another butcher) and Thomas Matthew (a painter), and also two men from Hythe, after which they went on a rampage through the town. A cask was thrown at men's doors, Thomas Edolph's lattice was pulled from a window, Thomas Beveridge's kitchen wall was pulled down, and a window pane belonging to Robert March was broken. Much wood was thrown over the cliff. This was not just indiscriminate destruction, however, because all those whose property the Bennetts damaged in their drunken spree were in the other faction.

Robert was questioned about this disorder, and also about writing letters to the men of Hythe asking them to hide the matter from the mayor. This consciousness of guilt did not get in the way of a strong sense of self-righteousness, because when asked to swear on the Bible that he would speak the truth, he refused such a ritualised test of his honesty:

> *but promised* before Master Mayor and the jurats *uppon his faith,* and
> *Swore, laying his hand upon his breast, by the living god, that he would say the truth, as well as though they should swear him upon a book*

The sense of righteousness in his pronouncement carries an echo of his father's declaration of faith. He was fined 6s 8d, and they were all bound over to keep the peace.

It was only a month or two later that he was called before the magistrates again, because his brother had broken his bond to keep the peace, and Robert was one of his sureties. The argument is recorded in unusual detail, although the *substance* of the complaint is not spelt out—presumably Robert was refusing to pay. It again raises the issue of *honesty*:

> Master Mayor upon occasion of speech, said to ... [Robert] that
> *He was forsworn, and that in this place!* Whereuppon ... [Robert] said
> "I defy all the world, or any that can so burden me." Whereuppon Master Mayor said
> "I do burden thee." And therefore, his words of defiance stretching to Master Mayor sitting in place of justice in the presence of the jurats and common council assembled, a matter odious and not sufferable, the ... jurats ... did adjudge him to be committed to ward, and there to remain [at] their pleasures ...

It was a full 11 days that he was in prison before he *yielded to his fault*. He was also fined again.

The incident that had brought Robert before the mayor (William Davies) on this occasion was a fight between John and another inhabitant, Richard Daniel. A widow described how

> in the dark evening ... by chance looking out of her doors after her girl (which she had sent for a pennyworth of tripe) [to check that] Byler's boy [did] not beat her; she saw Bennett and Daniel meet suddenly. Bennett struck Daniell with his dagger on his arm, whereat Richard Daniel, swearing a great oath, said to Bennett
> "Stand back, or else I will drive thee!"

John's complaint with Richard Daniel may have been partly over economic issues—perhaps that Richard was trespassing on tailors' territory. He was an agent in Rye for cloth exporters, even though he was not himself a tailor or woollen draper like John and his own brother Robert Daniel, but a wholesale fishmonger (*feter* was the local term for it). The conflict may also have involved political issues, which we will come to shortly.

There were other occasions on which Robert was punished for abusing the mayor—such as when John was accused of drinking in service time on Easter Monday—and he was frequently bound over to keep the peace. On one occasion he and John were even bound over to keep the peace against each other. There was also the thoroughly dishonest incident in 1574, when Robert and his fellow butcher Thomas Harris were fined for sending the shoulder of a dog instead of venison to a baker to be baked (perhaps for gentlefolk staying at one of the inns).

* * *

The brothers thus already had a reputation as troublemakers, but there was some reason behind the Bennett brothers' disorders in 1575. The problem was, they were outcrowd. A *common council* had been created in January 1575 out of the freemen—chosen by the magistrates—and only this select 24 men would henceforth meet at the fortnightly assemblies. Robert Bennett had not been chosen—and he the eldest son of a jurat! He did not object to the common council *itself*, since he was one of those who had assented to its creation (roughly 60% of the freemen did so). Such councils were common in the larger towns and cities, and in Rye it was created when the town increased in size, and then was abolished when it decreased again (1590). Its creation coincided with the organisation of some of the occupations into companies—the fishermen, tailors, mercers and shoemakers (the companies may have been created partly to exclude French immigrant artisans). These companies also ceased to exist—or at least were no longer mentioned in the records—when the town declined later in the century .

Even if Robert had no objections in principle to a common council, practical problems were likely to arise when it was first created, because whichever faction currently dominated the aldermanic bench (and most town's *did* have serious factional conflicts) had considerable control over the makeup of the council. This appears to have been Bennett's problem—the other faction was dominant.

The Bennetts were probably involved in an anonymous taunt against the common council, just before it was created, which focused on the brother (Robert) of the man with whom John fought, Richard Daniel. A cloth with 24 playing cards fixed to it—all knaves—was hung above the stairs in the court hall, and the initials RD CP (the latter presumably some insult) written on the knave of clubs, which was said to be the *foremost card*. RD was presumably the tailor Robert Daniel, who would shortly be made a common councillor, and who had his windows broken at this time. His brother Richard had also recently been made a freeman, in return for providing some services for the corporation. Another man whom Robert Bennett fought with on two later occasions had also just been admitted to the common council.

* * *

The Bennett brothers did not have to stay out in the cold for long. Only a year later a mayor was chosen from their own faction (William Tolkyn), and Robert Bennett was made a common councillor. The following year

The Story

John was appointed mayor's sergeant (by John Fagge, mayor and butcher), whose main role was to make arrests and execute writs—often for distraint (confiscation) of goods.

* * *

Was the rivalry between the two factions in the town determined solely by personal ties—marriage, apprenticeship etc.—and religious differences, or was there a socio-economic aspect to it? Back in the 1530s, the leaders of the catholic faction (as it was then) saw their faction as the *best and most substantial commons* (i.e. freemen), and they certainly had ties with local catholic gentry. They called the protestant faction *very simple and … [of] small substance, rude both in their communication and behaviour* (see page 79). So the catholic faction presumably included many merchants.

Similar socio-economic differences can perhaps be detected in the 1570s. Then, two-thirds of the 16 freemen described as merchants were probably members of the corresponding traditionalist, but now also protestant, faction, and half of these were rich. This faction's description of its opponents, the more radical protestants, as of *small substance* must have been something of a slur, since they was able to dominate local politics for a time (as mentioned above).

I would suggest that most of these radical protestants were, rather, the *middling sort*—a convenient term coined later in the 17th century for those who considered themselves to be the honester sort of independent artisans and smaller tradesmen, who tried not to be dependent on the patronage, or subject to the domination, of members of the elite. In the late 16th century the inhabitants of London were similarly divided into three groups by an anonymous author, as follows:

1. Merchants and chief retailers
2. Most part of retailers and all artificers
3. Hirelings

It is not easy identifying occupational differences between the factions—partly because people's allegiance is not always clear, and partly because the occupational terms themselves are so non-specific. For example, a *mercer* could be a merchant selling rich fabrics (and other things), or a petty chapman selling pins from his pack. A *brewer* could be the owner of a business, or his employee. A *tailor* could be an artisan, or a draper who dealt in large quantities of fabric.

In Rye in the 1570s, 3 of the 9 tailors were rich, suggesting that they were drapers, and all but one of these were members of the faction led principally by wealthy merchants; 6 of the tailors (two-thirds) were members of the less wealthy faction. The fishermen divided themselves between these factions at least for the purpose of mayoral elections—the socio-economic basis of their allegiance is less clear than for the tradesmen (except for some of those master fishermen who had become merchants and no longer engaged in fishing). I think there is, therefore, enough evidence to justify referring to the two factions in Rye as the *merchant* and *artisan* factions. Neither was made up *exclusively* of these types of people, but these groups seem to have dominated each of them.

* * *

The different characters of the two factions are dramatised in a so-called 'riot' which became the subject of two cases in the Court of Star Chamber in London—a court which dealt with large-scale breaches of the peace, and included members of the Queen's Privy Council amongst the judges. Some of the people involved in the witchcraft case also had links with 'rioters' and witnesses in this case—as will emerge later.

The issue at stake concerned the inheritance of a house—but it is striking that neither of the main protagonists actually claimed to inherit it. A large part of the struggle seems to have concerned power relations between the factions. It was a member of the merchant faction, a mercer and attorney named John Rolfe (and others), who initiated what may have been the first case—claiming that he and his family were in the house when the rioters assembled outside with loaded guns, and *the walls thereof broke down, and by the breeches entered the said house, to the great fear and terror of* himself and family. But when the defendant, John Hebblethwaite (and others), retaliated with his own case, it becomes apparent from the much more detailed evidence of witnesses that Rolfe's allies were actually the ones who started the trouble. Hebblethwaite was an attorney who used to be townclerk of neighbouring Lydd, and lived in Rye for a short time.

The Story

The *dramatis personae* of those involved in this *hurly burly* who are discussed in the text are listed in the table below, roughly in order of wealth:

Artisan faction		Merchant faction	
J Fagge (mayor, butcher)	£80		
		H Gaymer (jurat, feter)	£66 13s 4d
		[G Raynolds (jurat)	£40]
W Harmon (fisherman) †	£30	R Carpenter (jurat, brewer)	£33 6s 8d
		M Mills (jurat, Royal Purveyor of Fish)	£26 13s 4d
W Tolkyn (deputy mayor, feter)	£16 13s 4d	J Rolfe (mercer and attorney)	£15
R Bennett (butcher)	£10		
J Bennett (mayor's sergeant, tailor)	£6 13s 4d		
J Prowze (town gunner and innholder)	£6 13s 4d		
J Potten (fisherman) †	£5		
W Appleton (town clerk, vintner)	£5 * [sic]		
J Hebblethwaite (attorney, and ex-townclerk of Lydd) [briefly resident in Rye]	-		

* taken from 1571 tax list, because he was not included in the 1576 tax list

feter = wholesale fishmonger

† It is likely that George Raynolds had antagonised Harmon, which may explain his support for this faction (see p. 264).

Faith and Faction

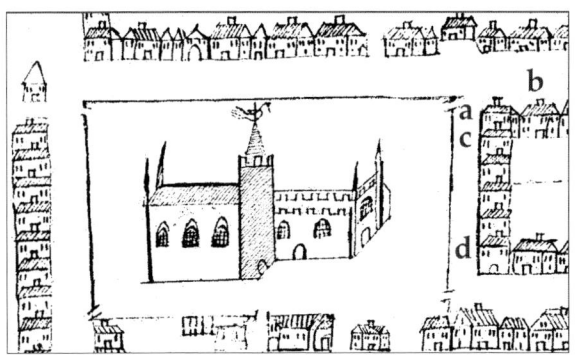

Key to houses

(not depicted realistically!):

a George Raynolds
b Matthew Mills
c William Harmon
d Henry Gaymer

One November evening in 1577, the wife of John Hebblethwaite was sitting with the wife of the town clerk, as well as her own daughter and servants, by the fire in the hall of one of the most substantial houses in Rye. Built around 1500, the house overlooks the churchyard, and appears today very similar (from the outside) to what it must have looked like then (see plate 7). Two strangers (not from Rye) broke in with swords and daggers drawn, announcing that they were re-possessing the house for the man who claimed to be the rightful heir to it.

The house had until recently belonged to the most senior jurat in the town, George Raynolds, who had been mayor several times, though his nomination for that role by the Privy Council twenty years earlier had once been rejected by the overwhelmingly protestant commonalty (as mentioned above) when he was 'servant' of catholic Queen Mary. He died leaving a will that was thought by some to have been tampered with. It disinherited his nearest heir—his nephew, who lived in Brodhurst, Kent—and stated that the house and adjoining property should be sold for charitable purposes. These included 40 coats of country russet and 40 shirts or smocks for the poorest children or adults of Rye, the cost of a new conduit head on Leasam hill and money towards the cost of some building for the corporation. There were also numerous small bequests for a wide variety of people (as was common among those testators, like Raynolds, who had no children). The person who had written the will was also named in it as executor—John Hebblethwaite. The only witnesses to the will were teenage servants.

Members of the merchant faction had been nagging Raynolds to finish his will right up to the evening that he died, knowing that he was old and ill. Perhaps all this nagging only goaded him into sticking his toes in, and refusing to finish it. They knew that a draft will was being written for him by John Hebblethwaite's servant Robert Convers (the future town clerk), and some thought that Raynolds might choose Hebblethwaite to be one of the executors. Raynolds told one witness, however, that he did not want *so many nasty heads of lawyers* to have his goods. He was in a quandary because his kindred were too poor to be executors. After his death, it was suspected that Hebblethwaite had inserted his own name as executor, and forged Raynolds' signature. The mayor, John Fagge (leader of the artisan faction) said that he did *not* think that Raynolds intended the residue of his goods to go to Hebblethwaite, even though he *did* think that Raynolds wanted Hebblethwaite to sell his lands and give the proceeds to charity.

The will had other peculiarities—there were very few bequests for the members of Raynolds' (merchant) faction, and several to members of the artisan faction! Two of the latter were overseers—though one was the mayor, John Fagge, and it was not uncommon for rich testators to ask the current mayor to be overseer, whatever their faction. Hebblethwaite claimed that he had *not* put pressure on Raynolds, and that the old man was *not* losing his senses (Rolfe had referred to his *imbecility*). But he did say that when Raynolds was ill in bed with the gout, unable to walk, he had been taunted by the jurat Henry Gaymer (feter, and later purveyor of the Queen's Fish), his erstwhile ally and current leader of the merchant faction. Gaymer scoffed at Raynolds (according to Hebblethwaite) for being old and not as 'fresh' as he, Gaymer; he also mocked his clothes. This behaviour had antagonised Raynolds. Perhaps the subtext of this mockery concerned the death of Raynolds' young wife whom he had married a couple of years' earlier, only for her to die a few months before he did.

As well as accusing Henry Gaymer of this taunting behaviour, Hebblethwaite said that Gaymer behaved lasciviously with women— *reputed to be a very incontinent liver with divers and sundry women, or at least brought many honest women into a slanderous report.*

Raynolds' wife had brought with her a dowry of valuable marshland, but after she died he was involved in litigation with her father over it, and Hebblethwaite was Raynolds' attorney. It was in this context that the latter persuaded Raynolds to let him write his will, on the pretext that if he died intestate, his father-in-law would reclaim the marshland. So perhaps the peculiarities of Raynolds' will resulted both from heavy persuasion by Hebblethwaite, as well as pique on the part of a confused and resentful old man.

* * *

After Raynolds' death, Hebblethwaite took possession of the house as executor of the will, and it was while he and the town clerk (William Appleton, vintner) were having supper with a neighbour, and only women and teenagers were at home, that the forcible entry was attempted (this was a traditional means of claiming ownership of disputed property, but litigation was increasingly seen as a more appropriate means of achieving the same end). His wife was turned out of the house by the strangers, and she fetched the deputy mayor, William Tolkyn, who (with the town gunner and keeper of the George Inn, John Prowze) managed to remove the sword of one of the men and had them both imprisoned.

When this tactic of forcible repossession failed, members of the merchant faction tried another an hour or so later. A maidservant from the house next door (which belonged to one of the jurats, Matthew Mills, house **b** in the sketch) came and asked to speak to Hebblethwaite's daughter. When the door was opened by Hebblethwaite's wife, five men—no strangers these, but inhabitants of Rye—rushed into the house, led by a man who *with a blow against [her] stomach ... carried her into the backside* [yard]. This man, John Rolfe (mercer, and one of the litigants), had brought a lease for the house signed by the disinherited nephew. The men were not armed, apart from the daggers that they always wore, but the town clerk's wife was hurt, and retreated to the upper chambers with the teenagers, while Hebblethwaite's wife called for help. Rolfe nailed up the front door with some nails brought by a servant of Henry Gaymer (leader of the merchant faction).

A crowd started to gather in front of the house—some witnesses said sixty people, some two hundred. Hebblethwaite and the town clerk arrived and tried to get into the house to rescue their wives and the teenagers, but Rolfe thrust a halberd (an axe blade on a long pointed shaft) through the hall window at the town clerk to prevent him getting in, who struck back with his rapier (there were weapons conveniently hanging on the walls of the parlour). The mayor (John Fagge, butcher) told everyone to keep the peace (or failed to do so, according to some witnesses) and then disappeared behind the church.

One of the mayor's servants came running excitedly down the street, crying *"They're in! They're in!"*. The town clerk and the Bennett brothers had climbed into the garret of the disputed house through

A halberd

the rafters from the neighbouring house (house **c** in the sketch), led by the latter's owner, William Harmon, fisherman. Descending to the parlour, they started fighting with Rolfe (his accomplices, strangely, are not mentioned—had they melted away?).

The people outside the house heard *one with a loud voice cry out within the parlour..."Kill him! Kill him!"*, echoed by another voice in the crowd outside crying *"Down with him! Down with him!"*. The witnesses agreed that the first was the voice of Robert Bennett, and the second that of John Potten, fisherman (the 'him' was of course John Rolfe).

Things seemed to be getting out of hand, and the jurat Robert Carpenter (brewer)—an ally of Henry Gaymer's—went to fetch back the mayor. Carpenter and Gaymer tried to persuade him to read the Proclamation of Rebellions to give the two of them authority to get the town clerk and the Bennetts *out by the ears, or they would fire the house* (they denied saying these words, but other witnesses confirmed it). To these jurats, it was the town clerk, the Bennetts, the Hebblethwaites and the crowd who were the rioters—whereas to John Hebblethwaite and his allies, it was the forcible entry of John Rolfe and company which constituted the riot.

Robert Carpenter was disgusted that the mayor, John Fagge, not only refused to do as he suggested, but lamely told the crowd to *do no more than they lawfully might* (so Fagge's opponents said). Fagge offered to pacify the situation by renting the house himself from Rolfe until the ownership question was settled—the crowd agreed (so Carpenter said), and Rolfe eventually also submitted and came out of the house. Carpenter thought this cowardly, and not the way to quell a riot. The witnesses agreed, however, that Fagge's action had the desired effect of restoring peace. Fagge thus appears to have conceded that Rolfe—or rather, his supposed landlord John Raynolds (yeoman)—had a serious claim to the property. John Raynolds himself had a very small part in all this litigation and strife—he was said to be poor, and others paid for the litigation.

John Rolfe's account of these events includes much more violence than the accounts of the others (although it is also rather non-specific)—giving a long list of the weapons with which the *very evil disposed and riotous persons* were armed—saying that they fought him for *two whole hours*, till he was *in despair of his life* (his supporters, however, said that the fighting lasted a quarter of an hour). In spite of his claims, nobody suggested that he had been wounded during the *hurly burly*. He needed of course to make a strong case against the others, because there is no doubt that his group and the two strangers initiated the violence.

The crowd seems to have been remarkably unanimous in their opposition to Rolfe, according to both plaintiffs and defendants. His reputation had already been shattered in godly Rye by the general belief that he had a former wife still living in Ipswich, whence he had come 16 years earlier. He said he had got a divorce from her, but nobody supported this assertion, and it was extremely uncommon for the church courts to nullify a marriage. Perhaps this was part of the reason why in spite of living in Rye for some years and being quite well off (taxed on £15 worth of goods), he had never been made a freeman.

Hebblethwaite claimed that Rolfe had got involved in the case because Gaymer, Carpenter and the town's preacher Richard Fletcher had *confederated together to set … John Rolfe awork to molest and trouble him … because [Hebblethwaite] will not lean to the bent of their bow and hang on their sleeves*. In other words, he would not do what they wanted. Gaymer and the others were also said to have paid for Rolfe's litigation in Star Chamber against Hebblethwaite (by contrast, mayor Fagge said that Hebblethwaite could no longer afford to employ his servant Robert Convers after this litigation because of its cost).

Hebblethwaite also claimed that Gaymer's associates had been loading guns for Rolfe's use in the house of the jurat Matthew Mills—next door—and leaving the gate open between the houses for access. These weapons would have been used to *murther* his associates, so Hebblethwaite said, if the mayor had read the Statute of Rebellions. Witnesses thought this unlikely, however, and the idea of a store of guns may have arisen when the town clerk and the Bennett brothers were escorted out of this gate and through Matthew Mills' parlour at the end of the dispute, and were astounded to see so *much* weaponry hanging on the parlour walls (they may also have chanced this accusation because it pinned the responsibility for riot firmly on the merchant faction).

John Bennett, mayor's sergeant, later imprisoned Rolfe, refusing to accept his sureties for bail that other witnesses thought adequate. Rolfe was apparently later acquitted by a local jury of a charge of assault (relating to this incident) before the Star Chamber cases were instigated.

We do not know the outcome of the Star Chamber cases, but the artisan faction appear to have got their way over old Raynold's will, since it remained in the form drawn up by Hebblethwaite.

* * *

The Story

This evidence suggests that those who saw themselves as having most authority in the town were the jurats from the merchant faction—in particular Henry Gaymer and Robert Carpenter. They would have taken control of the 'riot' if the mayor had not been obstructive, getting the families out of the disputed house *by the ears*. It was also them who expected Hebblethwaite to *lean to the bent of their bow and hang on their sleeves*, so he said. They were also accused of behaving in a domineering way—that Gaymer had said to his servant John Stace, *Stace if thou turn thy face from me this night, I will run thee through with my sword*, and that Gaymer had also said *in vaunting wise*, that *it should cost £500 rather than Rolf should have the overthrow, and that it would cost blood 'ere the controversy were ended*. When somebody said that Rolfe was *but a lubber*, Richard Fletcher, the minister, was accused of saying *Rolfe is another manner of man than you take him, for there is none of you all that dare meet with him abroad*. Hebblethwaite considered Fletcher to be *more like a soldier than a minister* (he admitted that he was a good preacher, just complained that he should practice what he preached!).

Nobody spoke of the mayor, John Fagge, in the same way. True, he was the richest man in the town, but he was just a butcher, related to other butchers and artisans, and was rich partly, at least, because he had profited from the dramatic expansion of the town's economy in the middle years of the 16th century. The opinion that he was rather weak as a leader was not seriously challenged by anyone. Even Hebblethwaite characterised him as *unlearned and unskilled in the laws of this realm* (a common claim by litigants, but curious when used of a magistrate!). But what he lacked in leadership qualities was perhaps counterbalanced by the greater numbers of his allies—though the crowd's support may also have reflected the fact that the town would benefit from the will because it bequeathed much to local charity.

Another contrast between the factions concerns sexual morality. John Rolfe was thought by others to be a bigamist, and Henry Gaymer was accused by Hebblethwaite of behaving lasciviously with women (even the minister Richard Fletcher was *suspected in London of having a bastard*, according to Hebblethwaite). These comments were no doubt the type of slurs that proliferate in Star Chamber cases, but they would not have stuck to John Fagge. It was while his faction dominated local politics that a determined effort was made to control whoredom and drunkenness in the town. *For the better avoiding of whoredom within the said town of Rye, for which no doubt God is highly displeased*, it was ordered in 1581 that single women who *shall be gotten with child, or found to offend that way* were to wear green and yellow partlets over their clothes (a partlet covered the upper part of the chest). This punishment was inflicted on eight women (mostly servants). If any failed to wear it on any occasion, they were to be *set in the Cage with god's yoke by the space of three hours*. The cage may have been the space under the stairs in the Court Hall which was used for similar punishments, and referred to by the same term, in other market halls—see plate 4. *God's yoke* was rarely mentioned—perhaps it was like the iron collar which was often used to punish offenders (particularly during market hours). In this instance women were targetted, although usually men were punished for sexual incontinency as well as their co-offendors. It was also decreed that alehousekeepers were not to admit any of a list of 12 common drunkards at any time, on pain of having their licence revoked.

The predominant mood in Rye at this period was puritanically severe—including a complete ban on the popular festivities and drama that had been a vivid component of local life until recently.

Members of the Fagge faction were certainly accused in Rolfe's very lengthy depositions of a wide variety of misdemeanours *other* than sexual ones—in particular, Robert Jackson (brewer, jurat and former town clerk), who attracted a large number of accusations, ranging from forging documents and stealing barrels of herrings to sleeping in church. This was in spite of the fact that he was not present at the 'riot'—but implicated because he was accused of receiving a silver cup bequeathed to him in the disputed will of George Raynolds (which he denied). Robert Bennett was said to have been indicted for murdering a boy—though if so, he must have been acquitted or pardoned. Several witnesses said that the town clerk (William Appleton) had persuaded a chandler (with threats) not to indict a well-off common councillor who had stolen candles from him, and he was also accused of counterfeiting a lease.

* * *

Widespread support for mayor Fagge amongst the freemen is indicated by their choice of him as mayor not only in this year, but in the two subsequent years as well. His election for a third term caused a furore because no mayor had held office for more than two terms for at least the previous century. About half the jurats refused to be sworn into office, and Fagge's supporters petitioned the Privy Council, asserting their right to choose him to be mayor, and pointing out that he was a *man of sufficient wealth to bare the same* (Fagge continued in office).

Many of his supporters among the *middling sort* would have been doing well during the current prosperity of the town, and no doubt wanted one of their sort as mayor. Having Fagge as mayor was therefore particularly important because there were few others who had enough wealth to carry the role—there were more rich people in the other faction (see table on page 90 above and page 177 below). There was another man in this faction who was nearly as rich as Fagge—the troublesome Robert Jackson, who paid tax on £60 worth of goods (it was he who was accused of receiving the silver cup). He was elected mayor in 1580 (in spite of opposition from the other faction, who declared that an outbreak of plague had deterred many freemen from taking part in the election).

* * *

The Bennett brothers may have been thorns in the side of the body politic, but they were clearly not isolated, indeed played a prominent role in the struggles of the artisan faction. When we return to the present in the next chapter—which for current puposes is 1607—it will be apparent that the Taylors also had allies, who were trying to undermine the case against Anne and Susan. The forbears of one of these had been involved in the factional struggles discussed in this chapter.

6 Attempts at Reconciliation

If Anne was so very godly, *what* was she doing meddling with Susan Swaffer—an unregenerate woman who followed the old ways in religion? It must have been with derision that Anne reported Susan as saying that because of her *unbelief it would be a long time 'ere [Anne] should enter into the kingdom of God*—an idea reeking of old ideas of purgatory.

George told in his letter sent to the magistrates as a substitute for evidence (see page 72) of a conversation with Susan which would have been laughable if it had not been so shocking, clearly expecting the jury to view it in the same way as he did. He had asked her:

> *How she knew whether they were good spirits or evil spirits?* And she told me
> *She thought they were good spirits, because she saw them continually in prayer.*
> I asked her *Whether she [saw] their prayer book?* and she told me
> *She did.* [I] demanded of her
> *What was contained in the said book, because ... I have heard that thou canst read.* And she told me
> *Yes, there was contained in the book the commandments of god, and the commandments of the divell.* I asked her
> *How she thought these spirits could be good, which had any thing to do with the divel's commandments.* She answered
> *She hoped they were good.*

Susan was perhaps being mischievous (if she really said this)—on another occasion she took a different tack, saying that *there was no manner of hurt with [the spirits], but continual prayer.* She must have been aware that moral ambivalence was one of the characteristics of the old world most hated by godly people, and a mixture of the commandments of god and the devil was still worse! *Because thou art lukewarm, and neither cold nor hot, I will spue thee out of my mouth* (Revelation 3:16). This passage is annotated: *nothing more displeaseth God than indifference, and coldness in religion; and therefore he will spew such out as are not zealous and fervent*—in the version of the Bible in English that was chained in every parish church in England. It is, incidentally, unlikely that she could read—she could not sign her name, which is usually taken as a likely indicator of being able to read. Perhaps George was just leading her on.

Susan was not of course simply a representative of the pre-Reformation world. She—or at least her husband—came from a village long known for religious radicalism, not from a remote rural backwater. But she does not behave as if she is aware of religious differences—in all the references to Anne in her examinations, there is barely a hint that Anne was particularly godly. She was not interested in defining her own beliefs against those of the godly—a characteristic of religious opponents at this period. I doubt that when she said spirit Richard wore a *surplice*, that she had any thought for the controversy that had been raging about this overgarment (a wide-sleeved, full white linen tunic)—godly people being of the opinion that ministers should wear ordinary clothes. For Susan, religion was just a way of life, not a matter of conviction.

How could Anne tolerate spending so much time with such an ungodly person? You would surely expect an eagerness on her part to reform this unregenerate woman. Yet she seems unconcerned—only interested in the spirits that visited Susan, without even paying very much attention to the question of whether the spirits were good or bad. They were messengers from the spirit world, that was the important thing.

* * *

Susan and her beliefs were of course no threat to the Taylors, so they could perhaps afford to take no notice. By way of contrast, take the mercer Thomas Fisher, son of the jurat of the same name, who was a recent convert to Catholicism. Fisher had apparently been talking about his conversion to his godly neighbours, and saying that the Pope was head of the Church of England—behaviour which seems hard to comprehend, given the recent terrorist attack on the Houses of Parliament that had been so narrowly averted (we are now back in 1606). It was only a couple of months since Guy Fawkes and fellow conspirators had been hanged, drawn and quartered. Had they succeeded in their catholic plot, they would have blown up the cream of the landed classes of England (and amongst the number of those killed, incidentally, would have been Thomas Hamon—dispatched before Anne Taylor's witchcraft reached him). The inhabitants of Rye were particularly affected by the plot because after it had been revealed, the government ordered that all shipping was to stay in port to prevent the plotters escaping overseas.

Was Fisher mentally unhinged in some way? Nobody suggested it, but then the witnesses were all for the prosecution. Fisher had been drunk, according to a barber, Robert Burditt, when he came to his house to be trimmed. There he found some neighbours discussing history. The schoolmaster, Samuel Lansdale (who would be in the jury which convicted Susan Swaffer the following year, and also future town clerk), was reading 'an ancient chronicle' that was in the barber's house. But the matter of contention between him and Fisher seems to have related to a different work—an early 16th century history of France by Paulus Aemilius. A passage (from one of these works) so amazed him—asking *if any would believe it*—that he read it out to the assembled company, which included, as well as the barber and his wife and Thomas Fisher, *one Master Taylor*, who was undoubtedly George (and another neighbour arrived later). George had been living in Rye for three years by this date. The passage concerned *a thing very strange and hardly to be credited with, that happened unto a king*—perhaps the deposition of a King by a Pope.

So Fisher found himself in this little nest of puritans, and got into an argument with Lansdale about the Pope. Lansdale

> termed the Pope's religion to be an antichristian religion, and the Pope Antichrist, at whose speeches ... Fisher being moved, seemed to seek for his dagger to strike him, but the company importuning them both to cease their speeches, they left off.

Lansdale went to tell John Bracegirdle, the vicar, but only found Mistress Bracegirdle at home, so he told her. It is not apparent that Bracegirdle did anything about it.

Fisher had reportedly been converted to Catholicism when he was in Dunkirk—probably on business—which was at this time ruled by the then superpower, Spain. It had only become accessible to English merchants since the Peace Treaty with Spain was signed in 1604 (this port had, incidentally, been one of Guy Fawkes' haunts in Flanders). One can imagine Fisher's eyes being opened to the extent of Spanish dominion in Europe. Thinking about how nearly the Fawkes' plot had succeeded, might he not have been bragging, in his drunkenness, to his poorer neighbours—who had probably never been to Dunkirk—that this was where the future lay? The power of Spain could not be halted—Fawkes' plot had been foiled, but the *next* one would succeed, and the English catholics would enable Spain to invade England (as had been intended by Fawkes' company). Why, the Spanish fleet could now anchor off Dover with impunity (since the peace treaty)! In somesuch manner he might have been enlightening these ignorants about what was likely to happen, and only *indirectly* saying what he believed. This seems a more comprehensible scenario than an outright declaration of belief.

Robert Burditt the barber (who was also the town's gunner) wrote down his deposition himself, not leaving the scribing to the town clerk (this a poor man, owning only £2 worth of goods). But it was not the inhabitants of Rye that reported Fisher to the authorities (other than to the vicar)—perhaps even these puritans were concerned about what repercussions such an act would have on the town. No, it was two clothiers from Cranbrook, in the Weald, who reported him to their local magistrate—for Fisher had been talking about his Catholicism even to these models of godliness. Wheels then started to turn, and the Lord Warden of the Cinque Ports, the Earl of Northampton, wrote asking for Fisher to be sent to him, *that the fountain from whence this contagion springeth may be further and more deeply sounded*. This the empty rhetoric of one who, in the late Queen's reign, had been deeply implicated in catholic plots to remove her; he was also one of those who negotiated the peace treaty with Spain (celebrated in the painting reproduced in plate 11). Robert Burditt and another inhabitant were deputed to take the prisoner to Dover Castle to be interrogated.

One of Anne's relations tried to influence matters. Noy Radford, her first cousin, told one of the Cranbrook clothiers that Fisher spoke to a Rye vintner 'and others' about his experience in Dunkirk. The vintner, however, denied that Fisher had said anything about the Pope being head of the Church of England, when asked by the magistrates to give evidence, *nor any speeches tending to the hurt of the king's majesty*.

Fisher was returned to Rye after his examination, to be imprisoned in the town gaol (he must still have been there while Susan was incarcerated). Not enough of a threat to be made an example of, he was left there, and died in prison in 1614.

* * *

Susan was not in the same league as Thomas Fisher junior. Religious differences between her and the Taylors do not seem to have been a great stumbling block—in fact the magistrates had to be on their mettle to try and prevent reconciliation between them. If Susan retracted her evidence against Anne, the case which the magistrates were building up would fall apart—no other witness had given substantive evidence against her. And at least one of the inhabitants was doing what he could to reconcile them.

The first people to try and get Susan to retract what she had said were, not surprisingly, the Taylors. Anne had joined Susan in prison in the summer of 1608, shortly before the summer Sessions of the Peace—

having returned to Rye at some point after fleeing the town to avoid the trial in December 1607. While in prison, she did her utmost to cajole Susan into retracting her evidence, according to a couple of other prisoners (who were there for only minor offences).

Susan must have been at a very low ebb, having given birth to baby Agnes a month or so earlier (presumably not in prison?). She lay in a window recess on the ground floor, by a grate which looked onto the road outside (the most likely window is shown in plate 9).

The magistrates took evidence of the women's behaviour from other prisoners in Baddings tower. One of these, a labourer, said that

> he hath seen Mistress Taylor go down unto the lower prison divers and sundry times where the said Susan did lie, and would pull and shut the loft door [i.e. to the upper floor] after her, and stay sometimes a quarter of an hour before she came up again.

Sitting in an upper floor window, he noticed that if anyone came to the grate where Susan lay, Anne would come upstairs again.

By the time a cutler named John Scragg arrived in prison, Anne had given up, and the two women did *fall out into vild and extreme words,* and did spend much of their time in *such brawling and scalding terms.* Susan reproached Anne bitterly, according to Scragg, resenting Anne's change in mood from cajoling to anger. His account is evocative and emotional in a way that the examinations of Susan herself never are (at least those recorded by the town clerk—this was written down by somebody else):

> "Are you she which would be a mother to me, if I would deny such words or speeches as before I had spoken? But since I was weary to hear you, and did tell ... your persuasions unto others, you now are thus angry with me. For at your first coming into prison, you did follow me up and down the house, from corner to corner; and [in] the place called 'little ease', there you did persuade me to deny all; and there you did promise me to do this and that for my life and enlargement, so I would deny all."
>
> Now ... to his thinking, Mistress Taylor did not greatly deny [those] speeches, but wix [waxed] by terms [i.e. broke into insults] in calling her *beggars womens*; and so to put her off ... from her talk in that matter, found other matter of vild words to pass the time.

Anne would be a *mother* to her—this severe puritan, similar in age to herself! The word may have been used in the broader sense of a good *patron,* but I wonder if Susan was thought to be in need of looking after in some way. Did she have some mental disability? This might help explain

The Story

Anne's lack of interest in reforming her, Susan's obliviousness to religious differences, and her oblique and unemotional style of speech.

Anne's shift to threatening behaviour is particularly evident in Susan's reference to the 'place called *little ease*'. Other, much larger, prisons—including the Tower of London and Colchester gaol—had cramped places of the same name where prisoners were incarcerated for particular punishment. In Colchester, it was a high alcove that was too low to stand up in, and could only be reached by ladder. So, having pursued Susan around the prison, Anne pushed her into this tight corner in an attempt to compel her to retract her accusations.

* * *

Scragg was in prison for only four days—'kept' in the lower room with Susan—but while he was there, he tried to do what he could to improve matters. He told Susan that if she retracted, *Master Taylor would get her a pardon, and get her some monies in her purse*. Susan's version of this was more romantic; perhaps she had heard about pardons from the balladsinger in the market place. She said he had told her that

> if she would deny that she had confessed against Mistress Taylor, and kneel down and ask her ... forgiveness, that then Master Taylor would procure her pardon, which she should have about her at the day of execution, in her bosom, to deliver for her discharge.

(as reported by one of the other ex-prisoners). Taking the pardon from her bosom on the scaffold would have been truly dramatic—and a lesson to them all!

Pardons were a regular part of the dispensation of justice at this period—a counterweight to the potential ferocity of the law—so it was not beyond the bounds of possibility that she might have obtained one, if George had pulled the right strings. However, the Taylors had given up on the idea. When George visited the prison, he rejected Scragg's attempts, calling her *bagges* and saying that he *would rather give [means?] to hang her*. Perhaps something happened which had changed the Taylors' minds.

John Scragg was not to be put off. Determined to play the good neighbour, he enlisted the Taylors' maidservant in the cause—Mercy Luck—asking her to speak to her master about *a pardon and other help for Swapper's wife*. But the maid

did return him answer, that her master or mistress did say
[Swapper's wife] was dangerous to meddle withall, for what soever was said to her, she would tell everybody again, and therefore they would not meddle with [none?].

Mercy was not from Rye, but with a name like that, she must have come from a godly family.

Scragg's efforts to mediate between these adversaries are remarkable, given that he was poor (taxed on £3 worth of goods in 1610). It was also hardly a sensible strategy for him, a prisoner, to arouse the wrath of the magistrates by attempting to restore peace and seek acquittal for both parties.

[Rye 13/17]

Scragg's poverty may underestimate his stature within the community, however, because his father, William (also a cutler), had been mayor's sergeant, and a member of the common council when Anne Taylor's father was still out in the cold. William had been rather older than Robert Bennett, and was active in the protestant cause when Queen Mary was on the throne. At least, he was summoned before her commissioners to answer charges regarding something religious (the details are not recorded).

It must therefore have been particularly humiliating that, during a time when the magistrates were particularly godly (1581), William was accused of committing adultery with the wife of the blacksmith Gabriel Gibbons (the Gibbonses had no children—could this have indicated some problem in the relationship?). They were to be carted round the town, and *tinged with a basin* carried before them. He begged to be let off—saying that he was an old man and this would ruin him. He offered to contribute to the town's works instead. He was removed from the common council, and nothing more is mentioned about other punishment.

Formerly there had been more honourable connections between William Scragg and the Gibbons family. Gabriel's father, a blacksmith like his son, was a jurat, and had been surety for William when he was summoned before Queen Mary's commissioners. Gibbons was also one of those hauled before the Privy Council for opposition to the Queen's regime. In fact the Scraggses, Gibbonses, Bennetts and Richard Ruck senior were all from the same protestant faction.

* * *

The Story

Somebody else was trying to get Susan to retract—the Vicar. We only know about his attempts from a short memo written in the town clerk's hand (*to whom* is not specified):

> Master Bracegirdle hath persuaded the prisoner to deny that [i.e. what] she hath confessed at her arraignment on Friday last, as Susan Swapper sayeth

The 'prisoner' must have been Susan herself, because Anne never did confess to anything. This would therefore have taken place back in December 1607, not long after Bracegirdle stopped attending the examinations of suspects and witnesses in this case. There is, however, no further mention of his intervention. In fact this vicar was remarkable in his ability to get on with all factions. Formerly, there had been endless disputes between vicars, preachers and magistrates—particularly when rather conservative vicars came into conflict with godly preachers appointed by the corporation.

Bracegirdle was, incidentally, remarkable for something else—translating the whole of one of the major works of late antiquity—Boethius' *De Consolatione Philosophiae*—into (mostly) blank verse (a mammoth task). He entitled the work *Psychopharmacon: The Mindes Medicine*. There had been frequent medieval translations of this work, the most recent being by Queen Elizabeth a few years earlier, but none into blank verse—an *honourable effort,* it has been called by a modern editor, *a labour of love;* he was an *excellent versifier*. He may have chosen blank verse because it was dedicated to the co-author of the first English play to be written in blank verse (Gorboduc)—Thomas Sackville, Earl of Dorset (depicted in plate 11):

> … This small token of my loyal affection, and gratitude … Who more fit or able to judge of this work, than your honour? Who have heretofore most gravely and prudently taken pains therein? What work more available to all estates, to persuade the mind to calm contentment in the sturdy storms of all crossing changes, than this author? Briefly the quiet establishing of my bodily estate proceedeth by means of your honour, and my mind's establishment by means of this author. If any object, I ought not employ myself so much in philosophy, and poetry: I answer this book containeth excellent grounds of divinity…
>
> Your Honour's servant at command,
> John Bracegirdle, Bachelor in Divinity

He did not have the work printed—*I write this privately, to signify my obedience and thankfulness, not to satisfy the curious.*

Sir Thomas was the patron of Rye vicarage, and Bracegirdle no doubt hoped that he would be rewarded with the living—which indeed he was, a couple of years' later. The Sackvilles were Sussex gentry of a relatively godly disposition, part of a group which were gaining power and status at the expense of the old guard of catholic aristocracy (of which Sussex was unusually well provided).

Bracegirdle was probably born in Cheshire, and he had cause to rue coming to Rye—four of his children died in five years. The pattern of his misfortunes was similar to that of the Taylors—he arrived a year before George Taylor did, and his last child died about the same month as little Elizabeth Taylor. If he had other children, they are not mentioned in the records.

* * *

The attempts by neighbours to undermine the case against Anne and Susan thus foundered on mutual resentments. But the trial of Anne Taylor did not anyway take place at the summer Sessions of the Peace in 1608, due to external interventions. During this hiatus, the evidence against her was piling up. A particular focus of concern for the magistrates was her and her mother's activities as cunning women. They were known to have healing skills, but such reputations could be double-edged, because cunningfolk were often suspected of being able to cause the diseases that they purported to cure …

7 Healers

If this were a historical novel, I might well have been advised to start differently. Keep it simple—use themes that have universal appeal. A godly elite, targetting a woman of the old religion, peddler of superstitious charms and amulets—yes, that is a familiar scenario. Would that history were thus straightforward! The stereotype not only does not fit Anne Taylor, she would have been utterly horrified to be thus depicted. Her godliness was of a harsher variety than that of the magistrates. She was a healer—but not one that used charms and amulets. She did not advise her clients to repeat latin prayers—2 *Ave Marias,* 10 Our Fathers, etc—nor charms in garbled latin, nor incomprehensible signs written on pieces of paper, nor ritualised rigmarole such as measured girdles.

It was actually Widow Bennett who was the more experienced cunningwoman of the two. *Widow Bennett of Rye ... had good knowledge to help the toothache,* so Mary Carpenter had heard, and *being grievously troubled with the teethache,* she went to her and *prayed her to help her.* In the event her treatment did not work (the widow said that Mary had to *believe* she could help her for it to work, which was a common claim among cunningwomen). The addition *of Rye* after the widow's name suggests that her reputation for being able to heal toothache extended beyond her home town. She must have specialised in treating women (as did many cunningwomen), since the interrogators referred to her patients as *she*. This was when they were questioning her about a drink which, they said, she had given to *certain persons taken with a bad disease.*

The interrogators also questioned her about predicting Thomas Hamon's death.

> Did not you at any time demand of old Stephen Frencham's wife, or of any other person, in the time of Master Hamon's sickness:
> *How he did?* and you being answered by Goodwife Frencham or some other person that
> *Now, god be thanked, he is somewhat amended,* did not you then reply and say,
> *By god, and if he ... did escape that sickness, you would* ~~be hanged~~ *lose your mark. For that you did know that he was taken at such a time and under such a planet as he could never escape it. And that he was taken under such a planet as Master Taylor's daughter was taken.*

Anne made a similar prediction (according to Susan): *[Hamon] was taken in such sort, and in such a bad day and ill hour, as he would never escape the same.* Both Hamon and Elizabeth died in July 1607 (buried on 29th and 4th respectively), so perhaps it was something about that month that Widow Bennett considered unlucky. Anne was talking in terms of shorter units of time—days and hours (this popular astrology will be discussed below).

Widow Bennett's prediction sounds rather threatening, until she brings little Elizabeth Taylor into the astrological picture. If the prediction applies to two different people, perhaps it is disinterested after all? The interrogators disperse this comfortable thought with the next question, concerning antipathy between Widow Bennett and the five-year old:

> Did not Master Taylor's daughter in her sickness revile you and your daughter Mistress Taylor, or any of you, with evil and wicked reproaches, terming you by the name of *?whoresbird divill* and *dog* or words to that effect?

Elizabeth was not Anne's child, and was only a 10-month old baby when her father married this new stepmother. Perhaps her mother had died in childbirth. Widow Bennett refused to answer the interrogators' question, and they then asked if she thought that either of Master Taylors' children had been bewitched, and if so by whom. To this she vouchsafed an answer—that *she doth not believe ...that they came any other wise to their death ... but by the handy works of god*.

Apart from this she denied all knowledge of the matters that she was asked about. Not content to see the town clerk write this down, she was audacious enough to write a comment *in her own handwriting* when the town clerk gave her the document to sign or mark (no other witness did this). In clear and assured writing—though interrupted by ink splodges and torn paper—she made the following challenging statement:

> to th[ese?] in torke[st?] causes nothing
> nor [i?]kan of [no] t[hi]ng by me anna
> bennet

She is saying that she has nothing to say to these distorted (*intorkest*) accusations (*causes*), and anyway knows (*kan*, from same root as *ken* and *cunning*) nothing about the matters referred to.

The Story

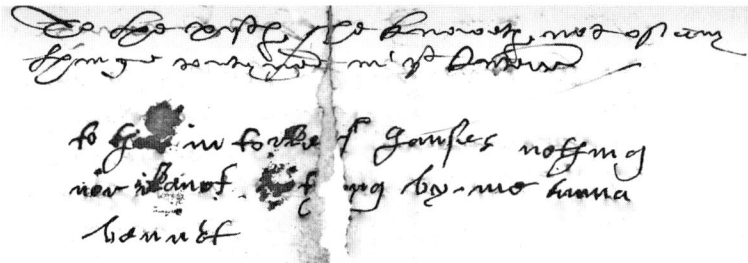

[Rye 13/21]

The verb *torkess*, deriving in part from the Latin verb *torquere*, to twist, was most frequently used to criticise other people's interpretations of the Bible, judging by the examples given in the OED (all from the 16th and 17th centuries). For example:

> Some sentence of Scripture .. must be turkist, and misshapen out of his native simplicitie

The implication is that the biblical sentence to which this author is referring is not just *twisted*, but *wrenched* out of its true meaning. Widow Bennet's use of *torkess* suggests that the language used in scriptural disputation came naturally to her, as it probably did to the other Bennetts, and at least one other Radford (her maiden name)—her nephew Noah Radford discussed the seditious speeches of the converted catholic Thomas Fisher with the Cranbrook clothiers who gave evidence against him (see above page 102).

It is striking that a shoemaker's daughter was able to write—and unusual that we have categorical evidence that she could do so (signing your name is usually taken as evidence of being able to read, but not necessarily of being able to write). There were numerous requests in wills for sons to be *kept to school*, but I have not found any for daughters.

Cunningfolk of course had to be able to read, otherwise what use were their conjuring books? Though it was a contemporary joke that this ability was often faked. One witness was asked if Anne or her mother had acquired the conjuring books belonging to *one Zacharias of Hastings*, which had been confiscated by the then vicar of Rye (the two women were not asked about this themselves). This was the same Zacharias who was accused in the 1590s of recommending cruel remedies for bewitchment (see above page 67).

***

Widow Bennett was thus asked questions specifically about her practice as a healer—in fact she was asked about little else—whereas the references to Anne's activity in this area were generally more indirect. For example, Susan said that Anne offered to give her some ointment to help her lame arm, after spirit Richard had gripped it on the first night that the spirits appeared to her. No doubt Anne would have inherited her mother's skills. This was not just a matter of learning them on the job, judging by an account by the son of a 19th century cunning woman. She passed her powers over to him in some way on her deathbed—so it was a spiritual gift, rather than just the accumulated training of years.

Someone who could heal could also use their powers to do harm, as the critics of cunningfolk complained, and from this point of view Anne would seem to have been less of a threat than her mother. But the interrogators never made a formal accusation against the old woman, and indeed only recorded the evidence of one witness against her—Mary Carpenter, who suffered from toothache. Goody Frencham was on a list of witnesses to be examined, but it does not appear that this was ever done. She may of course have refused to give evidence, but I get the impression that the interrogators did not really have their sights on Widow Bennett, even though an old woman would have been a more typical subject of a witchcraft accusation than a young one. There is also one suggestion of superstitious techniques being used by her when she asked Mary Carpenter for nail parings (as well as 2 shillings and 6 pence) for the cure that did not work.

***

Astrology in various forms played a central role in medical practice at this time—it was by no means an alternative therapy. One physician whom we know a lot about because he kept extensive notes—Richard Napier—drew up an astrological chart each time a patient came to see him. This showed the layout of the heavens at the time they fell ill, or at the time they came to see him. He could use it to decide what medication to prescribe, and also to reveal how serious the illness was, and how long it was likely to last (possibly of more interest to the patient, if they had little confidence in the cure). His practice was as busy as a modern GP's—about a quarter of an hour per patient—and his clients ranged from the nobility to the poor.

Napier was a clergyman, and had learned his skills from another astrologer—he had no formal training. But this was true of most practitioners (apart from surgeons, who were supposed to serve an apprenticeship). Medical training in the universities had only started in England in the later 16th century, and it was mainly based on the works of the ancient Greeks, particularly Galen. But university-trained physicians were not only few in number, they were extremely expensive, and only the very rich could afford them.

Widow Bennett may have been able to write, but I doubt that she drew up horoscopes for her clients. She did not need to, however—numerous cheap almanacs were printed each year, which provided essential information for cunningfolk (as also for most other people—in particular farmers, who needed to know when was the best time to do the various agricultural tasks of the year). Here she could find out which would be the good days, and which the bad, for carrying out a task, contracting an illness, giving medication, or whatever. The medieval idea of good and evil days was based on the phases of the moon, and they were so essential an ingredient of almanacs that when Thomas Middleton made the central figure in his *Inner-Temple Masque* (1619) a *Dr. Almanac*, the supporting cast were Three Good Days, Three Bad Days and Three Indifferent Days. These little books, sold by travelling chapmen, were well within the means of middling sorts of people, and were indeed the most popular literature after the Bible in the 17th century.

A Sussex critic of cunningfolk noted that as well as being *observers of times*—i.e. good and bad days, lucky and unlucky years—they claimed to help those *taken under an ill planet*. Indeed some cunningfolk specialised in dealing with people taken under an ill planet, and still in the late 19th century these practitioners were often known as *planet rulers*.

Being *taken under such a planet* sounds straightforwardly astrological—in other words the position of the planets in the heavens was thought to influence events on earth by correspondence. Planets could interfere more directly in life on earth, however. Thus, one man was *struck by a planet on his left arm*. If you were *planet-struck* or *blasted* you were likely to have been struck by sudden disease—paralysis, apoplexy—or death. Very like illnesses inflicted by spirits, in other words. Occasional deaths in the London Bills of Mortality, from the 1660s (drawn up by local women), included *planet* as a direct cause of death.

Planets had other similarities with spirits—one cunning woman in a witchcraft case said that planets came in several colours, *black, yellow, green and blue, and that black is always death, and that she saw the blue planet strike Thomas Fairbarne*. She denied that she had sent the planet. Fairies were also said to come in particular colours—a cunning man said that there were three kinds, white, green, and black, and that *the black fairies be the worst*. In 19th century Sussex there was a particular type of storm that was referred to as a *planet*, which parallels the idea that storms were caused by spirits. Capriciousness was everywhere—just as medieval saints sometimes seemed as spiteful as malicious spirits, so did planets.

Neither of the Bennett women actually mention planets interfering directly in this way. What they do mention is *planet water*—i.e. water made from herbs that had been picked at an auspicious time. Spirit Richard told Susan to *Go unto young Anne Bennett, and will her to send unto him some planet water*, with the implication that this was for Thomas Hamon, who had been sick for a day or two. It is curious that the *spirits* asked *Anne* for the planet water rather than the other way round. If the magistrates suspected that this planet water might have been used to kill Hamon rather than cure him, it is not mentioned.

When Anne got the message from spirit Richard, she poured some whitish water—about three or four spoonfuls—into a glass bottle, and gave it to Susan to carry up to him.

> And when [Susan] came again into the chamber, the spirit was not in that chamber but in the next chamber, where she saw him. So [she] did set the little bottle of planet water upon the table, and went down and told Mistress Taylor thereof.

Anne then had a little joke at Susan's expense, showing off her ability to know all that was going on:

> "I will lay a penny that the bottle is not upon the table". And [Susan] answered her,
> "I assure you it is there, for I left it there".
> "Nay," said she, "it is not there, go up and see." So [she] went up, and the bottle was not there, neither the said spirit.
> And then ... Mistress Taylor willed [her] to go gather her some herbs to make water, but she did [not] go for any.

Susan had had enough of being manipulated.

* * *

Another source of information for cunningfolk apart from almanacs was the fairies. Cunningfolk often attributed their skills to the fairies (it no doubt deflected attention from themselves, for one thing), and this is another area of similarity between them and the physician Richard Napier. He also used the services of a spirit, although he had the privilege of communicating with the Archangel Raphael rather than fairies. It was not always clear how to tell the difference, as a Sussex 'licensed physician' named Edward Poeton revealed in a tract deploring the activities of cunning people (he, of course, considered them all to be using the services of the devil). One illiterate and immoral practitioner who claimed to have the services of the angel Uriel admitted to Poeton, on enquiry, that he did not think that this spirit was one of the heavenly host, but was rather *a great prince of the Fayries*.

Incidentally, Poeton noted that it was true that the cures of cunning people were often more successful than those of physicians—but this was because they were helped by the devil, who might even appear to dissect the body of the sick person so that the practitioner could see exactly what was wrong! Indeed, the practical experience of cunningfolk may have resulted in their cures doing less harm than some of the invasive techniques of university-trained physicians, who relied so much on theory imbibed from the works of the ancient Greeks.

* * *

Did the curing activities of the Bennett women cause antagonism amongst other medical practitioners in the town? No medical practitioners gave evidence against Anne, and there are no indications of conflict between medical practitioners in Rye. If the Bennetts specialised in treating women, this may also have reduced competition with others. Making and administering medicines was a natural part of the housewife's role— 'receipt' books always contained recipes for medicines as well as food— and it would not be surprising if individual women gained a reputation for being skilled in curing particular illnesses.

The Royal College of Physicians (the members of which had received university training) claimed the authority to license practitioners—but they signally failed to assert their authority over those in London, let alone anywhere else.

Women were not licensed as medical practitioners by the corporation—but in all occupations requiring a licence, the corporation always favoured male householders over others—not only women, but also men who did not have a family to support. If a male householder died, his widow might well take over. And when the corporation *did* license a physician, it may well have been less to keep unauthorised practitioners out, than to make sure that *somebody* was available to care for the sick. As in the case of a certain *Master George who professeth the physick*, who was licensed to treat victims in a time of plague. Women were nevertheless employed to view the bodies, and lay out the dead.

There were a few surgeons in Rye, the first instances to be mentioned being French—Matthew Flory and William Gile (first names were always anglicised). Like some other refugees from Dieppe, they had more specialised occupations than English residents of Rye—Dieppe being at least ten time its size. In the later 16th century, however, some English inhabitants styled themselves *surgeons*. These had probably not been apprenticed to the trade, because they had had other occupations before— like the basketmaker Quintin Pye, and the tailor Andrew Ferguson.

Of as much concern as training was the *moral* stature of medical practitioners. Both surgeons and midwives were supposed to be licensed by the ecclesiastical authorities, affirming their probity. These Rye surgeons had their own ways of asserting their godliness—Quintin Pye appears as *Quintus Pious* in one entry in the parish register (a striking transformation!), and Andrew Ferguson as Forgadsonne (ForGodsSon?). Or maybe these verbal twists were just the churchwarden's little joke at the insufferable *sanctimoniousness* of these two—but my argument still stands. There is no doubt about William Gile's godliness—he had his children baptised with the godly names of *Hopewell* and *Repent* (giving his children English names suggests that he intended staying in England).

A sample of Quintin Pye's skills has been handed down to posterity in the form of a recipe for cleaning ulcers:

> A gallon of water; put in a handful of bendicke or humlocks and a handful of ke' sage and a handful of joun'wort. Seeth this to a pottle, putting in in the seething a pennyworth of allum; and this is a drying water for to wash any ulcer, approved.

Quintin Pye's Water was recorded by Samuel Lansdale (the schoolmaster mentioned in the previous chapter) in a book of recipes that he had inherited from others. This book had clearly been around for some time, because the earliest recipes are full of supersititious latin prayers and charms which would have been deplored by those inhabitants of Rye who professed godliness.

The Story

Anne's claims to godliness may therefore have stood her in good stead. She had in fact several sources of authority—inherited medical knowledge, having God on her side, and gentility—for she was not just one of the Bennett women, but *Mistress Taylor*. All well and good, if those around her believed her claims—but if they suspected hypocrisy, of which puritans were so often accused, the whole edifice might come crashing down.

* * *

Back in December 1607, when Susan was waiting in prison to be tried the next day, she sent for the town clerk's wife to come and speak with her (people in Rye always seem to be sending for each other—there must have been children and servants continually running between houses on these errands, though of course Susan had no choice). Margery Convers (the same woman quoted in chapter 4, who had a conversation with Anne on the day the apparitions were seen by the Taylors in the windows opposite) *did take a neighbour with her, and went unto the courthouse.* Speaking presumably through the grate, Susan *did tell [her] before her neighbour that*

> You, Mistress Convers, had a maid came unto Mistress Taylor for cure for her throat, and [she] took a candle, and did look in her mouth and made her gape, and looked upon her brows and in her nostrels, and said unto her
> *"Thou a sore throat! Thou hast a heat in thy stomach."*

—meaning full of pride and anger, haughty, impertinent, insolent. Susan went on:

> Whereupon the maid went to the cradle to see Mistress Taylor's child which was sick, and asked her how her child did, and Mistress Taylor was very angry with her, and swore,
> *"God's Soul! Dost thou take the upper hand of my child? I would thou shoulds well know, my child is better born than thou art, and comes of honourable parentage!"*
> And thereupon she gave her a great blow of the [shoulder, and told her,]
> *"Go thy ways, now. Thy throat is cured, I warrant thee!"*

Taking the upper hand, in its literal sense, meant taking a more prestigious seat at table—an issue that people got very heated about, and which was a frequent cause of strife. So perhaps the maidservant had been making comments about the sick child such as: how could Anne *really* be a godly person, if God had inflicted this illness on her child? Or, why could she not cure her own child, if she was so skilled at healing?

Anne had told Margery about this incident herself, when they had the conversation mentioned in chapter 4—on the day that both the maidservant and the child were buried. After Margery had said how sorry she was about the sickness and death of her maid, Anne had said

> Your maid was with me for a medicine for her throat, and I was as angry with her as ever I was with maid in my life! Then [Margery] asked her the cause, and [she] answered her,
> "Why, woman, she took the upper hand of my child!"

So Anne was much too concerned with status—her godliness (which was hollow, or she would not have sworn an oath) a mask for social climbing. *A puritan is such an one as loves god with all his soul, and hates his neighbour with all his heart*—as the saying went. Why, she did not even care about her husband and children! Here was Margery so full of feeling for her maidservant, and moreover said to Anne that she was *sorry for the death of [Anne's] children and likewise for the sickness of her husband*; to which Anne responded that she was *no whit sorry for the same, for as freely [god] gave them [her], as soon [she] gave them to god again*. Was this godliness, or lack of concern so extreme as to be unnatural? Margery quoted further comments of Anne's to show that she only wanted her husband's money:

> "Well, Master Taylor will leave me as free as he found me, for I have now no child, nor I shall have no more. And I think I will never marry widower again. I knew Master Taylor had a good portion of money and land, but I will stand to his brother's courtesy."

There are other suggestions that Anne did not care enough about her children (more understandable with her step-child, perhaps, but what about her own baby?). A butcher's wife said that Anne asked her for some powdered beef (i.e. salted) to make porridge for her sick child, and she thought it very strange to give such *very* tough meat to the child (beef was salted to preserve it after the general slaughter in November—there never being enough fodder to keep all the animals alive over the winter). After the woman gave Anne the meat (the *best* part), her arm went lame. Anne, however, said she had asked for *fresh* beef.

The Taylors themselves suspected that their children might have been bewitched, and asked Susan to ask the spirits whether or not this was the case. Susan said that if anyone had bewitched them, it was Anne herself.

The Story

* * *

Margery's depiction of Anne as a social climber is not in itself surprising, since Anne had managed to win a gentleman in marriage when she and her mother were in debt. But Margery herself only had the title *Mistress* by virtue of her husband's position as town clerk. She was a fisherman's daughter—sister of John Cheston, who left a *Spanish cushion of gold* to *my Sister Convers* (perhaps plundered from a Spanish ship?). Margery had been the wife of the previous town clerk, and Robert Convers did the classic career move of marrying his master's widow as well as inheriting his office. Convers had come from Berkshire as a 17-year old, to be apprenticed in Rye—perhaps the *John Convers* who had been an attorney in the town's court at the time was related, and had made the arrangements.

A notable social climber was Joan Breadcar or Bredkirk, another fisherman's daughter, whose father had not been well off (taxed on probably £10 worth of goods in 1557). She married another fisherman, John Styner, in 1580, and they had a succession of children. Styner did well—presumably from trade, since it was difficult making a living from fishing—and was later made a jurat (we will have more to do with him later). After John's death, Joan, now 47, went through a succession of husbands—she married Angel Shaw (the mayor's sergeant depicted in the tableau seen by the Taylors in the windows of the house opposite theirs) two months later, who died a month after that; she then married two 'gentlemen' in quick succession, Stephen Porter, deputy customs officer, and Philip Halsey, jurat, *my late wellbeloved husbands* as she calls them in her will! Her final husband was Robert Garrett, a Dover alderman. She died at the age of 65, very well off—though still having herring nets to bequeath, as well as an unspecified number of parts of ships and tackle.

So Anne's good fortune in the marriage stakes was not *extraordinary*. I might also mention the slightly bristly relationship between her and Susan over status. Ordinarily, the difference in status between them was emphasised whenever they spoke to each other by Anne's use of the familiar *thee* and *thou* to Susan (most of the time), while Susan always addressed Anne with the respectful *you*. But it was Susan of course who, when quoting the spirits, always referred to her as *young Anne Bennett*— thus denying at one swipe both her gentility and her married status. Susan could get the spirits to say what she dared not say herself.

Anne herself tells of some angels giving Susan a put-down for being presumptuous, in a comment that she volunteered at the end of her first examination. Susan had told her that:

> [One of] her spirits did will [Susan] that she should look up into the element, and she accordingly did look up, and did see appear unto her six candles, to her judgment. And after that there appeared unto her two angels in her chamber, and one of them had in their hand a ... fan. And the angel did let it fall, and ... Susan stooping to take it up, the angel gave her a box of the ear, rebuking her that she being a mortal creature should ~~meddle~~ presume to handle matters appertaining to heavenly creatures.

These were the angels whose coming, Anne said, was *to cut off the wicked from the yearth* (see above page 75). The fan may have been a winnowing fan to separate the wheat from the chaff (very Biblical, as were the candles—though there should be *seven*). Susan was presumably chaff.

* * *

Anne was not just an unneighbourly social climber. At the end of her evidence, Margery Convers made a much more explicit and serious accusation:

> Her maid in her death bed did confess that she had been with Mistress Taylor for her throat. And [that] ... she was never well after she came from thence, but presently [i.e. immediately] when she came home, fell sick in an extraordinary sickness, and so pined away a fortnight before she died. And this deponent doth verily believe that her said maid, named Philip Binwen, was bewitched to death.

So in spite of the neighbourly tone of this wide-ranging conversation between Margery and Anne, which occurred not long after the funerals of the maid and Anne's son, Margery thought Anne had bewitched her maidservant to death.

[Rye 13/25]

The Story

Margery may also have had her own motives for pinning blame on Anne—this deflected attention away from any responsibility that she herself might have been thought to have for the maid's death. Had the girl's parents accused her of lack of care? In the ague-ridden town of Rye, this might well have been a common problem for the masters and mistresses (or *dames* for those not entitled to the title *mistress*) of servants.

The apparent immediacy of Margery's account is deceptive—her evidence was recorded (by her husband) two years after the conversation, and just four days before the final trial in June 1609.

* * *

How important was Anne's role as a healer in making her a target for accusations of witchcraft? Not many convicted witches were referred to as medical practitioners, but this may under-represent the number of those who practised informally, as John Demos found in early modern New England. These women (mostly) may have been viewed with suspicion because of the implicit power which they held over their patients, as much as for any particularly dubious practices which they performed.

The Church was certainly critical of the superstitious activities of cunningfolk (men as well as women), and asked about them in their visitations. Many cunningfolk were indeed presented at the church courts—but these must nevertheless have constituted only a small proportion of the total, given that cunningfolk were thought to be as numerous as parish clergy. Moreover, those who were presented would be discharged if they denied the charges and got enough of their neighbours to support them (by saying that they thought the cunningperson was telling the truth).

* * *

The mood of the next chapter—still in the summer of 1607—is transformed. It is full of pranks, gift-giving, laughter, horseplay—puck-like behaviour which is perhaps more commonly associated with fairies in the modern mind than the vindictiveness which has been described hitherto. Though some of these pranks turn out to be not so amusing after all, and the gift-giving tallies rather too well with the words of the indictment and the statute, *...entertaining and feeding...wicked spirits...*

8 Entertaining Fairies

SPIRIT MARGERY: Sirrah Dick, doest thou know where I have been?
SPIRIT RICHARD: No.
SPIRIT MARGERY: I have been at Master Mayor's, to see if there be any manner of repentance with her [the mayoress], for her former life. And as thou thinkest, how I have made trial of her …? Two pennyworth of [Katherine] pears, some of them Master Mayor and Mistress Mayoress did eat, and the rest she set in a basin in her closet. [I have] brought them away … [look] … as goodly pears as ever I saw!

   What thinkest thou, Dick, I have left in the basin instead of the pears, a thing in the shape of a man's members! And I will … again … to see how she doth apply it, and what repentance is with her.

[Spirit Margery goes out, and returns again]

SPIRIT MARGERY: There is no ma[nner of repentance?] in her, Sirrah Dick, [for] [she] … came to the basin and set [it] … upon the board, and … conveyed the Things in the basin … [onto] plates. But it had been good for Mistress Mayoress that she had never … For she would make her know, before she had done with her, that she had highly offended her God.

The mayoress had apparently not noticed the metamorphosis when she served the pears on plates on the table! No, this ribald scene is not from a stage play performed before the rude multitude in Rye market, nor at a local inn—although it sounds as if it might have been. This is yet another instance of *what Susan said*, relayed by—of all people—the arch puritan George Taylor. He recounts it in his letter to the jury, introducing it with the words

> I beseech you mark ~~and think what credence is to be given to so lewd a person as this~~ how many devices this Swaffer's wife had. Which, if it please Master Mayor, he is likewise able to certify you (and Master Bracegirdle), what report she made upon her confession before them, concerning two pennyworth of [Katherine] pears which Mistress Mayoress should [i.e. did] buy.

Katherine pears were grown by the commercial fruit growers of Kent—who were a new breed, catering for the London market. So these pears were presumably bigger, and hence gave added value to, the traditional medieval joke of the phallic pear.

The Story

Perhaps the mayoress, Martha Higgons, had a reputation for being a seductress. You may recall that in June 1607 she—in her late twenties—had married her former husband, Thomas Hamon—aged 58—and then when he died 6 weeks later, she married (within a fortnight) his successor as mayor, Thomas Higgons. There do not appear to be any more explicit accusations of immorality in the records, but the spirits' ungodly attempt to control her behaviour suggests that it was not only puritans such as Anne Taylor who criticised her.

Did Susan really tell this lewd story about Martha to her husband, Thomas Higgons, and the vicar? This type of slander would more commonly have been written anonymously in the form of a ballad—on pieces of paper left lying around the town, or pinned up in public places. If she did say it—and George would hardly have written it down if he thought the mayor would contradict him—she must have expected people to believe that she was only relaying what the spirits had said, and would not therefore accuse *her* of the slander. But what effrontery!

* * *

This was not the only puck-like practical joke that the spirits played on the inhabitants of Rye. Interspersed with accounts of their aggression—Roger Swaffer's arm gripped so tightly that he was unable to use it for a time, as also the arm of a butcher's wife; one side of Thomas Hamon's body paralysed by the same means until he died—are tales of mischievous pranks, laughter, gift-giving. The spirits entertained the inhabitants of Rye with their antics—often at the expense of a particular person—while Susan in turn entertained the spirits with gifts (with the connivance of Anne).

There was the incident when *John Cheston and his wife have been feared this night, and like to be pulled out of their beds*. When Cheston himself was asked about this, he could not deny that he was thus troubled. Were the spirits punishing the Chestons for some objectionable behaviour (they appear to have been lying in separate beds, which might have been a source of complaint)? Perhaps this John Cheston was the brother of Margery Convers—but there was usually more than one man of this name in the town. In fact I think of John Cheston as a kind of generic term for inhabitant of Rye, because the parish registers have a continuous stream of these master fishermen—John Cheston juniors turning into John

Entertaining Fairies

Cheston seniors—and their wives and children; it is nigh impossible to identify individual households.

The Taylor household was troubled in a like manner. One night earlier in the year, when Susan was left in peace by the spirits, Anne reportedly told her that *if they have not been with you, they have been with me. For they have scrabbled about my pillows, and drawn them*. Unspeaking and invisible, these seem very different from Susan's familiars, although the implication is that they are the very same beings. The same night, while Anne's mother was sitting by the fire with her sick grandchild, *the doors did open and shett, nobody being there with them*. On another occasion, the Taylors' maidservant Mercy Luck was sat by the fire when her master was sick, and

> she ... was suddenly removed out of the chair where she set and flong into the fire, and did burn part of her neckecher. And then she did start up and went to bed.

A rational explanation might be that she had fallen asleep and tumbled into the fire. But these three incidents all occurred when somebody was sick—perhaps the spirits were making their presence felt because they were responsible for the illnesses—demanding attention.

These invisible, unspeaking sprites did not need a medium such as Susan to pass on their messages to other people. They were now in the public domain, and anyone could add their own interpretation of the spirits' pranks. Their exploits were no doubt enlarged upon in the alehouses of Rye, each speaker embellishing and twisting the story to give their own take on other people's behaviour and morals. People could say things that they would not dare say in their own voice—they were only the interpreters. What a profane invasion into godly Rye!

* * *

There is one deposition that is full of laughter, sometimes fiendish laughter. Curiously, it is the puritan Anne Taylor who is said to be laughing. The witness is a 50-year old grocer (one of the richer sort of merchant) from Sandwich named Thomas Tompkins. He had been incarcerated in Rye prison (probably for debt) while Susan was there, and needless to say, he claimed to be repeating what Susan had told him. But I suspect that quite a bit of his own invention has gone into it—perhaps in collaboration with Susan—because he presents an Anne Taylor that is

The Story

very different in character from the grave, judgmental woman described by those witnesses who were inhabitants of Rye. Presumably he did not know her, and was trying to ingratiate himself with the magistrates.

It was Tompkins who told the story about John Cheston being tumbled about in bed, which Anne—according to Tompkins—called a *pretty jest*. After recounting what happened, he said that she went on in bantering style:

> *"I pray thee, Sue, go up to the spirits to know who did it."* Whereupon [Susan] went up and there she saw the spirits. And one of the spirits said unto her …
> *"We know well enough wherefore you come; she need not to send you up to know who did it, for she knoweth who did it."* Whereupon one of the spirits called Richard … made a sign [with his] mouth unto … Susan
> [missing words]… unto the said John Cheston…
> Susan did at her coming down tell [Mistress Taylor]; whereupon she … said
> *"Did he do it?"* And fell in a great laughter.

All very inconsequential! Tompkins himself asked John Cheston if he had been thus troubled, and was told he had.

This laughter seems out of character for Anne Taylor because godly people deplored it, quite as much in themselves as in other people. It is unlikely, for example, that George was smirking beneath his beard when he recounted Susan's story about the pears (attitudes to laughter and the substantive reasons for deploring mirth will be explored further in the essay at the end of this book).

In Tompkins' other story—which is again about a prank, although it does not directly refer to the spirits—the laughter has turned fiendish:

> Upon a time, Mistress Taylor did set upon the board certain bread and meat for … Susan to eat, she having been about certain business before for [her]. And [Susan] … putting a piece of meat into her mouth, could not put the same in her mouth nor put her hand back again, but was forced against her will to dance up and down the house; and could in no wise stay herself until Mistress Taylor did bid her stay and come away. And this was done before Mistress Taylor's mother, and they both did laugh [at] her.

This female Svengali is cruelly preventing Susan—who probably could not afford meat herself (unless this just refers to *food*)—from eating the food that she has earned, and making her look foolish. The idea of using magic to make someone dance around the house was not original—there was a simple spell for this purpose in a contemporary conjuring book. All you needed to do was to write names on parchment and say *I conjure thee virgin parchment, by virtue of these names written in thee, that all the men and women in this house shall dance when I rehearse their names.* Not very useful, perhaps, but an excellent exercise in domination.

In this incident Anne has been metamorphosed from an ordinarily grave woman into the fiendish opposite—a cackling devil.

* * *

When the spirits first appeared to Susan, they had been frightening, certainly unwelcome—at least until she found that they could help her. By the summer of 1607 her attitude to them had changed to such an extent that she no longer waited for the spirits to appear of their own accord, but enticed them with gifts. She—and, according to her, Anne as well—left flowers and herbs for them in a window recess in the room frequented by the spirits in the Swaffers' house. This was about the same time as the Taylors were seeing apparitions in the windows of the house across the way from their own house—but those forewarnings of the destruction of the wicked seemingly had little in common with the transactions that took place on Susan's windowsill.

According to Susan, it was Anne who was most eager to ply the spirits with gifts:

> Mistress Taylor ... did make four nosegays and delivered them unto [her] to give unto the four Fayries, as she termed them. The which nosegays [Susan] did lay in the window, for that the familiars were not there at her coming. And afterwards they were taken [a]way as she thinketh by the spirits, for that no body else could come there, the doors being shet. And she further saieth Mistress Taylor hath diverse times sent them herbs to be laid in the window, which accordingly was done by [Susan]. And if [she] had stayed any long time from her, and not have fetched herbs to lie in the window, then Mistress Taylor would blame [her], and say that if you do anger them, you shall see whereto it will come.

All fairly innocuous, but there was a much more ominous occasion *when roses began first to bud out*:

> Mistress Taylor did give unto her little son which is dead, four roses. And did pray [Susan] to
> "*Carry up the child unto the spirits in the chamber*" ... And [Anne] named unto the child the spirits by their name, and willed him to deliver unto every one of them one. And that if he were afraid, he should lay them down, and then [Susan] should bring her child away.

The Story

Susan did as she was told, but the spirits were not there, so the child played in the chamber a while, before she carried him home again.

About two days later, Anne sent Susan with little George again, giving him two roses to give to the spirits Robert and Catherine. This time these spirits were there, but *when the child did see them, he cried out, and [squealed], and called to go down, and clung about [Susan's] neck.* The spirits went into the other chamber, and Susan carried the toddler downstairs, and took him to his mother, who said *"Alas! Poor child, thou wast afraid. How white he doth look!"*

> And afterwards when gillyflowers were ripe, [Anne] gathered four nosegays, and sent them by the child again to the four spirits. [The spirits were not there, so Susan] set down the child, and he played in the window with the nosegays. And of a sudden, the child spied them, and cried out, and squealed, and clong about [her] neck, and flung away the nosegays. And so [she] carried away the child, and told his mother what had happened ....

The child is almost being offered up to the spirits! Susan in fact thought that Anne had caused the death of her child by treating him in this way, as is evident from the words with which she preceded the above accounts of gifts of roses and gillyflowers:

> And as concerning Master Taylor's children that died, whereas Mistress Tayler did say that she doubted that [Susan] had bewitched her children … if any of them died by any evil means, they died by the evil dealing of her self. For she … saieth that afore midsomer last past when roses began first to bud out …

If Robert Pywall could die of fear without even seeing the spirits, how much more likely that a toddler would die after meeting them?

A reason why a cunning woman such as Anne would use a child to deal with spirits (though usually a much older child!) was because a virgin was thought to be able to see them when others could not—hence magicians' use of children as *scryers* to see spirits in a crystal ball. I wonder if this belief might also help explain why Susan was able to see the spirits, and Anne was not. Susan was certainly no virgin, but in so far as she was seen as an *innocent* (I have suggested above on page 103 that she might have been mentally disabled) she played the role of scryer to Anne's role as magician.

Entertaining Fairies

But these may all be slanders. The first, innocuous, story of leaving nosegays for the spirits was in Susan's first, innocuous, examination. The last two, by contrast—when Anne supposedly sent up her son to give flowers to the spirits—were in Susan's last examination, which was full of dark accusations against Anne. In the *alternative* version of Susan's first examination mentioned above (see page 51), it is Susan who gives the flowers—Anne is not involved at all.

* * *

Gillyflowers—clove pinks—were particularly popular at this period because of their strong scent (also called *gelofer*, from the French *girofle*, or clove). They were used to flavour wine (and also ale) as a cheap alternative to cloves—hence their nickname *sops-in-wine*. Roses and gillyflowers seem a different type of gift from the milk or cream that was conventionally left out for fairies. The latter would anyway have been more appropriate in a rural area, where one of the main problems that was blamed on fairies or witches was the failure of cream to turn into butter. Leaving milk and cream out for the fairies might gain their goodwill, and induce them not to interfere with the rest of the churn (butter-making by hand is a tricky process). Since Rye was more urban than most towns (not being surrounded by farmland), most inhabitants *bought* their butter, at the market held on Wednesdays and Saturdays at the Market cross in the Butchery.

A Gillyflower.

Giving roses and gillyflowers was anyway associated less with deflecting illwill, than expressing loyalty, as in feudal relations between lords and tenants. A red rose at midsummer had been sometimes used as a quitrent (as also in one instance three gillyflowers) which expressed a tenant's loyalty to his lord, as well as indicating that no other rents or services were due to him.

In those unsettled times, landowners valued military help from their tenants, defending their lands against encroachers, more than commercial rents—the latter were neither practicable nor lucrative. More recently, a curious twist to the custom of giving roses and gillyflowers by way of rent was reported by an (incredulous?) correspondent in the 1530s to the

The Story

Secretary of State, Thomas Cromwell. The dissolution of the monasteries was proceeding apace when monks at a Northampton monastery asked their tenants to pay their rent in roses and gillyflowers instead of the rent in cash and corn that they had been paying. Presumably they wanted a large quantity of sweetly smelling flowers for strewing or to make rose water—but perhaps there was also a suggestion that the *loyalty* of their tenants was more important to them than an economic rent. Who cared about income when the survival of the monastery was at stake? Henry VIII was dissolving those monasteries first whose members had a reputation for vice, and so the monks needed their tenants to speak up for their good name.

So Anne and Susan's attempts to create goodwill and loyalty in the spirits had precedents. Susan gives Anne the major role in presenting these gifts—perhaps Susan did not grow roses and gillyflowers in her garden. She does mention a few gifts which she gave on her own initiative—gifts that she could afford:

> She hath diverse times given [the spirits] water, and once bread. … the spirits did consume the water, and … when they left any water, the same was blackish, and the tub became spackled with white.

She always notes evidence that the spirits had taken the gifts. When the interrogators asked Anne about the bread and water, they assumed that she was the instigator.

* * *

Other gifts were demanded by the spirits, rather than offered by the women—always requests for objects that belonged to Anne. Cloth was particularly in demand, as when Anne was told by Susan:

> *"They do require you to send unto them half a sheet"*. And [Anne] … did accordingly deliver unto [Susan] half a sheet.
> And the same day in the afternoon, she sent her maid again unto … Susan to will her to come to her. And [she] came, … but did not bring the sheet. Then said [Mistress Taylor] unto her that
> *"If I had not given you the half sheet, I could have given you all my child's clothes that were in a tub,"* whereupon she said
> *"You may have the half sheet again, for they have not touched the same item,"* and so she went home and fetched the same.

'*All* my child's clothes'—Anne clearly thinks she will not need them because her child has died, and, as she told Margery Convers, she does not expect to have any more.

She implies that Susan wants the sheet for herself—why else would her child's clothes have been an acceptable substitute? They would surely not have been so for spirit Richard. At Anne's response, Susan decided that the spirits did not want the sheet after all—children's clothes were more desirable. Clothes were very expensive items for the poor.

For once, Anne's account of the incident was volunteered—Susan had not mentioned it. She did mention another demand for cloth from the spirits, however, that appears to carry a hidden threat:

> Richard her familiar willed her to go to young Anne Bennett, and demand of her a piece of cloth if it were never so old, of her length and of her breadth; or else a piece of inkle, or an old hairlace [ribbon] of that length, which accordingly she did.

Inkle was linen tape, which could be as wide as a girdle. Giving the spirits something that was the same length and breadth as Anne would put her in their power, according to old catholic beliefs. In the Middle Ages, this was often used in a positive way—you could, for example, have a sick person *measured for a candle* if you wanted to ask a saint to help them. That is to say, you take the length of them in a taper, coil it up with the wick left standing, and leave it burning in front of the saint's shrine. But what were Susan's intentions? There is no suggestion that she is offering help—so one can only assume that she (or the spirits) intend harm. So it is not surprising that Anne *refused to do the same, saying she had done too much already, as she doubted*. When Anne was asked about this incident by the interrogators, she confirmed that Susan had asked for the cloth—but added that there had been no mention of the spirits asking for it.

Susan was then asked again about what Anne had said (presumably because the bit about the half sheet had been volunteered by Anne). She embellished the story with further details—spirit Richard complaining that the piece of (linen) cloth was too small, and demanding a larger piece. Anne duly gave her a larger piece, and Susan laid it on the hemp that was stored in the garret, where it stayed for three days. Anne then asked her to fetch the piece of linen, and—far from being unused, as Anne had said in her own examination—it was *soiled* with clay on one end of it. So Susan *verily thinketh that the spirits did use the same … and Mistress Taylor* then said she did verily believe that the spirits had carried the same into the ground with them.

Two very different accounts—Anne recounting Susan's ruses to get things for herself, and Susan implying that Anne was if anything more involved in giving things to the spirits than she was. For the prosecutors, however, it did not matter who was the main instigator—all this gift-giving tallied well with the words of the 1604 witchcraft statute, repeated in the indictments of December 1607, which declared that *consulting, …entertaining,…feeding…any evil and wicked spirits*, was felonious.

* * *

Margery Convers thought, like Anne, that Susan was using the spirits' (supposed) demands for gifts to manipulate the latter. The two 'gentlewomen' were talking about sickness and death (in the conversation described in the last chapter), when Anne suddenly changes the subject:

> *"That Swapper was with her for the length of her husband in a sheet, were it never so old."* Then [I] said unto her again,
> *"I hope you did not give her the length of him in a sheet!"*
> *"Why"*, said Mistress Taylor again, *"she asked of me for the length of myself in a hairlace!"* Then said [I]
> *"Truly, Mistress Taylor, if you will be ruled by me, you shall give her nothing."* Then said she… again,
> *"She hath come to me for beef out of my pot, and diverse other things; and she came the other day for apples for one of them that was with child."* And I asked her whether she gave her any, and she said,
> *"I' faith, that I did, and a piece of sugar too!"*
> And then [I] asked Mistress Taylor *what they were that she sent the apples to*. And she said she *knews not what they were*. Then [I] asked [her] *whether they could speak*, and she said that *Susan Swapper sayeth that they can speak, and that they cry "Yangh Yangh"*.

So Anne is just Susan's dupe, being manipulated by Susan for her own ends—whether because she wants these gifts for her own use (as is suggested by Anne herself), or because she is going to give them to the spirits. Sugar was an expensive new commodity at this period.

Margery sounds as if she is sympathising with Anne, expressing solidarity with her against the wheedling of this poorer neighbour, advising her to distance herself from Susan and her spirits. If all the spirits can say is *yangh yangh*, they must be very minor spirits indeed (so

Margery implies)—not worth meddling with. It does seem rather a curious attitude in one that is accusing the other of witchcraft.

Susan herself had told the interrogators about the apples desired by the *spirit in the likeness of a woman great with child [who] did appear unto her in her house in the day time*. Unusually, Anne herself confirmed that Susan had told her about the *Fayries woman*, who also wanted a piece of sugar. She gave her three apples and the sugar *in regard she thought … Susan her self did long for the same*. The sugar was not mentioned either by Susan in her examination, nor by the interrogators when questioning Anne (they just quoted Susan's account). Maybe Susan thought it too much of a luxury item to be *really* requested by spirits, so she left it out.

* * *

Those apples for one of *them* that was with child—was Susan referring to the cravings of a pregnant spirit woman, or to those of her neighbour, Phyllis Swan? The spirit and human worlds seem now to be running in exact parallel—even merging with each other. Phyllis and her husband Robert had moved into the house between the Swaffers' house and that of the Taylors about the time the spirits first appeard to Susan, in Lent 1607. Phyllis deposed as follows:

> And the summer following when apples were green, … being young with child, she had a desire unto certain green apples hanging on a tree in Master Taylor's garden, standing over the summer house. And made [Susan] acquainted herewith, and said unto her
> "I would to god I had some of those apples".
> "Well," said … Susan, "I will help you with some of them anon." Then said [Phyllis],
> "My landlady, Goodwife Bennett, is in the garden. I would you would speak unto her for some of them."
> "Nay", said … Susan …, they being both in the house where [I] dwell. "I will send her away out of the garden with a powder!" [i.e. impetuously, in a rush]
>   And so … Susan departed and went presently home to her own house, and went up unto her garrett, and backened her hand toward … Widow Bennett, who presently came running out of the garden withall speed into her own house. And [Phyllis] did see her no more at that time. But … Susan went afterward and did bring her some of those apples.

Strangely, it appears that Phyllis wanted unripe apples—it was *summer … when apples were green*. Was this a symptom of the cravings of pregnancy, or because she wanted fairy apples (from that tree near the summer house), and therefore green was the appropriate colour?

Susan could simply have asked Widow Bennett to give her some apples for Phyllis. She prefers, however, to show off, demonstrating that she has power over her landlady by getting the old woman to run into the house *withall speed*. Presumably Widow Bennett thought that Susan was beckoning to her because she had encountered the spirits in the garret. It sounds rather undignified—Susan is clearly making fun of her.

If these apples were requested by a real woman rather than a spirit one, it would make sense of Susan's comment that the woman cut up one of the three apples that she had been given into quarters, and *flong [them] away*. This would presumably have been a tithe for the spirits, whose apples they were. The other two apples she ate.

More confusing than the case of the apples is spirit Richard's request for a *raw piece of powder [salted] beef*, which Susan obtained for him from Anne (did this have anything to do with the piece that Anne got from the butcher's wife, whose arm then went lame?). *He* then cut it into pieces and laid it in the window. At which point I give up all attempt at interpretation.

* * *

Finally, we turn to an incident which some people might have called a comical prank. But not the inhabitants of Rye. For them, it was a shaming tragedy.

On Monday 17th August 1607, Susan Swaffer was walking on the Strand (buying fish at the fishmarket?), when *there was speech given that Sir Thomas Waller was coming over Rye ferry. She seeing the people run to the ferry to meet him, amongst the rest she made all the haste she could to go to the ferry.* What was all the excitement about? There is mention of a *great troupe of men come to the town* and *great joy or triumph*—which suggests that Sir Thomas had come to take the musters (a review of the local militia). *Triumph* meant the pomp associated with an important event, particularly a military one (not necessarily involving a victory, as we would assume today). As Lieutenant of Dover Castle, Waller was the most important official in the Cinque Ports apart from the Lord Warden (who was not involved in the day-to-day running of the confederation).

> And coming to the ferryside, she did see standing underneath the further [wind]mill, one of her familiars named Richard, and [she] going towards the mill, he vanished away, and [she] did see him no more there. And she … standing amongst the people, of a sudden one pulled her by the coat, but she could not tell who it was. And the press of people being gone, [she]… went to Mistress Taylor's house and told her of it, and [Anne] blamed [her], and said you are never within.

The implication of Anne's comment seems to be that the spirits thought Susan should be paying more attention to them at home, and not gadding abroad.

Susan then went home, so did not see the terrible accident. Sir Thomas and his attendants must have proceeded to the gungarden for the official welcome, where, in the presence of the mayor and jurats of Rye and presumably numerous other people, the town's gunner, standing on the 'mount' on the gungarden, fired a cannon out to sea, accompanied by a blast on the trumpet. This achieved more than was intended—not only propelling a cannon ball, but unfortunately also part of the cannon itself, *that so brake and flew … [and] did streak [the gunner] upon the breast, and did carry away his right arm. By means of which forceable stroke, he presently died*, as the coroner's inquest found. *Robert Burditt, late gunner, … was slain, to the great sorrow, grief and lamentable spectacle of the beholders*, as was recorded in the town's Assembly book (Sir Thomas was not mentioned).

This was the very same Robert Burditt—a barber in everyday life— whose shop had been the scene of heated arguments about history and religion the previous year. He it was who gave evidence against the papist son of the jurat Thomas Fisher, and helped deliver him to the Lord Warden for interrogation.

Susan did not see the accident, but she heard the gunfire:

> Her husband being at home and wanting a shirt, [she] went up into her garret to fetch him one, and then she heard a great piece shot off, and the trumpet sound. [She] coming down from the garret with the shirt, said unto her self,
> *"Lord have mercy upon us, there is a great troupe of men come to the town, and great joy"*. And the spirit Richard spake and said,
> *"Aye, and as much sorrow"*.
> And then she turned about and saw him, and he went out into another chamber. And then [she] went to Mistress Taylor, and told her what she had heard. And she answered,
> *"Welcome, by the grace of god"*.

The Story

Was she saying that Anne welcomed the news? Susan afterwards recalled seeing the two male spirits walking up the gungarden earlier that day, and Anne said that it was a *token of his death*.

Unusually, Anne herself not only confirmed that Susan had told her about this incident, but quoted what Susan had said to herself and her husband. Susan saying *"Here is great joy or triumph at the coming in of Sir Thomas Waller"*, one of her spirits responded *"Aye, and as much heaviness at his going out"*. Joy and triumph—taking the musters would have been a celebration of the military strength of the Cinque Ports, and of their traditional role as defenders of the kingdom, at a time when the importance of this was being challenged. In remote parts of the country inhabitants might have been much less enthusiastic about the musters, involving as they did labour and the provision of arms (not bows and arrows these days, but guns). In the county town of Lewes, however, taking the musters was recently an occasion for fireworks—when the third Earl of Dorset, Lord Lieutenant of East Sussex, attended in person.

Guns were notoriously unreliable in those days, but this was indeed a terrible and shaming incident—dishonouring the town in the presence of one of the most important gentlemen in the region. How the country gentry would mock the attempts of mere merchants to proclaim their military importance!

Susan implies that the spirits knew what was going on—did they have some involvement in it? Apparently they did:

> Richard asked one of his fellows *where the brimstone was which lay upon the mantle of the chimpney*, and he answered, *he saw none*. Then one of the women said that *she had it*.

Brimstone is an ingredient of gunpowder. This interaction took place in Susan's presence (so she said) after she told spirit Richard that Anne flatly refused to satisfy the spirits' latest, threatening, request—for a piece of cloth *if it were never so old*, of Anne's length and breadth. If the latter request had been threatening, even more was the apparently irrelevant discussion about removing brimstone from the mantlepiece—which brimstone belonged not to the spirits, but to the Taylors.

Margery Convers wanted to know if Anne herself had had anything to do with it:

> *"It is reported about the town, that that day that my Neighbour Burditt was slain, that they did send to you for powder and brimstone"*. Whereupon Mistress Taylor called unto her mother which sat by her on the h[earth]

> "Mother, mother, hark, Mistress Convers s[aieth] ... brimstone in the con... that the Lord did show his mercy upon my Neighbour Burditt, that they sent unto us for gunpowder and brimstone!" Then said the old woman
> "~~Tush~~, they had that long before".

Gunpowder was manufactured locally, so it is possible that the Taylors traded in it and brimstone. The implication seems to be that Anne or the spirits had done something to the brimstone or gunpowder which caused the gun to blow up.

The corporation allowed Burditt's widow Martha and child to continue to receive his gunner's stipend of 40s a year while she remained unmarried. In spite of the divisions between the townsfolk, a tragedy such as this brought home to the inhabitants of Rye their shared interests, and the necessity of defending these against the slanders and incursions of outsiders.

* * *

This chapter has recounted a strange mixture of cynicism and belief. Susan clearly engaged in much subterfuge, using the spirits as a means of manipulating Anne. But her success in doing so partly reflected Anne's own obsession with the spirits, making her susceptible to demands. As we have seen, other witnesses confirmed Anne's intense interest in fairy treasure, and also the strange goings-on when she locked herself and Susan in the Swaffers' house and refused to let Roger Swaffer in. She herself talked of apparitions, and implied that they were connected with Susan's spirits.

Susan would not have got away with telling tales if other people had not been open to believing in them. In the classic study of intellectual aspects of belief in witchcraft, the anthropologist Evans-Pritchard noted that the Azande thought that most witch-doctors were frauds, but this did not undermine their belief that *some* of these people had real powers.

The godly Welsh knight William Vaughan thought that the fairies invoked by cunningfolk, like Susan's, were often real people:

> Yea, these seducing spirits [i.e. cunningfolk] aver, that they walk every week with the Fayries, that they have secret conference with Familiars. But in the end the Familiars fall out to be a pack of knaves of their own families.

Knaves was not just a term of abuse, but referred to male children or servants.

The Story

* * *

We have now uncovered a catalogue of increasingly alarming incidents piling up one after another in that summer of 1607. Around midsummer Susan visited Weeks Green in search of fairy treasure, and she and Anne may have been leaving gifts for the spirits in a window in the Swaffer's house; they may also have been conjuring spirits on the occasion that Roger was locked out of the house. About the same time apparitions appeared in the glass windows of Alexander Fowkes' parlour, which could be seen from the Taylors' first floor windows. There then followed a succession of suspicious deaths: George Taylor's daughter Elizabeth was buried on 4th July, and Thomas Hamon on 29th July, one side of his body having seemingly suffered a fairy-stroke. On 17th August Robert Burditt was blown up, with gunpowder that may have been interfered with by the spirits (and possibly by Anne). Finally, on 15th September, little George Taylor was buried (his death possibly a result of being sent to meet the spirits), as also the town clerk's maid servant (her death possibly also the result of Anne's treatment of her). It was less than a fortnight later that the magistrates first examined Susan.

By the time of the December Sessions of the Peace, therefore, some people in Rye may well have been getting seriously alarmed about the operations of the spirits in the town. If Anne had not escaped into Kent before the trial, no doubt she would have been convicted with Susan. But at that point events changed direction, because George Taylor succeeded in drawing in outsiders who were only too pleased to intervene. It is to them that we now turn. And eventually, to the final trial.

The story at this point changes gear, and we will not have anything to do with Susan for some time (while she languishes in prison)—but will return to her eventually…

9 Many Eyes Fixed upon this Case

From the mayor and jurats' point of view, the prosecution of Swapper's wife in December 1607 had gone without a hitch. And why should it not? They had stuck to the letter of the law, trying her on the witchcraft statute passed three years earlier, which made it a felony to *consult, covenant with, entertain, employ, feed or reward any evil and wicked spirit*. According to the statute, there was no need to prove that any harm had resulted to man or beast from these activities.

There was now just the other woman—Mistress Taylor—to bring to trial. She had evaded the first trial, you may recall, because she had for the past half year *essoigned herself from her dwelling house in place unknown in Kent*, out of the jurisdiction of their court. The magistrates were planning to hold a special sessions of the peace in the new year (see overleaf), when they received a bombshell from the leading lawyer of the county of Kent, Sir John Boys:

> We wish you to be well advised before you proceed to the execution of any, upon the statute of 1 Regis Jacobi …

In rather circuitous language, Boys argued that although the town's charter gave the mayor and jurats the right to *hear and determine all pleas of the crown* [i.e. major crimes] *except treason*, it did not mention the felony defined by the recent witchcraft statute, and therefore they could not try it. He went on to spell out the logical conclusion from this—that they could not try felonies defined by *any* statute! Such felonies could be tried by the *county* justices of the peace because these statutes always cited the commissions of the peace from which they derived their authority, but not town charters from which urban magistrates derived theirs.

The Rye magistrates were used to defending the town's privileges against attempts to infringe them, but this was a major challenge to their authority. Not many urban magistrates could try felonies, and if the right of the Rye magistrates to try some of these felonies was undermined, it would not be long before their right to try *any* was removed.

Sir John Boys was the grand old man of the Kentish legal world. In his 70s, he had been active not only as a lawyer, but as an MP (for Sandwich, Midhurst and then Canterbury), and sat on numerous parliamentary committees, pursuing issues both great and small. The various offices which he had held included being steward to five successive Archbishops of Canterbury.

Sir John followed up this challenge with a more immediate threat:

> And we write so much the rather unto you, because we have been required to grant a [writ of] *certiorari* for the removing of an indictment against Master Taylor's wife, which is informed us to be done upon former malice and hope of gain thereby.

This presumably concerned an appeal to the court of St. James, Dover, where Boys was a judge. This court dealt with miscarriages of justice within the Cinque Ports, amongst other issues, under the overall authority of the Lord Warden. Whom George was accusing of malice is not immediately evident, since we do not know who had preferred the indictment against Anne.

Not satisfied with this double whammy, Boys ended his letter with a finger pointing at the magistrates themselves:

> And thereuppon you have called an especiall Sessions [of the Peace], which we assure ourselves you will forbear to proceed therein, until it may be resolved upon that you may lawfully proceed therin, lest some former imputations laid to your town be verified.

Former imputations—was this a vague threat, or did he have something specific in mind?

This peremptory tone was not unusual in the letters from the many, mostly Kentish, lawyers that the magistrates had to deal with. With an *almost mystical reverence for the common law,* they were often somewhat disparaging towards the magistrates and town clerk of Rye, who had no legal training. The courts of many other towns were presided over by recorders who had been to the Inns of Court, but not in Rye. Robert Convers, the town clerk, was sometimes called *recorder*, but he achieved this position as it were by the back door—apprenticeship to an ex- town clerk of Lydd (see pages 89 and 91), and work as an attorney in the Rye court for private actions, where his namesake John Convers had also been an attorney when the teenage Robert arrived from Berkshire, back in the '70s. Other attorneys had even less claim to be trained for their role, since they held other occupations—two mercers, a barber, a chandler and a tailor, to name a few. So although the Rye courts were nominally common law courts, administering the same *common law of England* (rather than local custom) as the central courts in London, practice probably fell far short of what the common lawyers considered to be correct.

Apart from lack of legal training, there was another issue that prompted the common lawyers to view the Rye courts with a predatory eye. The Cinque Ports were only one of a number of jurisdictions — usually much smaller — that did not come under the umbrella of the central courts in London. The church courts had been the latter's main rival, and some of their work — including witchcraft — had been taken over by the secular courts around the time of the Reformation. At the other extreme, the numerous small manor and borough courts were nominally independent of the central courts, but judges in the latter increasingly undermined the authority of local justices during the 16th century. They encouraged merchants to use the courts in London rather than local courts *by upsetting judgments of municipal courts on technical grounds*.

These developments ran counter to the general charter of the Cinque Ports, which required their inhabitants to initiate all cases in courts inside the enclave (unless they concerned incidents that had occurred outside it). But as elsewhere, court officials tried to conform to the practice of the central courts to prevent their decisions being challenged. Sir John Boys was himself recorder for Dover, and had introduced to its criminal court a practice used in the county sessions of the peace.

* * *

It was not for another 3 weeks that Robert Convers (or possibly the Mayor, Thomas Higgons) wrote to the town's counsel, John Shurley, asking what they should do. Shurley was a Sussex lawyer who was more of a country gentleman than a committed common lawyer like Boys, even though he had had the rank of *serjeant-at-law* conferred on him (advocate at the court of Common Pleas). Convers had apparently taken the precaution of speaking to Shurley before the trial in December, which suggests on the one hand that the mayor and jurats thought there might be a problem with it, but also that Shurley gave them the go-ahead:

> Sithence which time we have received this enclosed letter from Sir John Boys, who certifieth us that we have no authority nor power by the said statute nor by our charter, to inquire of the said cause. Wherefore these are most earnestly to intreat and desire your advice and direction what is best for us to do in this case. I have entreated Master Thurbarne [a Kentish lawyer who was the town's other, less prestigious, counsel] to attend upon you for our further resolution herein

Shurley's answer has not survived (or may have been relayed verbally by Thurbarne). James Thurbarne was town clerk of the decaying Cinque Port of New Romney (and represented it briefly as MP), although, like many Kentish lawyers, he resided part of the year in Canterbury.

Having made his triple challenge, Boys apparently took a step back. If a case of malicious prosecution was brought in the court of St. James, it was not mentioned by correspondents, and the next surviving correspondence—the following summer—assumes that the trial *will* take place (it is possible that the appeal to the court of St. James was not valid because George Taylor was not a freeman of Rye). Anne had come secretly to Rye, and the magistrates, hearing of this, took the opportunity to imprison her in the town's gaol. This was the time when the altercations between her and Susan in prison were reported by John Scragg and others, as described in chapter 6.

This act of imprisonment provoked a response from no less a person than the Lord Warden of the Cinque Ports, Henry Howard, Earl of Northampton. The rhythm of his prose suits the even-handed stance that it presents:

> Master Mayor,
> A petition is exhibited unto me in the name of Mistress Taylor now a prisoner in the common gaol at Rye; whether she suggesteth that upon the unjust accusacion of a lewd woman, and some private displeasure conceived by yourself against her, she hath been by you committed and is still detained, albeit she hath tendered good bail and be by law bailable. As I like at no hand that authority be made a mask to revenge private injuries, so am I not credulous of every information I receive against the magistrates for due execution of justice. Yet in this case I could be well contented in respect of her sex and her present state, being now with child, and growen very weak by reason thereof, and the lothsomeness of the prison, to afford her all favour warrantable by law.

The accusation of malice is now pointing directly at the mayor himself—Thomas Higgons—who had taken over the mayoralty on the death of Thomas Hamon, and had of course married his widow Martha. But Northampton does not pursue this issue, concentrating instead on the question of bail. There is no other mention of Anne being with child, and indeed the magistrates later denied it.

The Lord Warden requested that the details be sent to Sir John Boys and the other most influential and active lawyer in Kent, Matthew Hadd, so that they could determine whether or not she could be bailed. He also wanted these two to *assist at this trial*, together with his deputy Sir Thomas Waller—*which request seems to me so reasonable as is not to be denied*. They were to be told when the trial would take place.

The magistrates responded within a week with a long letter. They explained that Anne had been indicted for aiding and abetting Susan, by *[delivering] to her divers things which she demanded for the said spirits,* and said that when she recently returned to Rye she

> used some outrageous behaviour upon her maidservant, for which behaviour and for divers other matters and suspicion concerning witchcrafts wherein as is informed she hath had some dealings ... come to light since her departure [she has been imprisoned].

There is no other record of the *outrageous behaviour on her maidservant*—which is striking given that Scragg mentioned enlisting Anne's servant Mercy Luck in his attempts at mediation at about this time. The only comparable incident concerned the *town clerk's* maidservant, whose death was laid at Anne's door by her mistress Margery Convers.

They went on to plead that they were not *tendered good bail* for Anne, and that the persons *named to be her bail we know to be very insufficient for the same* (i.e. they would not have been able to afford to pay the specified sum). Moreover, it was not the custom to offer bail to those indicted for felony, particularly if they were not clergiable (the right to avoid capital punishment if you were able to read). Anne was disqualified from this letout by being a woman, and it was anyway not available to those accused of witchcraft. Serjeant Shurley had also advised them that she should not be bailed. But they were nevertheless *ready, at the Lord Warden's request, to accept the said Anne's husband as her bail*.

In response to the accusation of *private displeasure*, the mayor complained that the lawyers who had been advising the Earl on this matter were acting for the Taylors—Master Hadd was George Taylor's counsel, and Sir John Boys had written to them on her behalf. Nevertheless, they were happy for them to advise about bail, and for Boys and Waller to be present at the trial, if the town did not have to pay for this. Hadd they did not want because they considered that he would not be sufficiently independent. Their own counsel, Thurbarne and Shurley, were needless to say *indifferently affected in this case*, and they would like them to be present too. They concluded *humbly submitting all our proceeding unto your honour's censure*.

The Story

Anne was indeed bailed in August 1608, her husband being one surety, and the others were—Rye magistrates! Namely Alexander Fowkes (George's trading partner) and the fisherman John Styner (who was illiterate, making no attempt to sign his name on the bond—see large cross below).

[Rye 1/8/99]

There were few rich inhabitants who were *not* magistrates, but it is striking that two of them supported the Taylors so far as to be willing to pay up if Anne defaulted again. I shall continue to refer to *the magistrates* as if they were all of one mind, for the moment, but the faultlines of faction will reveal themselves more clearly later on …

Anne must have been imprisoned again later, because the magistrates said that they had heard that the Lord Warden *doth take it in ill part that Mistress Taylor was not bailed upon [his] letters.*

* * *

If the magistrates of Rye hoped that the deferred trial was now finally to take place, they were to be disappointed. Further complexities lay in their path. From being almost petty tyrants in their own domain, they had become pawns in a much larger political game. The prime mover was the Earl of Northampton, no doubt prompted in part by Matthew Hadd, counsel to both himself and George Taylor.

No longer concerned simply over bail and miscarriage of justice, Northampton picked up on the issue which Sir John Boys had raised— whether the magistrates had the right to try the case at all. But the argument had changed slightly. As Matthew Hadd phrased it: *(I think) … the words of the [town's] charter do not extend to pleas of the crown futurly made.* By which he meant, that offences defined by statute *after* the last confirmation of the charter in the reign of Edward IV, could not be tried by the town's magistrates. Hadd concludes that the question of who is to try such cases must be decided by *those who have power by common law.*

Northampton wanted the advice of judges on this issue, and Thurbarne and Shurley drew up the case to present to them that autumn. The two judges considered it—and, remarkably, decided in *favour* of the privileges of the Cinque Ports. They upheld the right of magistrates in the Cinque Ports to try *all* felonies (except, of course, treason), whether defined by statute or not. The mayor and jurats might well have been surprised to find their way forward, seemingly, cleared of obstacles.

* * *

At last, the trial was to be held, on 5th December 1608. The court house must have been very crowded, with (presumably) Sir John Boys, Sir Thomas Waller, and James Thurbarne present (but not Serjeant Shurley), as well as the magistrates, mayor's sergeant, jurors, and of course the accused woman and no doubt sundry others. There was not much other business at the sessions—an inhabitant indicted by a tallowchandler (candlemaker) for practising chandlery without being apprenticed to the trade, two apprentices ordered to be whipped for pickeries (minor thefts), and a victim of theft ordered to 'prosecute the law' against another inhabitant who had been imprisoned on suspicion.

Anne stood at the bar (perhaps in her black gown and black hat), and when asked by the mayor's sergeant, Angel Shaw, whether she pleaded guilty or not guilty, answered *not guilty*. The usual legal formula followed—the mayor's sergeant asked her *how she wished to be tried*. To which the only acceptable answer was, *by God and the country* (i.e. trial jury). But she made no answer at all—*standing long time mute and refusing the trial of the country*—as the magistrates later told the Lord Warden. The dramatic implications of her refusal must have gradually entered the consciousness of those standing around, the general hubbub no doubt stilled, while the assembled company listened and watched for any intimation that she might give in.

Back in the early Middle Ages, the accused had real options as to how they might be tried. As an alternative to trial by jury, they could have chosen proof by ordeal (of fire, water or combat), when God rather than a jury would determine the outcome. But this was not an option in the 17th century, and refusing to answer in effect called the authority of the court into question.

Few accused persons took this route, because the punishment—*peine forte et dure*—and ensuing death meted out to such refusers was worse than death by hanging. They were pressed to death—weights being piled on top of them while they lay on the ground.

The usual reason why an accused person occasionally *did* adopt this strategy was when they expected to be found guilty, and wanted to prevent their lands being confiscated by the crown. If they had not actually been found guilty by a jury, such confiscation could not take place. One occasion when one of the accused suffered this torture for refusing to plead was in the Salem witchcraft case in New England at the end of the century.

It was not unknown for women to take this course. There was the notable case 20 years earlier when the catholic martyr Margaret Clitherow, step-daughter of a mayor of York, had refused to acknowledge that she had committed an offence when charged with the crime of harbouring catholic seminary priests in her house. By this means she wrong-footed the authorities, who had wanted to make an example of her, but did not want to be seen to inflict an inappropriate and cruel death on her. She refused the let-out offered to her of claiming to be pregnant, and embraced martyrdom.

It must therefore have taken considerable courage on Anne's part to stand silent at the bar, in the face of the importunity of Angel Shaw. But her reason (presumably suggested by her counsel) for remaining mute was clearly different from that of most people who used this strategy. How could the magistrates possibly inflict this terrible death on her, when their right to try the case had anyway been called in question? It was a humiliating position for the bench.

Why, with all these prestigious lawyers present, was there any need on Anne's part to challenge the authority of the mayor and jurats by refusing to plead? Perhaps there was a sense that although the presence of such lawyers and officials was intimidating to others at the court—in particular the jury—it was not clear what could be done if the jury *did* find her guilty, and the magistrates sentenced her to be hanged. In the Assize courts, it was not unknown for the judges to harangue juries (and even imprison them) for delivering the 'wrong' verdict; but these lawyers were not Assize judges.

Some discussion then took place in the courtroom (so the magistrates told Northampton) in which her lawyers made clear that they wanted the trial deferred yet again—*she and her counsel and friends agreed she should be tried before us, if Master Serjeant Shurley signified to Master Henden, then her counsel …that in his opinion she might be tried before us for the said offence*. An extraordinary excuse for yet more delays. The magistrates' right to try the case had already been upheld by two judges, and now one of the *magistrates'* counsel was to be asked the same question. The Taylors' counsel seem to be grasping at anything that could obstruct the trial process—and give George Taylor time to get the case removed to the court of King's Bench.

The penultimate paragraph of the magistrates' letter to Northampton appears to be answering objections made by him six months earlier. They said that no, Anne has not said that she is with child. *Concerning the prison where she remaineth, the same is made very decent and sweet, which at her coming thither was purposely made.* They ask him to *give patronage to our liberties which in this point has been untouched*, and if any *malice or maintenance … can justly be objected we shall most willingly submit ourselves to your Lordship's censure.*

This expression of innocence is somewhat belied by the last paragraph of their letter, because it appears that George Taylor is now also in prison. A merchant from Dover had sued George for non-delivery of Rye Billets (firewood)—he had only received 8 thousand of the 21 thousand promised. This case was mentioned earlier in connection with Anne cursing the mayor (see above page 61). The Dover magistrates had therefore written to those of Rye to apprehend him. There was an ancient custom of *withernam*, by which if they failed to produce the debtor or the debt, the other port could claim the debt against *any* Rye inhabitant who came within their jurisdiction (in the distant past the custom had been more widespread, but it was now confined to the Cinque Ports). So the magistrates had imprisoned George—*for want of bail* (again, the issue of bail—though there is no doubt that he was bailable).

* * *

The magistrates had reached an impasse. The following month they wrote again to Northampton, requesting permission to continue with the trial:

> In all ages parliament has made new felonies and no doubt of validity of charters made… we are burdened with a great charge in so long keeping the other poor woman already condemned in prison.

And as if Northampton did not know, they pointed out that Master Hadd was used by his lordship for his own counsel, so by implication his opinion was biased. But Northampton's response was more recalcitrant than ever, if phrased in terms of caring patronage:

> Master Mayor, I was desirous in a cause of this importance, that concerns the party in life and your corporation so near as the hazard of loss of your liberties, if [i.e. before] you should proceed to a trial of a crime you are not warranted by charter, to advise with counsel before I gave way to your request. Whose opinion I have since received, but in so doubtful a manner as I rest now less satisfied then before. For they tell me it is a late law, and an offence newly made felony, whereupon Mistress Taylor is indicted, and the matter questionable, whether you be by law warranted to proceed against her. Besides there be many eyes fixed upon this case, and that upon the event intend to draw a precedent from hence, that is like enough to give cause both to look into and to interpet charters more strictly than heretofore. Though the harm [being?] to your selves ... expect no assistance from me in defence of your proceedings. Yet so careful am I of your weal and the good estate of that town, as I may not so long as there is a fear conceived of an ensuing danger, give way or consent to any proceeding till that scruple be removed. Therefore, I pray you respite her trial till the Judges may be consulted withall, for it is better and more safe to support a little longer the charge of the other prisoner than upon a weak ground to proceed to a trial supposed not to be warrantable. Whereof I doubt not but you will be cautious and circumspect. And so I rest.
> Your very loving friend
> Northampton

With Northampton's threat that *you can expect no assistance from me*, and his demand that the case be submitted to judges *again*, the magistrates were back to square one. Thurbarne was somewhat bemused by this, writing in his illegible scrawl that *great labour is made to my Lord* (i.e. by George Taylor and his counsel); *my Lord is altered from his former course*. He suggested that they write to the rest of the Cinque Ports, whose charters were equally threatened by this issue, requesting their advice, and suggesting that they either present his Lordship with a petition, or with a case drawn up about the charter.

* * *

The magistrates wrote to the rest of the Cinque Ports in April 1609:

> the question ... doth concern every [one of us equally], and is of very great weight, being upon one of the most especial and main points of all the said Charters .... it may be dangerous to have liberties drawn in question, being so long time enjoyed in the like cases.

Sir John Shurley had vetted the letter (drawn up by Thurbarne), deleting a section which alleged

> some supposed alliance of the delinquent unto his Lordship's worthy lieutenant [i.e. Sir Thomas Waller] ... we cannot once suspect that any indirect c[onduct?] whatsoever can draw his worship to prejudice our rightful liberties.

This is the only mention of an alliance between the Taylors and Sir Thomas Waller.

The final version of the letter only hinted indirectly at what they saw as Northampton's lack of support for the privileges of the Cinque Ports:

> We are assuredly persuaded, that our most honourable Lord Warden will most graciously further us in the maintenance of all our Liberties; and that in his Lordship's time, so great a Liberty of the ports hitherto so long inviolably preserved, shall not receive any wound or blemish, much less overthrow.

This circular letter was taken from Port to Port, and included space for their responses. All were very willing to petition the Lord Warden. The Hastings' magistrates added that if the charter did not provide sufficient authority, they would like *a commission of the peace to be procured for the ports and members generally, as the justices of peace in the foreign [i.e. outside the Cinque Ports] have.* So that it could not be argued that their authority was on a different basis from that of the county JPs.

On the strength of this support from the Ports, the mayor and jurats of Rye asked Shurley and Thurbarne to attend on his Lordship, presumably in the hope that they could sway his opinion without going to the trouble and expense of organising a man from every Port to petition him.

This strategy was successful. A letter was taken to Northampton in London by an inhabitant of Rye named Master Young (presumably Matthew, foreman of the jury that had found Susan guilty), who, according to Thurbarne, took *exceeding pains in your business*, going repeatedly between the London residences of Northampton, Serjeant Shurley and Sir Thomas Waller,

> and at his request I have also sometimes accompanied him to my Lord's, and moved his Lordship in your behalf, and also to Master Serjeant Shurley, and we both have also often troubled Sir Thomas Waller about it. At the last, it is drawn to this conclusion that his Lordship is honourably pleased that you may persevere therein at your pleasure, which his lordship in some sort first intimated to me, and afterwards I perceived the same by Master Young, and

> after ... by Sir Thomas Waller himself, who [told] me expressly thereof, wishing ... that you be careful to proceed by advice of Counsel therin, that so the proceedings may the better be justified, which I doubt not of.

So everyone was agreed that his Lordship really *was* willing for the trial to go ahead. On the strength of this, Shurley said that he could be present if the trial was held a week after Whitsun, on the Monday or Tuesday—it should not be put off longer because he would then be required to attend the Sussex Assizes.

Thurbarne thought that the Ports should be told what was happening, since it looked as if a petition from all the Ports would not be necessary. They should be told that *his Lordship is pleased that you may proceed, doing it at your peril,* and that the Rye magistrates and their counsell have decided to proceed *if they shall like of it.*

Thurbarne ended his letter with a ticking off for the magistrates:

> I wish till the trial all temperate and mild behaviour towards Mistress Taylor, and that no speeches either of joy or desire of the trial may be used; but that quietly all things may be prepared against the time you shall appoint.

* * *

Northampton seems to have gone out of his way to try and prevent the magistrates from trying this case. He sounds like the voice of reason, listening to the points put to him by the lawyers, and arranging for Anne to get a fair trial (Susan is not mentioned). But would he not have better fulfilled his role as Lord Warden by getting the case removed to the court of St. James in the Cinque Ports, where any miscarriage of justice could have been investigated under his authority—and furthermore the privileges of the Cinque Ports would not have been called in question? The Lord Wardenship, however, involved conflicting loyalties—from the point of view of the Cinque Ports, he was their highest representative and should be furthering their interests in relations with those in the *foreign*. On the other hand, he was appointed by the King, and the government's interests were likely to run counter to those of a semi-autonomous region such as the Cinque Ports. During the 16th century the government had been increasingly successful at challenging the privileges of similar enclaves elsewhere in the country, and at drawing remote, lawless regions within more direct control from the centre.

A couple of decades earlier, anyone would have thought that Lord Henry Howard (later made Earl of Northampton) was an unlikely agent of the centralising state. Both his father (the Duke of Norfolk) and his brother had been executed as traitors by Henry VIII, who suspected them of planning to supplant his young heir. Queen Elizabeth later also mistrusted Howard—as well she might, since he was involved in plots to put Mary Queen of Scots on the throne in her stead, and bring England back into the catholic fold. But he was a consummate politician, managing not only to keep his head on his shoulders, but even inching into royal favour after the execution of Mary. He nevertheless still had to live on his wits, since he had no lands of his own (his father's having been confiscated), and resided with relatives.

Near the end of Elizabeth's reign he was an effective go-between in secret dealings—unbeknownst to the Queen—between her principal minister and King James VI of Scotland (the son of Queen Mary), smoothing the way for James' peaceful accession to the English throne after her death. James was immensely grateful, conferring on him not only the Earldom of Northampton and the Lord Wardenship of the Cinque Ports, but also (on him and his nephews) most of the Howard estates that had been confiscated at the executions of his father and brother. He made him a Privy Councillor, and ordered that henceforth he was to be given the precedence due to the son of a duke—status that was immensely important to a man who was bitter at having been out in the cold, abasing himself to inferiors, as he felt, for so long:

> To the place by birth my due .... your Majesty restored me   I am now admitted, though unworthy, by extraordinary grace to be your privy councillor. I was branded with the mark of reprobation; you have signed me with the character of trust. I was esteemed ... a man dangerous; you have trusted me with one of the strongest locks of your estate.

Howard was adept at flattery, but something of what he felt is no doubt evident in the words of this letter. James was rewarded on his part by hard work and loyalty, and a devotion to the interests of the government. Howard (now in his 60s) was one of the three most influential members of the Privy Council. And this I think goes some way to explain why this crypto-catholic nobleman—who was hugely disparaging of both merchants and puritans, let alone artisans—was furthering the cause of a puritan butcher's daughter.

* * *

The Story

Letters multiplied in May 1609—the month before the trial—and Thurbarne (the town's counsel) got increasingly irritable with the magistrates. They apparently wanted to defer the trial while they waited for the Ports' responses to the second circular letter, and he feared that it would then have to be put off till the autumn. He complained that *nothing hath prejudiced you in all this case but your own delays*, which seems a bit unfair, given the obstructions put forward by the Lord Warden and the common lawyers.

Putting off the trial might have been an attractive proposition to one member of the bench, however—the mayor, who was now Richard Portriffe (Thomas Higgons having died the previous October). Portriffe was in an invidious position because he was the *servant* or client of the Earl of Northampton, and would not have wanted to antagonise his lordship, who had granted him the sought-after position of Gunner in Rye (at 6d a day). This post did not require him to actually *man* a gun, unlike poor Robert Burditt (whose role had been lower in the hierarchy)—indeed, the cannon in question was apparently not now in Rye at all, but in London. Portriffe could also thank his patron for writing to the magistrates in 1605 objecting to 'his servant' being sent as bailiff for Rye to the annual Yarmouth herring fair.

Thurbarne wrote twice in one day to urge the magistrates into action.

> [I] have written twice in answer of your last letters …. in both which I have showed my opinion that it is best that a trial for Mistress Taylor be speedily had, and the rather because that in the delay danger may grow to your selves, and trouble, and …. it may be also very hurtful for her, the rooms being close and the air hot

and hence the issue of bail would resurface. He mentioned again that his lordship's instructions about bail had not been fully carried out, and in particular that George Taylor had not been told that the magistrates would accept bail. Furthermore, *Master Taylor doth labour very earnestly with Sir Thomas Waller and Sir John Boys to have allowance of a [writ of] habeas corpus to remove her body in the King's Bench*. If he succeeded, the case would be removed from the Cinque Ports to the court of King's Bench in London (which would contravene the privileges of the Cinque Ports).

* * *

A week or so earlier, an unfortunate incident had occurred, which dramatised the bristly relationship between the Rye magistrates and the Lord Warden. A messenger sent by his deputy, Sir Thomas Waller, had offended the mayor, Richard Portriffe, but the magistrates' response was over the top, perhaps expressing in actions what could not be said in their ever-respectful words:

> It hath something made this suit distasteful [wrote Thurbarne], especially to Sir Thomas Waller who hath showed his great love towards your town very much, that of late a messenger from [Dover] castle was imprisoned with you .... [and it is bruited] in the ports in disturbance of my Lord's authority. ... [the imprisonment] was only for this cause: that the messenger ... said [that the mayor] was no more known than Angel [Shaw, the mayor's sergeant] ....

Richard Portriffe might well have been somewhat sensitive about his status and reputation. A brewer like Thomas Hamon, he was not nearly as rich as Hamon had been (neither was he an MP), and he was only called *gentleman* by virtue of his office, unlike his gentlemanly predecessor, the merchant Thomas Higgons. Probably in his 60s, he had come to Rye from Cranbrook in Kent in the 1570s.

His reputation had been seriously dented in the 1590s when, in the role of chamberlain, he had been found guilty of embezzling (a charge investigated by the then Lord Warden). Fined 20s for his *false account*, it was ordered that his slate was then to be wiped clean— *from henceforth he is to be adjudged, holden and taken as a good member of this corporation*. He was nevertheless touchy about his reputation after this, as is testified by his three actions for slander later brought in the local court. One of these concerned a picture of him *with his heels upwards* (i.e. hanging by the heels, a symbol of perjury) on the walls of the courthall. This incident took place a few years later, and the issue may have been something new—but his former ignominy would still have been fresh in the minds of inhabitants (he had been *perjured* then in the sense of breaking his oath of office as chamberlain).

To return to the issue of the messenger. Sir Thomas Waller would have investigated the incident, reported Thurbarne, if he had been told about it, and he wanted to be told *the whole truth therein*. The particulars were to be sent as soon as possible, that his Lordship might also be told, who *is also incensed therein*. Thurbarne ended:

The Story

> I find my Lord very careful of your good in all things he can …. I wish that in all things … due respect be given to all that concern his lordship's authority, as so worthy a patron may be well pleased withall, which I persuade myself you will currently endorse.

Northampton was not one to forgive such insults to one of his servants, obsessed as he was with upholding authority and degree.

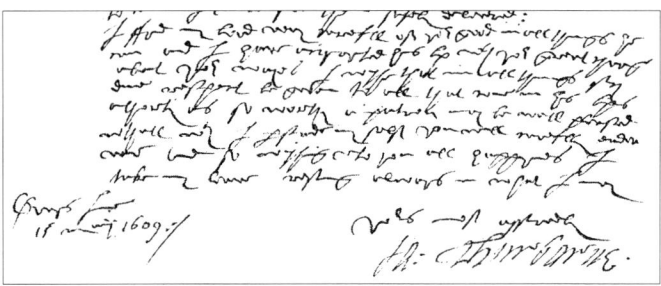

"I find my lord very careful …" [Rye 47/74/9 or 12]

The Ports' responses to the second circular letter were unfortunately very different from their earlier responses. Most of them echoed Northampton's phrase *at your peril*, and because the magistrates had phrased it more as if they were asking the advice of the other Ports rather than telling them what they were going to do, they all (apart from Sandwich) said that since it was a legal matter, they would have to ask their counsel. And unfortunately, as Thurbarne pointed out, the counsel for many of them was none other than Matthew Hadd, who was also counsel to George Taylor and his Lordship.

Thurbarne thought they should follow the advice of the Sandwich magistrates, and ignore the concerns of the other Ports:

> Only this we say, that in matters of like moment, wherein for law we make doubt, we take unto us the direction of our Counsel, and then proceed as the cause requireth, without acquainting any of our Brethren of the ports therewith

After this flurry of correspondence, there was just one more letter relating to this witchcraft case—an amiable note from Shurley:

> will be with you Saturday next for conference with you and Master Thurbarne touching that proceeding in cause… hearty thanks for good fish in London … always ready to do the best for you if I can.

The magistrates' presents usually consisted of fish—often turbot or John Dory, then as now considered the prime of seafish by connoisseurs.

* * *

The delays were finally at an end. Eighteen months after the first, abortive, trial of Anne Taylor, the final trial was opened at the summer sessions of the peace in 1609, and proceeded to a conclusion.

Four days before the trial, two final depositions were recorded by the town clerk, both of which alleged that Anne Taylor had caused death by witchcraft. These were the first explicit accusations of this kind by any witnesses—Susan only made accusations by innuendo. One deposition was by Margery Convers—quoted extensively in previous chapters—accusing Anne of bewitching to death her maidservant Philip Binwen. The other was by Martha Higgons, now twice widowed at the age of 30:

> Mistress Taylor in the life time of Master Thomas Hamon the husband of this deponent, did diverse and sundry times curse and speak evil words aswell of [him] as of [herself] ... Mistress Taylor did bear great hatred unto [him]

Martha said that she had heard Susan Swaffer at her trial (see page 59) and afterwards describe how her husband Thomas Hamon

> was taken and gripped by the members; and in such sort in truth was [he] taken and gripped, which was the cause of his death, as she verily believeth .... she verily believeth that Mistress Taylor did bewitch [him] ....his body was then likewise taken all black so that he had no feeling thereof and likewise one side of his head .... there are diverse persons can witness and testify the same.

That was the substance of the accusation—and she then made her mark at the bottom of the sheet, being unable to sign her name:

[Rye 13/25]

The Story

Robert Convers made a list of *the names of those that are ordered to be deposed*, which included four witnesses whose evidence had not been recorded. He made brief notes as to what their evidence concerned — including Widow Aldredge's opinion about Thomas *Higgons'* illness, *and whether she doth think that he was betwitched or not*. The others concerned Thomas Hamon's sickness and what Anne and her mother had said about it. These witnesses were bound over to appear and give evidence at the trial to be held on 12th June at 9.0 am.

Anne was tried on two indictments — the original one, and a new one preferred by Martha Higgons, accusing her of bewitching Thomas Hamon to death. So at last, the real issue was spelt out — and it was an accusation of *maleficia* that contemporaries would have recognised as a proper matter of witchcraft. And now that Martha was not married to one of the magistrates (at least for the moment …), there could be no complaint that one of them was involved in the case as both prosecutor and judge.

Anne pleaded *not guilty*, and requested to be tried by God and the country. The witnesses gave their evidence, the jury considered their verdict, and the foreman of the jury, Nicholas White, declared her *not guilty* on both counts. She was now a free woman.

* * *

What went on in that courthouse on 12th June 1609? Did the trial jury act on their own volitions, or were they pressurised? Did the magistrates want to save face (and defend the liberties of the Cinque Ports) by holding the trial, but not incur controversy (and further interference from outsiders) by having Anne found guilty?

One point stands out — the foreman of the jury was clearly a friend of the Taylors, because after the trial, Nicholas White, stood surety for Anne Taylor's good behaviour! He only stood surety in £50, being of middling wealth, so the magistrates would not have accepted him as a surety *before* the trial, when they were anxious that Anne should not escape again.

The Whites were an old Rye family — Nicholas had been born there, and if the parish register had gone back just a *little* bit further, we might have been able to check if that early protestant, Thomas White (a contemporary of Anne's protestant grandfather), who was accused of heresy just before the Reformation, was a relation.

The inclusion by the mayor's sergeant of a *friend* of the Taylors in the trial jury (sufficiently well-off to be foreman) contrasts with the inclusion of a rich *enemy* at the first trial. You may remember that Matthew Young, who was foreman of the jury in December 1607, had been involved in litigation against George Taylor. This suggests a change in the intentions of the magistrates. It is also possible that the paranoia that had been building up during 1607 had been subsiding, since there had been no (recorded) evidence of activities by the spirits—destructive or otherwise—in the two years since.

* * *

This witchcraft case was multifaceted, and it has taken over a hundred pages to tease out different threads in the story. Yet we have not revealed the strength of determination and feeling that must have driven the magistrates to doggedly pursue such a flimsy case. Was there a deeper cause than the arrival of spirits in 1607, which was the immediate trigger for the prosecution? And who *were* the accusers—more of the magistrates must have been involved than Thomas Higgons (husband of Martha), whom the Lord Warden charged with conceiving *private displeasure* against Anne, for them to put so much effort into it. But not *all* of them were involved, since three of the magistrates were prepared to stand surety for Anne—a role which could be expensive, given her history of fleeing from Rye to avoid the first trial. Still more curiously, two of her supporters were fishermen, who played no part in the artisan faction with which the Taylors and their forbears were so closely bound up.

We have been focusing closely on the details of the case itself. To get a clearer idea of who the accusers were, and why, we need to stand back, and cast our net wider, to look at events and relationships in the years preceding the case. It was the crisis years of the 1590s that hold the key—when Thomas Hamon was not only still alive, but mayor and MP for the town, and Mistress Taylor was plain Anne Bennett, and in her late teens. Hamon and his allies antagonised a number of the townspeople, and we will find echoes of these resentments in the reproaches later attributed to Anne (many of which were remarkably mild, in the circumstances).

The backdrop to these antagonisms was the devastating economic decay that set in towards the end of the 16th century, to which we must now turn.

10   Economic Decline

The dramatic economic contraction which hit the town of Rye from the late 1570s is more easily identified than explained. Stephen Hipkin has analysed its causes in detail. The key to the town's prosperity lay in its role as a port, and an indicator of its plummeting fortunes is provided by the decrease in the number of boats owned by Rye inhabitants. These nearly halved in the thirty years between the mid-1560s and mid-1590s, and more than halved again in the next thirty years up to the mid-1620s, when the numbers stabilised:

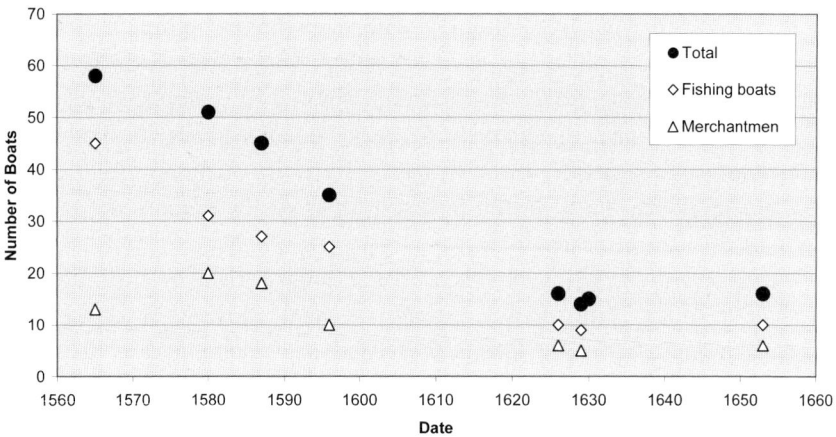

Source: Hipkin 1998-9: Table 1 p.114

At least as dramatic was the reduction in the number of shipments of goods in and out of the port. These may have been about a *third* in 1600 of what they had been in the 1580s. The chart on the next page includes the evidence of local customs duties (large black dots, overseas and coastal shipments combined), and also national customs duties (other markers), because neither series are complete (note that the national records only provide information on *overseas* shipments before 1600).

Economic Decline

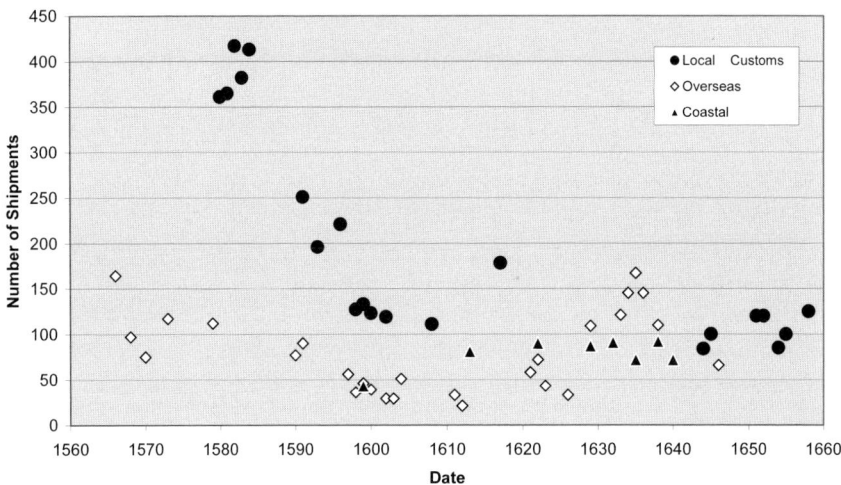

Shipments of Goods in and out of Rye 1560-1660
from the records of (a) Local Customs (black dots) and (b) National Customs (other)

Source: Hipkin 1998-9: Table 3 p.119

Overseas trade revived in the 1630s, as indicated by the diamond markers in the chart (there is a gap in the local customs duties at this date, because they were farmed out). But this was of little benefit to Rye merchants, since most of the goods—dominated by luxury textiles from Italy, such as cobweb lawns and tiffanies—were traded by outsiders. They were, however, carried in Rye boats.

What was responsible for this dramatic decline? The harbour was certainly starting to silt up in this period, and this was cited by contemporaries as the major issue. But the revival of fortunes in the 1630s indicates that silting-up cannot have been the whole story.

In truth, trade in and out of Rye harbour had always been changeable. Up until 1558, England had owned Calais, and Rye merchants provisioned this isolated bastion with food and woodfuel. After the loss of Calais, the merchants found other markets—the shifting arena of war on the continent encouraged the transit trade in cloth to be channelled via Rye and Dieppe. But London soon muscled in on this trade, and then the theatre of war changed again to Rye's detriment—Spain's war with England endangered shipping in the Channel (which affected coastal as well as overseas trade), and religious wars in France compounded the problems. The revival of trade in the 1630s was related to developments in the Thirty Years War (1618-48) on the continent.

The Story

If trading activity varied dramatically, the fishing industry was in terminal decline. Just in the fifteen years between 1585 and 1600 it probably declined by a third. The fishermen complained that the harbour, that had at one time been a safe haven for hundreds of ships, had become treacherous. The silt brought down by the rivers created hidden dangers, and the late 16th century storms wore away the shingle banks that protected the entrance to the harbour:

> the shore weareth lower .... therefore the force and rage of the sea hath more power to fall in here than ever heretofore it hath had ... We lose and are damaged among our sea craft, for want of good harbouring, in one foul night more than we are able in one whole year to get up again

They were worse off even than fishermen at Brighton and Hastings, which had no harbours, for there the effects of the storms could be avoided by simply dragging the boats up on the beach above the high water mark.

Merchants were of course also affected by the state of the harbour, but fishermen were less able to sustain the costs of these hazards, given their low profit margins. They also had other problems to contend with. The fishermen engaged in a number of other activities as well as fishing, all of which they relied on to make a living. Trade and the passenger service to Dieppe were perhaps the most important of these, and in these activities the fishermen were as affected by war on the continent as the merchants (only coastal shipments of seacoal from Newcastle to London were doing well).

Then there was privateering—the capture of ships and prisoners was an important source of income during wartime in the first half of the 16th century, when the enemy was always France. The corporation did well from the headmoney which the fishermen were expected to collect from prisoners—this in fact paid for most of the town's defences in that period. But the government did not want to give undue provocation to the new superpower, Spain, and so was reluctant to give out licences for privateering—indeed, on many occasions ships were forbidden to go to sea at all, in case they were needed against the enemy. If the fishermen could not engage in privateering themselves, they still had to suffer the piracy of foreigners.

And on top of everything else, there was the problem of illegal nets. Within the Cinque Ports the use of trawl nets was forbidden because they were thought to damage fish fry, and trammel nets were used instead. But there was fierce competition at this period from French and English trawl fishermen (increasing demand for fish from London being one factor here), whose nets

> so rake the seas that ... four boats ... have caught more sole than all our boats have taken in a whole year

Perhaps some pardonable exaggeration here. But trawling was taking over, and the Rye fishermen could ill afford the costs of completely new sets of nets.

By 1660, only 5% of taxed householders were described as fishermen, and another 31% as various other sorts of seamen. By this time the population had more than halved—from over 3500 in the middle of the 16th century to less than 1300 (in fact back to what it may have been at the start of the 16th century).

* * *

The corporation did what they could to improve what was most in their grasp—the state of the harbour. There had been ongoing harbour works, but a hugely ambitious project started in 1596 swallowed up vast sums. The intention was to make a cut from the river Rother to the Tillingham across marshland to the north of Rye, whereby the diverted water would increase the depth and scouring action of the Tillingham, and sweep out to sea the silt that had been making the quay at the Strand so hazardous for ships. The inhabitants were required to contribute labour to the work, and Anne Taylor's cousin Noy Radford was employed to play his drum to call them to the work, and back again.

On the face of it, a simpler option would have been to address the reason why the build-up of silt had so accelerated recently (in the long term, the decline of the harbour was of course inevitable, with the changing shape of the coastline). As was recognised at the time, this was primarily due to local gentlemen 'inning' their valuable marshlands to drain them (so much more valuable since the expansion of London), which prevented the silt brought down by the rivers from being deposited

The Story

on the saltmarshes. But persuading the landowners to desist from such a lucrative activity—although the corporation put great efforts into the attempt—was an abortive exercise.

All this work had little effect on the harbour, but much on the corporation expenses. Within three years, they had a major deficit, with no funds to repay it. This was in spite of contributions from various sources—including London, Kent and Sussex, and a local landowner. There were even problems in the first year, when it was announced in the assembly that the corporation was too poor to pay for a shipment of rye bought by the town's corn purveyor for resale to the inhabitants, and he was told to sell it where he could (a purveyor was appointed each year to buy corn for the town).

It was presumably a different shipment that the wife of a fisherman was referring to when she complained that the *wheat and rye which was late brought in by a Britton [Breton] was brought in against Master Mayor's consent*. Far from helping his poorer neighbours—she implied—the mayor was exacerbating their predicament. For this inflammatory comment her husband was fined the incredible sum of 20s—equivalent to a servant's wages for at least half a year—and if she did it again, she was to stand in the collar for two hours with a paper declaring her offence, and then carried to the cucking stool and ducked in the salt water three times. Her husband had also abused the mayor, but he just had to find sureties for his good behaviour. The picture below shows the cucking stool and pillory in the middle of the 19th century, when they were turned out from the disused room in Rye Church where they had been stored:

It is not clear what mechanism was used to duck the stool and woman in the harbour. The word *cuck* was an old word for shit—so the woman was being sat on a privy stool and washed, as a punishment for shitting on the inhabitants with her incontinent tongue. The corporation had ferocious punishments for scolding women—one that was used occasionally was to *wash [her] at the boat's tail*—that is to say, the woman would be dragged round the harbour at high tide behind a boat.

There were suspicions that some of the richer inhabitants were not doing too badly out of the town's predicament. They had already lent sums to the corporation for the harbour works—Thomas Hamon's contribution was much the largest at £280—and when it became evident that it would not be possible to repay the debts, and the creditors would not, or could not, increase their loans in spite of interest rates of up to 9%, it was decided to sell the most valuable properties (including the town's storehouse). The mayor, Thomas Hamon, bought the storehouse for £400, a building called the *Vine* (probably an inn) was sold to Stephen Harrison, and the custom house and ferry were also sold—so that by 1602, the corporation had virtually no rental income left.

Suspicions were also raised from another quarter about excessive claims and profits being made by the elite in Rye in connection with the provisioning and equipping of two ships for the war against Spain (there will be more about this expedition in the next chapter). The larger ship, the Hercules, was hired out to the Western Cinque Ports by its owners, who were inhabitants of Rye—as were the people who built, manned and provisioned it (at 150 tons, it was the largest ship ever built in Rye). One of the treasurers—a jurat from New Romney who was appointed to oversee the accounts—noted that *since they* [the ship] *came home* [from the expedition] *they have sold the ordnance* [large guns] *to [Thomas] Fisher of Rye for £110 19s, which cost us £137*. So Fisher (father of the catholic convert of the same name) got a very good deal.

The treasurer also noted that 'they' provided more provisions of beef, beer and bread for the ships than the Queen's allowance—indeed, there were 16 tons of beer left and 5000lbs of bread—probably more than would have been required for the additional month allowed for. The crews had made good inroads into the (salted) beef, but the stockfish (dried cod) was hardly touched (jokes about tough stockfish were common in plays of the period). There was also a complaint that the beer had been offered at 40s the ton, but Rye and Hastings now *make us pay 42s*, and that Captain Davies had at first proposed 40s a month for his wages, and *now he taketh £4 a month besides all his gettings* (he had actually asked for £5 when the ship returned, but was beaten down). Various other items from the ships had also been sold—including some to the town clerk of Rye, and the gunpowder to Thomas Fisher.

So there were a number of causes of complaint by the less well-off inhabitants against Thomas Hamon and his associates: that he did not have their interests at heart in these difficult times, that the richer inhabitants were stripping the assets of the town to line their own pockets, and that they were profiting from the provisioning and sale of goods from the Hercules—for whose setting up (as well as the hoy) all inhabitants had contributed with a local tax assessment totalling £200 the previous year. These members of the elite may, however, have later had cause to rue their unneighbourly behaviour, when it looked as if they had attracted divine or devilish retribution…

* * *

Historians like to punctuate their histories with crises, and the *crisis of the 1590s* may well be an over-used phrase—but not when applied to Rye. To the local troubles were added sharp increases in the price of bread, caused by an extraordinary run of harvests ruined by interminable rain (a Europe-wide phenomenon, and the start of the 'little ice age'). It was the poor and the middling sort who were particularly affected.

Linked to this crisis was a personal tragedy which epitomised for many of the inhabitants of Rye the troubles and conflicts of the time. It appears to expose an extreme callousness on the part of Thomas Hamon that puts the later scapegoating of Anne Taylor and Susan Swaffer by his associates in the shade—though there may of course have been extenuating circumstances which are not evident from the records…

This story—told in the next chapter—illustrates the increasing economic polarisation between the richer merchants and the middling sort—and the consequent political eclipse of the latter, the merchants riding high above the troubles of their opponents… for a time. The story also helps resolve the question of why two rich fishermen should have stood surety for Anne Taylor—when fishermen were not on the whole interested in the godliness which was such a distinguishing feature of her associates.

11 Thomas Hamon and the Crisis of the 1590s

It was a winter's day in 1596—a few years before the Swaffers came to Rye—when the captain of the *Hercules*, John Davies, came onto the Strand (quay) looking for witnesses. He used this ship—at 150 tons, by far the largest ship in the port—to carry merchandize, and was much more closely identified with the merchants who dominated the magistracy than the fishermen (he did not engage in fishing). Only a few months earlier he and his crew of fifty had sailed the *Hercules* back from Cadiz, where they had taken part in a daring exploit master-minded by the young Earl of Essex (this was the expedition mentioned in the last chapter). Cadiz had been sacked, and much of the Spanish fleet destroyed, thus putting off the launch of another Armada against the English heretics for another year. The Cadiz expedition was a triumph not only for the country but also for Rye and the western members of the Cinque Ports—whom they were representing since only one man was wounded and the artillery was little used.

But the immediate concerns of most of the inhabitants of Rye that winter were much more prosaic, if no less concerned with life and death. Davies had come onto the Strand to find people who had heard the *mutinous speeches* spoken there by a certain John Cotton, a day or two earlier.

Davies spoke to three master fishermen:

> "How now, my masters! How cometh it that Cotton hath thus dealt with Master Mayor?"
> One of them answered that *he supposed he was dronk*, and on (i.e. an) other ask[ed]
> *What the words might be?* Whereto John Daveys replied and said,
> "I understand, by honest men, the words were these, viz.that Cotton
> Wished that Master Mayor were hanged, and all those rascals and villeins that chose him."

The Story

There had been a problem at the mayoral election the previous August, when Thomas Hamon had been chosen for a second term. Fewer freemen than usual gathered at the cross in the churchyard on St Bartholomew's day to vote, because of a visitation of plague. This was not the first time such a problem had arisen—the election was held at the hottest time of year, when infection was likely to be at its height.

Cotton's alleged complaint, however, was not just that few people had been there to choose a mayor, but that those that did so were of bad character—*rascals and villeins*. The term *villein* still had connotations of serfdom at this time, so the implication was that their votes could be easily bought, because they were not as financially independent as freemen should be. They were just Hamon's hangers-on.

John Cotton was relatively poor and probably a newcomer to the town (nobody else had that surname), but what was more damaging to the corporation was that others shared his opinion:

The Strand (or quay)

> Whereto William Palmer [one of the master fishermen] said that
> *Diverse were of that mind, if they durst say so much.* Whereto John Davies said,
> *They were lewd speeches, for there were many honest men at the election of the mayor, for the whole Bench were there.*

So William Palmer, at least, did not dismiss Cotton's words as drunken abuse uttered in the heat of the moment—even saying that he and others agreed with them. He was a much more substantial inhabitant than Cotton—master of the fishing boat the William Besse (28 tons), and of middling wealth, he later became a churchwarden. Davies could not leave Palmer's words unchallenged, so went again to the Strand some days later to look once more for witnesses:

> Finding Henry Wayte and William Alexander there [the other two master fishermen to whom he had spoken previously], he demanded of them
> *If Palmer did not use such speeches as he hath before recited,* which they
> *affirmed to be true*

No-one spoke up in direct support of Palmer, but John Styner—the same rich fisherman and jurat who later stood surety for Anne Taylor—made a counter-charge against Robert Convers:

> Robert Convers in open sessions had reported that *all the fishermen were drunkards*, which John Davies
> *denied that any such words were used by him*. But ... Styner still confidently affirmed that ... *Robert Convers used those words*, and that *he would believe either [Davies] or ... Convers*.

At this time John Styner had not yet been made a jurat, and Robert Convers was not yet town clerk, but had the difficult role of constable. The 'open sessions' (i.e. sessions of the peace) mentioned by Styner had occurred only two days earlier, when a fisherman had been indicted for assaulting Convers, who was no doubt carrying out his duties as constable when the altercation occurred. Styner refers to *open* sessions because non-freemen would be there to witness the conflicts within the commonalty—unlike the usual fortnightly meetings of the freemen.

When William Palmer was questioned about his words, he did not try to deny them, saying that

> if the words which he spake were taken offensively, he is sorry therefore, for he protesteth that he had no evil meaning.

On this occasion Palmer was trying to be conciliatory, but he could be abusive. He was bound over to be of good behaviour, whereas John Cotton

> is adjudged to stand in the [iron] Collar with a paper declaring his offence the next market day, and to be bound for his good behaviour.

The fishermen did not just support Cotton with words—Palmer and another fisherman stood surety for him. Another man was prepared to say that *Cotton was as honest a man as ... [Stephen Harrison]*, the land chamberlain (to whom he had presumably been speaking). The magistrates considered that this *seemed to maintain Cotton in his lewd behaviour*. Harrison was one of those who had been profiting from the sale of the town's assets (see above page 161).

* * *

The Story

The controversy over John Cotton's remarks about mayor Hamon's election did not just concern fishermen. If we spend a little more time teasing out the strands of these cross-cutting conflicts, some surprising—indeed shocking—findings emerge relating to Thomas Hamon. After Styner accused Convers of calling the fishermen *drunkards*, a tailor spoke up—one of those non-freemen who had been at the recent sessions of the peace:

> Thomas Hills intruding himself into the company [of fishermen], *affirmed the words of … Styner*, which [Davies] *reproved in him, for that it was false which he said*.
> And [Davies] called … Hills *'knave' for that his false report*, who replied that *If he were a knave, he was the more fit to be his fellow*.

The reason Hills had been at the sessions when Convers slandered the fishermen was because he had himself been indicted, for helping a woollen draper or tailor—Simon Duron—escape from prison. Duron, together with a carpenter and sawyer, had been caught red-handed stealing four bags of barley (worth 16s) from a local gentleman, and at the recent sessions they had all been found guilty. In theory, death was the penalty for the theft of anything worth a shilling or more—but the rigours of the law were usually mitigated in practice. They all claimed *benefit of clergy*—originally restricted to the clergy, this loophole allowed those who were able to read to commute the death penalty for branding (for the first offence). But only Duron could read the *neck verse* (a literacy test taken from part of a psalm)—so he escaped the death penalty, but had his right hand branded. The others were sentenced to be hanged.

But perhaps they were banished instead, because their names do not appear in the burial register. This register was carefully maintained, with frequent annotations in the margin—even people whose names were unknown to the churchwardens were entered (for example *stranger*, *poor girl*, or *Frenchman*), and when there were no burials on one unusual day during the plague outbreak, a churchwarden has written *nothing*. The death of the daugher of one of the thieves (Richard Nightingale) had been recorded only shortly before, in October 1596, and the death of the daughter of the other (Lancelot Winter) would be recorded in December 1597. It is true that the men's banishment was not mentioned in the Assembly books—but perhaps this was not necessary, since they knew they were under sentence of execution. One of them, at least, was not living in Rye the following year, because the corporation was trying to avoid supporting his children—they granted his wife's mother a loft on condition that they would not be required to do so.

Thomas Hills had been acquitted by the jury of releasing Duron from prison, but could not find anyone to act as surety for his good behaviour, and so was banished from the town, not to return on pain of losing his ears. He was nevertheless back a year later, visiting his wife, but said that he was on his way to join his mother in Devon, so was allowed to stay for a month (there was frequent coming and going along the coast between Rye and the west country).

All part of everyday business at a 17th century sessions of the peace, perhaps. But the most extraordinary aspect of all this was that Simon Duron was the stepson of one of the richest men in the town—none other than the mayor, Thomas Hamon. So John Cotton's objectionable speech on the quayside that he *wished that the mayor were hanged*—spoken shortly after Duron's trial, and presumably alluding to it—was very close to home for Hamon (see above page 163).

* * *

Hamon was 29 when he had married Catherine Dearne, a month after her husband John died in 1578. The name was variously spelt Duron, Daron, Dearon, Deronne, Dearne, Dirne—John was presumably French, the only householder with this name. French names were typically anglicized, so Simon signed his name Dirne, and in his father's will it is spelt Dearne, while the town clerk wrote it in its original form, Duron, perhaps emphasising its foreignness.

Catherine already had six children when she was widowed, the first born when Hamon was only 12, so she must have been much older than him. A daughter was born a year after their marriage, but they had no more children, and their daughter Mary died in 1596 at the age of 17.

It was not unusual for a man to marry a widow who was older than him at first marriage, and then when she died, perhaps take a younger woman as his second wife. This made economic sense—the widow might bring wealth and trading connections (Catherine's husband had been a brewer, like Hamon himself); she would be an asset while he was establishing himself in his trade, because experienced in running a household and in assisting in the business; and her fertility might be declining, so they would not be overrun with children before the business was well-established. But Catherine no doubt lived longer than Thomas had bargained for, because she only died in 1607.

Thomas Hamon was born into a well-off family by Rye standards—they were in the top 7% of taxed households in 1557 (but not quite as rich as the jurat Robert Bennett, Anne Taylor's grandfather—taxed on £40 and £50 of goods respectively). Hamon's father (also a brewer named Thomas) had come to Rye sometime before 1549, when he was made a freeman, and Thomas junior was born in the same year. His father died, however, during the devastating flu epidemic of 1559, when the boy was only ten years old, and then his mother died when he was 17. She had meanwhile remarried, and after her death Thomas chose his stepfather to be his guardian.

When Thomas married Widow Duron, he was certainly not as rich as his father had been. A few years earlier, when he was 22, he was taxed on only £5 worth of goods in Rye (1571). Presumably some of his inheritance had been wasted (by his stepfather?) in the 12 years since his parents died. His marriage would certainly have benefited him, since the late John Duron had been one of the wealthiest inhabitants (taxed on £60 worth of goods just before he died), leaving lands to his three sons and even to one of his daughters. His eldest son John, another brewer, probably received more than the others, as was customary (in England), and brother Simon (the barley thief) was left a tenement (called Tanhouse), barns and lands in Wittersham, as well as 20s annually (when he reached 16) from his mother while she lived. The other two brothers were each bequeathed the same annuities. When John reached the age of only 24 he had a substantial business, judging by the size of the brewery on the Lower Street which he leased at this time:

> A brewhouse, malthouse, malt mill, three malt lofts and a chamber belonging to one of them, also a malt bin, the firkinhouse, cowpers house, hophouse, and stable under the hophouse together with half the backside ... [wherein] to lay his wood and other necessary things; with right of entry at the Budgegate ... with men, carts, horse and carriages between the hours of four in the morning and nine o'clock at night ...

But both brothers John and Simon declined in wealth over the next ten years. When Simon was stealing barley in 1596 (at which time the brothers would have been in their thirties), his elder brother was taxed on only £10 worth of goods, and Simon was near the bottom rung of the tax ladder—£2 worth of goods. By contrast, Thomas Hamon was taxed on £400 worth of goods at the same date (note that this tax list is not directly comparable with the tax lists of the 1570s—see appendix 2)!

Did Hamon bear some responsilibity for Simon's decline? Simon was underage when his mother married Hamon, and Duron's will stipulated that any such future husband must sign a bond to carry out the requirements of the will—a common provision, since a wife's property would belong to her new husband when she remarried. The overseers of the will should also have made sure that the children inherited their patrimonies. Altogether, the brothers' economic positions should have been much securer than Thomas Hamon's own had been when he was orphaned at the age of 17.

Was Simon simply a ne'er-do-well, a maverick, or a *Simple Simon*, that he got involved with stealing barley (a cheaper grain than wheat)? As a woollen draper who could sign his name and read the neck verse, he was not a simpleton. But the theft seems to have been an ad hoc affair—at least as he told it. A carpenter named Lancelot Winter came to Simon's house on 28th November and asked him to go with him to the Strand, where in the miller's house he found Richard Nightingale (sawyer) and two other men who were not from Rye. He agreed in the end to go with them over the ferry—but he did not know where (the miller's wife later said he told her they were going for butter and cheese). Lancelot told him *he should speed [fare] no worse than he did [at present]*. Nightingale was so drunk that he could go no farther than the ferry and there fell into the water.

The others broke open the barn door of local gentleman Master Swanne, and stole four sacks of barley—but they had been spotted by Swanne and it was near day, so they could not take it home (according to Lancelot Winter). They took some to the miller's house (the miller's wife admitted taking a bag of it), and some to Nightingale's (who remembered nothing—only that it was found at his bed's head). They then fled to various places, but Swanne caught them at Fleckley Ash (according to Winter). Simon said that some of the others went on another exploit from Monday till Wednesday, but he did not know what, and would not go with them. The miller's wife ground some of the barley on Sunday, and Simon had part of it.

Nightingale and Winter seem to have been persistent offenders—Nightingale had been whipped for pickeries recently, and Winter had been indicted the year before, probably for theft, and sentenced to be severely whipped. However a freeman, Richard Swanne, did act as surety for Winter. Swanne was disfranchised the following year for dissuading others from paying their market dues and complaining about the mayor.

The Story

He was reproved by another—*if any [man] had been mayor as long as this one, he would have been as ill spoken of as this one.* Richard Swanne replied *if any that should be mayor were worse th[a]n he that now is mayor, he wished that he were hanged at the Landgate.* That hanging theme again.

So Simon Duron stole barley because he needed barley—not just to profit from the very high prices of grains at this time. It was not just for himself—he must have married a year or two earlier, because a daughter (named after his mother) was born to him the previous year, and a son (named after his father) died the following year.

* * *

Many people desperately needed barley and other grains in 1596—relentless rain had resulted in a series of bad harvests (a Europe-wide phenomenon), which caused the price of bread to go skyhigh. In 1596 it was more than twice what it had been only 4 years earlier. When your daily bread consisted of just that—bread, beer and a piece of cheese if you were lucky—its price could determine whether or not the poorer sort could survive.

Their predicament was worsened by a long-term increase in the price of grains—a national phenomenon caused by the rise in population over the previous century. The agriculture of the time could not provide enough grain to feed the expanding numbers.

Wage rates increased very slightly during the second half of the 16th century, but did not keep up with the insidious increase in grain prices. If you average out the wild fluctuations in the price of bread, you see it moving relentlessly upwards, and the gap between that and wages getting ever wider from about the 1570s (see graph overleaf).

So in 1550, a tuppeny brown loaf (the bread bought by the poor) would have weighed 4lb, and wages were 9d a day (but work was only occasional); in 1596, the tuppeny loaf was less than half that weight—1½ lb—and wages were 12d per day. At least half these wages would have been spent on bread. The prices in the chart overleaf are for brown bread.

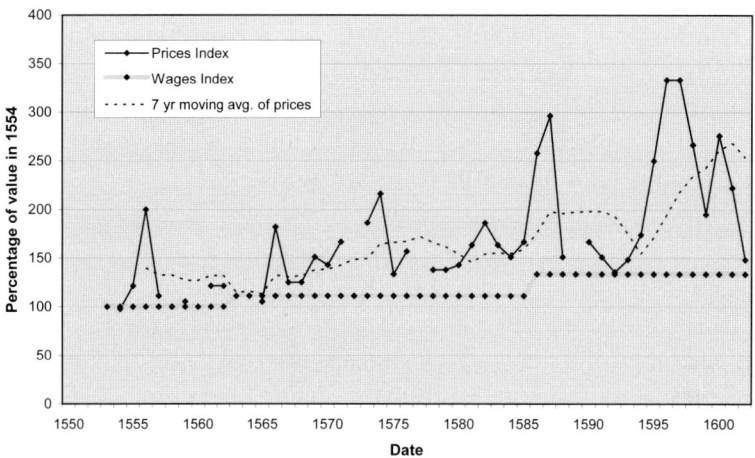

Price of Bread and Labourers' Daily Wages in Rye, 1554-1602
(expressed as percentages of price/wage in 1554)

Source: Rye 1/1-7 and Mayhew (1987): 170 (wages)

The predicament of the poor in Rye was not as bad as, for example, those in remote uplands in the north of England, where famine was prevalent at this time. But all grain had to be brought to the town by boat—since the land around Rye was not suitable for arable farming—and inhabitants had therefore to rely on the corporation's corn purveyor to buy shipments of grain for resale. There had been 70-90 shipments per year when Rye was populous in the 1560s and 70s. The government often complicated matters further for the corporation in times of dearth, since it tried to restrict the transport of grain to prevent local areas being depleted. When grain was scarce, the mayor and jurats had even been known to confiscate a shipment destined for somewhere else, giving the merchant the going rate for it and explaining to him and the government why they had gone to this extreme.

* * *

The story of Simon Duron is not quite finished. The following year, on 1st October 1597, there is a chilling entry in the parish register:

> Simon Deronne an housholder executed

The Story

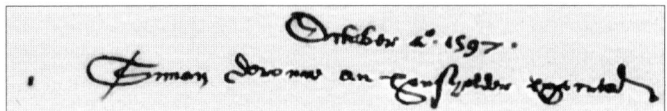

The churchwardens always noted if a deceased person was a householder. Simon had been convicted a second time of theft 5 days earlier, and since he had already received benefit of clergy for the first felony, he was sentenced to be hanged. No other details were recorded. 1597 was another year of dearth, nearly as bad as 1596.

This conviction is striking not only because people in Rye had been reluctant to prosecute criminals until recently (see page 66), but also because even in the Assize courts in Sussex, before the Queen's justices, grand juries threw out *three-quarters* of draft indictments for the most serious felonies (those for which benefit of clergy was not available). Duron and his accomplices (of the year before) were probably the only thieves in Rye to be sentenced to death (and not pardoned) in the second half of the 16th century.

Why had Hamon not done more to support his stepson during this time of dearth? A likely reason is revealed in the next chapter. But first to another scourge, which was not the less devastating for having been experienced several times in the town within living memory. Anne Bennett's family was one of those struck down by this calamity.

* * *

Was it the *Hercules* that brought the plague rats to Rye? Plague was rife in Spain, but was present in few other places in southern England at this time apart from Rye, and the war prevented merchant ships from going to Spain. Ports were common entrypoints for visitations of plague— *visitation* being an appropriate word, since the disease arrived suddenly, and it was not just the poor and weak who died from it. It was seen as God's punishment for sin, as the godly inhabitants of the nearby town Ashford spelt out when they sent £5 to be given to Rye's poor:

> it hath pleased God (for some cause to him best known) to visit your town with one of his great rods or scourges wherewith he often afflicted man for sin, whereof not long sithence we … of Ashford have had manifold experience, and as it pleased him of his great mercy then to raise us up many friends to have a fellow feeling of our miseries, and to contribute towards the necessitie of our poor (blessed be his name therefore), so it hath now pleased

him to move our hearts to contribute something (according to our small abilities) towads the relieving of the poor saints of God amongst you, the sum whereof is five pounds … And thus desiring God (for his Christ's sake) to look down mercifully upon you and in his good time to withdraw his heavy hand of correction from you, and to make both you and us truly thankful for all his mercies and loving kindnesses towards us … and to give us all grace and wisdom to make use aright of these his loving corrections upon us.

It was not just the ungodly, however, who were struck by the plague—the Bennett family were themselves one of those visited by it, as we know by the *P* written in the margin of the burial register next to Robert Bennett's name, in early 1597. Their house would have been one of those locked up with the locks, hasps and staples bought for the purpose. *Infected persons are for the most part shut up into their dwelling houses, and are not permitted to range abroad to the spoil of others,* noted the town clerk in September 1596; he thought this was why the outbreak was as yet *very little dispersed about the town*. The numbers dying trebled the following month, remaining at least as high in November, before declining in the cold weather of December which reduced the activity of the rat fleas.

The Bennetts' house would have been marked with a cross, as was directed during the outbreak in 1563, and a vessel of water left outside every other day, with food, subsidised if necessary by weekly payments from the rest of the inhabitants. Any dogs and hogs found roaming in the streets were to be killed to try and restrict the spread of infection, and a watch may have been kept at the Landgate—as in 1593—to prevent people going in and out of the town. Two women were licensed to view bodies, and Master George, *who professeth physick*, was hired for a year to minister to the people *to avoid thinfection of the plague, if god so please*. Roughly a quarter of the town's inhabitants died in this outbreak (not the worst in its history).

Another victim in the Bennett household was Anne's elder brother John, who died in November 1596, aged 22 (Anne was 19). His father asked in his will to be buried next to his son, in the Church by the north door (the father was 53 years old). Neither Goody Bennett's healing skills nor the family's godliness had managed to save them—although the women in the family survived. Widow Bennett carried on with the butchering business for a time after her husband's death (which was not unusual among widows—testators sometimes requested that their apprentices serve out their term with their widows).

* * *

The Story

Robert Bennett had not been doing so well in other ways by the time of his death. The value of his goods at this date was considerably less, at £43, than his tax evaluation of £120 the previous year—usually tax assessors underestimated a person's wealth, so they must have thought that he was much richer than he actually was. He died owing debts of £95 to the tanner Thomas Lashenden, to whom he presumably sold his hides. These debts no doubt had something to do with the betrothals arranged shortly afterwards between Widow Bennett and Lashenden, and between his son John and her daughter Anne.

Robert Bennett's decline in wealth was not just a tale of individual misfortune or mismanagement, but symptomatic of the decline of the butchers in the town in general since the 1570s. By 1598, none of them were rich enough to be jurats—11 of the 13 jurats were taxed on £100 or more, whereas none of the butchers were taxed on more than £50. This was so different from the late 1570s, when the butcher John Fagge was by far the richest man in the town (see page 90), and Bennett's uncle—another butcher—was also a jurat. And back in the '50s, Robert Bennett's father (another butcher) had been a jurat and one of the wealthier inhabitants.

This decline did not of course just affect butchers. When the port had been flourishing, the populousness of the town, and the number of travellers passing through, had boosted the service trades of brewing and baking, butchering and tailoring. If Robert Bennett's brother John, the tailor, had lived as long as Simon Duron, he would not have continued to flourish as he had done in the 1570s.

So when Anne Taylor declared (according to Susan) that she was heir to the money guarded by fairies in her garden, perhaps it was not just that she felt she should have inherited her grandfather's wealth, but that there was a more widespread decline that was somehow wrong, and could be reversed if you only had the right contacts in the spirit world.

* * *

The 1590s were thus a period of unmitigated disaster—at least for some inhabitants. Not all trades, however, were equally affected by the decline of the port and the harvest crises of the 1590s. Those which required capital—such as brewing and tanning—were better able to keep afloat than the others. A brewer needed costly equipment (after the introduction of hopped beer in the early 16th century)—a copper furnace, brewing tons etc.—which could only be acquired by those who either inherited them, as

John Duron did, or had the capital to buy them. Only a few people could afford to be a brewer or a tanner (such as Thomas Lashenden), whereas there could be numerous tailors. As the town's economy contracted, therefore, brewers and tanners would not have had to compete with many poorer rivals, as did the butchers and artisans.

Of course the richest inhabitants—be they brewers, tanners, mercers (those who dealt in expensive merchandise) or whatever—also engaged in general trading activities, and owned land, so it would not have been only their official occupation that determined their wealth. But the richer butchers had also owned lands in the middle of the century, and the Bennetts, for one, had had to sell their farm.

A rough idea of the effect of the downturn on the richest inhabitants (4% of those who were taxed) can be gained from the local tax assessments. These suggest—as I have argued elsewhere—that not only were the rich surviving better than the others, but, surprisingly, that they may have been doing at least as well in the mid-1590s as they had done in the 1570s (see appendix 2). It is unfortunately difficult to do the same exercise with inhabitants of middling wealth, because those worst affected would have disappeared into the realms of the untaxed, of whom there were many in Rye—about a third of all households in the town.

* * *

A widening economic gap had thus opened between the capitalist tradesmen and merchants on the one hand, and the ordinary artisans on the other. I would just like to explore briefly how this affected the balance of power between the factions. In the 26 years between 1583 and 1608, butchers were never chosen as mayor, and brewers were chosen in nearly half the years (including 6 years when Thomas Hamon was mayor). There was no point in electing someone as mayor who was too poor to support the role. In the previous 20 years (1563-1582), by contrast, brewers were only chosen as mayor twice, while butchers were mayor in 4 years (John Fagge in 3 of these years). With the decline of the butchers, therefore, the artisan faction was no match for the merchants—they did not have rich enough leaders to rival the Thomas Hamons and Thomas Fishers of the other faction.

So we find that whereas in the period 1576-1582, all the mayors had been from the artisan faction, between 1583 and 1608, by contrast, all the mayors were from the merchant faction, with the probable exceptions of 1585, 1592-3, 1597-8 and 1603.

The Story

There may have been another consequence for the power relations between the factions of the economic changes of the 1590s. There are suggestions that the poorer sort of freemen voted for the merchant faction. That is to say, the sort of freemen who were not as financially independent as freemen should be, and so *lean to the bent of* [the] *bow* of the richer sort *and hang on their sleeves* (in the words of John Hebblethwaite). These perhaps include those *rascals and villeins* who voted for Thomas Hamon in 1596, in the words of John Cotton. In the impoverished '90s, the merchant faction were likely to have gathered more poor hangers-on, thus strengthening their control of local politics.

There is a little evidence for this kind of social sandwich if we go back to the last time when some record of allegiance is available—the 1570s. In the disputed election of 1579, a slightly greater proportion of those of middling wealth voted for the godly butcher John Fagge than for his opponent, the brewer Robert Carpenter. Fagge was mayor during the 'riot' which led to the Star Chamber cases mentioned at the end of chapter 5 (see above pages 89-97), and his supporters wanted him to serve as mayor for a third term. It was in connection with this election that the names of his supporters are, very unusually, listed.

This list of Fagge's supporters, as well as the freemen not included on the list, can be grouped by wealth (using the tax assessment of 1576; see appendix 2). There is a problem in that those freemen *not* included among his supporters may not necessarily have supported his opponent. Indeed, a couple of these 'others' were definitely Fagge supporters (maybe they were out of town when required to add their signature or mark to the document in question)—and I have added them to his group.

Taking all the freemen who were either merchants or artisans (i.e. excluding the fishermen), I have rather arbitrarily grouped them in the chart below into 3 groups, with small groups of the poorer and richer freemen, and a larger group of those of middling wealth (see wealth categories overleaf). It is apparent that nearly three-quarters of the Fagge supporters are of middling wealth (total 51), with just over a quarter either poorer or richer than this. The 'others' have a larger proportion of poorer and richer freemen—just under half are in these two groups, and just over half in the middling group (total 49).

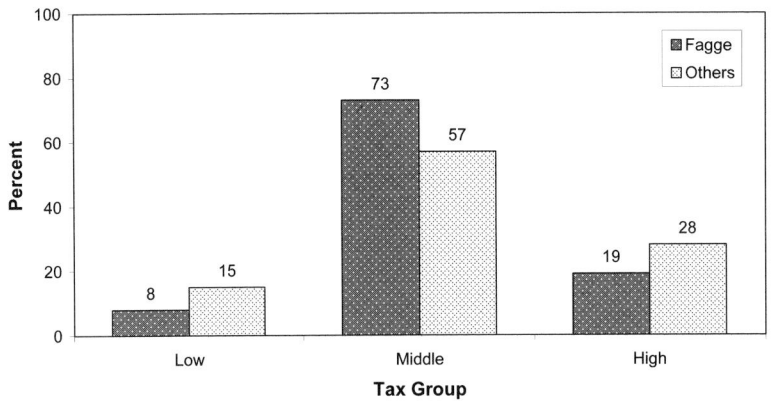

Wealth of Fagge supporters relative to other Freemen

Tax group	value of goods owned (see text)
Low	£1 - £2 10s
Middle	£3 6s 8d - £16 13s 4d
High	£20 - £80

Source: Rye 47/25 pt2/22 and Mayhew 1987: 277-84

The chart is problematic for the reasons given above, but this tripartite grouping I think suggests that factional allegiance roughly followed — with exceptions — the distinction made by contemporaries between the financially independent type of artisan — *the middling sort* — and those who were poorer or richer than these (see above page 88). More will be said about this 'social sandwich' in the essay at the end of the book.

* * *

Why have I left the fishermen out of this analysis of wealth groups among the factions? They do not display the pattern of allegiance suggested above for the different wealth groups among the tradesmen. The fishermen were a cohesive group — as they had to be, given their precarious way of life. Few master fishermen owned their boats outright, but owned parts in several, so that shipwreck would not have such a devastating effect on any one family. The profits from a fishing trip were at best very small, and they were divided equally according to each

The Story

person's input of labour or equipment—a *mansfare* of nets, contributed to a trip, brought the owner the same profit as a man's labour.

There was not therefore the same power relationship between richer and poorer fishermen that there was between the merchants and artisans. The merchants were not only able to exclude poorer competitors, they probably also had some control over the supply of raw materials to some artisans.

This discussion of differences between fishermen and tradesmen brings us back to the question posed earlier—why did two of the rich fishermen-jurats offer to stand surety for Anne Taylor in the witchcraft case? They evince few of the signs of godliness that was such a distinguishing feature of her associates. One indicator of this is their lack of enthusiasm for the current fashion of baptising children with biblical names (since the 1570s) including Abigall, Elias, Elnathan, Ester, Hanna, Ismael, Ithamar, Itai, Jonathan, Jhosepett or Josphet, Jonas, Josias, Judith, Moses, Nathaniel, Onesimus and Sallomon. Jonas (Jonah) Whale, son of the shoemaker John Whale, is particularly apt.

Use of these names would have seemed a dramatic break with the past, when names were generally drawn from a small pool—John, Robert, Thomas and William being particularly common for boys (there was more variety in girls' names), with John and Joan being the top favourites. Biblical names such as Joseph and Mary had of course always been popular, but if you exclude any biblical names used before 1560, use of the 'new' names (listed above) mapped out as follows: they had been used at least once by 15% (25) of merchants and artisans, 8% (8) of fishermen, and 5% (3) of those whose occupations I have not been able to ascertain.

Some of the new names are obscure, with only one or two references in the Bible—*Onesimus*, for example, was a servant of St. Paul, who in his letter to Philemon asks that the latter treat him as a brother; and *Itai* was one of King David's warriors (this baby did not last a year—perhaps he was a weakling, and his parents hoped that the name would give him strength). The use of such a name publicised to all and sundry that the parents of the child so named were intimately acquainted with the Bible.

The use of these new biblical names may have had an additional significance for the godly. It broke with the tradition of baptising children with the names of parents, godparents or other kin, which linked the child with the wider society, and confirmed her/his relationship with important others. By contrast, baptising a child with a biblical name not used by older people emphasised the child's link with God, one might say at the expense of earthly relationships. This may partly explain why such names were not popular with the fishermen—for them, strengthening ties with neighbours was more important.

The rich fishermens' lack of concern with godliness is also demonstrated by their illiteracy—you could only be familiar with the Bible if you could read. John Styner made no attempt to sign his name (usually considered to be evidence of ability to read) when he acted as surety for Anne Taylor, just leaving a cross as his mark. Robert Swayne also could not sign his name.

So this suggests that Styner and Swayne may have been motivated to support Anne Taylor more by a shared antagonism towards certain members of the aldermanic bench rather than because of any stronger bond with her or her faction. That the fishermen did have cause to criticise Thomas Hamon is evident from the dispute which opened this chapter (12 years before the witchcraft case), in which some of them had a large part to play. This group included John Styner, who refused to join with the other rich mariner present at the scene—John Davies—in castigating John Cotton for his abuse of the mayor Thomas Hamon. He instead made a point of expressing solidarity with the rest of the fishermen (see above page 165).

Robert Swayne had other reasons for antipathy towards the rest of the bench. We must briefly skip forward 12 years to 1608, when the magistrates were embroiled in defending their right to try the witchcraft case. At this time he got into a conflict with them about an unconnected issue—his purchase of a small shipload of seacoal, and then another of tar and firboards, without telling the mayor about them so that the freemen could 'have their parts' in the purchase of the same. Seacoal (i.e. coal dug up and brought by sea, as opposed to charcoal, the more traditional fuel in the south) was about the only trade that was booming at this time. Fishermen called in at Newcastle to buy seacoal after the summer fishery for cod and ling at Scarborough, and sold it in London (whose expanding population provided an ever-increasing demand for fuel) or Rye. Perhaps Swayne was too old and possibly sick to do the voyage himself (since he died shortly afterwards). Huge fines were inflicted on him of £1 for the seacoal, and £3 for the second shipload, and also because he *with very bad and evil speaches,…in deriding sort, greatly abused Master Mayor* [Higgons] *to his face* (the words are not recorded). He was apparently also dismissed from his juratship, though we only know about this because he appealed to the Brotherhood of the Cinque Ports (an annual assembly to which member ports sent representatives), who ordered that he be re-instated when he had apologised for his verbal abuse.

The Story

These conflicts occurred in the same month in 1608 when the magistrates reluctantly agreed to bail Anne Taylor at the behest of the Lord Warden, and Swayne's name was included as surety for Anne—and then crossed out, with *vacat* written in the margin. So he and Styner clearly had their own reasons for opposing the aldermanic bench.

* * *

To conclude—by the end of the crisis years of the 1590s, many of the inhabitants of Rye had become embittered and antagonistic towards Thomas Hamon and some others among the richer sort, as well as increasingly impoverished and powerless to do anything about it. Anne Taylor was clearly not alone in her antipathy towards Hamon—indeed her later criticisms and curses may have given voice to the views of others who *durst not say so much*, in the words of William Palmer.

The differences between the elite and the artisans—if not the fishermen—were accentuated in the 1590s by diverging religious outlooks, which will be discussed in the next chapter. It was this which may have prompted Thomas Hamon to distance himself from his stepson Simon Duron (and possibly, also, prompted Simon to refuse to seek help from his stepfather).

It seemed improbable that any of the elite in the 1590s—who must have been increasingly confident of their political and economic supremacy in the town—would feel so vulnerable to the curses of Anne Taylor as to formally accuse her of witchcraft. But retribution seemed to hit them in the following few years, and the balance of power between the factions consequently changed. This leads us finally (page 194) to pinpoint who exactly were the accusers in the witchcraft case. As Robin Briggs has noted, accusers in witchcraft cases were often those whose position had become endangered, striking back at those inferiors who now seemed to threaten their pre-eminence.

12   The Accusers

> … she did think that [Hamon's] lewd life would bring him to his end. And that he did never any man good but such as was of his Religion.

—another tantalising snippet of what Susan said that Anne had said, suggesting that Anne saw marked differences between her and Hamon's 'religion'. Indeed, the merchant faction in the 1590s seem to have been easing away from the godliness that had characterised the whole commonalty back in the 1570s—their less rigorous Protestantism suggested, in particular, by a more positive view of festivity. They were thus distancing themselves from the godly middling sort, who for their part showed signs of a more strident puritanism.

The elite may have been persuaded of the need for godliness back in the 1560s and 70s by the threatening international situation. The sight of boatloads of French protestant refugees arriving in waves from beleaguered Dieppe, and other French and Dutch towns, no doubt concentrated Rye minds on where the real enemy lay, and discouraged religious dissension. The fortified city of Dieppe—more than 10 times the size of Rye—embraced the Reformation in the early 1560s, like many other French towns (apart from a small catholic minority). During the previous decade they had strengthened their protestant resolve with the help of their contacts in Rye, as well as with smuggled copies of translations of scriptures, and Calvinist preachers sent from Geneva. It was said that:

> [the Dieppois] abhorred taverns and houses of ill-repute, masquerades, dice, and cards; the religious plays of Mid-August ceased for a time; and the new converts liked to compare the severity of their lives with that of the early christians.

According to one story, some Dieppois stealing taxes from a church in the rival catholic town of Arques wore white cassocks *in token of the purity of their faith*.

Wild scenes of image-breaking in the main church of Dieppe, and a bonfire built in the nave, displayed the religious fervour which inflamed some of the urban population. On a national scale, it was an incendiary mixture of this religious fervour amongst certain groups (particularly the urban artisans) with factional rivalry amongst, in particular, the nobility—rivalry that was exacerbated by the weakness of the new young King Charles IX—which took the country inexorably into the civil wars of religion. Both sides appealed to foreign powers—English and Spanish—and the Dieppois received an English garrison (ferried across from Rye), to defend them not only against their King's army, but also the surrounding catholic countryside .

The defence was unsuccessful, however, and when Dieppe surrendered to catholic forces, many of the inhabitants fled to England. Still more came over after the Massacre of St. Bartholomew's Day in 1572, when about two thousand protestants were killed by the catholic mob in Paris, and more in other towns (a reaction inadvertently set in train by the court's assassination of some of the protestant leaders). So the inhabitants of Rye had a sense of common cause with the refugees—particularly since the Pope had excommunicated the English Queen in 1570, and absolved her subjects of obedience to her. In these circumstances, for members of the merchant faction in Rye to quibble about excesses of godliness would have been unpatriotic.

The English government objected to the degree of protection which Rye corporation (like some other communities in the Cinque Ports) gave to those French mariners who attacked their catholic compatriots in the Channel (just as the corporation had also protected the Dutch protestant freebooters—the Sea Beggars—who preyed on the shipping of their Spanish overlords). As well as giving the privateers harbourage and food, the corporation defended their reputations and provided them with alibis when the Privy Council were trying to have them prosecuted for piracy.

Although the French had their own Church (i.e. community of worship) in Rye (as in some other towns), the community was not particularly separatist, and many of them established close personal ties with their English hosts. The future leader of the merchant faction, Robert Carpenter, was asked to be executor of the will of one godly Frenchman (a glazier), and he was overseer (in effect) of the will of another. A godly Frenchman who was made a jurat asked the mayor—another member of the merchant faction—to be overseer of his will. And of course Thomas Hamon's first wife, the widow Catherine Duron, was probably French. It is likely that Catherine and Jean Duron were married before he—or rather they—fled from France, since he does not appear to have been living in the town in 1557 (since he is not on the tax list for that year), and their first child to be born in Rye was baptised in 1561.

Relations between the inhabitants of Rye and the French immigrants were not always amicable—there was often rivalry between those who pursued the same occupation. But then the issue was straightforwardly economic rather than religious.

* * *

Some of the godly English inhabitants of Rye must have envied the French for having their own Church, in which they chose their own ministers and elders, and controlled all matters of worship, discipline and clerical dress. Such matters became the subject of acrimonious dispute between the English government and those of its subjects dubbed *puritans* (a new term of abuse from the 1560s).

In Rye, it was evident by the 1590s that religious differences were growing, when some people who had radical religious opinions were labelled *puritans* by their opponents. These differences focused in particular on the various ministers who served the town. The corporation had frequent conflicts with the vicars of Rye, over whose appointment they had no control (these conflicts were over both the appointment of officers and doctrinal issues). Some of these vicars were non-resident, and even when they did live in the town, the corporation generally also appointed at least one other preacher to give a lecture or sermon on a Saturday morning. These preachers in turn often aroused opposition from different groups amongst the townspeople (as well as from the vicar).

One such conflict surfaced in 1591, during the mayoralty of the leader of the merchant faction, Robert Carpenter. A *small sect of puritans, more holy in show than in deed, is sprung up among us*, complained the mayor and jurats. The 'puritans' were, so they said, trying to get the preacher appointed by the corporation, Richard Greenwood, removed for non-residence at his rural benefice.

Some of these 'puritans' were examined by the magistrates about some erroneous opinions that they were thought to hold, as well as for abusing the preacher, and one of them for striking him. One joiner accused another joiner as follows:

> I have heard Francis Godfrey say that *my Lord of Canterbury is but the Pope of England*, and call him *John of Canterbury*, and that the Book of Common Prayer which he alloweth to be said in the church is but *mass translated, and dumdogs to read it*; for those ministers that do not preach they call them *dumdogs* ....

> When they have been to sermon and be come home, will they say one to another:
> *"Have you been at church?"* *"Yea"* sayeth the other.
> *"Then you have heard mingle mangle [compair], as Latimer said in his sermon, as they call hogs to trough in his country"*.
> Upon a time Francis Godfrey did see Master Waylett pass in the street, he said to me:
> *"There is a dumdog, he doth starve at Guilford"*; and they call the Book of Common Prayer the *starving book.*

Waylett was minister at East Guldeford. Many of these opinions have the same earthy, abusive feel as those alleged to be held by the early protestants, and even the content has similarities. In the above quote, there is a reference to the early protestant Bishop and martyr Hugh Latimer, and the complaint about *dumdogs* brings to mind the alleged opinion of a Rye 'heretic' in the 1530s that *he had rather have a dog to sing for him than a priest* (though *dumdogs* was a very popular term at this period).

There was one opinion which might mark these puritans out as separatist in their attitude to other inhabitants:

> none ought not to pray except they have the gift of prayer, and that it is not lawful for them to join prayer with the wicked

One of the 'puritans' who was accused of abuse, and one who had struck Richard Greenwood, were punished for their misdemeanours, and Greenwood kept his position as preacher.

At first sight these 'puritans' seem of minor importance—there was a young joiner who was only just rich enough to be taxed (Francis Godfrey), a middle-aged shoemaker of middling wealth (John Baylie), a relatively poor French surgeon (William Gile, who would later be employed by the corporation to cure one man of a 'scald' head, and another family of some other illness), and another man (George Martin) of whom I have no details (perhaps he was an apprentice).

But there was also a servant (Richard Tate) of one of the richest merchants in the town—Robert Wood—whose godliness is indicated by the unusual names which he gave his children—*Convert* and *Renewed*. These are like the names given by the French surgeon, William Gile, to his children—*Hopewell* and *Repent* (what contrasting moods are expressed in these names!). Robert Wood had married the widow of one of the most prominent merchants in the French community, William Bucher, alias Guillaume Bucheret. William Gile, the surgeon, was not so poor by the time he wrote his will, ten years later, since he refers to land that he owned in Faversham.

In spite of the corporation's sneering reference to a *small sect of puritans*, therefore, the group was not as marginal as the complainants wanted to make out. The rich merchant Robert Wood was very much part of the establishment—he had been land chamberlain, was later made a jurat, and elected mayor in 1603 (dying two years' later). This does not necessarily imply that he saw eye-to-eye with the rest of the bench—far from it. The mayor and jurats sometimes seem to have invited important members of rival groups into their midst in order to absorb opposition. Once part of the magisterial bench, the new member owed loyalty to their brethren and were expected not to discuss matters with others, thus diluting their influence within their own group. This could be effective as long as the rival group was not so large or influential that it would dominate the magistracy.

For the same reason, these important people might be reluctant to take up the offer of a place on the bench—Robert Wood took six months before he took his oath, and another godly inhabitant, Peter Keling, twice refused the request to be a jurat when the other faction were dominant. The fisherman John Styner (who acted as surety for Anne Taylor) also refused when the offer was first made to him, a year after the altercation at the Strand described in the last chapter. He did accept five years later, however, when the other rich fisherman Robert Swayne was also made a jurat (1602). And Thomas Edolphe—a member of the merchant faction—frequently refused to be sworn as jurat when the artisan faction were dominant.

George Taylor was perhaps too big a fish to be absorbed in this way into the magistracy, and so the opposite tactic was used—the corporation refused even to make him a freeman, which would be a strong disincentive for staying in Rye at all.

It is often assumed that the responsibility of office put some people off—but there were economic incentives for merchants to join the bench, and anyone living in a port was by definition a merchant if they were wealthy enough. The mayor and jurats had the right to buy larger proportions of merchandize brought to the town by sea than others. According to a decree of 1572, the buyer could only have a quarter of the merchandize, the rest being divided amongst those who wanted it: for every freeman's part, a jurat could have double, and the mayor triple (and non-freemen could only have what was rejected by the members of the corporation).

The Story

Robert Wood was not the only puritan on the bench. The overseer of Wood's will, Richard Cockram, was called a *puritan* when he was mayor in 1610 (he had been made a jurat in 1604). The butcher and innkeeper Francis Daniel told some musicians who were staying in his inn that

> "We have a puritan to our mayor, and therefore you may play as long as you will at his door, but he will give you nothing."
> And that was the occasion that they stayed from playing and showing their music unto Master Mayor.

The mayor obviously did not like this aspersion, because Daniel was punished for the abuse.

* * *

We have learned something about the puritans, but as usual not much about the attitudes of members of the merchant faction, which are much harder to discern than those of their self-publicising opponents. Thomas Hamon was no papist, since it was during his mayoralty in 1600 that the mayor and jurats wrote to the Lord Warden complaining that the vicar, Roger Smith, had secret catholic sympathies, and had sent a crucifix enclosed in a letter to his father-in-law in London.

The mayor and jurats were even prepared to give limited support to a very radical puritan—the tailor Francis Brooke—who had an argument with vicar Smith about Brooke's non-attendance at church. Brooke was said to have been *transported … into this fury or passion of hard speech*, which might partly explain how he could declare that he would only pray for the Queen if she was *in the dominion of Christ his church*, and that if she was in the spirit of Christ, like he was, then she was the daughter of God, and he was her brother.

No doubt floored by this pronouncement, the vicar reported to the Lord Warden that Brooke had denied the Queen's supremacy over the Church of England (a treasonable offence). The Lord Warden then wrote in some concern to the magistrates—was Brooke not sound in his senses, or was there some other explanation?

The mayor and jurats hastened to reassure the Lord Warden that Brooke was no threat, and had indeed taken the oath of supremacy (after reading it carefully) in their presence. They continue (note the surprising phrase which I have italicised):

knowing of our own knowledge that Brooke is rather over precise in religion, having read more than he understandeth ... and ... having often found fault with Master Vicar his kind of teaching, wherein is small or no instruction *(which opinion in Brooke we condemn not)*, Master Vicar doth greatly envy [hates] the poor man ....
[with regard to attendance at church Brook says that]
he refuseth not to come to the church, but doth very often repair thether, and yet sith he receiveth no instructions in the church for the good of his soul, he doth sometimes absent himself from church and employeth himself to read the scriptures of God at home, wherein he can better inform himself then Master Vicar can.

Now, if it please your Honour, we have thought it convenient to describe unto you the quality and estate of this Brooke. He is by profession a tailor, and of late could not read but by his industry; having obtained knowledge to read English, he hath waded therein farther than his capacity can reach unto, whereby he hath over gone his sense and consumed himself by following the letter of the scriptures contrary to the intent and meaning thereof, to the detriment of himself only.

This reponse to the Lord Warden was partly to prevent him from interfering with their authority. On their own territory, they took a radically different stance towards Brooke, who had said that the mayor (Thomas Hamon) had the *spirit of the devil* and the vicar was a *false prophet* (his comments about the Queen were not mentioned in this report in the town's Assembly books). He was severely punished for these *intolerable abuses and mutinous misdemeanors*—imprisonment was to be followed by standing in the iron collar in the market with a paper upon his head declaring his mutiny and error, and then to be severely whipped. *If this punishment will not suffice, further order shalbe taken.*

Brooke was only just rich enough to be taxed in 1595, but he was substantial enough for the magistrates to appoint a mediator to settle a dispute between him and somebody else a couple of years earlier.

* * *

The mayor and jurats might not want a papist vicar, but they were very protective towards the converted catholic, Thomas Fisher (mentioned in chapter 6)—or perhaps rather towards his father, the jurat of the same name, who appears to have been in danger of being bankrupted by his son's debts. The magistrates tried to help Thomas Fisher junior avoid paying a huge debt of £45 which a merchant from Sandwich (Thomas

Tompkins) had lent him a year earlier when they were both in Ostend (there was a bill of exchange to prove it). The magistrates failed to apprehend Fisher when requested in numerous letters from the magistrates of Sandwich, who then sent them a huge bill which included a 4s fine for *themselves* for not *giving judgment against the defendant, the proof sufficiently made*.

The Rye magistrates claimed that Fisher had refused to come to Rye because he would be pursued by other creditors, and that he had sent a note to the mayor's sergeant (Angel Shaw) saying that he dared not meet him for a drink, for fear that Angel would arrest him. They later admitted, however, in a letter to the Lord Warden, that Fisher had in fact been in Rye prison all the time, and they curiously claimed to have thought that the plaintiff expected *them* to pay the debt and fine. They requested that the Lord Warden try and get Tompkins to withdraw his suit. Thomas Tompkins was incidentally the witness who gave the curious evidence against Anne Taylor when in prison in Rye, which presented her as uncharacteristically jovial—maybe he had catholic leanings like the man to whom he leant money, Thomas Fisher.

* * *

So Thomas Hamon's faction was not papist, and not puritan. But he and his allies distanced themselves more clearly from the hotter sort of godly inhabitants than members of the merchant faction had done for at least the previous couple of decades. One reason would have been a more relaxed international situation. An immense sigh of relief followed the dispersal of the Spanish Armada sent to invade England in 1588, even if the weather could take much of the credit for it (Rye had contributed a ship to England's defence, and may have been involved in the last engagement, when fire-ships from Dover began the breakup of the Armada). God had not smiled on Philip II's catholic crusade—which was good publicity for the protestants. And the French had acquired an astute new King, Henri IV, when the line of catholic Valois kings failed—a protestant, even if he found it expedient to convert to Catholicism. Toleration for protestants would follow in 1598 (Edict of Nantes), by which time some of the French refugees in Rye had started returning to France.

With the threat of invasion and of catholic aggression now receding, the merchant faction could defy the godly with some impunity. I will suggest an additional explanation for their decline in godliness and accompanying change in behaviour in the essay at the end of this book.

Thomas Hamon may also have had a more personal reaction against godliness, reflected in Anne Taylor's account of his attitude to his first wife, Catherine Duron:

> He [Thomas Hamon] had misused his other wife [Catherine Duron] greatly, which she knew very well. ... this woman which he married last [Martha Tharpe], should set at meat with him, and his old wife should set in the kitchen and pick the bones that this woman left, and be glad of them, if she could get them.

- thus Anne Taylor's view (according to Susan) of Hamon's relationships with his two wives (or what the relationships would have been like had he been married to both at the same time!). Perhaps Thomas Hamon's rejection of Catherine was not just something personal, but also a rejection of the godly fervour that probably characterised her, as well as her protestant compatriots. Hamon may thus have had religious reasons for refusing to support Catherine's son Simon, which tallies with Anne's statement that *he did never any man good but such as was of his Religion.*

One tell-tale characteristic of the late-16th century 'puritan' was their opposition to plays, music and festivity in general, as reflected in the accusation to which mayor Richard Cockram objected in 1610 (see above page 186). Patrick Collinson even called this period the *second* English Reformation, because of the suddenness and violence of the reaction amongst godly people against drama and festivity. Yet the merchant faction were *more* willing to have plays enacted in the town during the 1590s than earlier—which suggests that they were relaxing their adherence to godliness.

Many companies of entertainers had visited the town during the heyday of Merry England, at the end of the 15th and start of the 16th centuries. Some might just consist of a bearward and his bear (about once a year), others a company of actors, or perhaps some morris dancers. Usually they belonged to somebody or somewhere—either the servants of noblemen in their liveries, or actors from a particular town, who came to cry the banns for the town's annual play—giving a taster, in the hope that

The Story

people would come and watch it in their home town. One historian has remarked of these town (and village) productions that *it is remarkable that so few people could have produced so much drama.*

Rye had its own play of the Resurrection, which it put on at Easter, and for which the corporation paid the expenses of God's coat (in New Romney's play, this required 6 white sheepskins) and some plates. There is also mention of a stage. That is unfortunately all we know about it, except that the Rye players cried their banns in Lydd, New Romney and Sandwich, and visited those towns on other occasions.

At the little town of New Romney, there were not enough male inhabitants to take all the parts in their own play (seven stages were set up for the performance in 1555), so actors came from surrounding towns and villages—and a watch had to be set to protect property in the town of Lydd on playday, because everyone had left to see the play. New Romney was the administrative centre of the Cinque Ports, which presumably explains why it was chosen as the venue for these huge productions (at which nearly £30 was collected on 3 playdays in 1555). A Rye minstrel was thanked for contributing to the performance in New Romney in 1555.

No sooner had the number of visits by players to Rye peaked, than a decline set in—from about the 1520s (see chart overleaf). It reaches its nadir in the years when the corporation was notably godly, between 1560 and 1585. But from the later 1580s there is a distinct upward blip, when the merchant faction dominate the magistracy—the figures are not very large, but they regain about the level of the 1550s.

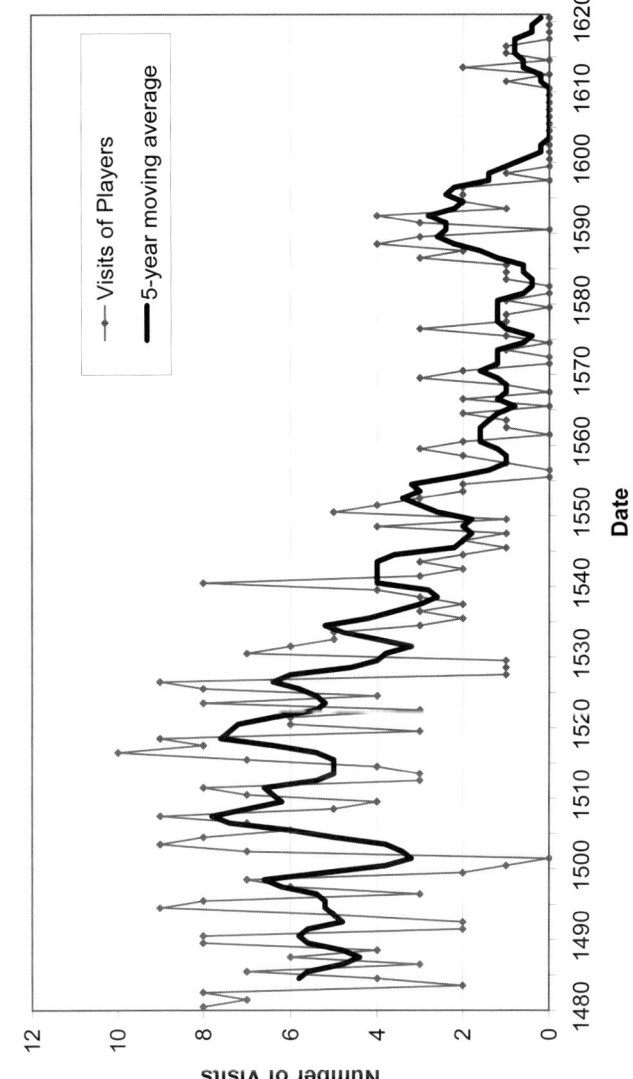

Source: Cameron Louis, *Records of Early English Drama: Sussex*, pp. 44-167.

The Story

The figures decline to zero again afterwards, although the merchant faction was still dominant, but this may have a different explanation. These numbers relate to payments to the players by the corporation, and it may have been thought more appropriate that the mayor should pay for the players himself when the corporation was bankrupt. What had often happened previously was that the mayor would pay the players initially when they performed before him and his brethren in his house, reclaiming the money later from the corporation. A performance for the inhabitants would follow—perhaps in a local inn—after the performance in the mayor's house.

The gradual rejection of drama in Rye thus started early—from before the Reformation—and was clearly associated with godliness. What is also evident is that these puritans were no ignorant philistines. They were rejecting on principle a flourishing festive culture which had involved most of the community.

* * *

It was in 1597—at the unpromising end of the blip (on the graph)—that William Shakespeare's company (the Lord Chamberlain's men) arrived in Rye, travelling the circuit around south-eastern England usually taken by the players of noblemen. Not all the Lord Chamberlain's men may have come—they could have been represented by a couple of players, performing a few songs and a jig for the populace of Rye. But they were paid the usual fee for actors, which was generally more than for musicians. It is also likely that the whole company came, riding with their props and costumes, because the theatres in London were closed. This was not for the usual reason of a summer outbreak of plague—but because of a furious reaction by the government to the production of a satirical play entitled *Isle of Dogs*—part-written by the young Ben Jonson (sadly, but not surprisingly, this play has not survived). Jonson and some players had consequently been imprisoned for three months—a rude introduction to the limits of government toleration. It was his first play.

If the company did perform a play, and if it was one by Shakespeare, which ones might they have offered? Shakespeare certainly wrote about subjects relevant to the town at the time. Only a year or so before he had written *A Midsummer Night's Dream*—but surely they would not have offered a comedy about *fairies* in godly Rye! Of the history plays, *Henry V* would have resonated with the town's experience of warfare with the

French, and of ferrying soldiers over the Chanel to fight at Agincourt—but this play had probably not been written yet.

Romeo and Juliet would have struck a chord in faction-torn Rye (though the play is unlikely to have been offered, at least because of its popery). Similar, and yet not—there were no family dynasties in Rye to compare with the Montagus and Capulets (and dynasties were also uncommon in other towns of the period). Powerful families were part and parcel of the honour of the gentry, but in a small community they could spell domination and disorder. The Rye factions were generally much more fluid.

The same surnames resurfaced amongst the jurats occasionally over the decades, but rarely would individual jurats who did share a surname be father and son. Of the jurats who held office in the second half of the 16th century (58), 6 were the sons of jurats. Two of these were the sons of John Fletcher—an extremely successful fisherman who was employed frequently as an intelligencer by Henry VIII in his French wars, and a very domineering man. Mortality rates were of course high in malaria-infested Rye, but nevertheless over half the jurats who left wills had sons living when they died (although some were young). So when Anne's father Robert Bennett was causing mayhem in the 1570s, I think it unlikely that he had ambitions to be made a jurat like his father had been.

Jurats were more often connected through marriage than father to son. In this period, 5 married the widows of other jurats, 4 married daughters, and about 2 married sisters (those who married more than one such have only been counted once). There were probably more, since it can be difficult when tracing relationships through women to negotiate the many remarriages. When the husband was an outsider, such a marriage enhanced his candidacy for office—as in the case of Thomas Higgons, who had been appointed by the government to supervise the customs house; he married the daughter of a jurat 9 years before being made a jurat himself, and later married Martha Tharpe/Hamon.

These ties through women could be seen as a more fluid connection than the hard-wiring of ties between father and son. How much more conducive to the peacefulness of the community to encourage links between families through marriage, than to emphasise patrilineal links which made families more exclusive! But there was a tension here between the ambitions of successful merchants like Thomas Hamon—whose concern to bear a son was no doubt bound up with a wish to found a family that would inherit his wealth and power—and the best interests of the community (he makes provision in his will in case his wife is with child). Family honour was likely to fan the flames of factionalism—the inhabitants of Rye may well have taken this for granted, and knew that marriage—as exemplified in Romeo and Juliet—could heal the antagonisms of faction (even if such marriages were generally within an individual faction).

* * *

I have been arguing in this chapter that the widening economic gap between the two factions shown in chapters 10 and 11 was mirrored by a polarisation in religious outlook. It is easier to point out the signs of godliness than a rejection of it, but there are suggestions that the merchant faction were easing away from godliness. Subsequent events may well have caused them to question whether this had been wise.

It is at last time to return to the witchcraft case, and the identities of the accusers. In the early years of the new century a series of disasters seemed to target—curiously—the richer members of the Rye bench, perhaps climaxing in 1606-7. The first disaster was the bankruptcy of the leader of the merchant faction, Robert Carpenter, in 1601, followed by his death a few years later, in 1606. Carpenter seems to have been not only powerful, but well-respected—even by his enemies. Frequently asked to be an overseer of inhabitants' wills (even by members of the opposing faction), he was not involved in the general mud-slinging that occurred during the Star Chamber cases relating to the 'riot' in the late '70s, even though he was very much part of the faction-fighting. He was not a target for accusations of sexual immorality—or at least lascivious behaviour—that were thrown at his fellow-faction member (and leader at this time) Henry Gaymer (*reputed to be a very incontinent liver with divers and sundry women, or at least brought many honest women into a slanderous report*). Sexual immorality was more often attributed to members of the merchant than the artisan faction—as one might expect—but not to Robert Carpenter.

Another prominent member of the merchant faction to be undone around 1606 was the jurat Thomas Fisher. Presumably as a result of his son's conviction for being a papist, his taxed wealth declined precipitately from £150 in 1595 to £6 in 1610 (in 1598 it had been £100). Considered rationally, this was his son's fault—but members of the merchant faction may have questioned what had caused his son to act in this way.

And what about the other events that occurred about the same time? Stephen Harrison drowned in 1605, soon after being made a jurat—Anne Taylor considered this godly retribution for his ostentatious clothes and behaviour (Thomas Fisher junior was also seen as a swaggerer). Harrison had been linked with the merchant faction back in the 1570s—when he was one of John Rolfe's witnesses in the Star Chamber case.

And of course there was the death of Thomas Hamon in 1607—at the height of his wealth and success, MP and frequently mayor of Rye, with a new wife and every hope of fathering an heir. Then the new mayor, Thomas Higgons, died 14 months after marrying the widow of Thomas Hamon, and the question was raised whether he was bewitched.

This cluster of events was surely enough to kindle paranoia. But as well as specific disasters, there was a general decline in the wealth of the rich in the early years of the seventeenth century. All those who were taxed on £100 or over (the 'rich') in 1596, and were also taxed in 1610, halved in taxed wealth, on average (mean), in these 15 years (if you exclude the extreme case of Thomas Fisher, the average decline is 49%; if you include him, the figure is 54%). The port's decline had finally hit the rich—the wars on the continent in the last decade of the 16th century were presumably a major factor.

Fate was too simple an explanation for these disasters. If one did not want to see it as God's punishment for evil living, then who more likely to be responsible than a sharp-tongued cunning woman from the artisan faction? One who had recently (1603) made an extraordinarily advantageous marriage to a godly gentleman (how had she managed that?), a man who as transpired during the protracted witchcraft case—was much too adept at pulling strings amongst the Kentish gentry. And did he, for his part, expect his marriage to advance his interests in the town?

* * *

There are more specific connections between the merchant faction and the victims and accusers in the witchcraft case. In particular, Robert Carpenter's daughter gave evidence against Anne Taylor and her mother. She said that Anne had often asked her to go to her house and talk with her (they were about the same age), and when she told her father about this

> he did admonish and warn [her] not to meddle … in any manner of wise with [her] … He said she was a bad person.

It is interesting, incidentally, that Anne was apparently so ready to socialise with someone whom she probably considered ungodly—Margery Convers was another such.

Elizabeth Carpenter/Bishop also told of a serious incident involving the Whitfields, who were landed gentry from Tenterden, and lived next door to the Taylors for a time.

> At a certain time [I was] at the house of Master Taylor when there was a controversy between him and Master Whitfield about a certain gate. Mistress Taylor [spoke words] against … Master Whitfield, and [I] said unto her
> *"I marvel that you and Master Whitfield cannot agree togethers"*. And she answered [me] again
> *"Agree with him? I shall agree with him well enough! For I will torment him all the veins of his heart"*. And [I] asked her
> *"Which way?"* And [she] said that
> *She had sent a messenger unto Master Whitfield's house that should torment them in all the veins of their hearts.*

Torment them in all the veins of their hearts—an expression just like one quoted by Susan Swaffer, that *Master Mayor and his [brethern would]…repent it a[ll] …vaines in their hearts, that he wold not [let her] husband to pass away his billets.* The gate may have been the subject of an action for trespass brought by George Taylor against Whitfield in 1604.

Clement Whitfield survived this, but his wife did not:

> my wife when she lay sick [did say] that Goody Bennett and her daughter Annis had bewitched her, and I could not persuade her to the contrary … for many times she did awake me suddenly in my sleep, and said to me,
> *"Look, husband, where Anne Bennett stands at my beds head, and she hath set me my time how long I shall live."*

He said in this letter to the magistrates that Anne Taylor and her mother *could no sooner see any of my children, but they did enquire in what manner my wife did fare*; they said they *knew her disease, and that it would cost her her life*, and that she would not live past Christmas. She died the day before Twelfth Night, 1605, after an illness lasting a year and a half. Unlike his wife, it would seem that Clement was not convinced that witchcraft was to blame, and did not give evidence. But he did leave Rye shortly afterwards.

This incident might seem unrelated to wider conflicts in Rye since Whitfield was such a short-term inhabitant. But his sister Margaret had married a very prominent member of the merchant faction back in the

'70s—George Raynolds, whose will provoked the riot between the factions in 1577 (see above p. 92).

Another witness who was Robert Carpenter's daughter-in-law just complained that Widow Bennett's cure for the toothache did not work.

These accusations against Anne and her mother by members of the merchant faction do not, it is true, refer to the disasters that I have mentioned as afflicting them at this time. But the crux of the accusation against Anne Taylor—that she had bewitched Thomas Hamon to death—had similarly not been made the subject of an indictment until two years after the magistrates first started collecting evidence. The interrogators did not even question the women about his death until two months after the first examination was recorded (and Susan did not mention it until they did question her), by which time over 13 thousand words of evidence had been collected.

Did they not mention the disasters because there was a vague sense of threat, but these had not precisely formulated? Or did they not want to spell the issues out—for one thing, it attributed considerable power to this woman, and corresponding weakness to those who had been struck down. It may also have highlighted their susceptibility in another way—if God allowed them to be thus destroyed, was it a consequence of their own sins? This might have been of concern not only to the evil livers, but also to those who perhaps felt blamed by others in the town for taking advantage when the corporation was deeply in debt—including the widow of Thomas Hamon because he had bought the storehouse, Stephen Harrison had bought the building called the *Vine*, and Thomas Fisher had bought the ordnance and gunpowder from the *Hercules*. The sufferings of the rest of the inhabitants had thus caught up with the rich. Was God also punishing them for becoming less godly, and distancing themselves from the bulk of the 'honester sort' of inhabitants?

One actor in this drama whose motivation I have not been able to uncover, although he was involved at every stage of it—a shadowy figure, writing everything down—is the town clerk, Robert Convers. His wife made one of the most serious accusations against Anne—of killing her maidservant—and he made notes in the evidence indicating which side he was on. He was not well off—taxed on only £20 in 1596, his rating had nevertheless increased to £30 by 1610.

* * *

The Story

The merchant faction had held sway over the magistracy and the town for the previous 25 years, but the various disasters that afflicted them resulted in the eclipse of their domination (at least for a few years). Just two months after Anne Taylor's acquittal, the one clearly 'puritan' jurat—Richard Cockram—was elected mayor, and kept the role for two terms (see above page 186). There was some vociferous opposition—from Matthew Young, whom we have already met as foreman of the jury at the first witchcraft trial (which Anne had avoided by fleeing into Kent), and as representative of the corporation in dealing with the Earl of Northampton in London about the magistrates' right to try the case (see above pages 67 and 147-8). He was objecting to being chosen chamberlain yet again, and unusually his complaints are recorded in some detail:

> Master Convers and Master Mayor were never friends till now, and for to do [me] a mischief he [Convers] procured him to be maior, for [I] looked to be a jurat long before this time, and to have been two jurats.

Never friends till now—a massive understatement!

What the mayor and jurats particularly objected to in Young's outburst was being called *fools and sots*—this was what was quoted in the Assembly Books. Perhaps it was another instance of the artisan faction being mocked as weak—the substantial members of the merchant faction on the bench having been struck down. *They are all fools, and two men do rule the whole town viz. Angel Shaw [mayor's sergeant] and Master Convers.* More intriguingly: *That one man had ruled as mayor this seven years and seven years*, by which he presumably meant Thomas Hamon, who had been mayor for an unprecedented 6 terms within a 12-year period. The implication of these comments is that the bench should be a band of equals, not some weak hangers-on dominated but one or two powerful individuals.

Matthew Young was disfranchised for his *great abuses and scandalous speeches*. In the long term his political career was not greatly affected by this, however, for he was re-enfranchised 4 months later (when he apologised), made a jurat 2 years after that, and was mayor 2 years after that.

The overall effect of Young's abuse was not to vilify a particular person, like most instances of verbal abuse against those in authority, but to undermine the authority of the whole bench, and to expose as a fiction their attempts to paper over the cracks in relations between them. The mayor and jurats wanted to be seen as a cohesive oligarchy, united in their strong control over those below, and Young's words exposed the fissures that went through the town from top to bottom. And encouraged dissidents to manipulate the antagonisms between them.

The new dispensation brought George Taylor into the commonalty, in August 1612, and his fee of 40s was halved in consideration of *the good service they expect the said George will hereafter do to this corporation*. Shortly after this he was employed to represent the town—with the vicar, John Bracegirdle—in negotiations about the state of the harbour, with the Commission of Sewers. It was noted in the assembly books that their work was *well liked of*. George's name often appears at this period in the list of attendees at the fortnightly assemblies—his status indicated by his position in the list, at the top, below Thomas Ensing, the most junior jurat. But then the following year (1613) his appearances become more infrequent, and he is sometimes fined for non-appearance.

Perhaps the other faction were making a comeback by this time, because Matthew Young was mayor, and the following year Martha Hamon/Higgons' latest husband succeeded him—Mark Thomas, who had paid the substantial sum of 50s for his freedom in 1609, and was chosen jurat the following December. The same day, seemingly, as he married Martha—thus bolstering his right to have a place on the bench.

* * *

And what about Susan Swaffer? She did better than Thomas Fisher junior, the catholic convert, who died in Rye prison in 1614. In spite of having been incarcerated in the basement of the prison since late 1607, and even having had a baby the following year, she was still alive in 1610. The magistrates could in principle have had her hanged after the baby was born—but I suspect that they were not really interested in doing so even before the balance of power shifted away from the merchant faction on the bench, and it would anyway not have been politic after the trouble over Anne Taylor's trial. When the King issued a general pardon in 1610, the magistrates asked their counsel whether her case was covered by it. John Shurley answered: *I think it is pardoned by the general pardon* and James Thurbarne agreed: *I am of Master Serjeant Shurley's opinion*. So at long last she as well as Anne Taylor was a free woman.

That is not the last mention of her. She was really too poor to appear in records other than the parish register, or in the context of crime or poverty, and so it is that we find her being interrogated about the possible theft of some woad in 1612. Not her theft, mind you—a fisherman and his wife, John and Bridget Hounsell, said that they were *acutting of [birch to make] brooms in the wood*, when they found a sack of woad (she thought it was dung). It was in the Swaffers' house that some of the woad was sold by Bridget to a kersey maker from Bethersden. The woad, however, belonged to a local shipwright, who had apparently lost it. There is no reference to a punishment for any of them.

The Swaffers indeed carried on into the next generation—or perhaps I should now say Swapper, since this nickname had clearly stuck. In 1633 a Jane Swapper—undoubtedly their daughter—married a Richard Ratlyf. Perhaps this was the daughter—never named in the depositions—who let Roger into his house that memorable day when he thought the devil was within, and his wife nowhere to be found (see above page 54). There is no other specific reference to Susan's children—although they certainly had more than one—before little Agnes was born in 1608.

* * *

When George Taylor was ill back in 1607 (see page 117), his wife thought he had not long to live (as reported by Margery Convers), so it is possible that this was the reason he only made a brief appearance in corporation affairs. He survived, however, until 1628, when he died in Rye, without leaving a will. In the 1618 tax assessment, the family was represented by the stalwart Widow Bennett, whose wealth had declined to a mere £12. She died a year before George did, at the grand old age of 83.

> Mrs. Ann Taylour widdow was buried on the 25th day of August in the year 1644

Quite a wordy and respectful entry in the parish register (although its maintenance was not such a time-consuming job as it had been when the town was populous). Anne was 66 when she died, by which time the country had been racked by civil war for a couple of years. It was the King's men-of-war and royalist privateers that the seamen and merchants of Rye had now to fear most in the Channel.

The people of East Sussex were not, however, as severely affected by the war as those in some other areas. Both gentry and non-gentry were more or less of one mind that the King was not to be trusted over his attempts during the previous decade to rule and collect taxes without consulting Parliament, and over his church reforms, which smacked of popery. So the experience in Rye would not have been as bad as in West

Sussex, where opinions were divided, and the people had to suffer warfare, and more billetting of soldiers and taxation to pay for the war than those in the east of the county.

A company under the command of Captain Cockram (son of the puritan jurat) was sent from Rye to help quell the opposition in the west. Both religious fervency and pragmatic determination motivated some of the soldiers, as voiced in a letter from John Coulton (and others) at Arundel to his fellow baptist Samuel Jeake (and others) in Rye:

> I will either see King Charles at his parliament or my self in heaven. What have I fought for this 32 years but assurance? I bless God I have it more then ever I had. Oh that I could enjoy my wonted communion with you; but I cannot, I have given my self unto the Lord and cannot go back.

Anne was poor by this time—she had been taxed in 1634 on a mere £4 worth of goods—though she did still own some property (including the three houses in Rye inherited from her father). The kinsfolk to whom she left legacies were all leatherworkers and butchers, as her ancestors had been. It was as if her marriage to George had never been—as she said, *he will leave me as free as he found me*—there is no mention of him or his relatives in the will. She had not remarried, and had no surviving children.

A few months after Anne's death, her main accuser, Thomas Hamon's widow Martha, died—when Anne's wish that *the right heirs might have the land* was probably realised. Since Martha did not have any children by Thomas Hamon, his sister Margaret's family, the Cokers, should have inherited all his land after Martha's death, according to the terms of his will. Margaret Hamon/Coker had been poor when her brother died—at least, her husband (said to be *of Rye*) had been taxed on a mere 20s worth of goods in 1595 (and £2 in 1598). Hamon had left her some leasehold land (not his valuable marshlands) in his will (*she paying rent*), as well as 40 ewe lambs, 10 wether lambs and one ram. By 1618, however, the Cokers had become relatively rich—taxed on £150 worth of goods—and their son Henry was taxed on £3. So perhaps she had, eventually, inherited the land.

Martha's third husband Mark Thomas was, however, doing better—taxed on £200 of goods in 1618, he was the richest man in town.

Epilogue

Our protagonists are dead, but the factions lived on. One of the handful of Radford cousins to whom Anne Taylor made bequests—Joseph—was briefly mayor in the 1680s. Still in the leather trades, he was a sadler, and the rest of this faction at this period were mostly butchers and artisans. The recently-deceased leader of the faction, Thomas Crouch, had come from a line of butchers all with the same name, though he may not have been one himself (he was just referred to as *jurat*). Then there were the descendants of John Peadle, tailor, who was one of those who gave one of his sons a biblical name in the 1580s—Moses. These two were a glazier (poor) and tailor. There was also a carpenter. Exceptions were two mariners, the customs collector (Robert Hall), and a merchant (Lewis Gillart junior) whose father had been a member of the other faction, but had partly disowned him, which possibly had something to do with his defection. The other faction consisted mostly of merchants, and were generally wealthier by the 1680s than their opponents.

Butchers and artisans—much the same occupations as had characterised the artisan faction in the 16th century, except that this faction was no longer the godliest in town. The religious polarity of the two factions had in fact *reversed*, as if somebody had flicked a switch sometime during the past two decades of civil war and interregnum. The capitalist merchants were now the religious radicals—*dissenters*—most of whom attempted to run their own religious assemblies, refusing either to take communion with less godly souls or to attend Anglican church services. The godliness of the artisan faction had been overtaken by the sectarianism of the other.

The contrasting religious stances of the two groups is illustrated by, on the one hand, Anne Taylor's seemingly innocuous bequest of £1 for the town's minister, John Beaton, in 1644. She clearly had no quarrel with his ministry. On the other, the fury of a young firebrand from the dissenting faction named Samuel Jeake—at about the same date, when he was in his late teens—against this same minister for burying a papist with the words *dear sister*:

> What fellowship hath righteousness with unrighteousness? What communion hath light with darkness? What concord hath Christ with Belial?

His opposition to the baptising of children of *visible unbelievers* by the minister led inexorably to him setting up his own baptist congregation, which *laid by the baptism of all infants,* and only baptised *believers making profession of their faith.*

* * *

Dissenters had a strong presence in Rye, as in many other towns in this period, and were persecuted by the government for holding religious assemblies of more than 5 people, and for allowing nonconformist preaching. Their troubles in Rye were exacerbated by members of the loyalist (artisan) faction, who wrote to the secretary of state, Sir Leoline Jenkins, complaining about the behaviour of the dissenters. The loyalists were seemingly oblivious to the dangers of inviting interference by outsiders into Rye's local jurisdiction—no doubt also attracted by the prospect of receiving a proportion of the fines inflicted on the dissenters. The spirited independence that had characterised the artisan faction for over a century had vanished—they were now closely linked to the government (referring to themselves as *in the King's Interest,* and their opponents, simply, as *fanatics*). They would soon be labelled *Tories,* as national parties emerged towards the end of the century, and their dissenting opponents *Whigs.*

By the 1680s, conflicts between the factions had deteriorated, becoming so destructive on occasion that ordinary town government was made impossible. Interference by the national government was a contributing factor. Many town corporations were still dominated by republicans after the restoration of Charles II, and King and Parliament had wanted these purged—particularly since a large proportion of MPs were returned by boroughs. The Corporation Act of 1661 had put this into effect—several of the dissenting faction in Rye were disfranchised.

This set a bad precedent for future conflicts in Rye because each faction, when it assumed control of the magistracy, created (or restored) new freemen from their own followers, and ignored ones created/restored by their opponents. It was a no-holds-barred contest—the low point reached, perhaps, in 1682, when the leader of the dissenters took advantage of the then mayor, Thomas Crouch, being out of town, to break into the town hall, seize the mayoral insignia and corporation records, and change the locks. The damning judgment of Sir Leoline Jenkins was that

> The height of disaffection and contumacy that appears to be in the generality of Rye is the greatest scandal that I know of in the whole government

But the lawlessness was not just the fault of the inhabitants. The Privy Council and the court of King's Bench gave conflicting judgments on which faction's choice of mayor should be allowed. The King's Bench declared the original disenfranchising of some of the dissenters not to be within the terms of the Corporation Act. This judgment would have given the dissenters the majority of freemen, but subsequently another royal order was issued in favour of the loyalists, and the dissenters finally gave in.

* * *

The relationships amongst the dissenters, and their business dealings, are described in some detail in the diary of Samuel Jeake junior, son of the baptist preacher of the same name, whose religious radicalism was of a much quieter variety than his father's. Jeake was a merchant and money-lender, and his experience was so different from the merchants of a century earlier that I would just like to point out the contrast—noting in particular the extraordinary resilience of the dissenting merchants, who survived the swingeing fines that were inflicted on them, and the occasional necessity of fleeing to London to escape arrest.

Jeake was a middleman who bought various goods for resale to customers in the surrounding countryside, and constant vigilance was required to prevent defaults on payment by them. The most lucrative trade was in linen imported from France, and when war with France was imminent in 1678, he cast around desperately for alternative sources of income. He found a solution—lending money at interest and negotiating bills of exchange (the precursors of bank cheques), particularly for those customers with whom he traded. Much of his money-lending was secured on property or ships ('bottomry')—such mortgaging having been recently made feasible by legal changes introduced in the 1650s.

Jeake's trade virtually ceased in the mid-1680s as a result of persecution, but the accession of William and Mary promised an end to the latter

> Feb 13 1689 The Prince and Princess of Orange proclaimed King and Queen .... So that now through the merciful Providence of God, we were freed from the fears of Popery and Persecution

This was not an end to Jeake's troubles, however—the outbreak of war with France again brought the prospect of financial ruin. But again Jeake was saved by new financial projects—this time introduced by the government to pay for the war with France. He got caught up in the excitement of the Million Lottery on his visits to London, which sought to raise 1 million pounds for the war in return for annuities secured by parliamentary guarantee. From buying lottery tickets it was a short step to investing in the newly created Bank of England. Like the Lottery, such investment in the new National Debt was considered a patriotic act (at least by the Whigs) to help finance the war against Louis XIV of France—an absolutist monarch who promoted the return to the throne of England of his fellow catholic James II.

When in London, Jeake attended the weekly meetings at the Bank, which may not have been unusual behaviour for small investors. Then there were shares to buy in the East India Company, and other companies. By 1699 Jeake was adept at trading in stock, and a fully-fledged participant in the Financial Revolution.

Jeake's trading success was no longer tied up with the fortunes of Rye—even before he moved into financial schemes, he sometimes avoided trading through the port by using Hastings, or even importing goods directly from France to Falmouth. Unlike the merchants of the 16th century, he was able to avoid the disaster of war on the continent by investing in the government's scheme for paying for that war (although the investment may not have fully compensated for the loss of overseas trade).

The merchants were now part of a national trading network, and could leave the butchers and artisans of Rye to their own concerns—Jeake paid £60 to be excused from future office in the town (with other conditions) in 1694. They were somewhat remote from the community of Rye, being both separatist in religion and separatist in their commercial dealings (on the whole), and I doubt that any suspicions of witchcraft practised by members of the other faction would have occurred to them. Samuel Jeake did have a lively interest in astrology, but pursued this in a remarkably systematic and even scientific manner—for one example of his approach, see page 16 above. He was not completely immune to the activities of spirits, however, as is evident from his account of a strange experience when staying with a friend, concerning some bedstaffs that had moved around the room in a *somewhat strange* manner (bedstaffs were stuck in the bedframe to hold the bedding in place):

The Story

I cannot yet resolve it into any other Cause, than the ridiculous and trifling actions of some of the meanest rank among the Infernal Spirits.

* * *

By the turn of the 18th century, the Whigs were consolidating their control of the magistracy, and radical fervour died down in Rye. Paul Monod has described how two families emerged to dominate the town—the Lambs and the Grebells (the latter an old Rye family, into which the Lambs had married). They maintained their dominance for the next century, interrupted only by challenges in the middle years which may have been set in train by the murder of one of the leaders of the oligarchy. This case harks back in its abnormality to the 1607 witchcraft case.

One night in Rye churchyard in 1743, a butcher named John Breads stabbed to death Allan Grebell (a jurat), mistaking him for the mayor, James Lamb (his brother-in-law). Although a murder trial had not been held in the town for the previous century (major crimes usually being referred to the Assize courts by this period), Lamb resolved to hold the trial there, in spite of attempts by the Lord Chancellor and one of the MPs to dissuade him. As in the witchcraft case, the mayor was both judge (with some of the jurats) and prosecutor (or at least, none other was mentioned).

Although Breads appears to have pleaded insanity, he was not only sentenced to death, but to be hanged in a cage on the salts outside the Strandgate. This method of displaying a criminal's decomposing body as a warning to others was a punishment usually reserved for the most notorious criminals.

Unlike the witchcraft case, the government did not intervene to stop the trial—presumably they thought that a show of strength, opposing the privileges of the Cinque Ports, was not required, since these days the Rye sessions court usually dealt with nothing more serious than any other urban court. And anyway the case was not flimsy as the witchcraft case had been. But no further hangings for homicide were seen in Rye.

Whether or not Breads' action was political, the removal of Allan Grebell, with his long-standing Rye roots, weakened the oligarchy. A rival faction—including many old Tories—asserted itself not long after, and opposed the oligarchy and their cosy corruption. Of particular concern was the £7860 which had been spent over three decades on harbour construction, with virtually nothing to show for it except profits for the oligarchs who had provided the loans and supplies for the works.

Thomas Lamb wrote to one of the Rye MPs intimating that at the impending parliamentary election they could no longer assure the MP's patron, the Duke of Newcastle, of having the borough in his pocket, unless something was done about the leader of the rival faction (Edwin Wardroper). An ally phrased their predicament rather differently, however, in a letter to the Duke:

> My Self and friends had Rather die fighting than be any Longer Meanly trampled upon. He [Wardroper] nor no man Living shall Lead me in Triumph Captive to the Conqueror till I have done my Utmost to Resist

The Duke of Newcastle sorted the problem out by dismissing Wardroper from his post in the customs service, and possibly by paying the corporation's debts of nearly £1000. The oligarchy were re-instated in full control. *No human power can shake* the influence of the Lamb family, reported an electoral agent who visited Rye in 1790. The other faction had been snuffed out, and there was to be no serious challenge to the Lamb oligarchy until the 1820s.

13 The Wider Context

This case was a one-off—there is nothing quite like it in the annals of English witchcraft. In less than a year, it had blown up from some rumours about fairies and buried treasure, to the making of a formal accusation of witchcraft. Most cases took decades to crystallize from suspicion to formal accusation. And if this prosecution had been initiated a couple of decades later, the accused women would have been in their 50s—a more typical age for people to be formally accused of witchcraft. Younger women in Germany—according to David Sabean—were often suspected of witchcraft, but were less likely to be accused for fear of repercussions. It was only when such women had become, perhaps, widowed and frail that their neighbours dared to make formal accusations against them. In Rye, some of the accusers were magistrates, so were less likely to be intimidated than their neighbours.

The political aspects of this case may also be unusual, although better documentation for other cases might very well modify this view—local politics (at least at the village level) does not generally reach the official record. Political factionalism in New England has certainly been linked by historians to witchcraft cases, and documentation there is better than in old England.

If it is unlike other English cases, neither does this case seem much like those continental trials where women (usually) were accused of flying to a witches' sabbath and engaging in devil worship. But not all European trials involved this type of accusation. There was considerable geographic variation in both the type and incidence of prosecutions in the epidemic of witch-hunting of the 16th and 17th centuries—which ranged from Scandinavia to Sicily, and from Russia to the European colonies in North America. Exploring the geography of witchcraft in fact reveals a striking pattern—as demonstrated by Brian Levack. When seen in this context, the Rye case seems less like an oddity, and similar to many other cases. The geographic pattern also suggests something about the dynamics of witch-hunting.

* * *

Levack's findings concern not so much why the extraordinary European witch-hunt happened at all, as why it was so extreme in some places, and relatively mild in others. There were dramatic contrasts in the intensity of prosecutions across Europe and white America. The total is very difficult to estimate, but may have been in the region of 90 thousand (maximum), with about half of these people living in the many, mostly small, states that made up the Holy Roman Empire, which was slightly larger than modern Germany. At the other extreme, to take a few examples, were the British Isles, with probably no more than 5 thousand prosecutions, and Finland, with about 700; in the English and Spanish colonies in America—other than New England—prosecution rates were very low.

The numbers of the accused who were executed also varied considerably—for example, 90% were executed in the Pays de Vaud, 38% in Norway and between a quarter and a half in England (of those whose fates were known). Overall, about half the people tried for witchcraft in Europe may have been executed—although this estimate does not include cases in German and Polish regions, where rates were probably higher.

The region where the prosecution rate was highest—the Holy Roman Empire—was notable for the lack of central political control over its myriad political units. It is this issue, together with the degree to which the legal system was centrally organised, that seems to be crucial in providing a general explanation for the geography of witchcraft. There was no hierarchy of courts in the Holy Roman Empire. Local authorities were certainly required to ask the universities for advice in trying witchcraft cases, but this procedure only exacerbated the problems, because universities were developing theories about witchcraft as devil worship and heresy which only inflamed local hysteria. The original accusers were mostly concerned about the harm which they believed had been inflicted by the supposed witch on the victims (*maleficia*)—as elsewhere in Europe—but when these ideas were leavened with ideas about devil-worship and heresy, they could prove a lethal mixture (elsewhere, it was often other types of officials who added the ingredient of devil-worship).

In addition, torture was often used to extract confessions and get the accused to name accomplices. Then the usual grimly repetitive narratives would be uttered, and the local elite would be confirmed in their worst fears. The accused—usually a woman—would tell how she had met a dark man when she was in a low state—perhaps ill and poor—and he had offered her money in return for sex. His nature was cold, and the money never materialised, but by this act of carnal copulation she renounced her baptism and sealed a pact with the devil. She flew to witches' sabbaths where they danced and feasted and worshipped the devil, sometimes doing orgiastic and blasphemous acts, which might include the killing and eating of babies. In addition, the devil required that they commit *maleficia*. There were some variations in the stories, but all had the same central theme of worship of the devil and renunciation of christianity.

Different regions of the Holy Roman Empire had varying prosecution rates which can also be related to Levack's theory. The worst area was south-western Germany, where several city states and other small territories were almost completely independent of all outside political and ecclesiatical control—this situation gave magistrates great freedom in their handling of witchcraft cases. Rates of prosecution were much lower in north-eastern Germany, where political units were much larger and less fragmented.

Another region in which central control was exceptionally weak was Poland, where some of the most intense witch-hunting occurred. Cases were generally tried in municipal courts, even though they were supposed to be tried in ecclesiastical courts, and the *municipal courts ... repeatedly violated all of the procedural rules that were designed to protect the accused*.

At the other extreme, in England, most cases of witchcraft and other felonies were tried by the King's justices, and not in local jurisdictions—other than, of course, in the Cinque Ports and a few other boroughs. And the relatively centralised legal system (by comparison with some other places) was reinforced by a rapidly centralising state, with a strong monarchy. An exception was during the Civil War, when Assize judges preferred to stay at Westminster, far from the fighting, and local justices and noblemen presided over trials.

In France the legal system was still more hierarchical than in England, with a regular system of appeals from local courts to provincial parlements, and thence to the parlement of Paris, and the latter, at least, provided a general dampener on the enthusiasm of prosecutors. But along the frontiers of the kingdom, in areas which were resistant to the efforts of the French monarchy to establish a centralised state, and where local courts operated with greater independence than elsewhere, some serious witch-hunting took place—along the north and east borders, Languedoc, the south-west, and Normandy. Overall, however, the prosecution rates were only slightly higher than those in England.

* * *

The right to use torture was an important factor in exacerbating witch panics, yet not as important as one might think. It was allowed in Scandinavia, but used sparingly, and prosecution rates were about twice those in England. The governments there tried hard to put a curb on witch-hunting, and to a great extent succeeded (all cases in Denmark had to be referred to the central courts after 1576).

By contrast, in Scotland torture was no more allowed than in England (without the permission of the Privy Council), but it was used extensively—usually in the form of sleep deprivation, which did not involve the use of identifiable instruments of torture. King James authorised torture in the case in which he thought he was a victim, but this did not apply to other cases. Local magistrates in Scotland were usually granted specific commissions to try witchcraft cases without any supervision, although some cases were heard before central judges in Edinburgh or on circuit. Execution rates varied markedly between these different types of courts—fully 91% of those tried by local magistrates were executed (of those where the outcome was known), with 57% for the Justiciary Court and only 16% for the Circuit courts (but these were only late 17th century). Overall, the proportion of witches executed in Scotland relative to the size of the population may have been about 12 times that in England. It saw one of the major witch-hunts in Europe.

Torture was permitted but rarely employed in Italy and Spain, which came under the jurisdiction of their respective Inquisitions. One might expect that the courts of the Inquisition would treat witchcraft severely—as a heresy—but it was in fact considered a very minor matter in both countries, and there were probably no more than 300 executions in the whole of this region. Moreover, these courts had strict procedural rules at this period. All over Europe, indeed, ecclesiastical courts generally put a brake on witch-hunting, because they had procedural controls, a hierarchy of courts, and the judges probably had less involvement in local conflicts. Increasingly, however, secular courts were taking over the jurisdiction of witchcraft cases from ecclesiastical courts.

* * *

The geographic pattern of witch trials is thus remarkably consistent—the most serious witch panics occurred in areas where the trials were conducted in local courts. Other factors may have been important in specific places, but none have such general application as this one—more examples could be cited from Levack's study. The town of Rye is thus only one example—even if an extremely small one—of a relatively autonomous jurisdiction on a country's borders where fears of witchcraft blew up suddenly and then multiplied. The town clerk was still listing new potential witnesses right up to the last trial, and Thomas Higgons was added to the possible victims of witchcraft. The kinds of irregularities that had been taking place in Rye were also by no means uncommon in the European context. As in Rye, members of political factions in some German towns used charges of witchcraft against their rivals' wives to advance their own political careers.

* * *

The main difference between Rye and the German towns was the absence of the pact-with-the-devil narrative—and indeed this has been presented as a major contrast between English and continental witchcraft in general. It has been argued that ideas about diabolism did not, as it were, cross the channel. Were these two 'types' of witchcraft, therefore, different phenomena?

The issue is complicated by the fact that judges in some countries—where witchcraft was defined as heresy—were expected to get a confession of a pact with the devil from the accused before they could obtain a conviction, whether or not *maleficia* had been alleged. But did they or the accusers believe in it? Disentangling the beliefs and motivations of the various participants in trials is notoriously difficult. One thing is generally agreed—that accusers everywhere were mainly concerned about the harm that they believed had been done to the victims by supernatural means (*maleficia*), whether or not they *also* believed that the accused had made a pact with the devil.

Another point which can, I think, be lifted clear of the tangle of issues is that there was no clear distinction between regions where trials involved diabolism, and other regions where they did not. There was usually a mixture of the two in any particular region. For example, in south-west Germany, where the larger trials focused on diabolism, there were also smaller trials that simply concerned *maleficia*.

At the other extreme, English trials were almost entirely devoid of diabolism, yet diabolism cropped up in New England—whose white population of course originated from England—but was not found in witch trials in English colonies further south. Diabolism was also present in witchtrials during the lawlessness of the English Civil War (though partly instigated by the self-styled 'witch-finder general', Matthew

Hopkins). Full-blown diabolism was rife in Scotland, where there was admittedly influence from Denmark through the King's wife—but attributing the character of essentially local scares to her influence surely gives it undue weight. In Spain, most cases were very minor—only involving *maleficia*—but there was a large Basque witch hunt in 1610 (near the French border) which involved the full witches' sabbath.

So there appears to have been a scattering of trials involving diabolism in areas where these beliefs were not otherwise prevalent— when, perhaps, a local community became convulsed by a witchcraft panic, and the fantasies became elaborated. Norman Cohn has shown that such nightmare fantasies have existed in Europe for over a thousand years, being applied to different out-groups on different occasions. The early Christians were accused by Romans of incestuous orgies and eating of children, and medieval heretics were accused of incestuous orgies and devil-worship—all of which were elements in the witchcraft fantasies of our period. I therefore think that it is inappropriate to say that in *this* area people knew about and believed in diabolism, and in *that* area they did not—these countries were all part of Christendom. When the paranoia took over, people did not have far to look to find fantasies that suited it (using the word *paranoia* in a very loose sense).

Perhaps we should be looking not only at how such ideas are transmitted, but also at the soil in which they flourish or die—the socio-economic context. To take a modern example, one area of southern Africa has seen the proliferation—since the 1960s—of beliefs in obscene and money-devouring familiars. These ideas were adopted from a neighbouring people, while the traditional animal familiars have played a much smaller role in modern witchcraft fears. These more recent fantasies have been shown by anthropologists to relate to the strains of wage labour and labour migration that, under apartheid, replaced the traditional subsistence agriculture. So it can be surmised that these people adopted these new beliefs because they reflected current concerns better than traditional beliefs. And when the new Christian Churches under black leadership identified witches with Satan, this was also woven into traditional non-christian beliefs—witches became identified with evil, where they had previously been more ambivalent. The endemic witch-killings still continue in the region.

* * *

The Story

I keep referring to paranoia—is this relevant to the Rye case, or indeed to others which involved political rivalry? Perhaps the accusers were utterly cynical—using a witchcraft accusation as a strategy to remove opponents. Even in this scenario, however, the strategy would only work politically if others considered the accusation to be believable. But the issue does not have to be cynicism or belief—surely the worst scenario is when those who are trying to undo their rivals are also fired by paranoid inclinations. And it bears repeating that the Rye case blew up very suddenly—if the process had carried on, rather than being stifled by outsiders, perhaps accusations might have spread further. If Anne and Susan had been hanged, would this have satisfied the accusers and silenced their opponents—or would it have further enflamed social conflicts in the town? In France peaks of official persecution of witches, far from pacifying village feeling, generated higher numbers of illegal killings.

* * *

Rye could thus be seen as one of many local communities convulsed by witch hunts in early-modern Europe, even if we only see the early stages of the process—when suspicions were still crystallizing—before it was interrupted by outsiders (this in itself is interesting, because the case reached the record book while suspicions were still fluid). Not very much is known about criminal justice in other self-governing communities in England, though a woman was executed for witchcraft in Norwich in 1588, five in Harwich in 1601, and three hanged at Faversham during the Civil War (the last two towns were very small).

The fundamental question remains—why were these communities convulsed in this way, and why was witchcraft central to these conflicts? In spite of the massive historical literature devoted to early-modern witchcraft in recent years, there is little agreement amongst historians on this question. How can we get anywhere near understanding a particular case, if the broader causes of this extraordinary social seizure are little understood?

This is no place to try and encompass this huge topic, but I would like to put forward a couple of general points, concerning the socio-economic context rather than the witch-hunt itself. Greater understanding can be achieved, I believe, if we spread our net even wider—outside the confines of early-modern Christendom.

Belief in witchcraft—in the narrow sense of the *power to harm others by supernatural means*—is found the world over, more or less, in developing societies: *from Africa to the South Seas, and from Asia to America*. The exception being nomadic peoples, who can *get away from one another when conflicts arise,* and so it is less essential to live in *amity and co-operation.* Perhaps witchcraft should not therefore be thought of as 'belonging' to any particular religion (nor as a pre-christian survival), but simply as a gut reaction to misfortune in certain circumstances. To focus only on issues peculiar to Christianity may limit our understanding of the phenomenon. In Europe, neither catholic nor protestant areas had a predominance of witchcraft cases—it was those unstable areas with marked religious divisions and conflicts which had the most.

To talk of a 'gut reaction' is not to deny that witch beliefs will be incorporated into people's religious and scientific ideas, but they are perhaps not *primarily* an intellectual matter. Consequently, education does not necessarily cause beliefs in witchcraft to evaporate. In the region of South Africa mentioned above, it was reported that *educated people ... cited Shakespeare to justify their beliefs,* and that someone who was educated at an English public school did not as a result abandon his belief in witchcraft.

Many historians do not favour this type of cross-cultural approach, associating it with *colonial-era functionalist social anthropolog[y], which should be relegat[ed] ... to the dustbin of history*—to take a comment from a recent book review by William Monter as an example. But early-modern Europe *was* a developing society which had concerns similar in some respects to third world societies today, so it may be counterproductive to rule out a broader perspective that includes such societies. Such an approach would move us away from thinking of witchcraft as a sort of cultural item which can be studied in isolation, and towards seeing it as an aspect of a certain kind of society.

There is a rather surprising contemporary who somewhat endorses this cross-cultural approach to witchcraft. The Kentish sceptic Reginald Scot was famous for writing a large tome denying the reality of witchcraft (it was this work which prompted James I to write his rejoinder). Scot claimed that the old women who were commonly accused of being witches were just suffering from melancholy—an emotional and physical condition that particularly afflicted old people—and their curses had no real effect on their neighbours. But he was less averse to belief in what he called *natural witchcraft*—the evil eye—which he identified as a common belief in Africa (though he did not believe in it himself).

* * *

The Story

What is it about developing societies that makes them spawning grounds for belief in witchcraft? Too large a question to be addressed comprehensively here, but there is a simple point that can be made, which is also relevant to the subject of the essay at the end of this book. I am first tempted to enter a *caveat*, because galloping globalisation and the development of international communications in developing societies in recent decades complicates the argument. But the creation of a few multi-millionaire globe-trotters in, for example, India, does not transform the rest of that society.

The distinctive characteristic of such a social world is that it is very *personal*. Today in the West we rely on so many impersonal services—police, banks, insurance, and many different types of communications, and we can safely assume that the price of an ordinary loaf of bread will not vary much in different parts of the country. In societies where bureaucracies are inefficient and markets are uncertain because the economy is not well-integrated, these things cannot be taken for granted. Everything has to be negotiated through other people. And if your enterprises fail, which is ever possible in such an unpredictable environment, it is essential that you can call on others to assist.

In this environment, people have to be experts in social relations. They also have to be willing to invest considerable time, effort and money or goods in tending relationships with significant others, or within the local community generally. Common methods of generating good feeling between people include gifts, hospitality, drinkings, festivities and similar social activities. The purpose is to establish a basis of goodwill so that when assistance (whether economic or political) is required in the future, allies will feel morally obliged not to betray trust at the crucial moment of need. These activities may seem very simple and inconsequential to westerners, who associate such activities with a very restricted domestic sphere—but they are essential techniques for the creation of what might be called the *good-will society* in less centralised societies.

The terms for these relations in early modern England were *good lordship* for hierarchical relationships, and *good neighbourhood* for the local community. These were not so much descriptions of existing social relations as ideals to aim for—the good will had to be continually reaffirmed and renegotiated in the myriad interactions of everyday life, as well as on occasions of special ritual significance. Popular festivities such as May games were thought to be one means of creating amity in a community, and I will look in more detail at another strategy for achieving it in the second part of this book.

Reducing quarrelsomeness was another objective. If good relations with others helped you run your life satisfactorily, then quarrels had the opposite effect—particularly in small communities. Hence the punishments in local courts for quarrelsome people (scolds, barrators). Christian ritual was important here—taking communion was (amongst other things) a celebration of the cohesion of the community, and was in this sense a spiritual version of more mundane types of social communion. It worked slightly differently from simple conviviality, however—you had to settle your quarrels with neighbours *before* taking communion with them (usually an annual event, at Easter), because harbouring unsettled quarrels in your heart would attract divine punishment. This was not always left to the individual conscience—church wardens in one Sussex parish complained to the church courts that their minister had admitted to communion an 'open contender' who would not reconcile his differences with neighbours. Taking communion with your neighbours was therefore about reducing conflict within the community, rather than an expression of how wonderfully cohesive it already was.

This point is still more evident in a custom which invoked the power of holy communion to suppress disorder in some towns before the Reformation. If a fight broke out, the *host* (consecrated bread) might be brought out of the church and held aloft—threatening divine vengeance on the brawlers if they did not stop fighting.

* * *

Throughout this book I have documented not only how disruptive factionalism could be in the town of Rye, but also the various efforts made by the inhabitants to control it. I have suggested that this may have been a reason for the absorption of leaders of rival groups into the magistracy, and for their lack of family dynasties (see pages 185 and 193 respectively). A similar rationale may have been associated with the creation of a common council in 1575—which caused such uproar among the Bennetts and their allies, as described above (page 87), because most of the initial members of the council (chosen by the mayor and jurats out of the freemen) were from the other faction. Henceforward the main body of freemen had no say in the administration of the town, apart from electing the mayor, until the council was abolished in 1590. Such councils (common in early modern towns) have been seen as undemocratic instruments of domination by some historians. But in a small community, where numerous personal ties link the common councillors with people outside it, democracy is perhaps of less significance than in a more anonymous context. Those outside may, indeed, have too *much* influence—pulling the councillors in different directions, and preventing them from working well together as a group. To facilitate the latter, some distance between them and the rest of the inhabitants can help—and their selection by the magistrates might be seen as creating this distance, as also the prohibition on them talking about council matters outside it. Which is not to deny that the structure could also be undemocratic.

Another means of reducing friction, it may be suggested, was to create interdependence between households by the widespread custom of sending out teenagers to serve in other people's households (see page 71).

More evidence of the overriding concern to maintain peace was the reluctance shown by victims of crimes to indict suspected criminals in Rye before the end of the 16th century (see page 66); this reluctance was also found elsewhere in England. A problem with prosecution on indictment and trial by jury in a local community is that these focus on a single issue, which is likely to exacerbate tensions where people interact in many different contexts, and so have many potential sources of conflict (*multiplex* relations). For example, I might have a quarrel with my neighbour over a shared fence, and think he is mistreating his apprentice who is also my wife's nephew, while he accuses me (a baker) of selling him underweight bread. In such circumstances, a new, major conflict will cause other grievances to resurface, and addressing only the most recent issue is likely to exacerbate the dispute.

The traditional method of settling disputes in the local civil courts (when mediation did not solve the problem) was *compurgation*—where the accused person was required to bring a specified number of neighbours to support him/her. This emphasised the restoration of peace at the expense of deciding the rights and wrongs of a particular issue. But the increasing influence of the common law courts made the use of trial by jury unavoidable, and it was used in trespass cases in the Rye civil court from about the 1560s.

* * *

If people are so dependent on the good will of others, it follows that they are likely to be very alert—hypersensitive?—to the possibility that these others do not bear them goodwill. If their enterprises are failing—the butter will not churn, the cow dies, goods are lost in shipwreck—perhaps it is ill will in others that is responsible. You may say that this is too much of a jump to make, from an essentially rational strategy—creating goodwill—to an irrational one, of attributing bad luck to the illwill of others. But people *did* sometimes think that misfortune had a personal cause—an intentional act directed at oneself—if not necessarily by a witch.

When storms hit Rye in 1572, throwing sand at the quay and heaping it on sandbanks in the harbour, the corporation decided that God was punishing the inhabitants for their immoral ways and their quarrelsomeness, and a programme of moral regeneration was instituted. The honest inhabitants were to take communion

> thereby to declare, to all the world, a general reconciliation of all offences whatsoever passed between every of the inhabitants of this town, as also to protest a godly, christian and steadfast love and unity between the inhabitants. And farther by such brotherly and Christian communicating togethers, to manifest their faith and godly agreement in the religion of Jesus Christ.

'Offences'—in other words to reconcile all parties who had quarrelled, where one had inflicted a wrong on the other. Thus communion had the same social significance in godly Rye as it had had before the Reformation, even if the remedy was to attend to one's spiritual state, rather than to use ritual in an instrumental way.

The 1550s and 60s had seen nearly everyone profiting from the town's prosperity, so the storms in the 1570s affected them all. Responses were not so harmonious later in the century when economic changes affected people in more diverse ways—benefiting some, while harming others. In this context, some people might attribute misfortune to the illwill of a neighbour—such as Anne Taylor—rather than to the hand of God correcting their own sins. A couple of years before the witchcraft case, when Thomas Hamon, then MP for the town, had been unable to get to Parliament because of lameness in one of his legs, the jurats phrased his predicament as follows:

> It falleth so out that it hath pleased God to lay his cross of lameness upon Master Thomas Hamon our mayor of Rye.

* * *

The Story

There is perhaps a more direct connection between witchcraft on the one hand, and patronage and neighbourly relations on the other, in the character of some of the witch fantasies of early modern Europe. The witches' sabbath was often more like a popular festivity, with feasting and dancing, than a diabolic ritual. For the Scots it was about eating and drinking and music and dancing. It is about *gorrovage* (uproar). Furthermore, *the Demonic Pact initiated…a standard feudal relationship*—in which the devil promised material rewards in return for the witch's loyalty.

* * *

Opinions were changing about how much reliance on patrons and neighbours was required for success in one's enterprises. I will be discussing this further in part 2, but would just like to consider some economic changes that bore directly on attitudes to misfortune—and hence witchcraft.

Fifteenth century England had consisted of a *loosely linked collection of regional economies*, with prices and wage rates varying considerably in different regions. The marketing of produce was tightly regulated (including the setting of 'fair' prices) to prevent the *cornering of the market in a vital commodity, which was all too real a threat in locally circumscribed markets*. At least two-thirds of households were oriented towards subsistence farming, but the average farmer was nevertheless much better off than he would have been a century earlier. The halving of the population since the Black Death had benefited tenants at the expense of landlords, by lowering rents because of an abundance of land, raising wages because of a scarcity of labour, and ending serfdom.

It would appear, therefore, to have been a rising demand for goods and services from a relatively comfortably-off peasantry in the later 15th century that quickened commercial activity. Prices started to rise, prompting greater specialisation in agricultural produce and maufactures by urban markets and their hinterlands. This in turn encouraged greater movement of goods between different areas, levelling out price variations and hence integrating local and regional economies. The country's plentiful water transport helped here—both coastal and riverine. Slowly but surely, all these factors interacted to create a broadly market-based economy by 1700. By this time, local famines were a thing of the past—as disparities between deficits and surpluses in different localities were ironed out.

In the south-east, the increasing demand from London provided a reliable market for different kinds of goods and services. The population was increasing, and with it demand grew for consumer goods from a broad swathe of the population in this region, not just the rich. So there were reasons why some people might feel that they could rely on the market to get their livings—and consequently did not have to rely so much on patrons and neighbours.

These changes did not affect everyone in equal ways, and it is likely that people were pulling in different directions—some thought they could rely on the market, others did not. Those that felt they did not need to depend so much on the goodwill of others might invest some of the (not inconsiderable) sums usually spent on hospitality and gifts in their own business. But then if they had distanced themselves from their neighbours, only to be crushed by disaster, perhaps the paranoia which on similar occasions in the past might have just taken the form of mild resentment, hit them with redoubled force ....

This is not to suggest that there was a simple connection between particular economic developments and witchcraft. I am just arguing that attitudes to *good lordship* and *good neighbourhood* were changing—a non-contentious point—and that this change related to concerns about witchcraft. I have mentioned some economic developments that were likely to have influenced these attitudes—another was the climate change that was decimating harvests across Europe in the later 16th century and increasing the sufferings of the poor (as it did in Rye). Rich landholders who could afford to store grain from one year to the next were not affected in the same way as their poorer neighbours—and were indeed reviled for hoarding, and selling it when prices were high, thus benefiting from others' sufferings. There was hence a widening gap between rich and poor in many areas, and scope for considerable disagreement about the necessity or otherwise of maintaining patronage and neighbourly relations.

This point is rather abstract—how does it relate to what was going on in Rye? The town's economic fortunes were of course idiosyncratic. As elsewhere in the country, there was a widening gap between rich and poor in the last couple of decades of the 16th century. But the port of Rye had its own problems—and the elite were only cushioned from these temporarily by their wealth. The turn of the century saw disaster hit the merchant faction—including some personal disasters for individual magistrates which may not have been directly related to the economic situation. What a cruel twist—continuing prosperity while the rest were suffering, followed by catastrophe!

And then one of the women from the other faction made the most extraordinarily advantageous marriage to a local gentleman, in a town where marriage—though usually to a widow or daughter of a magistrate rather than a granddaughter—was a means of access to the aldermanic bench. She and her mother were already known as wise women—had her powers helped her make this catch? So the elite saw the other faction gaining in influence just as they were losing their dominance over the magistracy. And Anne's cursing of Thomas Hamon encouraged opposition amongst others, perhaps threatening to revive the factional conflicts that had paralysed Rye politics in the 1570s and early 80s.

Other inhabitants also cursed him—as we saw in chapter 10—but if anyone was to be accused of witchcraft, she was the most likely target, and also probably the most feared. An accusation of witchcraft in effect denounced the evils of dissension, rallying people to the cause of social cohesion—an appropriate means of suppressing opposition to a regime. In this little semi-autonomous enclave, inhabitants needed to sink their differences to combat intrusions from outsiders—or so the elite could claim.

A century later, merchants no longer felt that their prosperity was closely tied with the fortunes of the rest of the town. This was expressed most clearly in the refusal of most of them to take communion with those inhabitants who did not belong to their select group. While they depended on the assistance of others in their group, they also felt enough confidence in the operations of the market and the various financial devices that had recently been created to dispense with the methods of achieving peacefulness in the community which had previously been so important.

***

I have not here made specific references to *good lordship* and *good neighbourhood* in Rye, but will return to explore these in more detail in the second part of the book, which is in a lighter, more discursive style than this chapter. In this essay, we will move out of the local arena for a time, to explore ideas presented in an eclectic selection of sources which are more informative on this subject than the local records.

Part 2

Of mirth and godliness

Essay

> If we shadows have offended,
> Think but this, and all is mended –
> That you have but slumber'd here,
> While these visions did appear.
>
> *A Midsummer Night's Dream V. i. 412*

Charming, innocuous, inconsequential, disarming. The playwright would seem to have us believe that these prankster fairies are of no more consequence than a dream. Today, it is easy to believe him. But at the turn of the 17th century, midsummer merrymaking—of which playing pranks on people was an essential part—was a contentious matter. Only three years after Shakespeare's death, in 1619, a riot erupted in Stratford over a maypole (amongst other issues)—the symbol par excellence of Merry England. And

> what are we to make of the godly Mrs. Barrington who came down into the hall where her family were celebrating a Jacobean Christmas? At the sound of the laughter and revelry, wrote an eye-witness, she 'changed her countenance, the tears ran down her cheeks, and she turned away'.

The likes of Mistress Barrington may have been in the minority among the gentry in Warwickshire, but in the south-east of England an increasing proportion of them espoused godliness, even if they were not necessarily strident about it. And godliness at this period *always* implied some degree of opposition to the types of festivities that had been customary at Christmas and Midsummer. James I had authorised the playing of some games on Sundays—as also Maygames—in his Declaration of Sports (a year before the riot in Stratford), but his attempts to compel the clergy to read it to their congregations four times a year met such opposition, according to an authoritative near-contemporary, that he withdrew the order. The same source (the Royalist clergyman Thomas Fuller) even suggested that many moderate men thought the Declaration of Sports (later enlarged and reissued by Charles I) was a principal cause of the civil war.

    The tales of fairies playing pranks on people in Rye are like the old festive culture returning by the back door—a culture that had been banished from the town 30 years earlier. No one person was responsible, the stories no doubt altered and embellished as they passed from one alehouse to the next. An ephemeral, ungodly crew haunted the town, their exploits beyond the reach of the magistrates.

Of mirth and godliness

* * *

Old-fashioned festivities were otherwise not much in evidence in godly Rye at the end of the 16th century. Back in 1556 and 1560, the corporation had actually contributed to the costs of making a breakfast for the May game, and of hiring minstrels to lead the procession at the fetching in of the May—when the young people went out to cut boughs and perhaps a tree to act as a maypole, around which they would later dance. But the magistrates drew the line at *disguisings*—when 'mummers' blackened their faces or wore masks, and mocked their neighbours with elaborate gestures while remaining *mum*. Two Rye inhabitants were fined for *going over mumming in masking* in the Christmas season of 1556. One of these characters was the future leader of the merchant faction, Henry Gaymer, who was also later accused of lascivious behaviour, and getting various (unnamed) women into ill repute.

The deathknell for these festivities in Rye tolled in 1578 when the corporation decreed that no-one was to *go out of the town in the mornings with drums, flags or otherwise, to cut down boughs in anyones woods, on pain of imprisonment*. It was in this decade that most such festivities ceased in the south-east of England—rather mysteriously, because there were no general government or episcopal orders banning them. Indeed, Queen Elizabeth enjoyed May Games (as had her father and grandfather), and her Privy Council even stepped in to countermand a local order banning them in Oxfordshire. There were a few other such local orders—like the one in Rye—but historians generally assume that the games were suppressed piecemeal by local worthies—godly magistrates or clergymen—as breaches of the peace.

* * *

So was that the end of the old festive culture in 16th century Rye? Not entirely. When Shakespeare's company visited in 1597, they were not dismissed with 11d for a pottle of wine as the Queen's players would be a few years later, but paid to perform before the mayor and his brethren. This company was one of several—as we saw in chapter 11—which performed there in the late 80s and 90s, reversing temporarily the steady decline in dramatic and musical performances that had occurred since the heyday of the early 1500s (ceasing almost entirely by 1580).

Given the controversy that surrounded drama and festivity at this period, this changing stance on the part of the magistrates was no minor

Essay

issue. I do not of course mean *all* the magistrates—it was a period when the merchant faction dominated the magistracy, and they actually had rather a history of religious variability. Catholic at the time of the Reformation in contrast to the Protestantism of the other faction, their religious stance became indistinguishable from the others in about the 70s, when the corporation displayed exemplary godliness. Then the merchant faction became less godly again during the 80s and 90s—or so I have argued—a time when they labelled some of their opponents *puritans*. A mayor from the artisan faction was later called a *puritan* because—according to his accuser—he would not pay musicians to play for him and his brethren. Maybe the artisan faction had become more radicalised at this period, but a case can be made (as argued in chapter 11) for considerable continuity in their stance over the 16th century.

What were all these changes in attitude about, on the part of the merchant faction? Such variability suggests some element of political strategy was involved. If so, the merchant faction must have had an eye on impressing followers and patrons, and challenging opponents. They would have assumed that the meanings implicit in their behaviour were obvious to these others. Is it possible for us to reconstruct what these meanings would have been?

This sounds as if I am only interested in the cynical aspects of their behaviour—but I think the approach helps us understand not only cynicism, but also belief. We cannot perhaps unlock the essence of religious faith, but we can explore the cultural meanings surrounding it— that contribute to its hold over people. And there is no doubt that making sense of godliness is a key to understanding the motivations of many of the inhabitants of Rye. Anne Taylor is a case in point. The records reveal complexities in her character—the strange mixture of strident godliness with an obsessive interest in buried treasure and the spirits found lurking around it, as well as her close involvement with her 'lewd' neighbour Susan. But she still remains shadowy, which—as I suggested in chapter 4—I think is tied up with the difficulty of understanding the strength and meaning of her faith. Much of this is about culture as much as individual character.

* * *

Where do we begin on this expedition to uncover cultural meanings? Local records are not a great help here, because useful as these are for telling us about the behaviour of the townspeople, they rarely tell us about their ideas. So I propose consulting an articulate contemporary—a certain William Vaughan—who does discuss ideas, on a variety of topics. I will be using a work of his—entitled the *Spirit of Detraction*—that is particularly impassioned, and his biographer in the ODNB thinks he suffered from religious mania at this time. But I think part of the book's strangeness to a modern, western reader is that he is concerned about issues that are very unfamiliar. It is about *laughter*—partly as an aspect of popular festivities—and it is this topic that I want to pursue in this essay. For Mirth and Godliness can be seen as contraries—interrogating the former helps draw the lineaments of the latter.

Eventually, we will return to Rye—and the ideas that have been gleaned from Vaughan and others will be used to interpret the values of the godly and their opponents, and the dynamics of factional conflict in the town.

Ritualised Speech

It may seem perverse to use William Vaughan as my informant, because he had little in common with the inhabitants of Rye, other than his godliness. He came from the other side of the country—Wales—where he was reporting from the front line in the war between Mirth and Godliness. A godly gentleman, magistrate and MP in a strongly catholic area, he suffered from the ridicule of his neighbours, and was driven to write a book about it because of the abuse he suffered when his wife was struck by lightning in 1608:

> I would stop the unpure mouths of prattling Momes ... who amidst their pots of drink, their pipes of tobacco, and idle fits of jollity, establishing the shallow foundation of their reports upon the flying and lying rumours of licentious libellers, declare that her death was caused by the Devil, or that the same Divell conjured up at mortal men's commands, took her away body and all, or at leastwise some principal part of her body, or some secret sin of hers or of his had caused God to punish them, or that it was a punishment of God for my severity of justice, as a godly magistrate.

A mome was a dolt, fool. It is not surprising that Vaughan should have feared that people would think his wife's extraordinary accident was a divine punishment, given the beliefs of the period. But what he is really upset about is the ridicule that he receives as a result.

Who were these 'libellers' that Vaughan complains about? He rages against *cursed copyholders* and *villanous vassals*—the common people who are *addicted to gossip-ales, bride-ales, and to bacchanales...* Gossip-ales and bride-ales—drinkings at christenings and weddings respectively—were some of the popular festivities that the godly railed against in the puritan tracts that tripped off the presses from the 1570s.

> These jolly fellows being driven to this exigent, doe confess, that corrupted custom brought them to such vicious habits. O cruel custom! O hateful habits! which work the fatal and final ruin of souls and bodies! Nevertheless, as there is no custom but may be altered, so for mine own part I cannot believe, that custom alone causeth man ... to carouse ... For some carouse of custom, some of wantonness and company.

He emphasises custom partly because—as many of the puritans acknowledged—those who engaged in such festivities thought they created *good neighbourhood.* They were believed to increase 'amity' between neighbours, and raised money for local causes (such as the church, or a neighbour who had fallen upon hard times—these were *church ales* and *bid ales* respectively).

But the main thrust of his critique is not against these poorer sort, but against *cavaleers and gentles of the first head*. That is to say, those more substantial gentlemen and nobles who behaved offensively to him. *The spirit of detraction stands very much upon his gentry*. His complaints about their extravagant speeches are similar to those he makes against the poorer sort—but references to divine tobacco (a new and expensive commodity) in the following passage indicate that he is talking about a different social level. In mocking fashion, he pretends to mourn the demise of tabletalk:

> Then farewell kind neighbourhood, farewell good fellowship, farewell tabletalk ...farewell all trencher-knights, and readers of other men's actions. As the body is nourished with good liquor ... so is the soul of man with the perfume of divine tobacco, and with the perfusion of detracting taunts. Take away these two ...what is man's life but a dry discourse, a solitary ghost, mortified with melancholy?

The high social status of his detractors is yet more evident when he imagines how they would try and rubbish his book. He evokes the voices of these bragging young bloods, engaging in elaborate wordplay that he likens to a game of tennis as they mock what he has written:

> I dare invite the whole crew of Archilochian cynics with their satires, iambics, and libels, with their so and so, with their vies and revies, with their *Fie, fie upon it, fie upon it*, to dash and blur it over, to taunt, to tear it, to fling their caps at it, to make tennis-balls and to bandy it away if they can [my italics]

So the writers of these libels would have known what iambic verse was, and perhaps that Archilochus was said to be its inventor.

But it is not just lighthearted ribaldry that he is complaining about, but something darker lurking behind the words. His focus of complaint changes gear, just as the ribald talk itself slides imperceptibly from joviality via insults to threats of physical assault:

> True Gentry scorns to brag, to bark, to backbite, to brave it out in time of peace, when cloaks do yield to gowns, when civil conference is expected, and cruel vaunts exiled into sathan's cell, there to rest, until the war-like drum summon them to try their quarrels in the open field against their country's enemies, with hands and not with tongues, with swords and not with words, with pikes and not with pens …

The jovial words carry within them a hidden threat to the authority of the godly magistrate from the followers of overbearing aristocrats:

> It is the part of a magistrate to esteem the windy detractions of licentious libertines, who with presumptious language dare brute abroad, that they can by their supposed familiarities with noble personages uncommission (or to use their own words unsaddle) any justice of his justiceship. I say it is his part to esteem such derogatory speeches, no otherwise then for bravados of a bribed brain, or bragging vaunts of upstart grooms, only to daunt pusillanious meacocks, which never saw the lions in the tower, nor understand the true scope, at which the state of England aims. Even as I never knew any man in all my life despised for his silence and sparing speech: so likewise I never knew any man degraded of his authority for his zealous endeavours on the Kings behalf.
>
>   Wherefore let this stand for a watchword to our country justices, that they be not terrified from welldoing, with the swaggering onsets of craking crocodiles. Let them put on their armour of patience …

The *lions in the tower*—the Tower of London—symbols of the power and majesty of the monarchy. The *true scope at which the state of England aims*— a country not fragmented by warring aristocratic factions, but ruled over by a King secure on his throne, served by grave and earnest magistrates. Vaughan is concerned to defend his own authority against his overpowering aristocratic neighbours and their clients, and their attempts to deprive him of his justiceship. He perceives the King to be his ally in this endeavour. Wales differed in this respect from the south-east of England, where gentry were not as domineered over by aristocrats as they had been. Fighting between the retainers of noblemen in Kent, for example, was rare after the first third of the 16th century.

Vaughan thus brackets together the flamboyant, domineering behaviour of aristocrats and their clients (retainers), with the excesses of good neighbourhood acted out by *cursed copyholders and villanous vassals*. *Villein* still carried connotations of serfdom, and a *vassal* was a client, so these and the copyholders are likely to be the impoverished tenants and clients of those very same noblemen—dependent on them for their good lordship. Two layers of merry fellows with the godly magistrate sandwiched between.

* * *

William Vaughan advocates silence and sparing speech as a counter to the wordplay of the noblemen and their retainers. A familiar example of such controlled behaviour is presented by Malvolio in Twelfth Night—trying to maintain his authority and gravity in the face of the joviality of the Lady Olivia's retainers, indigent relations and servants. Joviality that was of course customary on Twelfth Night, the culmination of the Christmas season. Maintaining your cool in a group who are convulsed by joviality requires a strong sense of ones own importance and weight, particularly if the joviality is customary on such occasions. Malvolio's implicit claims to gravity and virtue are, of course, undermined, and he is shown to be really a hypocrite consumed by social ambition (how could he be otherwise with a name like that?). But these were typical charges levelled at puritans—Anne Taylor was just such another.

* * *

Vaughan's diatribe against joviality and extravagant speech seems to a modern reader as over-the-top as Malvolio's pomposity. But joviality has long been a serious subject of study by anthropologists, because it plays such an important part in social relations in the third world. The anthropologist Radcliffe-Brown first identified social phenomena he termed *joking relationships* back in the 1940s. This referred to the type of behaviour that was expected or typical between people related in certain ways—most commonly those related by marriage, or through the female line in patrilineal societies. The type of joking can vary enormously—from light teasing, to ritual theft, lurid verbal abuse and violent horseplay. Similarly, the feeling of the relationships can vary—between, at one extreme, the relaxed easiness of light teasing, to, at the other, an uneasy ambivalence between potential enemies, where the joviality veers between defusing aggression and acting it out. Perhaps because of this variation, anthropologists have proposed a variety of explanations for this behaviour.

The explanation that seems most relevant to early-modern England (as will be demonstrated in a moment) concerns the use of jovial behaviour to oil the wheels of neighbourliness and mutual assistance (the *good-will society* that was introduced in chapter 12). This is most easily observed in the use of joking to create new ties in novel contexts in the third world—where traditional customs are adapted to new situations. Thus in the shanty towns of Namibia, unrelated neighbours sometimes define each other as joking partners (on the excuse of having 'appropriate' names), and provide mutual assistance to help each other survive in this harsh environment. At the other extreme, officials in state administration in West Africa sometimes give preference to those they consider to be joking partners—on the basis that their respective kinship groups or tribes recognise each other as joking partners. In this context, such favouritism by state officials would of course be labelled *corruption*.

> Joking relationships in West Africa are in fact deeply immersed in modern life and an integral part of public discourse.

Studies of such social phenomena continue to focus inordinately on Africa, although joking relationships are a much wider phenomenon. For example, in Lebanon, joking while playing cards on long winter evenings is characterised by

> tremendous mock ferocity, highly obscene language, ritualised insults, and a suspension of all the conventions of rank and respect

This contrasts with other contexts where there is

> strict observation of the sacred and hierarchical relationships between people...interaction is carried out through precise and appropriate verbal conventions of discourse.

Essay

How this worked in England can best be shown with an example. But there is a fundamental problem in studying ordinary speech at that period. Where is there evidence of everyday speech in a 'normal' context—that is to say, not in a stageplay, or in a context where somebody is trying to prove something? One contemporary text whose author was neither trying particularly to entertain, nor to make a point, is an account of a merchant's dinner party, taken from a French textbook printed in London in 1573. The author was an exiled French protestant who taught French to the sons of London merchants. His book is both written about a London merchant's family, and written for London merchants, so that his description would need to have met with their approval.

The merchant has arrived home with his brother-in-law after attending a wedding and going to see a maypole (so he is clearly no puritan). The conversation at the dinner table is nearly all banter:

guest	… As for me, I love the white of the hen; and you love the rump.	
father	You are a scoffer, as I perceive. Peter, fill me some wine …	
guest	I will not drink with you, for you put too much water in your wine.	
father	I shall not be so soon dronken.	
guest	What? will you be dronken?	
father	No, but it is the wine which maketh me dronk.	
guest	The faut is not in the wine, but in him which doth drink it.	
father	I am glad to see you merry. What, an ounce of mirth is better than a pound of sorrow, yea, and make good weight!	
guest	How would you weigh them? …	
[some more guests arrive: son John's godparents]		
father	… Gossip, you are welcome; and you also, my she gossip. How do you?	
godf.	So, so.	
father	Wherefore? Have you been sick?	
godf.	Yea, and of an evil sickness.	
father	What sickness hath taken you?	
godf	Lacking of money.	
father	Oh, take heed of that disease; for lacking of money is a pain which there is not the like ….	
	Where doth he take the sack to thrust in so much meat?	
guest	He is worse than an Epicure.	
godf.	There be found in the world such guts.	
guest	It is more pity that there is no more discipline among men.	
[end of the meal]		

father	...
	I drink unto all the company; thanking you that you have shewen unto me so much curtesy as to have come to my house; I am sorry that I am not able to make you better cheer.
guests	We do thank you, Sir, what better cheer could you wish?

A very light-hearted textbook! The conversation consists of badinage with almost no content—it is all about being merry together. The literal meaning of the words is unimportant, it is the manner of speech which carries the meaning—creating camaraderie.

At the end of the dinner party, the host and guests revert to a rather elaborate courtesy, which restores normality and ensures that nobody has the last word in the exchange of insults. In this instance the insults are innocuous—but one could imagine that in a real situation the boundary between acceptable and challenging insult might be less clear.

During the meal, the behaviour varies according to the company—the most extreme ribaldry is perhaps with the godfather—the 'gossip', i.e. the host's godsib or co-godparent. As the saying goes, *'Tis merry when gossips meet*. The term gossip was also used of friends, thus defining them as particularly close, and of the women who helped at childbirth.

The host's brother-in-law is another guest who is referred to elsewhere in the textbook as his gossip—if not a formal co-godparent at present, he might well be made one in the future, since relatives by marriage and through the maternal line were often asked to be godparents to children. Thus this use of spiritual kinship re-inforced ties which might fade away—they did not have the permanence, in particular the importance for inheritance, that patrilineal ties had. Through joviality, each made a claim on the other—demonstrating in a rather over-the-top way that they were such good friends that each would not take offence at the other's insult. The creation of individual ties of good neighbourhood thus complements the general camaraderie of festivity.

***

Joviality was not only a means of reaching out to make links with people—it could also be controlling. Joking is an example of ritualised speech, which puts brackets, as it were, around what is said, giving it a meaning that is separate from the content. So if you tell somebody some bad news in a very jocular way, they will probably take note of the jocularity first, and assume that the literal meaning of the words should not be taken seriously. Whatever is said takes its flavour from the jesting way in which it is expressed. Similarly, if you say something in a very deferential way to another person, their first impression is likely to be of your manner, and your actual words may be dimly perceived or at least only taken notice of secondarily. This is speech as a form of behaviour, which is used *not to report facts, but to influence people*. If we are not dealing with facts, it follows also that what is said cannot be true or false—an important point that I will return to later.

Using a particular mode of speech also restricts content—trying to have a serious discussion with people who, by their behaviour, insist that joviality is the dish of the day is difficult. And it is a hidden restriction—the disarming joviality of Malvolio's tormentors seems so natural and light-hearted, while he makes such heavy weather of it. Olivia berates him: *to be generous, guiltless, and of free disposition, is to take those things for bird-bolts that you deem cannon-bullets*.

It is rather like the uproar in the 1970s about use of the word *chairman* and similar terms, or simply *man*, for both genders—it was a highly-charged issue both for feminists and their opponents. Even if you were in favour of a change, it seemed over-the-top, excessive, to insist on changing the word to something like *chairperson*. The sexism was hidden in the vocabulary, and it seemed somehow offensive to bring it out into the public eye. How much more difficult must it have been in the 16th century to expose a form of control that was not just present in a few words, but permeated all speech?

I do not, however, want to overdo this idea that ritualised speech was a form of social control. The godly objected to joviality partly because it acted out—and so acknowledged—the domination of patrons and intrusiveness of neighbours, even if in a light-hearted way.

* * *

What was it about this period of history that made some people particularly disenchanted with Merry England? William Vaughan presents one possible view: as the monarch gained authority at the expense of the aristocracy, and the government extended its reach into the remoter corners of the land, there was less need for a gentleman to attach himself to an aristocratic patron for protection against the threats of other lords.

Another possible view was economic—which I have already discussed in chapter 12. With the quickening of the economy in the late

15th century (or later in remote areas such as Wales), the focus of landowners' interest was shifting from how much land you owned and how many people you could mobilise, to how much profit you could make. From this point of view, money spent on gifts and hospitality for allies (or potential allies) would be at the expense of more lucrative investments.

In these circumstances, loyalty to others might be regarded as of less value than independence and integrity. But it was no good advocating such changes in values unless you could convince others that you abided by them—and be sure that they would respond appropriately.

Plaindealing and Bodily Control

Godly people such as William Vaughan made efforts to defy the hidden social control of ritualised speech. They stood for plainspeaking—where words are used to carry no more than their literal meaning. No dramatisation—no tint of joviality—no *superfluous speeches*. A few plain words, spoken to the point. Straight facts, bare truth. *Silence and sparing speech*.

In practice, however, this was difficult to do, when others expected some degree of dramatisation. Joviality between allies of one sort or another was indeed only one example of ritualised speech—others were the dutiful respect expected by gentry parents from their children, and the elaborate courtesy and flattery expected by the monarch from his or her subjects. These different types of verbal behaviour characterised different types of relationships, and point up the contrasts between them:

> ritual abuse and politeness formulae are two sides of the same coin, and it is the clarity of this formal contrast which makes each effective: the use of one throws the other into sharp relief

More extreme examples of contrasting verbal behaviours in Lebanon have already been mentioned (see page 231). Of all these types of verbal behaviour, joviality was the most likely to cause offence.

The word for plain speech in early modern England was *plaindealing*, and the first example of its use (as one word) given in the OED is in the 1560s. It was originally just a term for honest trading—the opposite of false dealing and double dealing. Ballads about tradesmen were numerous, and plaindealing or its opposite was a popular term for depicting the character of tradesmen, and also of the age as a whole. There was a spate of such ballads in the early 17th century declaring either that *this is an honest age / This is a plain dealing age*; or, on the other hand:

> Plain dealing now is dead,
> And truth is so rare to find,
> That most men now are led,
> Contrary unto kind;
> When one man's just and sound,
> Whose words and deeds agree,
> A dozen may be found,
> That will from their promise flee.

Plain Dealing is a character in Thomas Dekker's play *The Whore of Babylon*, who is employed to ferret out the sins of the City. *I am Plain Dealing, and must speak truth. ... I'll not flatter the face, as painters do; but show all the wrinkles of it.* His main focus is on the *roaring boys* (as the young bloods are often called in ballads) at the ordinaries (eating places):

> Your gallants drink here right worshipfully, eat most impudently, dice most swearingly, swear most damnably, quarrel most desperately, and put up most cowardly.

Like William Vaughan, Dekker derides the extravagant speeches of these gallants: they would *walk boldly up and down strutting, laugh aloud at anything, talk aloud of nothing, so they make a noise, it is no matter*. He is actually referring to a newcomer, a gentleman just up from the country, but the implication seems to be that this is just a more extreme caricature of usual behaviour among the gallants. The content does not matter—everything is in the manner of speech. Contrariwise, the character Plain Dealing is concerned with the content—he *must speak truth*.

The concept of plaindealing was above all identified with candour—which could on occasion be interpreted as rudeness, an issue which the minister Nathaniel Hardy airs in his sermon before the House of Lords in 1646:

> Thrice Noble Worthies,
> If any thing were presented in this subsequent sermon, meriting your honours' acceptance; it must be that despised jewel of plain-dealing. ... I well know, reprehension to great men must be wrapped up (as we do pills) in sugar, that it may more easily be swallowed, and work before they think on it.

Of mirth and godliness

> We must come to your lordships … with soft and silken phrases … But yet withall, the great god who hath advanced you to nobility, hath engaged us to fidelity: it is not time for ministers to be cold or silent, when sins are bold, and sinners impudent.

When it was later published, he complained that when he preached this sermon, he had been

> branded … with the scandalous reproach of malignancy, … For what reason I know not, except … telling the truth.

A plaindealing judgment might be delivered by actions rather than words—*plain-dealing Death will strip him naked, and lay him open unto shame*—'him' being the *wicked politician, who … must of necessity vary himself a thousand ways to obey all winds, and second all tides*. So unlike the solid, unbiased, unwavering plaindealer.

Most of those using the word *plaindealing* approved of it—it was linked on occasion with *godliness* and *fervency*. The plaindealer's emphasis on truth and the literal meaning of words was undoubtedly appropriate for those who espoused the religion of the Word. Nevertheless it was not necessarily a good thing, to all people. The only time Shakespeare uses it is when the bastard Sir John calls himself a *plaindealing villain*, in *Much Ado about Nothing*. He is a plainspeaker, but a villain for all that. He stands aloof from good lordship, and the ritualised speech that that requires. He will not bend to seek his brother's love:

> I had rather be a canker in a hedge, then a rose in his grace, and it better fits my blood to be disdain'd of all then to fashion a carriage to rob love from any.

Perhaps the word smacks too much of the world of the artisan and the puritan—Shakespeare rarely refers to artisans except as figures of fun.

To some people *plaindealing* was a lower-order virtue which did not reach the heights of honour, loyalty, generosity … It was a kind of honesty that went with simplicity: an author complaining about the sale of offices declared that the *merchandize of a Christian is ingenuous simplicity and plain dealing*. But it was also not really a virtue if you were incapable of speaking in a more elaborate way—if you had not been to university to learn rhetoric, could not pen a sonnet, or even, perhaps, wield a pen. Bluntness was then not a choice, but the only mode of expression open to you. So plaindealing was a type of speech, or a behavioural stance, or, if you saw it that way, a type of virtue.

Honest, solid, unwavering—treating all customers with equal impartiality—these were the qualities of the plaindealing tradesman. His integrity and independence would not be compromised by the demands of his kin, neighbours and patrons—for what these people called *loyalty*, others might term *bribery and corruption*. But it was not only in the world of trade that such qualities were valued. The good reputation of a judge depended (in principle) on his being seen to dispense equal justice for all, and not to be subject to fear or favour; the country gentleman wanted to be seen to act with independent authority in his county community and in Parliament, not just following the dictates of an aristocratic patron; the medical practitioner wanted to be trusted as a dispenser of good treatments for all, not thought to capriciously do some people good and others ill. For all these types, a reputation for honesty and independence was desirable—other things being equal (which they were often not, as we will consider in a moment). And these qualities were, in principle, incompatible with the value of loyalty that typified *good lordship* and *good neighbourhood*.

This idea of adopting a shiny new ethic—it is of course not that simple. Other people may not see things the way you do—and even if they do, they may not believe your claims to honesty and integrity. Moral evaluations are underpinned by assumptions about gender, age, mind, body and so on—if your personal characteristics do not seem to fit your claims, people will not believe you. I will suggest briefly the kinds of issues that might be involved.

* * *

When plain, sparing speech was an outward sign of inner virtue, it implied that the speaker was capable of detachment from the demands of others, and could remain composed in the face of their emotionality and provocation. Their words did not, literally, inflame his blood. Blood was made up of different humours which were both physical substances and emotional states. Gravity was the essential characteristic of such a person. To the mature gentleman, gravity came naturally—it was the outer manifestation of the slightly melancholic temperament and cool blood associated with maturity, high status and masculinity. Such a person was slow to speak and to laugh because of his/her physiological state—but this quality was also a virtue to be cultivated:

> Open and loud laughter ... was a natural impulse to be resisted no less than the urge to scratch oneself or pick one's nose. Laughter was unacceptable because it was a sign of disturbed bodily control. [Those] most apt to laughter [were] children, women and the common people

– who also found it difficult to control their bodies, emotions, desires, speech and general behaviour. *Incontinent* was the word most often used to describe such a person—as succinctly expressed in the common term of abuse *whore of tongue and tail*.

In the church courts, incontinence was synonymous with adultery, but in the right place, it was not necessarily sinful. When a new freeman was sworn into the Rye commonalty, he was enjoined to *incontinently kiss the mayor*—behaviour that expressed the openhearted loyalty of the new member of the corporation. And what about the following commendation of incontinence; the speaker is telling another man not to cry:

> Commend these waters to those baby eyes,
> That never saw the giant world enraged;
> Nor met with fortune other than at feasts,
> Full of warm blood, of mirth, of gossipping.

Shakespeare is referring to gossips' feasts, or christenings—frequented more by women than men (particularly those women who had been present at the birth). He is more tolerant of female incontinence than were the authors of City comedies of the early 17th century, which dwell at length on leaky female bodies and uncontrolled emotions and desires. At the gossips' feast in *A Chaste Maid in Cheapside* (Thomas Middleton), the female gossips not only eat excessively and get drunk, but also wet the floor under their stools.

* * *

It was, however, the incontinent ones—regrettably—who did best at creating and maintaining the ties of good neighbourhood and good lordship. What use was a grave, virtuous old gentleman for creating an atmosphere of conviviality?

> the artificer and husbandman are sufficiently liberal and very friendly at their tables ... herein only are the inferior sort somewhat to be blamed, that being thus assembled their talk is now and then such as savoreth of scurrility and ribaldry, a thing naturally incident to carters and clowns, who think

> themselves not to be merry and welcome, if their foolish veins in this behalf be never so little restrained …. I might talk here of the great silence that is used at the tables of the honorable and wiser sort, generally over all the realm ….

Women gossipping at the standpipe, or at a neighbour's childbed, or warmblooded youth sent to serve in other people's households—these especially were the people who would forge the ties of good neighbourhood (so boarding school was often preferred by godly gentry for their children rather than serving in other people's households).

Above all, marriage created permanent ties between families—as reflected in use of the term *affinity* for a lord's retinue. Its members were linked to each other and to him by marriage. But such a tie was not set in concrete at the altar—it was a living relationship between the spouses, and between their relations. Crucial to its continuance was the sexuality of the wife—if relations between her and her husband went cold, the consequences could affect many more people than the married couple.

The sexuality of women thus had an important part to play in weaving the fabric of society—which no doubt partly explains why their 'incontinence' was so disparaged. Incontinence was desirable in women up to a certain point, and in the right context, but had to be prevented from going beyond acceptable limits (adultery could be seen as neighbourliness gone too far). This ambivalence made it particularly difficult to deal with. When contemporaries re-iterated *ad nauseam* that men are so superior to women, one might suspect that there was some snag that made it necessary for them to keep repeating it.

* * *

Even if women were generally considered to be incontinent, not *all* of them were characterised thus *all* the time. Olivia in Twelfth Night carries a certain gravity because she is a noblewoman, and also because she is in mourning for her brother's death—grief causes the body to close up (it is one of a multitude of factors that can affect the state of the body and mind). But for those who were thought consitutionally unfit for gravity, their claims to be grave, virtuous, sparing of speech, and constant, were not likely to be taken seriously. Their weak wills needed help—but there was a helper near at hand. Those godly ministers Dod and Cleaver articulated the problem and the answer:

> How great is his power, that can rule his own mind when wrongs and injuries be offered unto him; that can possess his soul with patience, when troubles and afflictions be upon him; that can mourn with godly sorrow when there is cause of heaviness; that can rejoice with christian gladness, when there is matter of comfort ... that is made able to dispose of his will, and affections, according as the lord his word, or works do call upon him to be affected? But no man can attain to this freedom by his own power, or by the might of any other creature; the word of God is that which must put us in possession of it

Turning to God helped those whose claims to virtue would not be taken at face-value—both to convince others that they meant what they said, and to strengthen their own wills. A godly gentleman could wear his religion lightly, but an artisan, and even more his wife, needed stronger defences. A reputation for godliness was essential.

When an artisan or a woman claimed to be able to be grave and slow to speak, they were in effect claiming higher status in the hierarchy of bodily states than would normally have been thought appropriate. But as plaindealers they were actually claiming more than that. Even a grave elderly man would have been incontinent in his youth—in the traditional system, a person's physical and emotional makeup was always changing, at the mercy of age, food, climate, emotions of self and others and any other aspects of the environment that might impinge on them. Instead, the plaindealer claimed to be always the same—they wanted to be respected as a grave person *all* the time—not subject to the vicissitudes that usually afflicted the humoral body and mind. To be able to claim autonomy, and authority over their own bodies and minds.

* * *

I have been arguing that joking and gossipping were used to create and maintain neighbourhood and patronage relations, and that this was underpinned by ideas about mind, body and social status. The godly emphasis on plain speech, gravity and truth opposed these ideas, and hence expressed defiance towards good lordship and good neighbourhood. The godly could not, of course, dispense entirely with the help of neighbours or the patronage of superiors, but they wanted a fundamental change in social relations. What form this change should take may have been difficult to visualise—so their rhetoric could be as strident as the reality was muddy.

Jovial speech is only one aspect of the contemporary controversy over popular festivities. But the discussion has introduced some key ideas which can now be used to interpret political strategies in Rye. So it is to Rye that we now return.

Back to Rye

There is nothing novel in suggesting that godliness and commerce were bedfellows at this time. The inhabitants of Rye typified godly plaindealers in the prosperous middle years of the 16th century. But problems with this interpretation arise towards the end of the century, when the merchants became less godly, while the artisans became more so—which mirrored the widening economic gap between rich and poor. If Protestantism had close links with Capitalism, why were these capitalists turning their backs on godliness? I would suggest that the mistake is to focus only on economics. Politics may also be important—just as both were aspects of patron/client relations.

Despite the rosy glow of benevolence surrounding the term *good lordship,* such relations were of course always unequal and involved some degree of domination. As William Vaughan made clear, the term was a euphemism. This is true of patron/client relations the world over—the clients always get the worst deal. It might therefore be expected that those at the top of a hierarchy with no-one to domineer over them would be more in favour of such relations, together with all the trappings of hospitality, gift-giving, festivities, joviality and ritualised speech. I think you could say that this was true (other things being equal, which they often are not) of the monarchy and aristocracy in England (at least after the Pope had been shown the door). Equally, the poorer sort at the bottom of the hierarchy—Vaughan's *cursed copyholders* and *villainous vassals* —had nothing to lose by having a patron, and everything to gain. It was the independent sort in the middle of the sandwich who—*if* they felt they could survive economically and politically without a patron—would prefer to defy such domination.

What has this got to do with Rye? If you take the town as a political arena on its own, the merchants at the top of the hierarchy are more likely to favour patronage relations than the artisans below them, because there is no-one to domineer over them in this limited setting. True, several of the elite in Rye had aristocratic patrons, but these were at some remove from the ordinary life of the town, and helped buttress the merchants' hold on authority and power relative to the bulk of the inhabitants (e.g. Richard Portriffe and the Earl of Northampton, William Davies and the

Lord Admiral, Francis Bolton and Sir Henry Guildford, Thomas Edolphe and Lord Buckhurst).

At the bottom are the *rascals and villeins* that John Cotton said made up Thomas Hamon's supporters amongst the freemen—a term not far removed from Vaughan's *villanous vassals*. The implication is that these were not as financially independent as urban freemen should be, and therefore susceptible to pressure. The pool of such impoverished freemen was likely to have increased in the troubled economic climate at the end of the century, relative to the prosperous middle years.

Another indication that the godly artisans in Rye formed the middle of a sandwich in the same way as Vaughan's godly gentry did in Wales, comes from the makeup of the factions. If you recall, the richer and poorer freemen were more inclined to favour the merchant faction (in the 1570s, at least, when relevant evidence is available), while those in the middle favoured the artisan faction. They were, indeed, the *middling sort*—a term that was popular with contemporaries (later in the century), but whose meaning has been argued over by historians. Perhaps the term could even have been relative to social context—the *middling sort* were the godly middle of a sandwich which could involve different groups in different places.

The elite in Rye may also have played up their role as patrons towards the end of the 16th century in order to justify their increasing wealth relative to the rest of the population. If they help particular followers, those followers will not complain—and others may also compete to be of their number. This was the period when more travelling companies of actors (servants of noblemen) were received in Rye, after 60 years of declining numbers. The mayor and aldermen were by this means advertising their espousal of festivity, hospitality and hence patronage. The reception of players might also have expressed connectedness with particular noblemen—thus, the catholic Earl of Arundel sent his players to Rye at least once a year before the Reformation, but after that time they were never received again.

A corollary of the elite's wooing of followers is that they felt their fortunes to be tied up to a great extent with the fortunes of the town. This contrasts dramatically with the attitude of the elite at the end of the 17th century. When the French wars destroyed a large part of the trade of Samuel Jeake and his fellow merchants, he did not go under, like the merchants a century earlier, but instead invested in the National Debt (created to pay for the wars) in the new Bank of England. He dealt in a variety of new financial instruments—which helped him to survive when, persecuted by Charles II's government (and his enemies in the artisan faction), he had to flee Rye and live in London for a time.

This new commercial confidence among the elite was mirrored by dramatic changes in the religious characters of the factions. These were not just different from a century earlier—they had reversed. The merchants were now the puritans—dissenters who would not even take communion with others in the town, let alone be their patrons (the social significance of communion has been mentioned earlier). The artisans—who had been such independent, godly, defiant spirits in the 16th century—had become stooges of the government. A radical transformation of a faction which had been characterised by religious fundamentalism since before Henry VIII's Reformation.

* * *

When Charles II returned as King of England in 1660, there sprung up in many places a spontaneous epidemic of maypoles to welcome him—expressive of the laughing, festive relationship of *good lordship* that was supposed to link him and his subjects (as well, of course, as rejection of the puritanism of the interregnum). But it was a very different kind of relationship from the *good lordship* of a couple of centuries earlier. In the 15th century the tail could, as it were, wag the dog—gentlemen could to some extent play noblemen off against each other, *shopping around for the most attractive protection of the moment*—because the noblemen needed political and military support against their rivals. In the centralised society of 17th century England, by contrast, there was no such room for manoeuvre—the festive celebration of *good lordship* merely endorsed the status quo. In effect, it promoted absolute monarchy (a danger only averted by the revolutions of the 17th century).

The social context is very different today. In the West we have little to fear from absolutism or dictatorships (assuming that Europe is not overtaken by complete economic collapse). In the current crisis of capitalism gone mad, financial whizzkids pursue fairy gold (it exists if enough people *believe* in it) and governments invoke spirits termed *financial markets* (they are only people, after all) with which to manipulate their peoples. One suggested contribution to remedying the situation has been to extend what has been termed the 'core' economy—that which does not involve financial transactions—beyond the household into the wider neighbourhood. In this context we would need to develop skills of neighbourly co-operation and dispute settlement, perhaps learning from ideas and techniques common in the Europe of the past and the third world today...

Afterword: the social sandwich and 20th century fundamentalisms

The discussion of mirth and godliness in this essay addressed certain characteristics that 16th century England shared with modern developing societies—such as patronage and joking relations (or so I have argued). In which case, did their godliness also share characteristics with some modern examples of religious fundamentalism? This would seem unlikely if you accept the theory put forward by the directors of the largescale Fundamentalism Project (University of Chicago)—that such fundamentalisms constitute a rejection of modernity. But they did not include the 17th century puritans among their sample, and *did* include examples of fundamentalism from developed countries. Arguments that are more commensurate with those used here have been presented by some anthropologists of Islamic fundamentalism. I would therefore like to indicate this very briefly—focusing in particular on early 20th century Islamic reformism in North Africa and Egypt. I should emphasise that none of the following comments relate to anything more recent than the 1980s (since when international communications and globalisation have become so very complex).

There are of course broad similarities between 16th century protestant godliness and early 20th century Islamic reformism (in North Africa, Egypt, Saudi Arabia). Both rejected the ritualistic religion of their opponents, a socially-embedded religion that was acted out rather than articulated in moral terms. A religion whose festivals were *concerned with the social punctuation of time and space*, and in the Islamic version, included ecstatic, sometimes mixed-sex dancing that was itself a mystic technique. These traditional Islamic rituals mixed sacred and profane in a much headier mixture than the simply profane festivities of 16th century England (though these were associated by contemporaries with catholic religiosity).

Both protestant and Islamic reformism sought a purer faith, involving a return to the religion of the scriptures, and a rejection of what were seen as superstitious accretions. With the help of the scriptures, each person could achieve a direct relationship with God, without the use of intermediaries—whether living holymen or dead saints. Both promoted a religion of the Word and of Truth. Many of the associated puritan social values were no more intrinsic to Islam than to Christianity:

> Islamic [i.e. fundamentalist] society rejects any space for conviviality and sociability ... this puritanism is profoundly modern and urban, in the sense that the most rigorous Muslim peasant society .... knows what it means to enjoy laughter, humour, song and poetry.

Not only were there similar principles between the two types of reformism, but the social background of the most extreme reformists was often similar. Many of them were artisans, small shopkeepers and traders, the lower levels of the professions, and, in the 20th century, office workers. These were people whose livelihood depended on skills, education, and a reputation for honesty and integrity—impersonal qualities that (as has already been discussed in this essay) sat uneasily with the ethics associated with kinship or patronage. This is not to say that people's choice of religious approach was determined by their way of life, but that the latter formed the context in which the choice was made.

Islamic reformism was not of course invented in the 20th century, for there were periodic outbreaks in previous centuries, of which 18th century Wahabism is only the most well known. Indeed Islam itself was *an urban religion conceived in a pastoral milieu* (and born in the townships of Najd), which by *proclaiming uncompromisingly that the allegiance of man is due to God alone* (a supra-tribal deity), defied tribal allegiances and kinship solidarity in the interests of a wider unity. The idea of the umma, an egalitarian community of the faithful, negates all divisions—by clan, tribe, class or nation.

The scripturalism typical of the towns contrasted with the mystic and ritualistic Sufism of the rural tribes. But Sufism was not peculiar to the rustics, for many of the urban poor in the 20th century—often rural immigrants—were active members of Sufi brotherhoods. The *'villagization' of urban culture is a phenomenon that has been observed by many sociologists*. These were unskilled people dependent on irregular employment—so a very different social group from the self-reliant reformists. One attraction of the brotherhoods was that they provided mutual support in difficult times. A perhaps less obvious feature was that devotions to living and dead saints could also be seen as a ritualistic expression of patronage relations—*[it] was God's own patronage network*. These people may have felt (implicitly) that their only hope of making a livelihood was through patronage from people, whether holy or not, who were better off. If so, it may not have been just wishful thinking, because the reformists also saw these people as receiving help from above:

> The brotherhoods were taken to be too close to powerful, 'feudal' rural class interests, too open to manipulation of the ignorant masses by the British, or the palace (the regime of King Farouk), or the upper bourgeoisie.... [They were] deeply linked with old alliances and social structures in the countryside and the city

It was thought that the British and the French *encouraged obscurantism in the subject population*, i.e. supported the Sufi brotherhoods as a bulwark against the less manipulable reformists. To the Islamic reformers, the religion of the Sufi brotherhoods

> represented forces from which they wished to free themselves .... along with poverty, clientelism, the power of rural notables, illiteracy, passivity, and all that was held to be responsible for Western domination ....

The reformists appear, in fact, to have often formed the middle of a sandwich (as I have argued the godly did in early 17th century England)—between the Sufi poor (and the rustics), and pro-Western secular elites. They wished to

> differentiate themselves ... from three different and unfavourably viewed outside groups: the non-Muslim West, the questionably orthodox, licentious and turbulent rustics; and the local ruling class, who the need for 'development' and technocracy inevitably pushes towards religious laxity

The stance of the elites was perhaps more varied than that of the other two social groups, though it has been said that the *secularism of the elites* was found *almost everywhere in the Muslim world, whether overt or concealed by Islamic labels* (this was written in and of the 1980s).

Could it also be argued that the religious laxity of the elites (both the traditionalists and the socially modernising nationalists) was associated with a less antagonistic attitude towards patronage and kinship relations than that of the reformists?

> 'Kin patronage' politics ... are far from exclusive to the Saudis .... the real structure of power in Syria and Iraq, if we look behind the façade of Ba'athist organization [is similar]. Traditional patterns of kinship and patronage are usually to be found behind party labels

Essay

Again, this relates to the 1980s. These political relations may not simply be traditional, however, but reconstituted versions of traditional modes of loyalty.

It may be objected that kinship and patron/client relations are here being conflated—the latter being more relevant to early modern England. But both are, after all, just different ways of organising social relations (if suited to different environments). And the language of kinship is creative—it has more to do with influencing people than with identifying biological relationships.

Conclusion (to the essay)

The death of Merry England that ballads loved to mourn was not really such a matter of sorrow as they made out. The jovial relationships that had smoothed the way for neighbours to help each other when times were hard, and patrons and clients to strengthen alliances when politics was unstable, became less desirable with the increasing centralisation of economy and polity. With the gradual development of an impersonal market and a strong central government, the need to nurture social relations was less keenly felt. Mockery—the most problematic aspect of such a need—was instead viewed as invasive, manipulative and an instrument of domination. It was the godly 'middling sort' who were particularly conscious of, and rejected, the joviality of those above and below them—even going so far as rejecting laughter among themselves. But opinions differed on this question, and political strategies in Rye presented a local variation.

These social phenomena were not peculiar to early modern England, and I believe that further comparison of 'joking relations' on the one hand, and religious fundamentalism on the other, between modern developing countries and early modern Europe would benefit studies of both. The limitations of early modern records as a means of studying everyday behaviour is counterbalanced by the advantages to be had from looking at a world that was so much less complex than that of today. England in particular offers something of a controlled environment in this respect, having been subject to neither colonisation nor recent invasion.

Appendix 1: Time Line

	Events in Rye		**National/International Events**
early 16th c.	Fishing, supplying Calais (England's last outpost in France) with food and fuel, and French wars, dominate activities in Rye; population about 1500.	1530s -40s	English Reformation; Henry VIII declares himself head of the Church of England; dissolution of the monasteries
		1542	New Act makes conjuring spirits or practising witchcraft to find treasure, harm a person or their goods, and some other activities, a capital offence; repealed 1547
1550s -70s	Trade increases with the decline of Winchelsea, and Rye becomes one of the principal ports on the south coast; population rises to at least 3500.	1553 -58	Mary I becomes Queen; returns the English church to catholicism for 4 years. Calais surrenders to the French.
		1558	Elizabeth I crowned queen
		1563	New Act: witchcraft a felony (capital offence) if results in death of victim (conjuring spirits to find treasure is no longer felonious)
1570s -80s	Immigration of protestants fleeing the wars of religion in France	1570	Pope declares Queen Elizabeth deposed and excommunicated
		1572	Massacre of protestants on St. Bartholomew's day in Paris
1575	Conflicts over new common council		
1576 -83	Artisan faction dominates the magistracy; storms batter harbour; attempts at moral reformation		
1580s -90s	Sudden economic decline in Rye, corporation in debt; widening economic gap and religious divergence between the factions	1585- 1604	War with Spain; 1588 Spanish Armada is dispersed by storms
1596	Cadiz expedition is profitable for Rye	1596	Raid led by Earl of Essex destroys another armada in Cadiz harbour

Appendix 1: Time Line

1596 -97	Mayor Hamon's stepson is convicted of stealing barley; there are protests about this and other matters. Plague.	1596-97	Atrocious harvests throughout Europe
	Some protestant immigrants return to France	1598	Religious toleration is granted in France (Edict of Nantes)
1600 -06	Disasters hit some members of the merchant faction		
1603	Elizabeth daughter of George Taylor born in Kent (February); his wife dies; he marries Anne Bennett, dau of Robert jun (December)	1603	James VI of Scotland crowned James I of England
1605	Taylors' son George born	1604	New Act: dealing with evil spirits for any purpose is felonious
1606?	Swaffers move to Rye		
1607			
Lent	Spirits appear to Susan when sick with malaria		
April June	Thomas Hamon's wife Catherine dies; he marries Martha Tharpe		
Mid-sum-mer	Gifts for spirits left in Susan's window; Susan goes to Weeks Green; possible conjuring in Swaffers' house; apparitions first appear in windows		
July	Thomas Hamon and George Taylor's dau Elizabeth die (buried 29th and 4th)		
Aug	Martha Hamon marries new mayor Thomas Higgons (10th); Robert Burditt (town gunner) blown up (17th)		
15 Sept	George, son of the Taylors, and the town clerk's maidservant are buried; the Taylors invite neighbours to see the apparitions		
26 Sep	Susan's first interrogation by the magistrates		

Appendix 1: Time Line

Oct - Dec	Evidence collected; trial held; Susan convicted; but Anne has fled into Kent	
1608 -09	Right to try case in Rye is challenged by common lawyers and Lord Warden of the Cinque Ports	
1608	More evidence collected; trial held in December; Anne refuses to plead	
1609	More evidence collected; trial held in June; Anne is acquitted. Artisan faction make a come-back.	
1610	Susan is pardoned	
1612	George Taylor is made a freeman, and represents the town with the vicar in negotiations over harbour works	

Appendix 2: Local Tax Assessments

These were raised on goods or rental income of property in Rye, whichever was the greater—for inhabitants, this would be goods. Some lists only give the tax, without the value of the goods being taxed. The ones listed overleaf are those referred to in the text.

The frequent tax assessments must have been impressionistic, but they give a very rough idea of relative differences in wealth, as viewed by the tax assessors—see table below for 1576 and 1596 (the assessments most frequently referred to in the text). These are both shown in the same table for convenience rather than for the purpose of comparison—see discussion of problems with the latter below. Note that the number of households taxed in 1576 is likely to have been a far smaller proportion of the total population than in 1596.

	% of taxed population	
Taxed goods	**1576**	**1596**
£1-2	32	40
£2.5-9	42	22
£10-19	16	9
£20-99	10	21
£100-400		8
Total	100	100
Total number of taxed households	420	416

Comparing different tax lists is problematic. Graham Mayhew (1987: 139-42) has pointed out that the assessments for the rich in the 1590s were much nearer their actual wealth than those in the 1570s. Using probate inventory totals as a comparator suggests that for those taxed on £20 or more, the 1596 tax asssessments were closer to actual wealth by a factor of about four than the figures for 1576. So an assessment of £200 in 1596 would have been comparable to one of £50 in 1576. For those taxed on less than £10 (minimum £1), the relation to actual wealth at the two dates is much the same (for £10-19, the factor is about 2). In 1596, 4% of the taxed population (16) were assessed on £200 or over, and in 1576, 2% (8) on £50

Appendix 2: Tax Lists

or over, suggesting that the rich had not as yet been hit hard by the town's decline. Further details in Gregory 1991: 41-3.

Date	Source	Tax rate and purpose (if given)
1553	Rye 1/1/22ff	6d in the £ on goods
1557	Rye 1/2/8ff	6d in the £ on goods
1571	Rye 1/4/88ff	6d in the £ on goods
1576	Rye 1/4/228ff	12d in the £ on goods; see Mayhew 1987: 277-84
1596	Rye 1/6/30vff	4d in the £ on goods (for £200 for setting forth of ship and hoy for Cadiz expedition)
1598	Rye 77/6	1d in the £ (for wages for the MP, T. Hamon)
1604	Rye 1/7/535ff	tax only (no details)
1610	Rye 77/7	2d in the £ (£100 to mend jetties and pay debts)
1618	Rye 1/10/73ff	?4d in the £ (for erecting a jetty)
1634	Rye 1/12/105ff	4d in the £
Parliamentary taxes:		
1657	Rye 82/81	tax only (for loans to the unpaid soldiers in Rye)
1660	Rye 82/82	Poll tax and tax on land and goods of the richest inhabitants (for demobilisation of the army)

Notes

Abbreviations

APC	*Acts of the Privy Council of England, 1542-7*
BL	British Library
EP	BL Sloane MS 1954 ff.161-93 (paginated separately)
ESRO	East Sussex Record Office
GM	Mayhew, Graham (1987) *Tudor Rye.*
HMC13	Royal Commission on Historical Manuscripts, 13th Report, Appendix, part IV
IGI	International Genealogical Index: a database of genealogical records compiled by the Church of Jesus Christ of Latter-day Saints
KHLC	Kent History and Library Centre
KT	Thomas, Keith (1971) *Religion and the Decline of Magic*
LoW	Lord Warden of the Cinque Ports
LP	*Letters and Papers, Foreign and Domestic, of the reign of Henry VIII*
M&J	Mayor and Jurats of Rye
PRO	The National Archives: Public Record Office
PROB	PRO PROB: Probate records in the National Archives
Rye	ESRO Rye Corporation Manuscripts
TNA	The National Archives
WSRO	West Sussex Record Office

The numbers on the left below are page numbers. Demographic details are from Rye parish registers (ESRO PAR 467/1/1/1-2) unless specified otherwise, and many are also included in the Names Index. Plays which lack an author are by Shakespeare.

Preface

xi *work of the devil:* Malcolm Gaskill notes that decaying ports on the East coast were particularly keen to invite Matthew Hopkins to search for witches during his witchfinding campaign in the 1640s; pp. 179-85.

xiii *often noted:* Hill 1962: preface; Lamont 17.

xv *Master Beveridge:* Rye 47/75.

Part 1: The Story

Prologue

1 *17thc town plan:* see p. vi; Rye 132/15.
18thc brick facades: GM 14.
whitewashed: Armstrong 82.
dunghills, dogs, pigs: GM 42-8.
wooden chimneys: GM 176-7; Brandon 144.
Camber, harbour: GM 14, Mayhew 1984: 111.

14th century: Martin et al 42.
2 *sandstone:* Seward 220.
gallows: Monod 14.
subsiding cliff: Martin et al 21-3.
Rother, Romney and Winchelsea: Draper et al 12, 14; Martin et al 4; 300 years' earlier, Old Winchelsea had probably been the most important port on the south-east coast, Eddison 79.
trade transferred: GM 6-7, 236.
3 *busiest ports:* Hipkin 1998-9: 116-28; GM 237-44, 252-8.
passenger service; posts: GM 37-8.
curious cache: Rye 13.
4 *social dramas:* Turner 1957: 91ff.
Van Dyck travelling to London: Royalton-Kisch 8-9; 86, 88, 90, 92.
escaping: Cust 84.
no market for landscape drawings: Royalton-Kisch 21-2, 29, 54.
5 *bad road; ironmasters:* Fletcher 1975: 5-7; Furley 489.
daily cavalcade: Brent 1975: 40; GM 38.
'as stale as Rye fish: PRO SP12 284/88, quoted in Hipkin 1998: 127.

Chapter 1: Approaching Rye

6 *someone else in Swaffers' house:* Robert Pywall, Rye 1/7/535ff (tax list).
Snapper: Butler 1862: 26.
called 'Swaffer' by GT: Rye 13/6 letter.
where GT came from: Berry 1830: 162-3; KHLC QM/SI (1597).
origins of 'Swaffer': Wallenberg 96; Reaney and Wilson 435.
three Susan Swaffers: IGI.
7 *Swaefa:* Robb and Chesler 630.
Berkshire; quoting G Taylor: WSRO Ep. II/5/6/189v; Rye 13/6 examination.
Jane Swapper: 25/7/1633.
GT's siblings: Berry 1830: 162-3.

8 *Roger's siblings:* KHLC p181/1/1A.
9 *farms in the weald; shaws:* Brandon chap. 4; Brent 1976: 38-40; Zell 1994: 11.
farms on the downs: Brent 1976: 26-30.
'nothing else but a desert: Lambarde 191.
shunned by larger gentry: Zell 1994: 91; Celia Fiennes thought them a kind of 'yeomanly gentry', (in the late 17th century); 136.
clay soils cold: Brent 1976: 41-4.
cottages erected: Brent 1978: 49-51.
wood and water: Brent 1978: 41; Brandon & Short 201.
cattle farming: Zell 1994: 106-8.
industries: Brent 1978: 42, 54; Zell 1994: 92.
'was by trade: Brent 1978: 47, 49.
10 *mainstay:* e.g. in Rye in 1590: wages were 12d a day, employed perhaps half the year, 4d a day perhaps spent on bread for household (6 lbs.); see pp. 170-1.
criminals: Herrup 13.
'the people be given: cited in Herrup 11 (BL Lansdowne MS 53/164-5); Lower 1861: 230.
'people bred: Norden 176.
'Indigenae; 'on the downs: Aubrey 1847: 11.
11 *dairying in west country:* Zell 1994: 107.
radicalism in pastoral areas: Fletcher 1975: 61-62.
end 15th century: Lutton 172.
attitude, doctrines: Thomson: 239-50.
evangelists: Davis 1983: chap. 4.
barking dog: Thomson 181.
earthy, eccentric: Lutton 181-4.
death by burning, Antwerp contacts: Mayhew 1982: 140-1.
12 *martyrs; Fishcock:* Davis 1983: 123-9, 126-7.

godly names in Weald: Tyacke.

ungodliness: see e.g. Collinson 1980: 186-8 on Cranbrook.

'wicked liver; 'lewd: Rye 13/5, 6: letter.

measuring: Adair 39-40; Kieckhefer 103; see p.129.

Sussex catholicism: Fletcher 1975: 94-102.

13 *'less concerned with:* Bossy 1965: 223, 225; Duffy 2005: chap.1.

harvest: Brent 1976: 32, 1978: 51; Bushaway 107-11.

Sussex catholics: Manning 151-65, 221-71; Fletcher 1975: 98-102; Herrup 22.

Montagu: Cross 145; Fletcher 1975: 99.

neighbourhood: Davis 2000: chap. 7; Bossy 1973; Wrightson 2002: 75.

large vs small farmers: Brent 1976: 34-5; Thirsk 2000: 78-9; Wrightson 2002: 198-201.

14 *rise in wheat prices:* Clay Vol. 1: 40; Wrightson 2002: 128-31.

not as well-populated: Brent 1976: 35-37, 1978: 51-2.

London expanding: Clay Vol 1: 20.

Rye imported wheat: Brent 1976: 41, 1975: 38, 46; GM 239; Rye 47/78.

Roger senior and William Swaffer: KHLC QM/SRc 1596/15.

William beaten up: Knafla 54, 126 (1602) 192 witness/accuser; KHLC Q/SR 1 no.6 (1600), Q/SR 3 no. 11 (1602).

15 *'charged with:* KHLC Q/SR 4 no. 7 (1603).

migrating out: Zell 1994: 85.

wages high; main export: GM 155; 241.

specialised: he also imported 6 tons of wood in Jan. 1608; Rye 66/76.

George Taylor: Berry 1830: 162-3, pedigree and coat of arms; KHLC QM/SI 1597; stepmother, see p. 79;

marriage to Anne Bennett, by licence, Dunkin 44.

paid no more in tax: Rye 1/7/535ff (1604).

burials exceeded baptisms: Brent 1975: 46.

16 *fièvre ague:* OED

Samuel Jeake: Hunter & Gregory 1988: 107-16, 51-2, 55; quote 116.

'one of the most deadly: Dobson 165.

'in as great numbers: Lang 22, quoted in Dobson 175.

brackish water: Dobson 175

'the large quantity of: Hasted Vol 7: 253-4, quoted in Dobson 175.

'all the infections: The Tempest II.ii.1082.

'evil in winter: Lambarde 181; quoted in Dobson 175.

17 *Rye: water had to be piped; payments:* Brent 1975: 46; GM 29-30.

'to see the fashions: examination of John Baber, Rye 47/75.

largest town: Mayhew 1984: 109.

townhouses: Brent 1975: 50

Lewes market: Brent 1975: 47, 1976: 30.

more than one child: and Agnes.

Smallhythe: Draper et al 174.

Nicholas King: Rye 13/14.

lighters carrying: GM 237-8.

18 *marsh lookers:* Brent 1978: 50.

'wealthy but not healthy: Blome 1673: 122, quoted in Dobson 175; see also Brent 1978: 50.

stock from Wales, butchers as agents: Brent 1976: 46, Brandon & Short 180.

ferry, portcullis, market: GM 14, 35, 41-2.

Court Hall and town administration: Armstrong 82; for town officers and freemen, see GM 91-127. For a short time a common council was created out of the freemen, which will be discussed later.

19 *at least 149 freemen:* calculated from Graham Mayhew's list (see GM pp. 277-84) plus some recorded as voting for Fagge in the mayoral election of 1579, but for whom no record of their being made free survives – presumably because they were freeborn (total 19), see GM 19.

too poor to be taxed: GM 140-1.

Swaffers' and Taylors' houses: by a process of elimination, I think these three houses must have been the current 4-9 Lion Street. The houses were in the Butchery (which was mainly to the west of Lion Street and the market when their houses were built, sometime before the middle of the 16th century), opposite a house belonging to the King's Purveyor of Fish, so not along one of the side alleys that existed then, but facing Lion Street; these three houses and a fourth had watercourses (i.e. drains) in 1564, so were presumably not divided by a side alley; the Taylors had a consider-able amount of land (they were having an orchard planted, and there had been a slaughterhouse, barn and herber on the site in 1564), which suggests that they had the house at nos. 4-6 Lion Street: its garden went across the back of their house and the other two (the fourth has not survived), and a rear extension ('range') was built onto it at about the time that George and Anne married; Martin et al 26-7, 212-3; ESRO HBR/1/1540 (1607 and 1622); PROB 11/49/143 (1567); Rye 13/1, 15, 19.

20 *medieval in layout:* Brandon 143; Pearson 60.

parlour: Chatwin 36; Pearson 90. This description of the rooms is sourced from the records of this case, apart from the shops, for which see Martin et al 212.

roofs; weasels: GM 177; Rye 13/3.

Chapter 2: Susan's Story

In this chapter quotations are from Rye 13/1 unless otherwise stated.

21 *'pestilential vapours:* Hasted 1797-1801: vol. 7 pp. 253-54.

'great shake: Rye 13/6 letter.

common term: see e.g. *Early English Books Online.*

'fresh-incomers: Short 69, quoted in Dobson 175.

22 *fatalities:* Dobson 175.

colder, Thames: Fagan 103, Anon. 1608.

staples: Thirsk 2007: 221-22, 236.

'sick a bed: Rye 13/3.

likely time: Walsh 1566; Briggs 1976: 449; Latham 102; Wilson 450; Pitcairn Vol. 1 pt. 2 pp. 52, 56.

rail: Willett and Cunnington 66-68.

23 *ghosts and protestantism:* KT 702-5; Gordon; eclecticism of popular religion, Lewis 2002: 88.

unburden: KT 712-18; Caciola 86; Gordon 93; Latham 144.

limit: Schmitt 179-81; Caciola 66-68.

addressing spirits: KT 717.

24 *noisy spirit:* Plot 206-10; Gordon 92.

'took hold of her: Rye 13/7; this quote is from a later examination, by which time the spirits had acquired names.

25 *'How can a man die:* much quoted in medical works, this saying originated in an Arabic medical treatise; Northcote 37-38; Cogan 32; Bullein 5v; Rohde 44.

febrifuge: Cogan 1584: 33.

Sussex remedy: Friend 375; a similar cure was used in 14th century Italy, when it had to be picked before sunrise Wilson 339; Grieve 704.

'he did take hold: this and the next three quotations are from Rye 13/3.

Notes

26 *cunningfolk and fairies:* KT chap.8 and p.727; EP p.50; Penry 32; Walsh; Rosen 51; Wilby 52, 87; Pitcairn Vol.1 pt.2 pp. 51, 53-4.
Faustus: see e.g. KT 564.

27 *manual:* Hill 1946: 73.
'Mistress Taylor said: Rye 13/3.
Williams: Rye 13/15.
George's account: Rye 13/6 examination; see also Halliwell 15.

28 *Anne's account:* Rye 13/5.
monasteries: KT 279-81.
loans: Wrightson 1982: 52-53.

29 *Halifax:* LP 12 pt2 1537 nos. 316, 339, 369.
apples and fairies: Wimberly 64-5; MacKillop 19, 180; Briggs 1959: 115.

30 *P. Swan; 'things that Susan:* Rye 13/19, 7.
stone cellars: GM 180; Martin et al 90-4.
J Shurley; clay: Martin et al 220; Rye 13/7.

31 *thyme:* Northcote 181; Friend 4-5; Woodward 123.
burial grounds: Wilson 340.
summerhouses: Hutton 1996: 252, Amherst 32, 52, 74, 83, 112.
arbour/harbour/herber: McLean 1981: 172.

32 *'for which cause:* Davies 2003: 95; see also Kittredge 204, Beard 73, Latham 144-47, MacKillop 180, Jessopp 99.
folklorists: e.g. Simpson.
'my Dad; spate: Simpson 23; KT 280.
'There be many: LP 13 pt.1 1538 no.786.

33 *Sussex artisans:* Calendar of Patent Rolls, Ed. VI, vol.1 (1547) p.185.
cross- and hill-digger: KT 279-80.
witchcraft statutes: KT 525-27; Davies 2003: 4; the 1563 statute is transcribed in Newton & Bath 233-6.

conjuration necessary: Beard 55, Kittredge 1929: 205-11.
experienced : KT 280-81, Davies 2003: 93-95, 120, 175; Halliwell 15-16.
conjuring books: KT 270.
secular courts: civil cases for debt and some types of slander were also now actionable in the central secular courts, Outhwaite 15.
treasure trove: Hill 1936: 185-237.

34 *licensed:* Hill 1936: 253-55.
thief-detection: Davies 2003: 3-4, 10-11; KT 256-7.
'nor knew not what: Rye 13/3.
hits something: Rye 13/6 examination.

35 *'You take and look:* Briggs 1976: 9.
pregnancy: for an example of a pregnant woman acting as a scryer, see Walsham 2006: 305 (on scryers, see p. 126).
George too: Rye 13/6 examination.
fear cause of death: Macdonald 158, 181-82; Graunt 11,17, 70.

36 *prosaic Roger:* Rye 13/3.

37 *about a mile:* Rye 47/51.

38 *farmhouse:* ESRO W/A10/31.
Lashendens: Rye 58/11, injunction from the court of Chancery at Dover; later litigation in Rye civil court, Rye 33/17/210-11, 35/52 (1603-4).
broken off: an additional reason for the Bennetts' withdrawal was probably the accusation against John Lashenden of begetting a bastard; this was the subject of a slander case in the church courts in 1600-01, the evidence for which is equivocal; WSRO Ep.II/5/6/269-70, 299.

40 *largest houses:* GM 174.
Susan's mark: her mark on her third examination is a chaotic squiggle.
handwriting: of William Tharpe or Thorpe, see Rye 60/10/107.

41 *legality*: see p. 139.

pamphlets: Cockburn 1985: 98-100; Sharpe 1996: 94-102.

familiars: Sharpe 1996: 100 'ever-developing lore of familiars'. I am grateful to Miranda Chaytor for her suggestions about familiars and links between fairies and ghosts.

civil war imps: Gaskill, e.g. 50-1; for similar in Rye, see HMC13/215-6 (1645).

northern counties: Bath 145; PRO ASSI 45/1/1, mostly transcribed in Raine.

no depositions (evidence) retained: Cockburn 1985: 11.

42 *shamans:* Lewis 1986: 78, 88-89. This comment is not intended to imply anything about pre-christian survivals (for which, see e.g. Wilby).

noises: Rye 13/3, 7, 14.

weasels: Rye 13/3; Briggs 1967: 65-71.

fairies generally: KT 724-34; Latham; Briggs 1959.

faireses; town clerk: Simpson 53; WSRO Ep. II/5/6/189v.

size: Latham 68-80.

euphemisms: Latham 52, 101, 104, 174; Wilby 95

deflect malice: KT 728; Aubrey 1881: 29; Spence 12.

43 *fairy colours:* Latham 83-88; Wimberly 64-5; Walsh 1566; Wilby 62; MacKillop 177.

pinching: Latham 120; Briggs 1959: 51; Chappell 80.

typical victim: Latham 148-62

fairies as ghosts : MacKillop 177-8; Latham 44-46; Wilby 56; Wilson 303.

Bessie Dunlop: Pitcairn Vol. 1 pt. 2 pp. 51-58.

purgatory; 'theologians; ghosts known: Schmitt 180-81; Caciola 66-68; Gordon 97.

44 *fraud:* see also KT 732-33, Davies 2003: 95.

origin: All I can suggest as models for the other spirits—Robert, Margery and Catherine—are the town clerk and his wife for the first two—his age would be appropriate, in his late 40s.

money collected: see e.g. Rye 147/1/14-17 (1525-26).

hat: Jones 1995: 207.

chalice: Farmer 342-3; Jones 1995: 82 (picture), 220.

according to George: Rye 13/6 letter.

45 *saint's whiteness:* Jones 1995: 231.

reached heaven: Schmitt 1998: 204-05.

flat cap: Willett and Cunnington 133.

Switzerland; capricious: Gordon 88; Briggs 1989: 24 (France).

Chapter 3: The Interrogators

46 *nearly half the men:* GM 19, Dulley 50.

harvest; seasick: Brent 1975: 41.

names of boats: Rye 1/8/64, Rye 47/53.

Winchelsea castle: Seward 219-20

Herring Fair: Dulley 43.

Robert Swayne's trade and sons: ESRO W/A12/339 (1609).

47 *Thomas Hamon:* PROB 11/110/493.

Martha Tharpe: b1575, but then d1582; she was probably another child born with the same name, but not entered in the register of baptisms because her name was there already (this was common); married by licence, Dunkin 58.

more successful: Hasler Vol.1 p.305.

efforts to promote: Fletcher 1975: 251.

Thomas Higgons: GM 125, Rye 66/72-77.

W Tharpe: he was made a jurat in the same year that his daughter Martha married Thomas Hamon.

48 *'butchers, bakers:* Rye 47/81.

status of JPs: Fletcher 1975: 127-8.

one or two JPs: Cockburn 1985: 93.

'but as she heard: Rye 13/5 q15.

49 *'she was altogethers:* Rye 13/5 q2.

'her swear: Rye 13/7 q5.

oft repeated: Wilby 90-1; Wilson 449; Aubrey 1881: 29, 102; Latham 128.

'she had said nothing: Rye 13/1.

jointly: Collinson 1980: 195.

white wand: KT 312-13.

50 *'what the four; 'the eldest; 'Mistress Taylor:* Rye 13/1.

31 Questions: Rye 13/4, 5.

names of the spirits: Rye 13/5 q4.

why she had not told: added to interrogatory Rye 13/4 as q18.

51 *statute; magic:* KT 525; Davies 2003: 9.

contrasting version: If this was a legal document, the official heading has been omitted. It is headed *The confession of certain persons concerning the spirits appearing at Rye*, which suggests that the copy was not made by an inhabitant of Rye; the handwriting is contemporary. BL Harleian MSS 358/188; transcribed in Butler (the only major error is rendering *Swapper* as *Snapper*).

appeal court: see p.138.

52 *Roger's examination:* Rye 13/2, 3.

'Lewd and wicked: Rye 13/5 q19.

'to the intent; 'at her sister: Rye 13/1; Rye 13/14.

53 *'Mistress Taylor:* Rye 13/8.

54 *'he coming; 'they came:* Rye 13/3, 9.

'then he went in: Rye 13/3 q5.

Mittimor: i.e. Michenor.

Mistress Taylor's chamber: i.e. the one not let to the Swaffers.

55 *hemp:* Thirsk 2000: 83.

'true it is: Rye 13/7 q9.

'she saieth: Rye 13/12 q20.

'there was common: Rye 13/9; the Moores lived opposite the Taylors, Rye 13/5 q30.

56 *'she hath very well:* Rye 13/9.

'in the house: Sloane 3851 f.129. Another version of this ritual (early 17th century) is quoted in Briggs 1953: 456, 459-60, where she suggested that it had a more popular origin than the rituals used by intellectual magicians, though some rituals were undoubtedly taken from translations of latin magic books (Davies 2003: 122-3).

57 *suggestion:* Sloane 3851 f.90.

first examination; 8 thousand: Rye 13/1; 13/2-9.

30 mins: Cockburn 1985: 110

argue it out: Herrup 141-2.

couple of pages: see PRO ASSI 45/1/1.

58 *most boroughs:* Sharpe 1999: 35-6.

privileges: GM 91.

St. James: see p.268.

'The said; second examination : Rye 13/8; 13/7 q8.

turkeys: Thirsk 2007: 254.

59 *'Mistress Taylor did then:* Rye 13/8 and next quote

stroke: derived from 'fairy stroke', MacKillop 177.

'Neither upon: Rye 13/6 letter.

60 *gaol:* An accused person would normally be imprisoned after they were first examined, but if the magistrates were not sure what to do, they may have waited until after Susan's second examination; Cockburn 1985: 93.

'little ease': Rye 13/17; Holloway 586; Mayhew 1984: 122-3.

'also she sayeth: Rye 13/8.

Jeremy Talhurst: of East Guldeford; Rye 47/80.

61 *Calais billets:* Rye 1/4/154-5; GM 241; Hipkin 1998: 118.

tenth of the annual exports: see tables in GM 242, 255.

court case: Rye 47/75, plaintiff James Hughesson.

'if wood is delivered: Rye 1/8/47v.

avoid paying: Rye 1/5/210v (1590).

double dues: Rye 1/3/76 and licence required from the mayor 1/4/120v.

'draw up a bill: Rye 1/8/10.

62 *two other actions:* plaintiffs M Young, Rye 33/17/398, and G Brooke, 47/75. He was a defendant in 4 more cases in 1608/9, Rye 35/56.

litigious: e.g. there were at least 118 actions initiated by Rye inhabitants in the town's court in 1603-4, that is about 1case for every 3 taxed households; Rye 33/17/193v-250.

accusations go back decades: Levack 151and Sharpe 1999: 109-10.

indictments: Rye 47/75.

statute: transcribed in Newton & Bath 237-9.

James I and statute of 1604: Maxwell-Stuart 38-40; his involvement closely linked with politics, 34-8.

Scot: The Discoverie of Witchcraft.

Macbeth: Booth.

63 *detecting imposters:* Maxwell-Stuart 45-6.

little change at Assizes: Gibson 2008: 127; only 5% of the extant Home Circuit Assize indictments for witchcraft concerned dealing with spirits (36 out of 794), and half of these came from the Matthew Hopkins witch hunt during the Civil War, Walsham 2006: 312.

pomp: Cockburn 1972: 65-7.

mayor's sergeant: GM 98.

grand jury's role: Herrup chapter 5.

grand jury: The grand jury consisted of five feters (wholesale fishmongers), two brewers, a baker, tanner, cooper, pumpmaker, shoemaker, basketmaker, tailor and two unknown (from this list of potential jurymen, a smaller number would have been pricked to serve).

bill of error: Rye 47/75; they had probably heard of a *writ of error*, which was used by the court of King's Bench to upset the decisions of local courts on technical grounds; Baker 25.

threw out: Herrup 114 (1625-40).

64 *Sussex physician:* EP foreword.

other occasions; betrothed: indictments in Rye 47/75; Rye 58/11.

Lashendens: Rye 13/27; on the other hand, there was the extraordinary case of the Taylors' ally Alexander Fowkes, jurat, and two servants of John Lashenden's, trying to resist the efforts of the mayor's sergeant, Angel Shaw, to distrain Lashenden's goods; Shaw had them indicted for assault and battery in July 1609; Rye 1/8/166v, 47/75. Lashenden had lost a debt case brought by a yeoman of Burwash in Rye court, and was adjudged to owe him the huge sum of £191 plus £5 costs, Rye 35/56 (includes inventory). JL said he had paid back £110 of it.

65 *felony cases in Rye:* GM 208-9.

indictment 1563: Rye 1/3/5v. There were only 10 formal accusations of witchcraft—1% of all indictments for crime—in East Sussex in the first half of the 17th century, Herrup 27.

poor law: Wrightson 2002: 215-21.

refs. to banishment: Rye Assembly books (Rye 1/1 etc.); suspected felon acquitted and banished, e.g. 1/5/317.

66 *'to the intent:* Rye 47/3.

formal accusation and *proclamation:* Cockburn 1985: 91, 43; banishment is specified in the town's charter for those suspected of felony whom no-one comes forward to prosecute; Holloway 143.

ears: e.g. Rye 1/2/20, 34v, 1/6/c220, 1/7/361v.
currier: Rye 1/4/119, 47/2.
67 *Mother Rogers:* Rye 47/50.
trial and trial jury: Herrup 131-64.
68 *MY debt case:* Apr-May 1607, Rye 33/17/398, 35/55.
MY East Guldeford: Rye 1/6/165 (1597).
MY made free: Rye 1/8/93, 133v; made chamberlain same year.
'*he looked to be:* Rye 47/78, 1/8/180v.
marriage: to Margaret widow of John Fisher, jurat; Dunkin 57.
fled; verdict: Rye 47/75, 1/8/73v.
69 *benefit of the belly:* Cockburn 1985: 121-3.

Chapter 4: Anne Taylor

70 *no evidence:* very occasionally allowed in the Assize courts from the end of the 16th century, Cockburn 1985: 107.
71 *fifth child:* Berry 1830: 163; parish registers of Shadoxhurst, KHLC p332/1/1, and Rye.
'*I have now:* and next quote Rye 13/25.
servants, spoil: Mertes 53-4 (a custom universal among medieval nobility, ended by late 17th century); Fletcher 1975: 34, 38 (gentry); Dod and Cleaver 173, 290, 292, 368; these godly authors, however, preferred that parents should cultivate some detachment from their children, rather than that they be sent out to be disciplined by others 50-51, 56. In Rye it was assumed in 1574 that every household would have a servant (*viz.from 14 years and upwards*) available to help with removing sand from the Creek (presumably excluding the poorest households), Rye 1/4/198v. On servants in Rye, see Mayhew 1991.

'*as freely:* Rye 13/25, and next 2 quotes.
'*picture of death:* Rye 13/5 q29.
72 '*My masters:* Rye 13/6 letter.
appeal court: see p.138.
'*About midsummer;'very ancient:* Rye 13/6 examination, letter.
73 *Susan's report:* Rye 13/7 q8.
drummer: e.g. Rye 1/4/156v (1573), Louis 134 (1609).
Indian dye: on expensive red dyes in the early 16th century, see Jardine 31.
'*Master Harrison:* Rye 13/13.
'*the picture:* Rye 13/5 q30.
'*the shadow:* Rye 13/6 letter.
74 '*a shape of a man:* Rye 13/5 q30.
apparitions in the sky: Walsham 1999: 181-94, 326-34.
'*some apparitions:* Rye 13/5 q29.
call down; 'two gentlewomen: Rye 13/7 q7.
75 *lack of belief:* Rye 13/5 q30; Rye 13/6 letter.
'*diverse sights:* Rye 13/22.
seer's foot: Wilby 99; Sloane 3851 f.129v.
taken to court: Rye 47/75.
'*the two angels:* Rye 13/5 q31.
a general sense: KT 166-70; Clark 1997: chap22; Jue 259; Gribben 58.
76 *common view:* Firth 109-123.
annotated bibles: Gribben 58.
until eleven months: Rye 13/6 letter.
typical of the Civil War period: Firth 195-203; KT 167-70.

Chapter 5: Faith and Faction

78 *Faith and faction in Rye in the 1530s:* has been analysed in depth by Graham Mayhew (1982).
tried for heresy: Welch 63; WSRO Ep I/10/5 f9r.
illicit books: Mayhew 1982: 141.

'and some of them: PRO SP 1/124/23; LP11 1424 (1536).

'best and most substantial: PRO LP12 pt2 no.505; SP 1/124/21, SP 1/113/106-9.

79 *15th century lollards were mostly artisans:* Thomson 249.

step-grandfather: Berry 1830: 162-3; quitclaim from John Taylor of Willesborough, gent, and wife Bridget (widow of Thomas Fletcher), Rye 139/69 (f. 85b); see Bridget Ruck in the Names Index; d1619 St. Alphedge, will KHLC DRb/P/wr/19/Pt II/62.

similarities: Hunt 87.

'not the very body: PRO SP 1/113/106-9 (and other quotes on this page).

80 *prison:* Elton 86.

refused to accept; Fleet prison: Mayhew 1982: 74-5.

Ravensdale: Foxe Vol 3 p.947; married and 2 children baptised 1553-5.

R Bennett made CW: Rye 147/147.

81 *lamp re-hung etc:* Rye 147/147-152v; for the previous removal of Catholic furnishings in the late 1540s and early 1550s, see GM 68-71.

Crispin: Farmer 93.

altars etc taken down: GM 75-7.

coronation: no description of what was worn by the barons at Elizabeth's coronation has survived; Manwaring Baines 4-7.

expenses: Rye 60/7/201.

82 *Bennett's will:* PROB 11/49/143.

prosperous: GM 14-22, 235-7.

'so satisfied: Rye 1/4/236 April 1576.

hats and caps decree: Rye 1/4/195.

83 *'this unseasonable:* Rye 1/4/121-2.

preacher: GM 77-90; and chap 11.

welcomed: GM 84-5.

poor people from France: GM 82.

84 *members of factions:* GM 64-6, 127-37; *a caveat:* it will be apparent from what follows that by the 1590s, at least, Thomas Hamon was no longer a member of what had been the 'protestant' faction. Mayhew characterises the latter faction as particularly godly in the later 16th century, but does not identify socio-economic differences between the factions.

'rivalry; 'dark side: Adams 34; I am using the word in a broader, less perjorative sense than Adams does (and contemporaries did).

85 *Wills of William and John:* ESRO W/A7/217 (1573), 147 (1579); John's later role as mayor's sergeant would also have been lucrative, Rye 57/7.

'night of illrule: Rye 1/4/214v-215v; GM 224-5.

'but promised; 'Master mayor: Rye 1/4/218v, 223v.

86 *yielded:* Rye 1/4/225; GM 220.

'in the dark evening: Rye 1/4/224.

agent: GM 258.

drinking in service time: HMC13/52.

against each other: Rye 1/4/119v.

87 *shoulder of a dog:* Rye 1/4/183v.

common council: Rye 1/4/187v; GM 103-5. For a different approach, see Hipkin 1995(b). See also pp. 217-8.

assented; companies: Rye 1/4/193; GM 165-8.

24 playing cards, windows broken: GM 104; Rye 47/12/3.

R Bennett vs Thomas Fogler: Rye 1/4/214, 303v.

88 *Mayor chosen etc.:* Rye 1/4/245v, 267 (1576 and 7).

Daniel bound over: Rye 1/4/284v.

catholic gentry: GM 66.

middling sort: Wrightson 1994: 41-45; for Norwich, see Reynolds 9.

anonymous: quoted in Wrightson 1994: 42; Stow 479 (included with Stow's *Survey of London*).

89 *rich:* the 10% of taxed households taxed on £20 or more (see appendix 2).

Star Chamber cases: The documents referred to below are in the category PRO STAC 5, apart from Rye 137/36 – Rolfe's plea, or a copy of it - which is missing from the PRO (part of the latter is transcribed in GM 128-9). Specific references are given for quotes, and for items mentioned by only one or two witnesses.

may have been the first case: Rolfe wanted the house back from Fagge, who still held it (Rye 137/36 and see below); Hebblethwaite did not have any reason to initiate a case, except in retaliation against Rolfe's case.

'the walls thereof: Rye 137/36.

90 *hurly burly:* PRO STAC 5 R34/21.

wealth: i.e. the value of their goods in Rye taxed in 1576 - see appendix 2 for details, and p.177 for a more comprehensive analysis of differences in wealth between the factions.

91 *the house:* This house is known today as St Anthony's (described in Martin et al 257-8). Identification is based on layout of the wards (for which see GM 144): the house of Mathew Mills was on one side of Raynolds' house (see p. 93-4), and that of William Harmon on the other; since the latter was in Middlestreet ward and the former in Baddings ward (GM 280-1), these houses must be on the south-west corner of the churchyard.

servant of Queen Mary: this suggests clear links with the merchant, ex-catholic faction. Mayhew considers that Raynolds was committed to neither faction - presumably because he left so many bequests to members of the artisan faction in his will, GM 128; this is discussed on p. 92.

George Raynolds' will: ESRO W/A7/67v.

nagging: R34/21 M Beveridge; M and J Mills, R Fletcher, H Gaymer.

92 *Hebblethwaite town clerk:* H32/29 pt2.

'so many nasty: R34/21 J Edolphe.

kindred too poor: R34/21 L Phillips.

residue of goods: R34/21 J Fagge.

other faction: R Jackson, W Appleton, W Tolkin, W Allen, J Persall; overseers J Fagge and L Phillips. Bequest for H Gaymer - *accomplishment of a promise made between him and me.*

not uncommon: e.g. Fagge's own will, which had 5 overseers, including R Carpenter, PROB 11/66/24; Robert Daniell asked Fagge to be his executor in 1579, ESRO W/A7/210; see also p.194.

he had not put pressure; imbecility: R13/6; Rye 137/36.

leader of merchant faction: according to Graham Mayhew, GM 131.

not as 'fresh'; 'reputed to be: R13/6; H32/29 pt1.

litigation with Whitfield: R34/21 M Mills.

93 *neighbour:* R Jackson

traditional means of claiming ownership: Baker 203-4.

Prowze arrested stranger: H76/38.

halberd; weapons found in parlour: H76/38; R34/21 R Carpenter.

'They're in!: R34/21 R Fletcher minister of Rye.

94 *allegiance of W Harmon:* as a 'cousin' of G Raynolds, it was thought possible that he might be made one of the executors or overseers of his will, but G Raynolds told J Edolphe that he would not do this because Harmon had sued him over something; ESRO W/A7/67v; R34/21.

'one with a loud voice; 'down with him: R34/21 J Carpenter and R Fletcher.

'out by the ears; 'do no more: H76/38.; H32/29 pt1.

'very evil disposed: Rye 137/36.

95 *general belief*: H 76/38.

divorce: Wrightson 1982: 100

'confederated together: H32/29 pt2.

no longer afford: R34/21 J Fagge.

gate: installed when Queen Elizabeth stayed in the town a few years' earlier, presumably for her entourage, since she herself stayed in Gaymer's house (*Green Hall*), which was beyond Harmon's house; GM 35-6.

'murther'; sureties adequate: R13/6; R34/21 L Phillips and R Fletcher.

Rolfe acquitted: R34/21 R Carpenter.

96 *'Stace if thou*: and next 2 quotes, H76/38.

lubber: big, clumsy, stupid, idle fellow.

'more like a; 'unlearned: H32/29 pt2, pt 1.

'suspected H32/29 pt2. Also one of the Thomas Fishers (merchant faction) was presented in the church courts for sexual misconduct with Joan Peadle in 1601; WSRO Ep.II/9/9/80v.

'for the better avoiding; drunkards: GM 205-7, 12; Rye 1/4/345, 360.

97 *partlet*: Willett and Cunnington 61.

god's yoke: probably a reference to Matthew 11.29.

collar: see e.g. pp. 160, 165, 187.

ban: see p.190-1, 225.

variety of crimes: R34/21, witnesses J Carpenter, W Davies, S March, S Harrison, W Mellow and others.

silver cup: R34/21 R Fletcher; Rye 137/36.

furore: Rye 1/4/307; Rye 47/25 pt2/22.

2 terms: mayors of Rye are listed in Vidler 158-60; mayors and jurats in the Tudor period in GM 273-6.

98 *'man of sufficient, 1580 election*: Rye 47/25 pt2/22.

Chapter 6: Attempts at Reconciliation

99 *unbelief*: Rye 13/5 q31.

'How she knew; 'no manner of hurt: Rye 13/6 letter

god and the devil: see also KT 568; Wilby 117-20.

Bible, Geneva: Berry 1969.

100 *surplice controversy*: Rye 13/1; Como 243; Coffey 1.

Burditt's deposition: Rye 47/70/5; he was paid by the magistrates to write letters in 1603, Rye 1/7/509v.

101 *chronicle*: *Polychronicon*, written by Ranulf Higden, monk of Chester in the early 14th century. It was a very popular chronicle of universal history, printed several times around the turn of the 16th century, so this copy may have been in Rye for a long time! ODNB

Paulus Aemilius: De Rebus Gestis Francorum. This must have been printed in Latin or French, because although frequently reprinted, it had not been translated into English. Perhaps it had been acquired from one of the many French Protestant refugees who fled from persecution in France intermittently during the later 16th century.

'termed the Pope's: examination of Lansdale Rye 47/70/2.

Guy Fawkes' haunts and Spanish fleet: Haynes 43, 72.

102 *the following three paragraphs*: Rye 47/70/3-8; one of the clothiers (Roberts) is described in Collinson 1980: 191.

Lansdale: attorney e.g. Rye 1/9/457v.

prison: Rye 1/9/475v.

103 *cajole*: Rye 13/16, 17.

'he hath seen: Rye 13/16.

loft door: i.e. door to the upper floor.
'fall out into; 'are you she: Rye 13/17.
brawling: i.e. verbal abuse.
104 *'little ease':* Gaskill 55; Haynes 6; Ballads 1867: 275.
'Master Taylor; 'if she would deny: Rye 13/17, 16.
pardons: Cockburn 1985: 126-8.
'bagges: Rye 13/17 [i.e. baggage?].
105 *'did return:* Rye 13/17.
godly name: see pp. 178, 184.
Scragg and Gibbons: GM 207, 73. Being carted was a common punishment for adulterers, GM 222.
106 *'Master Bracegirdle:* Rye 13/17.
honourable: Kaylor & Streed 6, 13.
Queen: Kaylor & Streed 10.
'This small token: Kaylor & Streed, dedication.
107 *patron:* Kaylor & Streed 6, 8.
old guard; Cheshire: see p.13; ACAD.
Sessions of the Peace: not apparently held at all in summer 1608.

Chapter 7: Healers

108 *'Widow Bennett:* Rye 13/18.
common claim: KT 249.
'certain persons; 'Did not you: Rye 13/20 q12, q4.
109 *'was taken in such sort:* Rye 13/7.
'Did not Master: Rye 13/20 q7.
'she doth not: Rye 13/20 and 21 q8.
'to these: end of Rye 13/20.
110 *signing name evidence of ability to read:* see e.g. Spufford 181. The signature of another butcher's wife was more assured than those of Anne Taylor or Margery Convers (see pages 77, 119); Joan Harry, Rye 13/10 (her husband Anthony was taxed on £30 in 1610).
school: e.g. A Harry ESRO W/A7/194, R Daniel W/A7/210.
able to read: Davies 2003: 69-71.

'one Zacharias: Rye 13/23 q3.
111 *ointment:* Rye 13/7 q1.
inherited: Davies 2003: 70, Wilson 34.
powers; list; only one: Woodward 199; Rye 13/26; but see Whitfield letter, 196.
old woman: Levack 149-51.
superstitious techniques: Wilson 422-3; Chapman 293.
astrology, Napier: MacDonald 25-30.
112 *surgeons, training:* Pelling and Webster 175-7, 204.
good days: Capp 1979: 28, 57, 230; KT 349-52; Wilson 199; Mason 17, 85; Means 73-4.
most popular; critic: Curry 21, KT 349; EP 24.
ill planet; planet rulers: KT 757-8.
'struck by: Thompson 148.
blasted; Bills of Mortality: KT 757; Graunt 346
black, yellow: Flower: Examination of Anne Baker.
113 *'the black fairies:* Walsh.
storm: Rock 1862: 189.
auspicious time: Chapman 293.
'Go unto; 'And when Susan; 'I will lay: Rye 13/8.
114 *cunningfolk:* see note on p.258.
Raphael: MacDonald 16-18.
Poeton: not university trained.
'a great prince; dissect: EP 36, 49-50.
housewife's role: For a good description from the late Middle Ages, see Rawcliffe 184-5.
physicians: Pelling and Webster 168-71, 182-85; see also Beier 4-5.
male householders: e.g. Rye 1/3/76, 1/4/217v.
115 *'Master George:* Rye 1/6/83; also M Flory in 1579, Rye 1/4/308; and another freed from quarterly charge for licence to practice if he will treat the poor Rye 1/8/199v.

view the bodies: GM 48.
Size of Dieppe: Merk 134-5.
licensed: Pelling and Webster 179-80, 226-7 and 234.
'a gallon of water: Frewen 606/88, 91v.

116 *hypocrisy:* Patrick Collinson called hypocrisy *the kind of key signature for everything else attributed to Puritans* Collinson 2008: 27-8.
'did take a neighbour: and next 3 quotes Rye 13/25.
very heated: e.g. Manningham 164.

117 *oath 'God's soul':* Dent called such an oath 'monstrous blasphemy', 149.
'A puritan: Manningham 219.
'no whit: and next quote Rye 13/25.
'courtesy: her meaning is unclear - it sounds as if she is referring to the inheritance custom *courtesy of England*, but this relates to men, not women; Baker 230.
powdered beef: Rye 13/10.
fresh beef: Rye 13/12 q30.
asked Susan; if anyone: Rye 13/7 q7; Rye 13/8.

118 *cushion:* John Cheston PROB 11/133/821, 55/223 (1619 and 1573 respectively).
John Convers: e.g. Rye 33/14 (1575).
Joan Breadcar: see Names Index; Dunkin marriage licences: m1609 Angel Shaw, m1618 Robert Garrett (1609 to Halsey apparently void); 'Mr. Haulsey m Mrs. Porter' in Rye register of marriages 1611; wills: Stephen Porter gent ESRO W/A13/83 (1610); Philip Halsey jurat PROB 11/130/181 (1617), 'she brought him all, and she should have it'; Joan Garrett wid. PROB 11/152/375 (1627); Hull 388.
Stephen Porter: deputy customs officer, Rye 47/75.

119 *'One of her spirits; 'to cut off:* Rye 13/5 q31.

very biblical: Matt. 3:12, Luke 3:17; another example Collins 1980: 178.
'Her maid in her: Rye 13/25.

120 *not many:* <10% in Europe, Briggs 2002: 127-8; Davies 2003: 12-13.
practised informally: Demos 81-84.
church courts: Davies 2003: 12-18; perhaps surprisingly, the attitude of the church courts at this period was much the same as it had been before the Reformation; KT 325-6.
numerous: KT 291-5.

Chapter 8: Entertaining Fairies

121 *'Spirit Margery:* Rye 13/6 letter.
arch puritan: GT was not unusual: Lake and Questier 2002: xiii.
Katherine pears: Thirsk 2000: 102.

122 *'John Cheston:* Rye 13/13; Chappell 80; Kittredge 214-7.

123 *'if they have not; 'doors did open:* Rye 13/1.
'she was suddenly: Rye 13/19, witness Phyllis Swane.

124 *'I pray thee:* and next quote, Rye 13/13.
'I conjure thee: BL Sloane MS 3851 f.135.

125 *'Mistress Taylor:* Rye 13/1.
'when roses: and next two quotes, Rye 13/8.

126 *Pywall:* who dug for treasure before Susan did, see p.35.
scryers: KT 274, Walsham 2006: 304-5, Aubrey 1881: 100.
popular: Rohde 116.

127 *gillyflowers:* Friend 118, 248.
milk: Addy 141, Wilson 107-9.
problems blamed: Aubrey 1881: 29-30.
tricky: (particularly if the cows were illfed) Wilson 109.
market: GM 41.
rent of a red rose or gillyflowers: Hazlitt 33, 53, 91, 269, 299, 163.

military help: Carpenter 1992: 281-7.
Northampton: Friend 500.

128 '*She hath diverse:* Rye 13/1.
'*They do require:* Rye 13/5 q24.

129 '*Richard:* Rye 13/1 and next quote.
measured: Adair 39-40.
confirmed: Rye 13/5 q24.
embellished: Rye 13/7 q6.

130 '*verily:* Rye 13/7 q6.
indictments: Rye 47/75.
'*That Swapper:* Rye 13/25.
expensive: Thirsk 2007: 49.

131 '*spirit in the:* Rye 13/1.
'*Fayries woman:* Rye 13/5 q22.
'*And the summer:* Rye 13/19.

132 *green apples:* Wimberly 64-5.
tithe for the fairies: Wilson 16.
'*raw piece:* Rye 13/1; see p. 117.
'*there was speech:* Rye 13/1.
Waller role: Peck 1982: 44.

133 '*And coming:* Rye 13/1.
pulled by the coat: Bessie Dunlop was similarly pulled by the apron by her familiar; Pitcairn Vol. 1 pt.2 p.52.
'*that so brake:* Rye 1/8/54, 56.
'*Her husband; 'token:* Rye 13/1.

134 '*Here is great:* Rye 13/5 q26.
triumph: Rye 13/5 q26; musters Lewes '*Richard asked:* Rye 13/1.

135 '*It is reported:* Rye 13/25.
gunpowder made locally: Brent 1978: 42; gunpowder/saltpetre, Ponting.
Martha Burditt: Rye 1/8/56.
Azande: Evans-Pritchard 183-95.
'*Yea, these seducing:* Vaughan 202; he said that 'in time of Popery' masters and servants manipulated each other by invoking fairies that 'haunted butteries and cellars', p.205.

136 for a fuller chronology, see appendix 1.

Chapter 9: Many Eyes on this Case

The individual documents in bundle Rye 47/75 are not numbered.

137 '*essoigned:* M&J to LoW 28/07/08, HMC13/140, Rye 47/71/17.
'*We wish you to be well:* and next two quotes; J Boys to M&J 03/01/08, HMC13/136, Rye 47/71/8.
felonies: Sharpe 1999: 35-6.
Sir John Boys: Hasler 476-7.

138 *writ of certiorari:* Baker 129.
St. James: called a court of Chancery from the mid 16th century, but it had broader functions; no records survive before 1615; Murray 104-19.
The alternative version of Susan's examination mentioned on p. 51 could have been recorded for this appeal (Murray 114), and would have been particularly suitable for George's purposes, since it hardly mentions Anne at all, and has none of the vitriolic comments attributed to her in Susan's third examination. Condensed versions of his and his wife's accounts of the apparitions in the windows are also included in the document.
'*almost mystical; recorders trained:* Clark 1977: 292, 143, 281, 283.
Berkshire: WSRO Ep. II/5/6/189v.
attornies: Rye 33/14-16.
Rye courts: Jones 1967: 361.

139 *other jurisdictions; church courts:* Baker 25-6; Outhwaite 15.
'*by upsetting judgments; tried to conform:* Baker 25-6.
cases within enclave: GM 91.
Boys introduced practice: Clark 1977: 289.
'*sithence:* [R Convers] to J Shurley 24/01/08, HMC13/137, Rye 47/71/7.

Notes

Serjeant Shurley: Hasler 378-9; he was active in Parliament as MP for Lewes.

140 *James Thurbarne:* Hasler 502; Clark 1977: 287.

not valid: Murray 106.

secretly to Rye: M&J to LoW 28/07/08, HMC13/140, Rye 47/71/17.

'Master Mayor: LoW to M&J 22/07/08, HMC13/139-40, Rye 47/71/16.

Anne not pregnant: there may have been a confusion with Susan (e.g. from R Convers to J Shurley 24/01/08, HMC13/137, Rye 47/71/7).

Matthew Hadd: was high steward of Dover castle, and *eventually held most of the important legal offices in Kent*, Peck 1982: 44-5; he served as legal counsel for several Kent towns, Clark 1977: 275-6.

141 *'delivering to her:* M&J to LoW 28/07/08, HMC13/140, Rye 47/71/17.

maidservants: see pp. 104-5, 119.

not available for witchcraft: Sharpe 1996: 90.

142 *Anne Taylor bailed:* Rye 1/8/99.

'doth take it in ill part: they had heard from Mathew Young that Sir Thomas Waller had reported this; M&J to Thurbarne 13/05/09, Rye 47/74/7.

'the words of the charter: from M Hadd, addressed 'To whom it may concern', (nd), Rye 47/75.

143 *wanted advice of judges:* M&J to Thurbarne (nd), Thurbarne to M&J 26/10/08, M&J to LoW 26?/02/09; Rye 47/75.

decision of the judges: M&J to LoW (nd), Rye 47/74/4; M&J to LoW ?26/02/09, Rye 47/75.

other business: Rye 1/8/125v.

'standing long time: M&J to LoW 26?/02/09, Rye 47/75.

counsel allowed: on possibly only 3 occasions, Cockburn 1985: 108.

ordeal: Baker 63.

peine forte et dure: Cockburn 1985: 72; 23 suspects stood mute in Home Circuit trials 1558-1625, and the only woman was probably reprieved, Langbein 74-6.

144 *Salem:* Boyer and Nissenbaum 8.

Clitherow: Lake and Questier 2011: 88-93, 106-8.

'she and her counsel: M&J to LoW 26?/02/09, Rye 47/75.

145 *non-delivery of billets:* M&J of Dover to M&J of Rye 07/02/09, Rye 45/75.

withernam: Murray 218, 223.

'in all ages: M&J to LoW ?/03/09, Rye 47/75.

146 *'Master mayor, I was desirous:* 10/03/09, Rye 47/66/1.

'great labour: Thurbarne to M&J (nd) Rye 47/74/3.

'the question: M&J of Rye to rest of Cinque Ports 27/04/09, Rye 47/74/13.

147 *vetted the letter:* Shurley to M&J ?/04/09 and edited letter to Ports (nd), Rye 47/75; see also M&J to Shurley 24/4/09, Rye 47/75.

'We are assuredly: Rye 47/74/13.

Hastings: Rye 47/74/13.

asked Shurley and Thurbarne: M&J to Thurbarne (nd), Rye 47/75; M&J to Shurley 08/05/09, Rye 47/74/8.

148 *'and at his request I have:* Thurbarne to M&J (nd), Rye 47/74/6.

date of trial; 'I wish till the trial: Thurbarne to M&J (nd), Rye 47/74/6.

conflicting roles of LoW: Hasler: 300.

Northampton: Peck 1982: 6-13; 22-3.

149 *'To the place by birth:* Peck 1982: 6.

flattery; obsession wth honour: ODNB.

letters multiplied: Rye 47/74/8, 6, 7, 10, 9 or 12, 2, 5, 1, and Thurbarne to M&J 22/5/09, Rye 47/75.

150 *'nothing hath prejudiced:* Thurbarne to M&J 22/5/09, Rye 47/75.

Portriffe client of LoW: Rye 1/8/27v.

gunner; cannon in London: Peck 1982: 43-4.

objecting: LoW to M&J 16/06/05, HMC13/132.

'I have written twice: 23/05/09, Rye 47/74/2, 5.

'Master Taylor doth labour: Rye 47/74/5.

151 *'It hath something made:* 13 or 15/05/09, Rye 47/74/9 or 12.

Richard Portriffe: sold lands in Cranbook to Alexander Weller (PROB 11/88/35 1596); married in Cranbrook 1572 (IGI); in Rye tax list 1576; children baptised in Rye from 1588.

embezzling, 'from henceforth: Rye 1/5/273, 337.

slander: Rye 35/50, 33/17/97v, 106.

'the whole truth: 13 or 15/05/09, Rye 47/74/9 or 12.

152 *Ports' responses:* M&J to Ports 21/05/09, Ports to M&J 22/05/09; Rye 47/74/10 and 9 or 12.

'Only this we say: Rye 47/74/9 or 12.

'will be with you: 06/06/09, Rye 47/75.

153 *often turbot and John Dory:* good turbot, brill and Dory from Rye, Fiennes 139.

depositions of Higgons and Convers: Rye 13/25.

154 *list of witnesses:* Rye 13/26.

trial June 1609: Rye 1/8/156-7.

indictments: Rye 47/75.

Thomas White: see p.78.

Chapter 10: Economic Decline

157 *farmed out; luxury textiles:* Hipkin 1998: 139 n23, 131-4.

trade changeable: Hipkin 1998: 108, 122-3, 128.

158 *declined by a third:* Hipkin 1998: 128.

'the shore weareth: Rye 99/5, quoted in Hipkin 1998: 117.

worse off than Brighton; sustain costs: Hipkin 1998: 127-8, 130; 1995(a): 244.

privateering; headmoney: Mayhew 1984: 109, 121-4.

159 *suffered piracy:* Hipkin 1995(a): 243.

illegal nets: Hipkin 1998: 127, 129-30.

'so rake: quoted in Hipkin 1998: 129.

1660 tax list: Rye 82/82.

population: Hipkin 1998: 108; GM 19-20.

harbour works; play his drum: GM 265-9, 26.

inning: Hipkin 1998: 117, 1995(a): 243; GM 264-5.

160 *contributions:* GM 268.

too poor to pay; 'wheat and rye: Rye 1/6/140, 142.

161 *cuck:* the derivation is spelt out in a contemporary ballad, Rollins 1929: vol. 1 p. 193; see Gregory 1985: 235.

boat's tail: Rye 1/7/468, 488v, 569 (9-10 women 1603-5).

loans and selling of assets: GM 268-9.

the Vine: Also known as the White Vine; Rye 1/7/309; presumably the building now known by this name at 24-5 High Street, which at that time was used as an inn, Martin et al 145.

treasurer; 'make us pay: GM 1984 120-21; KHLC CP/Br/21, 15.

stockfish jokes: Seager 297.

162 *tax to pay for ship:* Rye 1/6/30ff.

crisis: see e.g. Underdown 1986.

Chapter 11: Thomas Hamon and the Crisis of the 1590s

163 *used the Hercules:* Rye 47/44.

Cadiz: Mayhew 1984: 120-1.

'How now my masters: Rye 47/54.

164 *problem:* Rye 47/54; also a problem in 1580, GM 132.

easily bought: Aubrey 1881: 302; 'villain' = bondservant, slave.

Notes

John Cotton poor: taxed on £1 worth of goods in 1596 (the lowest category).

'Whereto William Palmer: and next 2 quotes, Rye 47/54.

Palmer churchwarden, Besse: Rye 47/53, 1/8/40v; taxed on £10 in 1596 (see taxlist on p.252).

165 *constable:* Rye 1/6/98v.

sessions: Rye 1/6/93v.

'if the words: Rye 47/54.

abusive: Rye 47/78 (1609), when hauled before the magistrates for mistreating his wife, and Rye 1/9/496v (1614).

'is adjudged: and next 3 quotes, Rye 47/54.

Palmer stood surety: Rye 47/54.

166 *found guilty:* Rye 1/6/96-96v, 106v.

worth a shilling: Baker 432.

benefit of clergy: Cockburn 1985: 117-20.

167 *loft for mother:* Rye 1/6/210.

Hills banished; back: Rye 1/6/99, 227.

West country: GM 239, 241.

John Duron: eldest child born 1561 (John Jun.); 6 children named in his will, PROB 11/60/297 (1578).

not unusual: in a sample of first marriages by London tradesmen, a quarter married widows; Wrightson 1982: 81.

168 *TH sen. made free:* GM 115.

mother remarried (Alice); guardian: Richard Stace (1559); Rye 1/3/149v.

will of J Duron: see above.

'A brewhouse: GM 163 / Rye 139/28.

169 *examination of S Duron:* Rye 47/54.

pickeries, indicted: Rye 1/6/88, 29.

surety: Rye 1/6/53.

170 *'if any man; rain:* Rye 1/6/59v; Hoskins 107.

long-term increase: Wrightson 2002: 116, 128-9.

prices and wages: The price of bread (or rather, the weight of e.g. a tuppenny brown loaf) was set according to the current price of wheat in Rye, and daily wage rates were set for labourers working for the corporation.

at least half: see p.255.

171 *famine 1596-7:* Appleby 112-5, Wrightson 2002: 199.

shipments: Hipkin 1998: 123, 125.

depleted: HMC13/29.

confiscate: Brent 1975: 46.

172 *S Duron convicted:* Rye 1/6/178.

grand juries; only thieves: Herrup 114; GM 208.

rife in Spain, entrypoints, not just the poor: Slack 76, 66, 7, 158-9.

ships stayed, 'it hath pleased: HMC13/112, 113.

173 *'infected persons:* Rye 1/6/83.

plague outbreaks of 1563 and 1596: GM 47-8.

Master George: Rye 1/6/83.

roughly a quarter: GM 47.

John died: during the plague outbreak, although his name was not marked with a P in the burial register.

carried on butchering: pays her dues for butchering in Jan. 1605 (long after her daughter has married George Taylor); Rye 65/84.

testators: e.g. PROB 11/39/325 John Colbrand 1557.

174 *value of goods; tax:* ESRO W/A10/31, B2/234; 1596 tax list.

indebted to Lashenden: Rye 58/11.

Bennett's uncle: John Sharpe, ESRO W/A7/147 (1579), will of brother John.

costly equipment: GM 162-3.

175 *elsewhere:* Gregory 1991: 41-3.

untaxed households: GM 140-1.

list of mayors: Vidler 158-60.

176 *'lean to; 'rascals:* see pp. 96, 163.

list of supporters: Rye 47/25 pt2/22.

1576 tax and occupations: GM 277-84.

couple of others: John Bennett, Robert Jackson and Thomas Colbrand.

177 *shared ownership:* Dulley 47-50.

178 *biblical names:* Gregory 1985: 273-83; both instances of 'Onesimus' were French: son of W Gile (baptised 1595), and nephew (O Harry) of Andrew Harry, ESRO W/A7/194 (1580).

179 *parts:* more on this on p.185.

'with very bad; dismissed: Rye 1/8/94v, 100; Hull 387.

180 *'vacat':* Rye 1/8/96v, 98.

endangered: Briggs 1989: 59.

Chapter 12: The Accusers

181 *'she did think:* Rye 13/8.

size of Dieppe: Merk 134.

boatloads: on the French refugees in Rye, see GM 79-90.

embraced: Merk 92-3.

'The Dieppois;'in token: Merk 97, 107.

wild scenes: Briggs 1998: 18; Merk 90, 101.

national: Gwynn 19-21.

182 *English garrison:* Merk 108, 110.

massacre: Briggs 1998:23-4.

government objected; sea beggars: GM 86-7, 79-81.

183 *French church:* GM 87-8.

personal ties: Andrew Harry ESRO W/A7/194 (1580); Anthony Cog [i.e. Coq] PROB 11/ 75/346 (1590); George Syre (ov. William Davies) PROB 11/58/10 (1576).

rivalry: GM 84-5.

'puritan' first used: Fletcher 1975: 61.

vicars and preachers: GM 78-9.

'a small sect: Rye 1/5/216-7; HMC13/98-100 / Rye 47/43. The M&J were complaining to the Lord Admiral, whose chaplain Greenwood was, in the hope that he could use his influence to counteract the threat.

'I have heard: HMC13/99.

184 *Waylett minister:* Rye 47/70.

dumdogs: the term was much used in early printed books from about the 1540s (see *Early English Books Online*), including Jewel's *Second Book of Homilies*, which was ordered to be read in churches; used in Norwich, Reynolds 61; it is a quote from Isaiah 56:10 'his watchmen … are all dumb dogs, they cannot bark; … loving to slumber'.

'none ought: HMC13/99.

joiner: HMC13/99; in 1591 he had been called 'glazier and joiner', when he took an apprentice whose uncle and guardian was the godly jurat R Wood; Rye 1/5/231v.

John Baylie shoemaker: Taxed on £10 in 1598; he took many apprentices: Rye 1/4/266v, 374, 1/5/147v, 1/6/271v.

scald head: Rye 1/6/196, 169.

servant of Wood: Rye 1/5/214v.

Wood rich: taxed on goods worth £400 in 1596; will PROB 11/106/235 (1605).

W Bucher: had links with the godly faction back in the 1570s, when he was said in the Star Chamber case to be one of those who assembled outside the disputed house to help dispossess Rolfe; PRO STAC R34/21, R Carpenter, R Fletcher and S Harrison.

185 *Gile will:* William Gill PROB 11 121/414 (1613); Hopewell born 1590.

Wood took 6 months: chosen in August 1595, he took his oath the following March, Rye 1/6/30-31.

P Keling: Rye 1/5/115, 232 (1587 and 1591); although he is not recorded as voting for Fagge in the 1579 election, he asked in his will for the godly jurat R Wood to bring up his son, with another overseer from Lydd; PROB 11/80/120 (1592).

J Styner: refused, Rye 1/6/249v; accepted with Swayne Rye 1/7/435.

T Edolphe: GM 93-4.

economic incentives: decree 1/4/120 (1572); disputes over this regulation include: R Swayne (see p.179) and Thomas Brown (a non-freeman wanting to buy corn), Rye 47/75.

186 *'We have a puritan:* HMC13/144 / Rye 47/77. Musicians were better tolerated than players in some contexts, Louis xxxix.

crucifix: HMC13/121-22 (1600).

F Brooke: Rye 1/6/257, HMC13/120-21.

'transported, letter: HMC13/120.

187 *'knowing:* HMC13/121.

'spirit: Rye 1/6/257.

mediator: Rye 47/51.

Thomas Fisher jun.: Rye 47/70/17, 41-2, 44, 50; also 19, 20, 27, 29, 32-4, 37, 45-6, 52-3; also papers relating to a debt of £80 owed by Fisher to a man of Dover.

188 *sigh of relief:* GM 90; Firth 150-2.

Rye contributed: Mayhew 1984: 119-20.

189 *'He had misused; 'he did never:* Rye 13/8.

Collinson: 1986: 11, 27.

visits: Louis xxxvii-xxxix

190 *'it is remarkable:* Louis xliv

sheepskins: Louis xlvii; Gibson 1996: 144.

not enough; 7 stages: Gibson 1996: 219, 138.

watch at Lydd; admin centre: Gibson 1996: 219, 216.

£30, Rye minstrel: Dawson 206-8.

192 *mayor paid first:* Louis xxxvii-xxxviii and e.g. pp. 84, 86.

Lord Chamberlain's men: usual circuit, Louis xxxix.

usual fee: 20s for players of the Lord Chamberlain and the Queen. The fee varied according to the status of the patron and the size of the group, but for the same patron, players' fees were often about double, or a bit less, that of minstrels. This was just payments by the corporation - players would expect to be paid by the audience as well. Louis xxxvii-xxxviii.

Isle of Dogs: Ackroyd 307-8.

when written: probably not before 1599, Taylor 4-5.

193 *ferrying:* Collard 14-16.

popery: Friar Laurence.

dynasties rare other towns: Archer 243.

domineering man: John Fletcher, a protégé of Wolsey; Mayhew 1982: 146-8; Collard 18-9.

sons living: GM 116.

will of T Hamon: PROB 11/110/493.

194 *heal antagonisms:* Bridget Ruck, George Taylor's stepmother, crossed factions, her first husband Thomas Fletcher being prominent in the merchant faction (see Names Index); Joan Breadcar may be another one.

bankruptcy: Rye 47/61; Rye 1/7/357v.

overseer: T Chiswell ESRO W/A11/221 (1603), exec for A Harry W/A7/194 (1580); all the following are PROB 11: A Cog [i.e. Coq] 75/346 (1590), J Fagge 66/24 (1583), W Davie 61/485 (1579), J Dounck 63/172 (1581) and J Bruster 79/436 (1592).

'reputed to be: see p.92.

Fisher and Harrison: see pp. 100-1, 262, 265, 272.

195 *Higgons died:* Rye 13/26 (witness to be asked about possible bewitchment).

'he did admonish: Rye 13/24; daughter Elizabeth married Michael Bishop (son of jurat Henry).

196 *Whitfields:* next door, 1604 tax list; sued by G Taylor for trespass in 1604, Rye 33/17/216, 35/52. Born 1548 in Tenterden, m Mary dau of William Blunt Esq., Berry 1830: 54 (pedigree and coat of arms).

'At a certain time: Rye 13/24.

'Master Mayor: Rye 13/8.

'my wife when: Rye 47/74/11. The Bennett women also predicted the death of T Hamon, see pp.108-9.

197 *sister Margaret:* born Tenterden 1549, father John (who drowned himself in 1585), Berry 1830: 54.

Tenterden was closely linked to Rye, as its 'limb' within the federation of the Cinque Ports; Draper et al. 174.

Carpenter's d-in-law: Mary wife of William, Rye 13/18.

made notes: Rye 13/17; see p. 119.

198 *'Master Convers:* Rye 47/78.

'fools and sots: Rye 1/8/180v.

'They are all fools: Rye 47/78.

re-enfranchised: Rye 1/8/198v; jurat 1611; mayor 1614.

199 *George Taylor made free:* Rye 1/9/338v, 351-v, 417v, 473; Rye 47/84.

'well liked of: Rye 1/9/352.

Fisher died: Rye 1/9/474.

pardon: Rye 1/8/73-v, 156-7 and 256.

'I think: HMC13/147-8.

200 *'acutting:* Rye 47/84.

civil war; men of war: E. Sussex of one mind, and not as severely affected as the west, Fletcher 1975: 256, 270.

201 *'I will either:* from Arundel; Frewen 4223 p. 70; Coulton calls himself 'clericus under Capt. Cockram', p.71.

A Taylor's will: ESRO U1/233 (1644); the slaughterhouse may still have been used in 1723, Martin et al 27.

Hamon's will: PROB 11/110/493.

Epilogue

202 *Joseph Radford:* Hunter & Gregory 32; Monod 122.

The characteristics of the factions: Monod 106-17; Hunter & Gregory 28-30, 61. Members of the factions are listed in TNA SP 29/413 (letter from Crouch, Gillart and Radford to Sir L. Jenkins, 24 June 1680), and the occupations are here taken from a 1660 tax list (Rye 82/82). Only those owning £100 or more of goods (or £5 or more in rental income) were means-tested for this list (others paid a poll tax). Of those in this rich group who were still there in 1680 when the list of faction members was drawn up, 10 were members of the merchant faction, and only one was a member of the artisan faction (Crouch). Gillart and Hall were either not there or not taxed in 1660. Other freemen are also listed who apparently did not ally themselves with either faction. The relative wealth of poorer inhabitants can be ascertained from a more inclusive tax list (this just gives a figure for the tax, not the value of goods being taxed) drawn up three years earlier in 1657 (Rye 82/81).

Lewis Gillart defected: Monod 111.

Anne Taylor's will: ESRO original will Bundle U1/233 (1644).

'What fellowship: ESRO Frewen 4223 p.63v, quoted in Fletcher 1981: 150.

203 *opposition:* Fletcher 1981: 149-51 / ESRO Frewen 4223 p.68v.

Restoration politics see e.g. Hutton 1985.

wrote to: Monod 118; particularly Robert Hall, the customs collector.

fines: Watts 226-7.

factional conflicts: Halliday 132-35; Monod 117-28; Hunter & Gregory 30-2.

change the locks: Hunter & Gregory 32; Monod 121; Halliday 134.

204 *'The height of:* quoted in Hunter & Gregory 30; CSPDom 1682, 354. Rye was not the only town to suffer such disturbances, as Paul Halliday notes: *Division had not been unknown before 1640, but never had it been so dangerously persistent as in the decades since;* p.3.

conflicting judgments: Hunter & Gregory 31-2; Halliday 133-5; Monod 122-3.

Jeake's trading activities: Hunter & Gregory 14-19, 32-33, 57, 61-66.

mortgaging: Wrightson 2002: 276.

'Feb 13 1689: Hunter & Gregory 195.

205 *financial projects:* Murphy 204-8, 211, 215-17; Hunter & Gregory 69-72.

avoiding Rye: Hunter & Gregory 62.

did not compensate: Murphy 217.

excused: Hunter & Gregory 34.

Jeake and astrology: Hunter & Gregory 11-21, 73-6.

206 *'I cannot yet:* Hunter & Gregory 117.

Whigs in control; challenges: Monod 155-73, 179.

the murder of Grebell: for the story see Monod 10-36; more specifically 13, 25, 29-31, 11, 27, 34.

rival faction: Monod 223-35.

£7860 had been spent: Monod 226.

207 *'My self and friends:* Monod 230.

'no human power: Monod 233.

Chapter 13: The Wider Context

208 *younger women; took decades:* Sabean 1984: 108-9; Levack 149-51; Sharpe 1999: 109-10.

political factionalism: Demos 315-86, Boyer and Nissenbaum esp. 92-109.

usually women: Levack 141-9.

geography of witchcraft : Levack 210-42. Levack's argument about centralisation is here pursued rather more single-mindedly than he does – he gives weight to a number of other factors.

209 *total prosecutions and execution rates:* Levack 20-24, 218, 221, 237.

Holy Roman Empire: Levack 188-9, 212-14, 100-2.

usual story: Larner 1981: 11; Briggs 1989: 83.

210 *different regions:* see note above.

'municipal courts: Levack 231-2.

procedure in England : Levack 219-20, 99-100.

Civil War: Gaskill 121, 200.

France: Briggs 1989: 45-6; Levack 216-7, 97-8.

211 *torture, Scandinavia and Scotland:* Levack 223-4, 218-9; Larner 107-9.

Scotland: procedure and execution rate: Levack 219-20, 98-9, p.108 n.86; Larner 197.

torture, Italy and Spain: Levack 204.

Inquisition, procedure and execution rates: Levack 239-41; Ginzburg 126; Henningsen xxvi.

procedural controls in ecclesiastical courts,but secular courts taking over: Levack 88-95.

local courts: Levack 97, 102-3.

212 *Rye, new witness list:* Rye 13/26, 27.

German political factions: Midelfort chs5-6; see also Quaife 149-50; like M Young in Rye, pp.68, 147.

cross the channel: Levack 218.

confession of pact: Larner 145-6.

accusers concerned about maleficia: Levack 182-3, 186-7, 153-6; Quaife 127; Briggs 1989: 14-9.

smaller trials: Levack 188-9.

diabolism in New England: Levack 188, 221-3; Larner 22.

213 *English Civil War:* Gaskill.

diabolism, Scotland and Spain: Levack 219-20, 237-9.

nightmare fantasies: Cohn xi-xiii, Levack 35-40.

money-devouring: Kuper 2001.

214 *illegal killings:* Briggs 1989: 43.

self-governing communities: Macfarlane 1970: 297, Sharpe 1999: 92-3, Gaskill 167-8.

215 *'from Africa:* Mayer 1970: 45; see also Larner 22.

'get away: Cheater 226.

catholics and protestants: Levack 111, 122-4; Quaife 115, 121-2; Briggs 1989: 36-8; Sharpe 80.

included in intellectual ideas: e.g. Bacon on the evil eye (1627): 251, (1972): 24.

'educated people: Niehaus 187.

public school: Kuper 2001.

'colonial-era: Monter 2004: 107.

'natural witchcraft': Scot 398-400.

216 *very personal:* for 15th century England, see Carpenter 1992: 281-7.

good-will society: this is Bourdieu's *good faith economy*, but broadened to include a more developed society than he discusses, Bourdieu 171-97; Peck 1990: chaps. 1 and 2.

good lordship/neighbourhood: Hunt 130-5; Underdown 1985: ch. 3; Stone 124-5; Westfall; Heal conclusion; Wrightson 1982: 51-65; Wrightson 2002: 82, 85-86; Trevor-Roper 13-16.

217 *barrator:* a quarreller, either by multiplying law suits or verbal or physical brawling, OED.

eucharist and social cohesion: Bossy 1973: 140-3; see also Duffy 7, 125-7; Wrightson 1982: 54; Rubin 73-6.

held aloft: James 1986: 18-27, 23 n.21.

218 *undemocratic:* in relation to Rye, see Hipkin 1995(b); for Kent, see Clark 1977: 139-40.

elsewhere: Durston 306-11.

compurgation: Baker 64-5.

trespass: and trespass-on-the-case, Rye 33/14-15.

219 *'thereby to declare:* Rye 1/4/121-2.

'It falleth so out: Rye 47/70/11.

220 *gorrovage; 'the demonic pact:* Larner 152-5, 148; see also Clark 1980: 98-127; Briggs 1989: 81; Wilby 85-9, 240, 177.

'loosely, 'cornering: Wrightson 2002: 129, 111.

economic specialisation; water transport: Palliser 5-6, 2.

no more famines: Clay Vol. I pp. 103-4.

221 *increasing demand:* Palliser 5, 4; prices began rising before the population did, indicating that the latter was not the only cause, Wrightson 2002: 128.

increasing integration of English economy: Palliser 9-10, 5; Wrightson 2002: 109, 53, 99-100, 171-81; Brandon & Short 132.

costs of hospitality and gifts: in medieval London, the custom of leaving 1/3-1/2 of moveables to charity (to benefit the merchant's soul) was followed quite strictly, Thrupp 177-9.

attitudes to good lordship changing: Stone 94-97; Wrightson 1982: 59.

climate change: Palliser 3; Fagan 90.

widening gap: Briggs 1989: 72.

Part 2: Essay

Of mirth and godliness

224 *riot in Stratford:* Sisson 187.

'what are we to: Thomas 1977: 81.

increasing proportion: Clark 1977: 124, Collinson 1986.

Declaration of Sports: Hill 1964: 193, 195; Malcolmson 11.

225 *making a breakfast:* Louis 115, 117.

'going over; lascivious: Louis 116; see p. 92.

Notes

'*go out of the town:* Louis 126 / Rye 1/4/302 May 1579.

festivities ceased: Hutton 1994: 113-32; Collinson 1986: 8-12, 14.

no orders banning: Hunt 135; Clopper 292; Johnston and Husken 96-7; Hutton 1996: 268.

countermand: Govett 23.

Shakespeare's Company: see p.192.

227 '*I would stop the unpure:* Vaughan: Epistle Dedicatorie (to the Lords of the Privy Council).

228 '*cursed copyholders;* '*villanous vassals:* Vaughan 118.

'*addicted;* '*these jolly fellows;* '*cavaleers:* Vaughan: Preface to the Reader.

'*the spirit of detraction;* '*then farewell kind:* Vaughan: 329, 81.

229 '*I dare invite:* and next two quotes, Vaughan 112, 328, 331.

Archilochus: a Greek poet who used iambic verse for his satires, OED.

230 *noblemen in Kent:* Clark 1977: p. 3-33, 112; on Sussex: Fletcher 1975: 54.

Malvolio, Anne Taylor: e.g. *Twelfth Night* II.iii; see pp.116-7.

Radcliffe-Brown: 1940 and 1949.

231 *joking can vary:* Tamari 217.

good-will society: see p.216.

shanty towns: Sylvain 222-23.

West Africa: Diallo 184-7, 195.

'*joking relationships:* Hagberg 201.

'*tremendous:* Gilsenan 1996: 186, 182, 183.

232 *wedding and maypole:* St. Clare Byrne x-xiii, 17, 20-34.

'*as for me:* St. Clare Byrne 25-34.

233 '*Tis merry:* Jonson 12-13; Rollins 1929: vol.2 174-79.

term gossip: Bossy 1973: 132-4.

spiritual kinship: Fletcher 1975: 38, 52; Lynch 31, 57, 60-61; Macfarlane 1976: 144-45.

234 '*not to report:* Bloch 22 quoting Austin 234; see also Parkin 1984: 345-7.

hidden restriction: Bloch 5-6.

'*to be generous: Twelfth Night* I.v.85.

235 *period of history:* Carpenter 1997: 52-64, 263-5; 1992: 244.

plainspeaking: for detailed analysis of the extreme plainspeaking practised by the Quakers, see Bauman 1983, particularly chaps. 2, 4, 8.

dutiful respect: Houlbrooke 144-5; Wrightson 1982: 115.

'*ritual abuse:* Parkin 1980: 62

236 *ballads on plaindealing:* e.g. Chappell I: 261 and 355; Rollins 1929 vol I: 109, 117, 190, 207, 251, vol II: 117; 1922: 365.

'*this is an honest:* Rollins 1922: 406.

'*plain dealing now is dead:* 'Knavery in all Trades', Rollins 1922: 413.

'*I am Plain Dealing:* and next two quotes, Dekker II.i.104, 124, 71, 83.

237 '*Thrice Noble Worthies:* Hardy.

'*plain-dealing Death:* Carpenter 1629: 62.

godliness and fervency: e.g. Trapp: Gospel according to St. Mark VI.19, Younge 601.

'*plaindealing villain; 'I had rather: Much Ado About Nothing* I.iii.25.

Shakespeare on artisans: Ackroyd 275; I do not mean to imply that Shakespeare was unconcerned about this issue – plainspeaking plays a large part in *King Lear*.

lower-order virtue: e.g. Rollins 1929 vol. I: 117, 190.

'*merchandize:* Boccalini 169.

238 *incontinence and the humoral system:* Paster Introduction and Chap. 1; Gregory 1985: Chap. 7; Beier 31, 163.

239 '*open and loud:* Thomas 1977: 80.

incontinence was low class: Paster 121.

'whore of tongue and tail': WSRO Ep.IV/3/1/8; Ep. II/5/11/22; also Ep. I.11.13.34v.

'incontinently kiss: Holloway 145 (Rye custumal).

'Commend: King John V.ii.56

gossips' feasts: Capp 2003: 50-1; Scotland: Todd 145-7.

City comedies: Paster 53-55.

240 *'the artificer:* Harrison 1968: 131-2.

'women creating ties: Capp 2003: 50-3; Peck 1990: chap. 5.

sent to serve: Wrightson 1982: 74; Fletcher 1975: 38, 100; Mertes 52-7, 191; similar strategies in other cultures: Emecheta 36-7 (Nigeria, Ibos) and Maher 81 (Morocco).

grief closes the body: Paster 34.

241 *'How great is:* Dod and Cleaver 46.

patronage always involves domination: Seymour-Smith 219.

sandwich: see also Hill 1972: 340.

urban patrons: Stone 7-8; Archer 241; Patterson 7, 87, 235.

243 *Rye patrons:* Hipkin 1995b: 319; HMC13/80, 132, Rye 1/4/129, 1/8/28, ESRO W/A11 f87; although magistrates forbidden to have patrons in the Cinque Ports, Hull 291.

1570s makeup of factions: see p.176-7.

travelling companies: see p.191; Westfall; Louis xliii.

Jeake: see p.205.

244 *epidemic of maypoles:* Hutton 1996: 236, 1994: 223, 225-6; I think there is a more direct relation between maypoles and *good lordship,* but exploring that would require another essay.

'shopping around: Carpenter 1992: 599; see also Mertes 133, 137.

suggested contribution: see e.g. the New Economics Foundation 2011.

245 *Fundamentalism Project:* Marty and Appleby: Introduction. The contributors to this work do not necessarily reflect the views of the editors according to Sonn 1992.

concerned with: Gellner 52; see also 51, 161, 215.

mixed-sex dancing: Gellner 125-6, 142, 162-3; Maher 94-7.

Catholic religiosity: see e.g. Hall 10; Gardiner 61; Hutton1994: 99-102.

246 *'Islamic society:* Roy 197, see also 80, 82.

social background: Gilsenan 2000: 217-8, 232, 261; Ruthven 317, 337; Caplan 49; Tapper 61.

18th century Wahabism: Gellner 51; Ruthven 273-82.

'an urban religion: Ruthven 355.

Najd: Gellner 82.

Umma: Roy 71; Ruthven 356.

Sufism and social status: Gilsenan 2000: 90, 230-34; Roy 88.

Sufism similar: Gellner 80.

'villagization: Ruthven 349.

'it was God's own: Gellner 215.

247 *'The brotherhoods:* Gilsenan 2000: 231-2.

'encouraged obscurantism: Gellner 148; see also Maher 21 re: Morocco.

'represented forces: Gilsenan 2000: 232.

'differentiate themselves: Gellner 68.

'secularism of the elites: Ruthven 358.

'Kin patronage: Ruthven 356-7; see also Roy 52.

248 *reconstituted:* Roy 200; Gellner 70.

language of kinship: Gellner 29-30, 70; Roy 200; Carsten.

Bibliography

1 Manuscripts

British Library

Additional 11401	*Psychopharmacon*: a translation of Boethius' *De Consolatione Philosophiae* by John Bracegirdle.
Harley 358 no. 47 f.188	*The confession of certayne persons concerninge the Spirittes appeareinge at Rie.*
Sloane 3851	Tracts on Magic.
1954 ff.161-93	*The Winnowing of White Witchcraft*, by E[dward] P[oeton] (paginated separately).

East Sussex Record Office, Lewes

Rye Corporation MSS

Rye	1	Assembly Books (including records of Sessions courts etc.)
	13	The Trial of Susan Swapper and Anne Taylor for witchcraft
	33	Court of Record: Rolls and Books
	35	Court of Record: Plea Rolls
	47	General Files (correspondence, depositions etc.)
	57	Custumals and Precedent Books
	58	Miscellaneous documents
	60	Chamberlains' Account books
	65	Receipts: The Great Box (dues for land-based trades)
	66	Receipts: The Lesser Box (dues for sea-based trades)
	77	Rate Books (local tax assessments)
	82	Parliamentary taxes, army and militia rates
	132	Maps and plans
	137	Deeds relating to Rye
	139	Draft deeds relating to Rye
	147	Churchwardens' Accounts

Parish records   PAR 467/1/1/1-2   Rye parish registers 1538-1635

Frewen 606   Book of recipes and remedies
        4223 Letter book of Samuel Jeake I

Historic Building Records   HBR/1

Lewes Archdeaconry Probate Records
    W/A   Registers of Wills
    W/B   Registers of administrations
    U1   Original Wills

Kent History and Library Centre, Maidstone

Bishopric of Rochester
    Consistory Court   DRb/P/wr/19/Pt II   Wills Register

Parish register of Shadoxhurst   p332/1/1
Parish register of Headcorn   p181/1/1A

Cinque Ports Archives   CP/Br   Papers re: Cadiz expedition, 1595-8

Quarter Sessions Records
    QM/SRc Recognizances
    QM/SI   Indictments
    Q/SR   Sessions Rolls

West Sussex Record Office

Archdeaconry of
    Lewes   Ep.II/5   Deposition books
                Ep.II/9   Detection books
    Chichester   Ep.I/11   Deposition books
                Ep. I/10 Court Act books and Instance books
Exempt Deanery of Pagham and Tarring
                Ep.IV/3 Deposition books

The National Archives: Public Record Office

ASSI 45/1/1	Assizes: Northern and North-Eastern Circuits: Criminal Depositions and Case Papers
MPF 1	Maps and plans
PROB 11	Prerogative Court of Canterbury: Wills registers
SP	State Papers
STAC 5	Court of Star Chamber proceedings (Elizabeth I)

Unpublished Thesis

Gregory, A. 1985. Slander accusations and social control in late 16th and early 17th century England, with particular reference to Rye (Sussex), 1590-1615. D.Phil. thesis in Social Anthropology, Univ. of Sussex.

2 Printed Sources

Abbreviation

SAC   *Sussex Archaeological Collections*

Place of publication is London unless otherwise specified.

ACAD. *A Cambridge Alumni Database.* ed. J. L. Dawson for Cambridge University Library; available at http://venn.lib.cam.ac.uk/Documents/acad/index.html.
Ackroyd, P. 2005. *Shakespeare: the biography.*
Acts of the Privy Council of England, 1542-7.(ed.) J.R.Dasent, 1890.
Adair, J. 1978. *The Pilgrims' Way: shrines and saints in Britain and Ireland.*
Adams, S. 1982. Faction, clientage and party: English politics, 1550-1603. *History Today* **32: 12**, 33-9.
Addy, S.O. 1895. *Household Tales with other Traditional Remains collected in the counties of York, Lincoln, Derby and Nottingham.*
Amherst, A. 1895. *A History of Gardening in England.*
Anon. 1608. *The Great Frost: cold doings in London, except it be at the lotterie.*
Appleby, A.B. 1979. Diet in 16th century England: sources, problems, possibilities. In Webster, pp. 97-116.
Archer, I.A. 2000. Politics and government 1540-1700. In *The Cambridge Urban History of Britain, Vol.2: 1540-1840* (ed.) P. Clark. Cambridge, pp. 235-62.
Armstrong, J.R. 1974 (1961). *A History of Sussex.*
Aubrey, J. 1847 (1656-91). *The Natural History of Wiltshire.* ed. J. Britton.
—. 1881 (1686-7). *Remaines of Gentilism and Judaism.* ed. J. Britten. Folklore Society.
Austin, J.L. 1961. Performative utterances. In *Philosophical Papers, etc.* Oxford, pp. 233-52. ed. J.O. Urmson & G. J. Warnock.
Bacon, F. 1627. *Sylva sylvarum: or A Natural Historie in Ten Centuries.*
—. 1972 (1625). *Essays.* Intro. by M.J. Hawkins.
Baker, J.H. 1979. *An Introduction to English Legal History.* 2nd edn.
Ballads. 1867. *A Collection of 79 Black-letter Ballads and Broadsides, printed in the reign of Queen Elizabeth between the years 1559 and 1597.*
Bath, J. 2008. The treatment of potential witches in north-east England, c.1649-1680. In Newton & Bath, pp. 129-45.
Bauman, R. 1983. *Let Your Words be Few: symbolism of speaking and silence among 17th century Quakers.*
Beard, C.R. 1933. *The Romance of Treasure Trove.*
Beier, L.M. 1987. *Sufferers and Healers: the experience of illness in 17th century England.*
Berry, L.E. (ed.) 1969 (1560). *The Geneva Bible.* Wisconsin.
Berry, W. 1830. *County Genealogies: pedigrees of the families in the county of Kent, collected from the heraldic visitations and other authentic manuscripts.*

Bloch, M. 1975. Introduction. In *Political language and oratory in traditional societies* (ed.) M. Bloch, pp. 1-28.
Blome, R. 1673. *Britannia*.
Boccalini, T. 1626. *The New-founde Politicke*.
Booth, R. 2008. Standing within the Prospect of Belief: Macbeth, King James, and witchcraft. In Newton & Bath, pp. 47-67.
Bossy, J. 1965. The character of Elizabethan Catholicism. In *Crisis in Europe 1560-1660* (ed.) T. Aston, pp. 223-46.
—. 1973. Blood and baptism: kinship, community and christianity in western Europe from the 14th to the 17th centuries. In *Sanctity and Secularity: the church and the world* (ed.) D. Baker. Studies in Church History. Oxford, pp. 129-43.
Bourdieu, P. 1977. *Outline of a Theory of Practice*. Cambridge. trans. R. Nice.
Boyer, P. & S. Nissenbaum. 1974. *Salem Possessed: the social origins of witchcraft*. Cambridge, Mass.
Brandon, P. 1974. *The Sussex Landscape*.
Brandon, P. & B. Short. 1990. *The South-East from AD1000*.
Brent, C.E. 1975. Urban employment and population in Sussex between 1550 and 1640. *SAC* **113**, 35-50.
—. 1976. Rural employment and population in Sussex between 1550 and 1640: part 1. *SAC* **114**, 27-48.
—. 1978. Rural employment and population in Sussex between 1550 and 1640: part 2. *SAC* **116**, 41-55.
Briggs, K. 1953. Some seventeenth-century books of magic. *Folklore* **64**, 445-62.
—. 1959. *The Anatomy of Puck: an examination of fairy beliefs among Shakespeare's contemporaries and successors*.
—. 1967. *The Fairies in English Tradition and Literature*.
—. 1976. *A Dictionary of Fairies; hobgoblins, brownies, bogies and other supernatural creatures*.
Briggs, R. 1989. *Communities of Belief: cultural and social tension in early modern France*. Oxford.
—. 1998 (1977). *Early Modern France, 1560-1715*. Oxford.
—. 2002 (1996). *Witches and Neighbours: the social and cultural context of European witchcraft*. Oxford.
Bullein, W. 1579. *Bullein's Bulwarke of Defence: against all sicknesse*.
Bushaway, B. 1982. *By Rite: custom, ceremony and community in England, 1700-1880*.
Butler, G.S. 1862. Appearance of spirits in Sussex. *SAC* **14**, 26-32. Transcription of Harleian MSS No. 358 f. 188.
Caciola. 2000. Spirits seeking bodies: death, possession, and communal memory in the Middle Ages. In Gordon & Marshall, pp. 66-86.
Calendar of the Patent Rolls, Edward VI. 1924-29.
Caplan, L. 1987. Introduction. In *Studies in Religious Fundamentalism* (ed.) L. Caplan, pp. 1-24.
Capp, B. 1979. *Astrology and the Popular Press: English almanacs 1500-1800*.

—. 2003. *When Gossips Meet: women, family and neighbourhood in early-modern England*. Oxford.
Carpenter, C. 1992. *Locality and Polity: a study of Warwickshire landed society, 1401-99*. Cambridge.
—. 1997. *The Wars of the Roses: politics and the constitution in England, c. 1437-1509*. Cambridge.
Carpenter, N. 1629. *Achitophel, or, The picture of a wicked politician*.
Chapman, A. 1979. Astrological medicine. In Webster, pp. 275-300.
Chappell, W. (ed.) 1874. *The Roxburghe Ballads*.
Chatwin, D. 1996. *The Development of Timber-framed Buildings in the Sussex Weald: the architectual heritage of the parish of Rudgwick*.
Cheater, A.P. 1989 (1986). *Social Anthropology: an alternative introduction*. 2nd edn.
Clark, P. 1977. *English Provincial Society from the Reformation to the Revolution: religion, politics and society in Kent, 1500-1640*. Hassocks.
Clark, S. 1980. Inversion, misrule and the meaning of witchcraft. *Past and Present* **87**, 98-127.
—. 1997. *Thinking with Demons: the idea of witchcraft in early modern Europe*. Oxford.
Clay, C.G.A. 1984. *Economic Expansion and Social Change: England 1500-1700*. Cambridge. 2 Vols.
Clopper, L.M. 2001. *Drama, Play and Game: English festive culture in the medieval and early-modern period*. Chicago.
Cockburn, J.S. 1972. *A History of the English Assizes 1558-1714*. Cambridge.
—. 1985. (ed.) *Calendar of Assize Records: Home Circuit Indictments Elizabeth I and James I. Introduction*.
Coffey, J. & P.C.H. Lim (eds) 2008. *The Cambridge Companion to Puritanism*. Cambridge.
—. 2008. Introduction. In Coffey & Lim, pp. 1-18.
Cogan, T. 1584. *The Haven of Health*.
Cohn, N. 1975. *Europe's Inner Demons: an enquiry inspired by the great witch hunt*.
Collard, J.A. 1997 (1978). *A Maritime History of Rye*. Rye.
Collinson, P. 1980. Cranbrook and the Fletchers: popular and unpopular religion in the Kentish Weald. In *Reformation Principle and Practice: essays in honour of A. G. Dickens* (ed.) P.N. Brooks, pp. 173-202.
—. 1986. *From Iconoclasm to Iconophobia: the cultural impact of the second English Reformation*. Reading.
—. 2008. Antipuritanism. In Coffey & Lim, pp. 19-33.
Como, D.R. 2008. Radical Puritanism, c. 1558-1660. In Coffey & Lim, pp. 241-58.
Cross, C. 1976. *Church and People 1450-1660: the triumph of the laity in the English Church*.
Curry, P. 1989. *Prophecy and Power: astrology in early modern England*. Cambridge.
Cust, L. 1900. *Anthony Van Dyck: an historical study of his life and works*.
Davies, O. 2003. *Cunning-folk: popular magic in English history*.
Davis, J.F. 1983. *Heresy and Reformation in the south-east of England, 1520-59*.
Davis, N.Z. 2000. *The Gift in Sixteenth-century France*. Oxford.

Dawson, G. 1965. *Records of Plays and Players in Kent 1450-1642*. Malone Society Collections Vol. VII.

Dearn, T.D.W. 1814. *An Historical Topography and descriptive account of the Weald of Kent*. Cranbrook.

Dekker, T. 1955 (1607). The Whore of Babylon. In *The Dramatic Works of Thomas Dekker* (ed.) F. Bowers. Vol. 2. Cambridge.

Demos, J.P. 1982. *Entertaining Satan: witchcraft and the culture of early New England*. Oxford.

Dent, A. *The Plaine Mans Pathway to Heaven*.

Diallo, Y. 2006. Joking relationships in western Burkina Faso. *Zeitschrift fur Ethnologie* **131**, 183-96.

Dobson, M.J. 1998. Death and disease in the Romney Marsh area in the 17th to 19th centuries. In *Romney Marsh: environmental change and human occupation in a coastal lowland* (eds) J. Eddison, M. Gardiner & A. Long. Oxford, pp. 166-81.

Dod, J. & R. Cleaver. 1612. *A Godlie forme of Householde Government*.

Draper, G., with contributions by D. Martin, B. Martin & A. Tyler. 2009. *Rye: a History of a Cinque Port to 1660*. Chichester.

Duffy, E. 2005 (1992). *The Stripping of the Altars: traditional religion in England c.1400-c.1580*. 2nd edn.

Dulley, A.J.F. 1969. The early history of the Rye fishing industry. *SAC* **107**, 36-64.

Dunkin, E.H.W. 1902. Calendar of Sussex Marriage Licences ... from the Archdeaconry of Lewes, August 1586-March 1642/3. *Sussex Record Society* **1**.

Durston, G. 2004. *Crime and Justice in Early-Modern England, 1500-1750*. Chichester.

Eddison, J. 1998. Catastrophic Changes: a multidisciplinary study of the evolution of the barrier beaches of Rye Bay. In *Romney Marsh: environmental change and human occupation in a coastal lowland* (eds) J. Eddison, M. Gardiner & A. Long. Oxford, pp. 65-87.

Elton, G.R. 1972. *Policy and Police: the enforcement of the Reformation in the age of Thomas Cromwell*. Cambridge.

Emecheta, B. 1978. *The Bride Price*.

Evans-Pritchard, E.E. 1937. *Witchcraft, Oracles and Magic among the Azande*. Oxford.

Fagan, B. 2000. *The Little Ice Age: how climate made history 1300-1850*. New York.

Farmer, D.H. 1978. *The Oxford Dictionary of Saints*. Oxford.

Fiennes, C. (ed.) 1949. *The Journeys of Celia Fiennes*. ed. C. Morris.

Firth, K.R. 1979. *The Apocalyptic Tradition in Reformation Britain, 1530-1645*. Oxford.

Fletcher, A. 1975. *A County Community in Peace and War: Sussex 1600-60*.

—. 1981. Puritanism in 17th century Sussex. In *Studies in Sussex Church History* (ed.) M.J. Kitch, pp. 141-55.

Flower, M. 1970 (1618). *The Wonderful Discoverie of the Witchcrafts of Margaret and Phillip Flower ...* Leicester.

Foster, J. 1891. *Alumni Oxoniensis*. available from British History Online at http://www.british-history.ac.uk/.

Foxe, J. [1875]. *Acts and Monuments [Book of Martyrs]*. ed. J. Cumming.

Friend, H. 1884. *Flowers and Flower Lore*.

Furley, R. 1874. *A History of the Weald of Kent*.
Gardiner, H.C. 1946. *Mysteries' End: an investigation of the last days of the medieval religious stage*. Newhaven, CT.
Gaskill, M. 2005. *Witchfinders: a seventeenth-century English tragedy*.
Gellner, E. 1981. *Muslim Society*. Cambridge.
Gibson, J.M. 1996. "Interludum Passionis Domini": parish drama in medieval New Romney. In *English Parish Drama* (eds) A.F. Johnston & W. Husken. Amsterdam and Atlanta, GA, pp. 137-48.
Gibson, M. 2008. Applying the Act of 1604: witches in Essex, Northamptonshire and Lancashire. In Newton & Bath, pp. 115-28.
Gilsenan, M. 1996. *Lords of the Lebanese Marches: violence and narrative in an Arab society*.
—. 2000 (1982). *Recognizing Islam: religion and society in the modern Middle East*. revised edition.
Ginzburg, C. 1983. *The Night Battles: witchcraft and agrarian cults in the 16th and 17th centuries*.
Gordon, B. 2000. Malevolent ghosts and ministering angels: apparitions and pastoral care in the Swiss Reformation. In Gordon & Marshall, pp. 87-109.
Gordon, B. & P. Marshall (eds) 2000. *The Place of the Dead: death and remembrance in late medieval and early modern Europe*. Cambridge.
Govett, L.A. 1890. *The King's Book of Sports*.
Graunt, J. 1676. *Natural and Political Observations mentioned in a following Index, and made upon the Bills of Mortality*.
Gregory, A. 1991. Witchcraft, politics and 'good neighbourhood' in early 17th century Rye. *Past and Present* **133**, 31-66. Reprinted in *New Perspectives on Witchcraft, Magic and Demonology*. Vol. III: *Witchcraft in the British Isles and New England*, (ed) B. P. Levack (2001), pp. 99-134.
Gribben, C. 2000. *The Puritan Millennium: literature and theology, 1550-1682*. Dublin.
Grieve, M. 1976 (1931). *A Modern Herbal*. Harmondsworth.
Gwynn, R. 2001 (1985). *Huguenot Heritage: the history and contribution of the Huguenots in Britain*. Brighton.
Hagberg, S. 2006. The politics of joking relationships in Burkina Faso. *Zeitschrift fur Ethnologie* **131**, 197-214.
Hall, T. 1660. *Funebria Florae*.
Halliday, P.D. 1998. *Dismembering the Body Politic: partisan politics in England's towns, 1650-1730*. Cambridge.
Halliwell, J.O. 1841. *A collection of letters illustrative of the progress of science in England : from the reign of Queen Elizabeth to that of Charles the Second*.
Hardy, N. 1647. *The arraignment of licentious liberty ...*
Harrison, W. 1968 (1587). *The Description of England*. Ithaca NY.
Hasler, P.W. 1981. *The House of Commons, 1558-1603*. The History of Parliament Trust. 3 Vols.
Hasted, E. 1797-1801. *The History and Topographical Survey of the County of Kent*. Canterbury. 12 vols.

Haynes, A. 2005. *The Gunpowder Plot.*
Hazlitt, W.C. 1999 (1874 and 1909). *Tenures of Land and Customs of Manors.* Epsom. Enlarged edition of *Fragmenta Antiquitatis*, by Thomas Blount (1679).
Heal, F. 1990. *Hospitality in Early Modern England.* Oxford.
Henningsen, G. 1980. *The Witches' Advocate: Basque witchcraft and the Spanish inquisition (1609-1614).* Reno, Nevada.
Herrup, C.B. 1987. *The Common Peace: participation and the criminal law in 17th century England.* Cambridge.
Hill, C. 1962. *Puritanism and Revolution.*
—. 1964. *Society and Puritanism in Pre-Revolutionary England.*
—. 1972. *The World Turned Upside Down: radical ideas during the English revolution.* Harmondsworth.
Hill, G. 1936. *Treasure Trove in law and practice from the earliest time to the present day.* Oxford.
Hill, T. 1946 (1563). *A most briefe and pleasant treatise ... to dress, sowe and set a garden.*
Hipkin, S. 1995a. Buying Time: fiscal policy at Rye, 1600-1640. *SAC* **133**, 241-54.
—. 1995b. Closing Ranks: oligarchy and government at Rye, 1570-1640. *Urban History* **22**, 319-40.
—. 1998-99. The maritime economy of Rye, 1560-1640. *Southern History* **20/21**, 108-42.
Holloway, W. 1847. *The History and Antiquities of the ancient town and port of Rye, in the county of Sussex. with incidental notices of the Cinque Ports.*
Hoskins, W.G. 1968 (1953-4). Harvest fluctuations and English economic history, 1480-1619. In *Essays in Agrarian History* (ed.) W.E. Minchinton, Vol. 1, pp. 93-105.
Houlbrooke, R.A. 1984. *The English Family 1450-1700.*
Hull, F. (ed.) 1966. *A Calendar of the White and Black books of the Cinque Ports, 1432-1955.*
Hunt, W. 1983. *The Puritan Moment: the coming of revolution in an English county.* Cambridge, Mass.
Hunter, M. & A. Gregory (eds) 1988. *An Astrological Diary of the 17th Century: Samuel Jeake of Rye, 1652-99.* Oxford.
Hutton, R. 1985. *The Restoration: a political and religious history of England and Wales, 1658-67.* Oxford.
—. 1994. *The Rise and Fall of Merry England: the ritual year 1400-1700.* Oxford.
—. 1996. *The Stations of the Sun: a history of the ritual year in Britain.* Oxford.
International Genealogical Index: a database of genealogical records compiled from several sources (mostly parish registers) by the Church of Jesus Christ of Latter-day Saints (the Mormon Church).
James I. 1924. *Daemonologie (1597)* and *Newes from Scotland (1591).*
James, M. 1986. Ritual, drama and social body in the late medieval English town. In *Society, Politics and Culture: studies in early modern England.* Cambridge, pp. 16-47.
Jardine, L. 1996. *Worldly Goods.*

Jessopp, A. 1896. *Random Roaming and other Papers*.
Jewel, J. 1571. *Second Book of Homilies*.
Johnston, A.F. & W. H:usken (eds) 1996. *English Parish Drama*. Ludus: Medieval and Early Renaissance Theatre and Drama Vol.1. Amsterdam.
Jones, D.J. 1995. Saint Richard of Chichester: the sources for his life. *Sussex Record Society* **79**.
Jones, W.J. 1961. Chancery and the Cinque Ports in the Reign of Elizabeth I. *Archaeologia Cantiana* **lxxvi**, 143-51.
—. 1967. *The Elizabethan Court of Chancery*. Oxford.
Jonson, B. 1976 (1631). *The Staple of News*. ed. D.R. Kifer.
Jue, J.K. 2008. Puritan millenarianism in old and New England. In Coffey & Lim, pp. 259-76.
Kaylor, N.H. & J.E. Streed (eds) 1999. *John Bracegirdle's Psychopharmacon: a translation of Boethius' De Consolatione Philosophiae*. Tempe, Arizona. Medieval and Renaissance Texts and Studies Vol. 200. Edition of BL Add. MS. 11401.
Kieckhefer, R. 1976. *European Witch Trials: their foundations in popular and learned culture, 1300-1500*.
Kittredge, G.L. 1929. *Witchcraft in Old and New England*. Cambridge, Mass.
Knafla, L.A. 1994. *Kent at Law, 1602: the county jurisdiction: assizes and sessions of the peace*.
Koestler, A. 1969 (1964). *The Act of Creation*.
Kuper, A. 2001. Enemies of the people: where witches - and witch-hunters - still ride. Review article. *Times Online 08/06/2001*.
Lake, P. & M. Questier. 2002. *The Antichrist's Lewd Hat: Protestants, papists and players in post-Reformation England*.
—. 2011. *The Trials of Margaret Clitherow: persecution, martyrdom and the politics of sanctity in Elizabethan England*.
Lambarde, W. 1970 (1570). *A Perambulation of Kent*. Bath.
Lamont, W.M. 1969. *Godly Rule: politics and religion, 1603-60*.
Lang, W.D. 1918. *A Map Showing the known Distribution in England and Wales of the Anopheline Mosquitoes*.
Langbein, J.H. 1977. *Torture and the Law of Proof: Europe and England in the Ancien Régime*. Chicago.
Larner, C. 1981. *Enemies of God: the witch-hunt in Scotland*. Oxford.
Latham, M.W. 1930. *The Elizabethan Fairies: the fairies of folklore and the fairies of Shakespeare*. New York.
Letters and Papers, Foreign and Domestic, Henry VIII. (ed.) J. Gairdner et al., 1895.
Levack, B.P. 2006 (1987). *The Witch-Hunt in Early Modern Europe*. 3rd Edn.
Lewis, B. 2002. Protestantism, pragmatism and popular religion: a case study of early-modern ghosts. In *Early-Modern Ghosts* (ed.) J. Newton. Durham, pp. 79-91.
Lewis, I.M. 1986. *Religion in Context: cults and charisma*. Cambridge.
Louis, C. 2000. *Records of Early English Drama: Sussex*. Toronto.
Lower, M.A. 1861. Old Speech and old manners in Sussex. *SAC* **13**, 209-36.

Lutton, R. 2010. Heresy and heterodoxy in late medieval Kent. In *Later Medieval Kent, 1220-1540* (ed.) S. Sweetinburgh. Woodbridge, Suffolk, pp. 167-88.

Lynch, J.H. 1986. *Godparents and kinship in early medieval Europe*. Princeton, N.J.

Macdonald, M. 1981. *Mystical Bedlam: madness, anxiety and healing in seventeenth-century England*. Cambridge.

Macfarlane, A. 1970. *Witchcraft in Tudor and Stuart England: a regional and comparative study*.

—. 1976. *The Diary of Ralph Josselin, 1660-1683*.

MacKillop, J. 1998. *Dictionary of Celtic Mythology*. Oxford.

Maher, V. 1974. *Women and Property in Morocco*. Cambridge.

Malcolmson, R.W. 1973. *Popular Recreations in English Society 1700-1850*.

Manning, R.B. 1969. *Religion and Society in Elizabethan Sussex: a study of the enforcement of the religous settlement 1559-1603*. Leicester.

Manningham, J. 1976. *The Diary of John Manningham of the Middle Temple, 1602-03*. Hanover, N.H. ed. R.P. Sorlien.

Manwaring Baines, J. 1968. *The Cinque Ports and Coronation Services*. Hastings Museum Publication No. 18. 3rd edn.

Martin, D. & B. Martin, with J. Clubb & G. Draper. 2009. *Rye Rebuilt: regeneration and decline within a Sussex port town, 1350-1660*.

Marty, M.E. & R.S. Appleby (eds) 1991. *Fundamentalisms Observed*. Chicago. Fundamentalism Project Vol.1.

Mason, J. 1612. *The Anatomie of Sorcerie: wherein the wicked impietie of charmers, inchanters, and such like, is discovered and confuted*. Cambridge.

Maxwell-Stuart, P.G. 2008. King James' experience of witches, and the 1604 English witchcraft Act. In Newton & Bath, pp. 31-46.

Mayer, P. 1970 (1954). Witches. In *Witchcraft and Sorcery: selected readings* (ed.) M. Marwick. Harmondsworth, pp. 45-64.

Mayhew, G. 1982. Religion, faction and politics in Reformation Rye: 1530-59. *SAC* **120**, 139-60.

—. 1984. Rye and the defence of the narrow seas: a 16th century town at war. *SAC* **122**, 107-26.

—. 1987. *Tudor Rye*. Falmer.

—. 1989. Order, disorder and popular protest in early modern Rye. *SAC* **127**, 167-87.

—. 1991. Life-cycle service and the family unit in early modern Rye. *Continuity and Change* **6**, 201-25.

McLean, T. 1981. *Medieval English Gardens*.

Means, L. (ed.) 1993. *Medieval Lunar Astrology: a collection of representative medieval Texts*. Lampeter, Dyfed.

Merk, C. 1909. *A History of Dieppe*. Paris.

Mertes, K. 1988. *The English Noble Household, 1250-1600*.

Midelfort, H.C.E. 1972. *Witch-hunting in South-Western Germany, 1562-1684: the social and intellectual foundations*. Stanford.

Monod, P.K. 2003. *The Murder of Mr. Grebell: madness and civility in an English town*.

Monter, W. 2004. Recontextualising British witchcraft. *Journal of Interdisciplinary History* **35**, 105-11. Review article.

Murphy, A.L. 2006. Dealing with uncertainty: managing personal investment in the early English National Debt. *History* **91**, 200-17.

Murray, K.M.E. 1935. *The Constitutional History of the Cinque Ports*. Manchester.

New Economics Foundation, The. 2011. *The Great Transition: social justice and the core economy*. available at http://www.neweconomics.org/publications/the-great-transition-social-justice-and-the-core-economy.

Newton, J. 2008. Introduction. In Newton & Bath, pp. 3-27.

Newton, J. & J. Bath (eds) 2008. *Witchcraft and the Act of 1604*. Leiden.

Niehaus, I., E. Mohlala & K. Shokane. 2001. *Witchcraft, Power and Politics: exploring the occult in the South African Lowveld*.

Norden, J. 1610. *The Surveyor's Dialogue*.

Northcote, R. 1912. *The Book of Herbs*.

Outhwaite, R.B. 2006. *The Rise and Fall of the English Ecclesiastical Courts, 1500-1860*. Cambridge.

Palliser, D.M. 1983. *The Age of Elizabeth: England under the later Tudors 1547-1603*.

Parkin, D. 1980. The creativity of abuse. *Man (N.S.)* **15**, 45-64.

—. 1984. Political language. *Annual Review of Anthropology* **13**, 345-65.

Paster, G.K. 1993. *The Body Embarrassed: drama and the disciplines of shame in early-modern England*. Ithaca NY.

Patterson, C.F. 1999. *Urban Patronage in Early Modern England*. Stanford, California.

Pearson, S. 1994. *The Medieval Houses of Kent: an historical analysis*.

Peck, L.L. 1982. *Northampton: patronage and policy at the court of James I*.

—. 1990. *Court Patronage and Corruption in Early Stuart England*.

Pelling, M. & C. Webster. 1979. Medical practitioners. In Webster, pp. 165-236.

Penry, J. 1960 [c.1587]. *Three Treatises concerning Wales*. Intro. by D. Williams. Cardiff.

Pitcairn, R. 1833. *Criminal Trials in Scotland, from AD 1488 to AD 1624*. Edinburgh. 3 Vols.

Plot, R. 1676. *The Natural History of Oxfordshire*. Oxford.

Ponting, C. 2005. *Gunpowder*.

Quaife, G.R. 1987. *Godly Zeal and Furious Rage: the witch in early modern Europe*.

Radcliffe-Brown, A.R. 1940. On joking relationships. *Africa* **12**, 195-210.

—. 1949. A further note on joking relationships. *Africa* **19**, 133-40.

Raine, J. 1861. Depositions from the castle of York, relating to offences committed in the northern counties in the seventeenth century. *Surtees Society* **Vol. 40**.

Rawcliffe, C. 1999 (1995). *Medicine and Society in later medieval England*.

Reaney, P.H. & R.M. Wilson. 1991 (1958). *A Dictionary of English Surnames*.

Reynolds, M. 2005. *Godly Reformers and their Opponents in Early-Modern England: religion in Norwich, c. 1560-1643*. Woodbridge Suffolk.

Robb, H.A. & A. Chesler. 1995. *Encyclopedia of American Family Names*.

Rock, J. 1862. Old Sussex Harvest customs, and peculiarities of speech at Hastings. *SAC* **14**, 186-90.

Rohde, E.S. 1974 (1922). *The Old English Herbals*.
Rollins, H.E. (ed.) 1922. *A Pepysian Garland: blackletter broadside ballads of the years 1595-1639*. Cambridge.
— (ed.) 1929. *The Pepys Ballads*. Cambridge, Mass. Vols 1 and 2.
Rosen, B. 1969. *Witchcraft*.
Roy, O. 1996. *The Failure of Political Islam*. Cambridge, Mass. trans. Carol Volk.
Royal Commission on Historical Manuscripts (ed.) 1892. *Thirteenth Report, Appendix, part IV: the manuscripts of Rye and Hereford corporations*.
Royalton-Kisch, M. 1999. *The Light of Nature: landscape drawings and watercolours by Van Dyck and his contemporaries*. Exhibition catalogue.
Rubin, M. 1991. *Corpus Christi: the Eucharist in late medieval culture*. Cambridge.
Ruthven, M. 2000. *Islam in the World*.
Sabean, D.W. 1984. *Power in the Blood: popular culture and village discourse in early modern Germany*. Cambridge.
Schmitt, J.-C. 1998 (Fr: 1994). *Ghosts in the Middle Ages: the living and the dead in medieval society*. Chicago.
Scot, R. 1964 (1584). *The Discoverie of Witchcraft*. Intro. by H. R. Williamson. Arundel.
Seager, H.W. 1972. *Natural History in Shakespeare's time: being extracts illustrative of the subject as he knew it*. Buckinghamshire.
Seward, D. 1995. *Sussex*. A Pimlico County History Guide.
Seymour-Smith, C. 1986. *Macmillan Dictionary of Anthropology*.
Sharpe, J.A. 1996. *Instruments of Darkness: witchcraft in England, 1550-1750*.
—. 1999 (1984). *Crime in Early-Modern England, 1550-1750*.
Short, T. 1750. *New Observations, natural, moral, civil ...*
Simpson, J. 1973. *The Folklore of Sussex*.
Sisson, C.J. 1936. *Lost Plays of Shakespeare's Age*. Cambridge.
Slack, P. 1985. *The Impact of Plague in Tudor and Stuart England*.
Sonn, T. 1992. Review of *Fundamentalisms Observed* (ed.) Marty & Appleby. *Journal of Asian Studies* **51**, 869-71.
Spence. 1948. *The Fairy Tradition in Britain*.
Spufford, M. 1974. *Contrasting Communities: English villagers in the 16th and 17th centuries*.
St. Clare Byrne, M. 1949. *The Elizabethan Home: discovered in two dialogues by Claudius Hollyband and Peter Erondell*.
Stone, L. 1979 (1977). *The Family, Sex and Marriage in England 1500-1800*.
Stow, J. 1598. *Survey of London ... Also an apologie ... concerning that citie ...*
Tamari, T. 2006. Joking pacts in Sudanic West Africa: a political and historical perspective. *Zeitschrift fur Ethnologie* **131**, 215-43.
Tapper, R. & N. Tapper. 1987. 'Thank God we're secular!': aspects of fundamentalism in a Turkish town. In *Studies in Religious Fundamentalism* (ed.) L. Caplan, pp. 51-78.
Taylor, G. (ed.) 1982. *Henry V*. Oxford.

Thirsk, J. 2000. Agriculture in Kent, 1540-1640. In *Early-Modern Kent 1540-1640* (ed.) M. Zell. Kent History Project, 5. Woodbridge, Kent, pp. 75-103.
—. 2007. *Food in Early-Modern England: phases, fads, fashions 1500-1760.*
Thomas, K.T. 1973 (1971). *Religion and the Decline of Magic: studies in popular beliefs in 16th and 17th century England.* Harmondsworth.
—. 1977. The place of laughter in Tudor and Stuart England. *Times Literary Supplement,* 77-81. January 21.
Thompson, C.J.S. 1928. *The Quacks of Old London.*
Thomson, J.A.F. 1965. *The Later Lollards 1414-1520.*
Thrupp, S.L. 1962 (1948). *The Merchant Class of Medieval London, 1300-1500.* Michigan.
Todd, M. 2000. Profane pastimes and the reformed community: the persistence of popular festivities in early-modern Scotland. *Journal of British Studies* **39**, 123-56.
Trapp, J. 1647. *A Commentary or Exposition upon the Four Evangelists.*
Trevor-Roper, H. 1983. Foreword. In *The Lisle Letters (abridged)* (ed.) M. St. Clare Byrne. Harmondsworth, pp. 7-27.
Turner, V.W. 1957. *Schism and continuity in an African society: a study of Ndembu village life.* Manchester.
Tyacke, N. 1979. Popular puritan mentality in late Elizabethan England. In *The English Commonwealth 1547-1640* (eds) P. Clark, A.G.R. Smith & N. Tyacke, pp. 77-92.
Underdown, D. 1985. *Revel, Riot and Rebellion: popular politics and culture in England, 1603-60.* Oxford.
—. 1986. Review of *The European Crisis of the 1590s* (ed.) P. Clark. *International History Review,* **8**, 484-7.
Vaughan, W. 1611. *The Spirit of Detraction.*
Vidler, L.A. 1934. *A New History of Rye.* Hove.
Wallenberg, J.K. 1934. *The Place-Names of Kent.* Uppsala.
Walsh, J. 1566. *The Examination of John Walsh ...upon certayne Interogatories touchyng Wytchcrafte ...*
Walsham, A. 1999. *Providence in Early Modern England.*
—. 2006. Angels and idols in England's long Reformation. In *Angels in the Early Modern World* (eds) P. Marshall & A. Walsham. Cambridge, pp. 134-67.
Watts, M.R. 1978. *The Dissenters: from the Reformation to the French Revolution.* Oxford.
Webster, C. 1979. *Health, Medicine and Mortality in the Sixteenth Century.* Cambridge.
Welch, C.E. 1957. Three Sussex heresy trials. *SAC* **95**, 59-70.
Westfall, S.R. 1990. *Patrons and Performance: early Tudor household revels.* Oxford.
Wilby, E. 2005. *Cunning Folk and Familiar Spirits: shamanistic visionary traditions in early modern British witchcraft and magic.* Brighton.
Willett, C. & P. Cunnington. 1954. *Handbook of English Costume in the 16th Century.*
Williford, J. 1645. *The examination of ... Joan Williford ... at Faversham in Kent.*

Wilson, S. 2000. *The Magical Universe: everyday ritual and magic in pre-modern Europe.*

Wimberly, L.C. 1927. *Death and Burial Lore in the English and Scottish Popular Ballads.* Lincoln, Nebraska.

Woodward, M. 1938. *The Mistress of Stantons Farm.*

Wrightson, K. 1982. *English Society 1580-1680.*

—. 1994. Sorts of People in Tudor and Stuart England. In *The Middling Sort of People: culture, society and politics in England, 1550-1800* (eds) J. Barry & C. Brooks, pp. 28-51.

—. 2002 (2000). *Earthly Necessities: economic lives in early modern Britain, 1470-1750.*

Younge, R. 1638. *The Drunkard's Character.*

Zell, M. 1994. *Industry in the Countryside: Wealden society in the sixteenth century.* Cambridge.

Names Index

Brief biographical details (or the person's involvement in the story) are given for inhabitants of Rye, including date of death where known (d=burial or death, m=marriage, b=baptism). Demographic details are mostly from Rye parish registers (ESRO PAR 467/1/1/1-2), in which burials are more complete than baptisms.

Appleton, William, vintner, town clerk, d1589; involved in riot of 1577, 90, 93

Aubrey, John, 10-11

Beale, Goodwife, 56-57

Beaton, John, mid-17th century minister of Rye; 202

Belveridge, Thomas, customs officer and jurat (briefly); target of Bennett disorders, 85

Bennett family, 105, 110

    Bennett women; dual betrothals, 38; as healers, 108-14; accused of bewitching Mary Whitfield, 196

    Anne, dau of Robert jun, see Taylor

    John, tailor, brother of Robert jun., mayor's sergeant, d1579; 97, 110; disorders, 85-8; involved in riot of 1577, 90, 93-5

    John, jun., brother of Anne Taylor, d1596; 173

    Robert, jun., butcher, father of Anne Taylor, b1543, d1597; 38, 97, 105, 173-4, 193; disorders, 85-8; involved in riot of 1577, 90, 93-5

    Robert, sen., butcher, jurat, d1567; 31, 79-82, 154, 168, 174

    Widow, Anne, dau of Thomas Radford, shoemaker, b1544, m1568 Robert jun, d1627; 19, 74-5, 131-2, 173, 200

    see also Bennett women

    William, son of Robert sen., d1573; 85

Binwen, Philip, maidservant of Margery Convers, d1607; asked Anne Taylor for medicine, 71; bewitched to death, according to her mistress, 119

Bishop, Elizabeth, dau of Robert Carpenter, m1594 Michael (tailor, son of jurat Henry); witness against Anne Taylor, 195-6

Boethius, 106

Boys, John, Sir, lawyer; writes to Rye magistrates on behalf of Anne Taylor and challenges their right to try the case, 137-43, 150

Bracegirdle, John, vicar of Rye, d1613; 48-9, 72, 101, 106-7, 199

Breadcar, Joan, dau of John, m1580 John Styner (d1609), m1609 Angel Shaw (d1609), m1609 Stephen Porter, gent, deputy customs officer, (d1610), m1611 Philip Halsey, jurat, (d1617), m1618 Robert Garrett of Dover, d1627; social climber, 118, 267

Breads, John, mid-18th century butcher, murderer of Allan Grebell; 206

Names Index

Brooke, Francis, tailor, d1627; verbal abuse of, 186-7
Browne, Anthony, Viscount Montagu, 13
Burditt
  Martha, wife of Robert; 135
  Robert, barber and town gunner, d1607; gives evidence against Thomas Fisher jun (catholic convert), 100-2; blown up by faulty gun, 133-5
Bucher, William, alias Guillaume Bucheret, French merchant, d1580; 184; involved in riot of 1577, 272
Carpenter
  John, brother of Robert; 264, 265
  Robert, brewer, leader of merchant faction, jurat, d1606; 176, 182-3, 194-6, 199; involved in riot of 1577, 94-5
  Mary, wife of Robert's son William, yeoman; toothache not cured by Widow Bennett, 108, 111, 196
Chaytor, Miranda, 259
Cheston, John, fisherman, d1619; brother of Margery Convers, 118; target of prank by spirits, 122-4
Clitherow, Margaret, catholic martyr (York); 144
Cockram
  Richard, jun., d1650; captain of regiment in Civil War, 201
  Richard, sen., merchant, jurat, d1613; 197; 'puritan', 186
Coker, Margaret, dau of Thomas Hamon sen, b1547, m William Coker; 201
Convers
  John, attorney in Rye court, d1593; 118
  Margery, wife of Robert, sister of John Cheston; 118, 122, 129, 134, 196; views the apparitions in the windows, 71; accuses Anne Taylor of bewitching her maidservant to death, 116, 119, 153; talks with Anne about gifts given to spirits/Susan, 130
  Robert, town clerk, yeoman then gentleman, born Berkshire, apprentice or servant of John Hebblethwaite then of Francis Bolton, townclerk, and marries his widow Margery; d1620; 20, 71, 95, 139; wrote will of George Raynolds, 91; career 118; not university-trained 138; assaulted when constable, 165; motivation, 197
Cotton, John, fisherman, d1606; abuses mayor, 163-7;
Coulton, John, soldier in the Civil War; 201
Crispin and Crispinian, saints, 81
Crouch, Thomas, late 17th century jurat ; 202-3
Daniel
  Francis, butcher and innkeeper, d1621; 186
  Richard, feter and Rye agent for London cloth merchants, brother of Robert, d1588; fought with John Bennett, 86-8
  Robert, woollen draper, d1579; target of abuse when common council created, 86-7
Davies
  John, fisherman/merchant, captain of the *Hercules*, d1612, 14 or 16; 163-5, 179
  (or Davy), William, jurat, fisherman, 86
Dorset, Earl of, *see* Sackville, Thomas
Dunlop, Bessie, Scottish cunning woman who dealt with fairies, 43

Names Index

Duron
  Catherine, wid of John sen, m1578 Thomas Hamon, d1607; 167, 182, 189
  John, sen, brewer, d1578; 167-9, 175
  John, jun, brewer, son of John sen, d1607; 168
  Simon, woollen draper or tailor, son of John sen, d1597 (hanged); 166-7, 170, 172, 180
Edolphe
  Joan, wife of Thomas; 264
  Thomas, jurat, d1595; 185; target of Bennett disorders, 85
Elizabeth I, Queen of England, 13, 81, 106, 149, 225
Ensing, Thomas, jurat; 199
Evans-Pritchard, E.E., 135
Fagge, John, butcher, jurat, leader of artisan faction, d1583; 88, 174-5; involved in riot of 1577, 90, 92-6; and disputed election of 1579, 97, 176-7
Fawkes, Guy, 100, 101
Fishcock, John, of Headcorn, protestant martyr; 12
Fisher
  Thomas, jun, merchant, son of jurat of same name, catholic convert, d1614; 265; interrogated, 100-2; sued for debt by Thomas Tompkins of Sandwich, 187-8
  Thomas, sen, merchant, attorney in Rye court in 1570s, jurat d1616; 161-2, 194-5, 197
Fletcher
  John, fisherman, jurat, intelligencer for Henry VIII, d1546; 193
  Richard, preacher, later Bishop of London (father of the dramatist John Fletcher); 194; involved in riot of 1577, 95-6
Flory, Matthew, French surgeon, 115
Forgison, Andrew, taylor then surgeon, d1605; 115
Fowkes, Alexander, Royal Purveyor of Fish, jurat, trading partner with George Taylor; 74-5, 142, 261
Fowler, Robert, fisherman, jurat; 81
Frencham, (Margery d1616?), wife of Stephen, mercer; 108, on a list of witnesses to be examined, 111
Gaymer, Henry, feter, Royal Purveyor of Fish after M Mills, jurat, leader of merchant faction, d1596; 194, 225; involved in riot of 1577, 90, 92-96
George, Master, physician, 173
Gibbons
  Gabriel, blacksmith, d1597; 105
  William, blacksmith, jurat, d1598; hauled before Mary I's Privy Council for opposition to religious policy, 105
Gile, William, French surgeon, d1612; 115, 'puritan', 184
Gillart, Lewis, late 17th century merchant; 202
Godfrey, Francis, joiner, d1598; 'puritan', 183-4
Godsmark, Henry, feter, d1619; foreman of grand jury in 1607, 63-4
Grebell, Allan, mid-18th century merchant, jurat, murdered by John Breads; 206
Greenwood, Richard, preacher, 183-4
Hadd, Matthew, lawyer, counsel to Lord Warden, Taylors, and many of the Cinque Ports, 140-2, 145, 152

Names Index

Hall, Robert, late 17th century customs collector and government informer; 202

Hamon
  Martha, dau of William Tharpe/Thorpe b after 1582, m1607 Thomas jun, m1607 Thomas Higgons, m1609 Mark Thomas, d1645; 47, 60, 122, 189, 199, 201, 259; prefers indictment against Anne Taylor for bewitching Thomas Hamon to death, 153-4
  Mary, dau of Thomas Hamon, b1579, d1596; 167
  Thomas, brewer, jurat, son of Thomas sen, b1549, m1578 Catherine Duron wid of John sen, m1607 Martha Tharpe dau of William, d1607; 60, 72-5, 193-4, 219; sudden death of, 47-8, 153-4; suspected of being bewitched to death, 58, 153-4; death predicted and possible cure, 108, 113; causes of complaint against, 162; abused by Cotton, 163-4; fails to support his stepson, 166-9, 172; his religious stance, 181, 186-90
  Thomas, sen., 168

Harmon, William, fisherman; involved in riot of 1577, 90, 93

Harris (most of the numerous Harrises seem to have been French, and butchers, after Andrew, glazier, died)
  Edward, butcher, d1598; 85
  Joan, wife of Anthony, butcher; 117, 266
  Thomas, butcher, d1624; 87

Harrison, Stephen, tailor, jurat, d1605; 73, 161, 165; interrogated about 1577 riot, 195

Hebblethwaite
  John, ex-town clerk of Lydd, lawyer; involved in riot of 1577, 89, 91, 94

Henden, Master (Serjeant Edward?), lawyer and counsel for the Taylors; 144

Henry VIII, King of England, 11, 33, 46, 77, 78, 79, 128, 149, 193, 244

Higgons
  Martha, see Hamon
  Thomas, customs officer, merchant, innkeeper, jurat, m1592 Christian Didsbury dau of William jurat, m1607 Martha Hamon wid of Thomas, d1608; 47, 122, 139-40, 150-1, 154-5, 193, 195, 201, 212

Hipkin, Stephen, 156, 263, 276

Hounsell, John, fisherman, and wife Bridget; 199

Howard, Henry, Earl of Northampton, Lord Warden of the Cinque Ports 1604-14; 102, 140, 142-50, 152, 198, 243

Jackson, Robert, brewer, jurat, interrogated about 1577 riot, 97

James I, King of England (and VI of Scotland), 62, 81, 215, 224

Jeake
  Samuel, jun., late 17th century merchant, dissenter, d1699; 204-5
  Samuel, sen., town clerk, dissenter, d1690; 201-2

Jonson, Ben, 12, 44, 192

Keling, Peter, merchant, jurat, d1592; 185

King
  Elizabeth, sis of Susan Swaffer and wife of Nicholas, lighterman; 17, 42, 52
  Nicholas, 17

Names Index

Lamb
  James, mid-18th century merchant, jurat, prosecutor and judge in murder case; 206
  Thomas, son of James, merchant, jurat; 207

Lambarde, William, 9, 16

Lansdale, Samuel, attorney, schoolmaster, later town clerk; 115; in trial jury in 1607, 67; gives evidence against Thomas Fisher jun, 100-1

Lashenden
  John, tanner, son of Thomas, d1625; 258, 261; betrothed to Anne Bennett, 38; member of grand jury in 1607, 64
  Thomas, tanner, d1604; creditor of Robert Bennett jun, betrothed to Widow Bennett, 38, 174-5

Luck, Mercy, servant of the Taylors; 104, 123, 141

March, Robert, butcher, d1582; target of Bennett disorders, 85

Margery, Mother, 65

Margery, spirit, 121

Martin, George; 'puritan', 184

Mary I, Queen of England, 12, 80, 91, 105, 196

Mathew, Thomas, painter, briefly jurat, d1589; 85

Mayhew, Graham, 84, 263

Michenor, Elizabeth, wife of Nicholas, labourer, ex-wife of Robert Pywall; witness of Roger Swaffer being locked out, 55-6

Mills, Matthew, jurat, Royal Purveyor of Fish; involved in riot of 1577, 93, 95

Montagu, Viscount, *see* Browne, Anthony

Moore, Anne, wife of John, labourer, neighbour of Swaffers and witness of Roger Swaffer being locked out, 54-6

Newcastle, Duke of, *see* Pelham-Holles, Thomas

Northampton, Earl of, see Howard, Henry

Palmer, William, fisherman, 164-5, 180

Paulus Aemilius of Verona, chronicler, 101

Peadle, Moses, glazier, and Aaron, tailor and innkeeper, late 17th century; 202

Pelham-Holles, Thomas, Duke of Newcastle, mid-18th century government minister and patron of various inhabitants of Rye; 207

Phillips, Lucy, attorney, overseer with the mayor of G Raynolds' will; evidence, 264-5

Poeton, Edward, Sussex physician, author of manuscript deriding cunningfolk; 63, 114

Portriffe, Richard, brewer, jurat, client of Lord Warden, mayor at last two trials of Anne Taylor, d1614; 150-1

Prowze, John, former fisherman, town gunner and innkeeper of the George, d1598; drew map of Rye harbour, x; involved in riot of 1577, 93

Pye, Quintin, basketmaker then surgeon, d1616; 115

Pywall, Robert, former tenant in Swaffers' house and gardener for the Taylors, d1605; 41; digs for treasure, 27-8, 34-6

Radford
  Anne, dau of Thomas, *see* Widow Bennett
  Joseph, sadler, cousin of Anne Taylor, jurat in the 1680s; beneficiary of her will, 202

Names Index

Noah, first cousin of Anne Taylor, involved in case against Thomas Fisher jun, 102; town's drummer, 159
Ravensdale, Thomas; protestant martyr, 80
Raynolds
   George, jurat, d1577; client of Mary I, his appointment for a second time as mayor rejected by commonalty, 80; his house and will as focus of riot in 1577, 91; brother-in-law of Clement Whitfield, 197
   John, yeoman of Brodhurst, Kent, nephew of George; disinherited by latter's will, 94
   Richard, saint, 44
   Richard, spirit, 24, 41, 43-4, 100-1, 113, 121, 129, 132-4
Rogers, Mother, 67
Rolfe, John, mercer, attorney in Rye court, d1590; involved in riot of 1577, 89-90, 93-7
Rubens, Peter Paul, 4
Ruck
   Bridget, dau of Richard, b1539, m1561 Thomas Fletcher jurat (d1568), m John Taylor father of George, d1619; 263
   Richard, jurat, step-grandfather of George Taylor, d1557; 79-80, 105
Sackville, Thomas, Earl of Dorset, 106-7
Scot, Reginald, 62, 215
Scragg
   John, cutler; tried to reconcile Susan and Anne when all were in prison; 103-4, 106
   William, cutler, John's father, d1584; 105
Shakespeare, William, 192-3, 215, 224, 237, 239

Sharpe, John, butcher, jurat, uncle of Robert Bennett jun; 174
Shaw, Angel, yeoman, town drummer and later mayor's sergeant, d1609; 73-4, 118, 143-4, 188, 198
Shurley
   Sir John, serjeant-at-law, counsel to Rye corporation, 41, 139-41, 143-4, 147-8, 152, 199
   John, sen., 30
Smith, Roger, vicar, 186
Styner, John, fisherman (was apprenticed to John Cheston sen), jurat, d1609; 46, 118, 165-6, 179, 185; stood surety for Anne Taylor, 142
Swaffer / Swapper
   family, origins of, 6-8, 14-15, arrival in Rye and layout of house 17-20, religious outlook of, 12, 100, 102; succumb to malaria, 21-4; children, 200
   Agnes, dau of Roger, 69, 103, 200
   Jane, dau of Roger, 7, 17; m1633 Richard Ratlyf; 200
   Roger, sawyer employed by, and tenant of, George Taylor; account of the spirits 25, 27, 34, 35, interrogation of, 52; called a *wicked liver*, 52 locked out of his house, 53-4, 56
   see also Swaffer family
   Roger, sen., yeoman, 15
   Susan, wife of Roger; called a *lewd woman*, 12, 121, 140; spirits appear to her, 22-8; goes to Weeks Green, 37-9; only person to see the spirits 41; her description of them 22, 42-5; her story rehearsed 48-51; accusations against Anne, 58-60, 196; in prison 59-60, 102-5; trial and verdict, 62-4, 67-9; and

298

the apparitions, 74-6; and
moral ambivalence, 99-100; and
lewd story, 121; tells of pranks
played by the spirits, 121-3,
132-5; manipulates Anne, 129-
30, 134-5; alleged account of
death of mayor, 153; pardoned,
199-200
 see also Swaffer family; Swaffer,
Susan and Anne Taylor
   William, sawyer, brother of
Roger, 14
Swaffer, Susan and Anne Taylor, dig
for treasure 26-7, 34-36; attend to
the spirits, 52-7; nature of their
relationship, 26, 99-100, 118-9;
attempts at reconciliation fail,
102-6; quarrel in prison, 103-5;
leave gifts for spirits, 125-32
Swane, Phyllis wife of Robert, sailor,
neighbours of Swaffers and
tenants of Taylors; tale of fairy
prank, 123; desires green apples
when pregnant, 131-2
Swayne
   Henry and John (d1615),
fishermen, sons of Robert; 46
   Robert, fisherman, jural, d1609,
46, 185; dispute with rest of
bench, 179
Talherst, Jeremy, of East Guldeford;
60, 62
Tate, Richard, servant of Robert
Wood; 'puritan' who struck the
preacher, 184
Taylor
   Anne and George; their garden,
29-31; see apparitions in
windows of house opposite,
and godliness of, 71-7; predict
the end of the world, 75-6;
attempt to get Susan to retract,
102-5; attitude to the not-so-
godly, 99-102, 196; suspect their
children were bewitched, 117;
petition the Lord Warden, 140,
146
   Anne, b1577 dau of Robert
Bennett jun, m1603 George sen,
d1644; 20, 34, 41-2, 48-9, 134-5,
202; gives advice and help to
Susan Swaffer 23-4, 36-8, 111;
interrogation of 50-1; takes
charge, 51-7; alleged evil-
speaking, 58-60; indicted and
escaped, 62, 68; godliness of,
71-7, 117; her godly but
disorderly forbears (Bennetts),
79-88, 93-5; as healer, 116-7,
120; as social climber, 116-8;
accused of causing death by
witchcraft, 60, 119, 153, 195,
196; manipulates Susan, 103-4,
113, 124-5; allies of, 104, 106,
142, 178-9; 154; in prison and
issue of bail, 102-5, 140-2, 145;
refuses to plead, 143; verdict,
154; on Hamon's religion and
wives, 181, 189
 see also Taylor, Anne and George;
Swaffer, Susan and Anne
Taylor, Bennett women
   Elizabeth, dau of George sen and
his previous wife, b1603
Shadoxhurst, d1607; 58, 71, 73,
107, 109, 136
   George, jun., son of George sen,
b1605, d1607, 58, 71, 126, 136
   George, sen., gent and wood
merchant, son of John of
Willesborough, m1591 Joan
Burrow of Boughton, sons John
and William died, dau Eliz
b1603, m1603 Anne Bennett of
Rye, son Geo d1604, son Geo
b1605, dau Eliz and son Geo
d1607, d1628; 21, 42, 44, 59,
101; origin of, 6-7, 15, 79; hires

299

gardeners 27- 8, 34, hears Susan's story, 48, attempts to get case removed to another court, 51, 72, 138, 140, 150-1; economic conflicts with Rye magistrates 60-1; involved in litigation 61, 67, 75, 145, 261, 274; sickness of, 117; recounts lewd story, 121-2; allied with Sir Thomas Waller, 147; in prison, 145; not told that bail would be accepted, 150; has same counsel as many of the Cinque Ports and Lord Warden, 152; made a freeman and represents town with the vicar, 198-200

John, gent, of Willesborough, later St. Alphedge, father of George, m Bridget dau of Richard Ruck (Rye jurat), d before 1619; 15, 79

Tharpe
Martha, *see* Hamon
William, jurat, father of Martha Hamon, d1625; 47; makes copy of Susan Swaffer's first examination, 40, 259

Thomas, Mark, merchant, jurat, 3rd husband of Martha Hamon; 199, 201

Thurbarne, James, New Romney, lawyer, counsel to Rye corporation; 139-41, 143, 146-8, 150-3, 199

Tolkyn, William, feter, jurat, d1603; 88; involved in riot of 1577, 93

Tompkins, Thomas, grocer of Sandwich; witness against Anne Taylor, 123-4; creditor of Thomas Fisher jun, 188

Turner, Victor, 4

Tyndale, William, 11

Van Dyck, Sir Anthony, 4, 60, 63

Waller, Thomas, Sir, Lieutenant of Dover Castle; 132, 134, 141, 143, 147-8, 150-1

Wardroper, Edwin, mid-18th century town clerk and customs collector; 207

Waylett, John, minister of East Guldeford; 184

Whale, John, shoemaker, d1615; 178

White
Nicholas, feter, d1615; foreman of jury that acquits Anne Taylor, 154
Thomas, innkeeper, d1555 or 56; accused of heresy, 78

Whitfield, Clement, gent, brother-in-law of George Raynolds, neighbour of Taylors, sued by GT for trespass, his wife Mary accused the Bennett women of bewitching her; 196-7

Williams, Philip, tailor d1612; gardener for the Taylors, 27, 29

Wood, Robert, merchant, jurat, d1605; 184-6

Young, Matthew, yeoman; creditor of George Taylor and foreman of trial jury in 1607, 67; represents Rye corporation in dealings with the Lord Warden, 147-8; abuses mayor and jurats and temporarily disfranchised, 198-9

Zacharias of Hastings, cunningman, 67, 110

General Index

amity, 215, 216, 228
abuse, in speech, verse or behaviour, 48, 151, 160, 163, 179, 186, 198, 231, 271; *see also* joking
Antwerp, 4, 11
Arundel, 14, 201, 243
Ashford, 6, 172
astrology, 16, 108-9, 111-2, 205
Bible, 11, 29, 85, 99, 110, 112, 141, 178, 179
Brighton, 158
Cadiz, 163
Calais, 61, 157
Canterbury, 6, 137, 140, 183
catholicism, 12-13, 80, 100, 101-2, 188
catholics, 13, 43, 80, 101
centralisation
   economic, 220, 234
   political, 148-9, 229, 234, 244
   uncentralised societies very personal (the 'good-will society'), 216, 231; *see also* good lordship; good neighbourhood; misfortune; quarrelsomeness
Chichester, 13, 14, 33, 44
Cinque Ports, 146, 182, 190, 196
   Brotherhood of, 179
   charter, 58, 137, 139, 142, 145-7
   court of St. James, 138, 140, 148, 268
   jurisdiction, 58, 139, 210
   MPs, 47
   officials, 132
   privileges, 58, 80, 81, 143, 147-8, 151, 206
   regulations, 84, 159
   traditional role of, 134
   western, 161, 163
   withernam, 145

Civil War
   English, 11, 24, 76, 210, 213-4
Colchester, 104
common law, 138, 142
compurgation, 218
constable, 14, 88
courts
   Assizes, 41, 51, 57, 62, 63, 65, 144, 148, 172, 206, 210
   central, in London, 139, 218
      King's Bench, 145, 151, 204
   church, 49, 95, 120, 139, 217, 239
   local (civil), 139, 218
   Quarter Sessions, 17, 139
   Star Chamber, cases of riot in 1577, 89-95
Cranbrook, 11, 12, 102, 110, 151
cunningfolk, 26-7, 32, 34, 42-4, 67, 107, 110-4, 120, 126, 135, 195
customs duties, national, 156
developing societies, *see* centralisation
diabolism, 62, 209, 210, 212, 213
Dieppe, 3, 83, 115, 157-8, 181-2
Dover, 61, 72-3, 101-2, 118, 132, 138-9, 145, 151, 188
Dunkirk, 101-2
East Guldeford, 18, 68, 184
faction, artisan, 89, 92, 95, 97, 155, 175, 185, 194, 195, 198, 202, 203, 226, 243, 244
faction, merchant, 89, 91, 92, 93, 95, 175, 181-3, 185, 188, 189, 190, 192, 194, 195, 196, 197, 198, 199, 221, 225, 226, 243
factionalism, 84, 194, 208, 217
Faversham, 81, 185, 214
Flanders, 101
France, 60, 61, 80, 81, 83, 101, 157, 158, 182, 188, 204, 205, 210, 214

301

fraud, 44, 135
godliness, 12, 71-3, 75-7, 102, 173,
    178, 181-2, 184, 188, 192, 194, 202,
    224, 226-7, 237, 241-2,
    moral reformation by the
        corporation, 96-7
    and literacy, 109-10, 179
    of surgeons, 115
    dissenters, 203-6
    compared with early 20th century
        Islamic fundamentalism, 245-8
good lordship, 84, 216, 221-2, 230,
    237-9, 241-2, 244; *see also*
    centralisation; patronage
good neighbourhood, 13, 84, 216,
    221-2, 228, 230, 233, 238-41; *see also*
    centralisation; quarrelsomeness
Hastings, 67, 110, 147, 158, 161, 205
Headcorn, 7, 8, 12, 15, 17
illness,
    cures for, 12, 24-5, 27, 42, 67, 108,
        111, 113, 115-7, 129, 184
    diagnosis, 58, 111-2, 114, 116-7
    fear, as a cause of death, 35
    inflicted by saints, 45
    influenza, 168
    malaria, 16, 21, 120, 193
    plague, 38, 115, 164, 166, 172-3,
        192
    planet-struck, 112-3
    prediction of death, 108-9, 196
    stroke, 59
    'troubled with treasure', 27-8
    see also spirits, illnesses caused by
indictment, 51, 62-3, 65-7, 130, 138,
    154, 172, 197, 218
Isfield, 30
Italy, 157, 211
joking, 122, 124, 224, 227, 229-31,
    233-4, 235, 239, 241-2, 245-6;
    see also speech, ritualised; abuse
judges, 57, 62, 89, 139, 143, 144, 146,
    210, 212
    Inquisition, 211

Scotland, 211
juries
    grand, 63, 64, 65, 82, 143, 172
    trial, 57, 63, 65, 67, 68, 72, 95, 99,
        121, 143, 144, 154, 167, 218
Justices of the Peace, county, 48, 137
Kingsnorth, 6
lawyers, 92, 138, 139, 140, 141, 144,
    148, 150
lollards, 11, 79
London, 3-6, 14, 18, 22, 35, 80, 82, 88,
    104, 112, 114, 121, 147, 150, 157-60,
    179, 192, 204-5, 220, 229, 232
Lydd, 92, 190
magic, 49, 51, 124
    conjuring books, 56-7, 110, 125
medical practitioners, 108-119, 184
'middling sort', 88, 97, 177, 181, 243
misfortune, belief in personal cause
    of, 215, 218-20
names
    biblical, 178
    godly, 12, 115, 184
New Romney, 140, 161, 190
Newcastle, 158, 179, 207
Northampton, 128
patronage, 84, 88, 145-6, 220-21, 226,
    234, 238, 241-3, 245-8
    clients, 80, 84, 91, 150, 196, 229-30,
        242
    patrons, 39, 84, 103, 107, 150, 152,
        207, 242-4
plaindealing, 235-8, 241-2, 245;
    see also speech, plain
Playden, 4, 82
Privy Council, 10, 80, 89, 91, 105,
    149, 182, 204, 211, 225
proclamations of suspected felony,
    66, 217-8
Protestantism, 12, 181, 226, 242
protestants, 11, 23, 78, 80, 83, 84, 182,
    184, 188
puritanism, *see* godliness

puritans, 77, 101-3, 116-7, 121, 122-3, 150, 183-6, 188-9, 192, 197, 201, 226, 228, 230, 232, 237, 244-6
quarrelsomeness, belief in need to reduce, 217-8
Reformation, the protestant, 11, 84, 128, 181, 192, 219, 226, 243, 244
River
  Rother, 1, 2, 17, 18, 68, 159
  Tillingham, 1, 159
Romney Marsh, 2, 16, 18, 47
Rye,
  assembly, 160
    assembly books, 65, 133, 166, 187, 198, 199
    common council, 86, 87, 217
    common court (civil), 68, 218
    customs duties, 18, 61, 156, 157
    customs officer, 47, 193, 202, 207
    economic decline, 83, 156-62
    freemen (commonalty), rights of, 19; 185
    mayor and jurats, rights and election of, 19, 185; authority, 57, 137, 143-5
    disputed election in 1579, 97, 176
    riot in 1577 (Star Chamber cases), 89-95
    sessions of the peace, 57, 62, 102, 107, 136-8, 143, 153, 165-7, 206
    witchcraft accusations in (before Taylor/Swapper case), 65-7
Sandwich, 123, 152, 187, 190
Scotland, 43-4, 62, 149, 211, 213
servants, 14, 19, 91, 93, 95-6, 116, 120, 152, 160, 178, 184, 189, 230, 243
  maidservants, 65, 71, 88, 93, 104, 116-7, 119, 120, 123, 128, 136, 141, 153, 197
  male, 135
South Downs, the, 9

Spain, 13, 101, 102, 157, 159, 161, 172, 211, 213
speech
  plain, 235, 237, 241; *see also* plaindealing
  ritualised, 227; *see also* joking; abuse
spirits, 58, 99-100, 130-1, 205-6
  appear to Susan Swaffer, 21-26
  guarding buried treasure, 29-36
  at Weeks Green, 36-40
  angels, 75-6, 114, 119
  apparitions in windows, 49, 72-5, 77, 116, 125, 135-6
  conjuring, 26, 33, 51, 56, 62, 136
  devil, 23, 26, 32, 44, 45, 54, 59, 99, 114, 187, 200, 208, 210, 227
    pact with, 44, 212, 220
  fairies, 26, 29, 33, 42-4, 49, 56, 113-4, 120, 125, 127, 131, 135, 174, 192, 208, 224
    gifts left for, 125-32, 141
    Queen of the, 39, 43, 44
  familiars, 40, 41, 43, 50, 123, 125, 133, 135, 213
  illnesses caused by spirits, 24-5, 42-3, 52, 57, 59, 111, 117, 122, 132, 153
  legal treatment of those who deal with spirits, 49, 62, 137
  names of spirits, 24, 41, 44, 50
  noisy spirits, 24, 42, 52-3
  pranks, 121-4, 132-5
  see also Richard, spirit; Margery, spirit
torture, 60, 144, 209, 211
treasure, buried
  searching for, 23, 26-9, 32-7, 40, 42, 44, 48, 62
  legal status of, 33-4, 51
  moral right to, 34-5
Prosecution of Susan Swapper and Anne Taylor for witchcraft accusers, 194-7

and death by witchcraft, 60, 109, 117, 119, 153, 195, 196
compared with other cases, 57, 65, 208, 214
correspondence over, 137-53
examinations and depositions, quotations from, chaps. 2-8, 153-4, 181, 189, 196
  size of, 3, 51, 57
indictments related to statute of 1604, 62
input by magistrates (and vicar), 48, 50-2, 57-8, 62, 67-8, 102, 106, 138-47, 151, 154-5, 197
  jurats supporting Anne Taylor, 142, 178-9
legal issues over, 41, 57, 137-52
trials, 63, 143, 153
verbal abuse, 160, 163, 179, 186, 198, 231
Weald, 5-9, 11-15, 37, 102
Weeks Green, hamlet near Playden, 36-9, 48, 82

Willesborough, 6, 7, 8, 15, 79
Wiltshire, 10
Winchelsea, 2, 54, 75, 82
witchcraft
  maleficia (causing harm by supernatural means), 62-3, 154, 209-10, 212-3, 215
  and religion, 215
  cross-cultural approach to, 215
  statutes (England), 33, 62, 139, 142-3
  see also misfortune; witch trials; prosecution of AT and SS for witchcraft; Rye, witchcraft accusations in
witch trials, in Europe and New England
  geographic pattern of, 208-13
  and urban politics, 208, 212
writs, 88, 138, 150, 261
Yarmouth, 46, 150